Otros títulos publicados por Editorial *A Contracorriente*:

Marisol Montaño, Alejandro Solomianski y Sofia Wolhein (eds.), *Otras voces. Nuevas identidades en la frontera sur de California (Testimonios)*

Ana Peluffo (ed.), *Pensar el siglo XIX desde el siglo XXI. Nuevas miradas y lecturas*

Andrea Matallana, *El Tango entre dos Américas. La representación del tango en Estados Unidos, 1910-1939*

Brantley Nicholson y Sophia McClennen (eds.), *The Generation of '72: Latin America's Forced Global Citizens*

Carlos Aguirre (ed.), *Militantes, intelectuales y revolucionarios. Ensayos sobre marxismo e izquierda en América Latina*

Carlos Aguirre y Javier Villa-Flores (eds.), *From the Ashes of History: Loss and Recovery of Archives and Libraries in Modern Latin America*

Emilio del Valle Escalante (ed.), *Teorizando las literaturas indígenas contemporáneas*

Laura Prado Acosta, *Los intelectuales del Partido Comunista. Itinerario de Héctor Agosti (1930-1963)*

Diana Moro, *Sergio Ramírez, Rubén Darío y la literatura nicaragüense*

Raúl Diego Rivera Hernández, *Del Internet a las calles: #YoSoy132, una opción alternativa de hacer política*

Adrián Scribano, *Sociología de las emociones en Carlos Marx*

Ariel Goldstein, *Prensa tradicional y liderazgos populares en Brasil* (En prensa)

Alejandro Sánchez Lopera, *José Revueltas y Roberto Bolaño: Formas genéricas de la experiencia* (En prensa)

Paulo Drinot (ed.), *La Patria Nueva: Economía, sociedad, y cultura en el Perú, 1919-1930* (En prensa)

Insurgent Marcos
The Political-Philosophical Formation of the Zapatista Subcommander

Nick Henck

Raleigh, NC

© 2016 Nick Henck

All rights reserved for this edition for:
© 2016, Editorial *A Contracorriente*

ISBN: 978-1-945234-03-39

No part of this book, including the cover, may be reproduced without expressed permission from the editor.

Library of Congress Control Number: 2016944203

Library of Congress Cataloging-in-Publication Data: pending

ISBN 10: 1-945234-03-2
ISBN 13: 978-1-945234-03-3

Copyediting and layout by Julie Steinbacher
Cover art: *Subcommander Marcos with Political-Philosophical Influences*, 2016. © by Dan Carman. Reproduced with permission of the author.

This work is published under the auspices of the DEPARTMENT OF FOREIGN LANGUAGES AND LITERATURES at NORTH CAROLINA STATE UNIVERSITY.

Distributed by the University of North Carolina Press, www.uncpress.org.

For John F. Drinkwater, for all his years of generous mentoring, and Neil B. McLynn, for his unstinting efforts in furthering my career in Japan, and in fond memory of my dear friend William J. Snell (1959-2015)

"La integración intelectual a un entorno ajeno tiene algo de naufragio. Al aceptarlo, ¿se recusa todo lo anterior? No necesariamente."
[Juan Villoro, *De Cartago a Chiapas: crónica intempestiva*]

"Intellectual integration in alien surroundings has elements of the shipwreck. Does acceptance mean casting aside everything that went before? Not necessarily."
[Juan Villoro, *From Carthage to Chiapas: An Untimely Chronicle*]

Table of Contents

Acknowledgments	ix
Introduction	11
A) The Approach and Organization of the Book	18
Literary formation	27
Marxist (and) Leninist Formation	47
A) The Fuerzas de Liberación Nacional (FLN)	47
B) Rafael Guillén's Thesis	55
Structural Marxist Formation: Louis Althusser and Nicos Poulantzas	75
A) Louis Althusser	84
B) Nicos Poulantzas	127
Post-Structural, Post-Marxist Formation: Michel Foucault	161
A) Discourse as War or Words as Weapons	168
B) Power and Resistance	171
C) Genealogy	182
D) Grand Narratives	194
E) A Miscellany	196

Dogs Not Barking: Gramsci (and Others)   217

    A) Student Writings   219

    B) Guerrilla Writings   224

    C) Rebel Writings   228

    D) Perceived Affinities between Marcos and Gramsci   229

    E) Divergences between Marcos and Gramsci   236

Conclusion   245

Appendix I: The Althusserian Preamble to Rafael Guillén's Thesis   255

Appendix II: The Preface to Rafael Guillén's Thesis   257

Appendix III: Subcommander Marcos' *Letter to Adolfo Gilly*   259

Works Cited   267

Index   303

Acknowledgments

First and foremost I would like to express my gratitude toward my home institution, Keio University, for generously granting me a two-year sabbatical, without which the completion of this book would have dragged on for many more years. In particular, I would like to thank my colleagues in the Law Faculty in general, and those in my department in particular, not only for picking up the slack in my absence but indeed for all their support over the last decade.

I am also indebted to Keio University's library staff, especially those working in the Hiyoshi Media Center, who aided me considerably in acquiring the books and journal articles which I needed to complete this project. In a similar vein, I am also appreciative of the efforts of those working at the International Institute of Social History (Amsterdam) for helping me to obtain certain obscure, and therefore difficult to access, works.

Further deserving of my profound gratitude is Greg Dawes, editor of Editorial *A Contracorriente*, whose enthusiasm for, faith in, and commitment to this project ensured that the publication process was an entirely pleasurable one. Moreover, I should like to thank the two anonymous readers for taking the time to read and comment upon my manuscript. The second reader merits particular thanks for his concrete suggestions regarding improvements and for his general words of encouragement.

It would also be remiss of me not to take this opportunity to commend Dan Carman for the excellent artwork that adorns the cover of this book. When I commissioned this piece from him, supplying him with only the sketchiest of outlines as to what it was that I had in mind, I could never have envisioned such a perfect outcome.

Material from two chapters of this book has been previously published elsewhere. Almost the entirety of Chapter 1 formed part of a longer article entitled "Subcomandante Marcos: The Latest Reader," published in the journal *The Latin Americanist* (June 2014), 58(2), 49–73; while Chapter 5, excepting the initial two paragraphs, previously appeared as an article entitled "The Subcommander and the Sardinian: Marcos and Gramsci," published in the journal *Mexican Studies/Estudios Mexicanos* (Summer 2013), 29(2), 428-458. I would therefore like to extend my deepest gratitude to both *The Latin Americanist* and *Mexican Studies/Estudios Mexicanos* for generously allowing me to republish this material here.

Finally, but by no means least, words of apology as much as of gratitude: to my wife, Yasuko, who may be forgiven for thinking that she had earned a reprieve from my fascination with Marcos after I published my biography of the Subcommander back in 2007 … alas not!; and to our little boy, Louis, who I pray will one day understand why his dad felt he had to spend so much time with his head stuck in books or staring at the laptop, reading and writing about a mysterious masked man who lives a world away.

Introduction

As the Zapatistas' military leader and spokesperson, the world's most recognizable revolutionary icon in a generation (i.e. since Che Guevara), a shining beacon of the anti-neoliberal globalization and anti-capitalist movements,[1] and arguably "the best Latin American writer today,"[2] Mexico's Subcommander Insurgent Marcos (to give him his full title) has, deservedly, been the subject of numerous books, book chapters, encyclopaedia entries and articles.[3] And yet, despite a plethora of pages having been devoted to the Subcommander, there has been to date very little examination of his political-philosophical formation and the extent to which this may have informed his discourse.

The Subcommander himself, when asked specifically in a 2007 interview with Raymundo Reynoso, "Who is Marcos, how was he formed, what formed him?," replied that prior to the Zapatista uprising

> There were two large aspects to Marcos. One, that of the orthodox left, and later the one which resulted from the process of digestion and modification which the indigenous communities provided.[4]

Unfortunately, the Subcommander failed to elaborate any further in the interview on this "orthodox left" aspect of his formation. Elsewhere too, he has described himself in a similar way, telling one interviewer that "We were closed-minded, like any other orthodox leftist…," and on another occasion recalling his "orthodox way of seeing the world in terms of 'bourgeois[ie] and proletarians.'"[5] Again, however, in these instances too Marcos fails to expand on his leftist orthodoxy. Indeed, the fullest account Marcos has provided us with concerning what precisely this entailed can be found in a May 1994 interview, where he talks of the "interweaving" and "exchange" that took place "between the proposals of the guerrilla group, the initial group of the EZLN, and the communities," whereby

> the most orthodox proposals of Marxism or Leninism, theoretical concepts or historical references—for example, that the vanguard of the revolution is the proletariat, that the taking of state power and the installation of the dictatorship of the proletariat is the aim of the revolution[6]—were confronted by an ideological tradition that is, how can I say this, somewhat magical. It is magical in one sense, but very real in another ... [W]e were confronted by this reality, the Indigenous reality .... Ultimately the theoretical confronted the practical, and something happened—the result was the EZLN.[7]

Here, once again, Marcos emphasizes his orthodoxy, although in this instance he is rather more specific concerning what strain of leftism he subscribed to, stipulating it was Marxism-Leninism (as opposed to, say, Trotskyism, Stalinism, or Maoism). Moreover, we see the Subcommander echoing this in another interview, where he also describes this "confrontation," describing it this time as a "...process of translation from the university Marxist-Leninist culture to the indigenous culture," adding that "this translation was more of a transformation."[8]

Aside from these few brief declarations however, any significant elaboration on the part of the Subcommander himself concerning his left-wing formation has been notable by its absence. This stands in sharp contrast to Marcos' numerous and fairly detailed utterances concerning the actual "confrontation" that took place between "the most orthodox proposals of Marxism or Leninism" on the one hand and "Indigenous reality" on the other, regarding which the Subcommander has elaborated on significantly. For example, in his 1995 *Letter to Adolfo Gilly*, Marcos relates how:

> Our square conception of the world and of revolution was badly dented (*abollada*) in the confrontation with the indigenous realities of Chiapas. Out of those blows, something new (which does not necessarily mean "good") emerged, that which today is known as "neo-Zapatismo."[9]

Moreover, in an interview he granted only two days after the date of his *Carta* (October 22), the Subcommander elaborated further:

> When the families of the villagers enter the Zapatista army, they start the process of cultural contagion, forcing us to reformulate politics, our way of seeing our own historical process, and the historical process of the nation .... We had a very square notion of reality. When we collide with reality, that square gets very dented (*abollado*). Like that wheel there. And it

starts to roll and to be polished by the contact with the people .... Then, when they ask: Who are you? Marxists, Leninists, Castroists, Maoists, or what? I don't know. Really I don't know. We are ... a hybrid, of a confrontation, of a shock, in which, I believe fortunately, we lost ...[10]

Similarly, earlier that same year Marcos had already told Alma Guillermoprieto (1995, p. 39) that:

we faced the choice of continuing with a traditional guerrilla structure, or *masificando* and putting the strategic leadership in the hands of the people. Our army became scandalously Indian, and there was a certain amount of clashing while we made the adjustment from our orthodox way of seeing the world in terms of "bourgeois and proletarians" to the community's collective democratic conceptions, and their world view.

Finally, when interviewed by Manuel Vázquez Montalbán (2002, p. 476), Marcos recalled:

We came to the forest as a classic revolutionary elite in search of ... the proletariat in the classic Marxist-Leninist sense. But that initial approach was not adequate to deal with the reality of the indigenous communities. They have a different substratum, a complex prehistory of uprisings and resistances. So we modified our approach interactively ...

The EZLN was ... created out of a ... culture shock, which then went on to produce a new discourse ...

Unsurprisingly, Marcos' comparatively extensive discussion of the transition of the EZLN from a traditional left-wing guerrilla to an armed indigenous movement has resulted in commentators tending to echo and therefore amplify this emphasis. Thus we have the following, to cite but two, fairly recent examples. Kara Zugman Dellacioppa (2009, p. 125) has written that:

Zapatismo is a political vision and movement born in the heart of indigenous Mexico in the 1980s, when four urban guerrillas set out to construct a revolutionary army. During this period, the urban guerrillas were transformed by the indigenous communities they were attempting to organize. In this "trans-cultural dialogue," Guevarism and Maoism were modified and in some cases rendered unrecognizable as the politics of the urban guerrillas passed through the indigenous cultural lens and were rearticulated by the indigenous communities.

So too, Alex Khasnabish (2010, p. 225) writes that "Marcos and the other urban *guerrilleros* arrived ... with the ideological discourse of Marxism ...," adding that "this encounter [between the guerrillas and the indigenous] resulted not in the revolutionizing of the Indigenous communities but rather in the defeat of Marxist dogma at the hands of these indigenous realities ..."

Of course, such an emphasis is not *per se* necessarily a bad thing; however, what has tended to transpire is the near total eclipsing of any discussion of Marcos' Marxist past in favor of focusing on the Subcommander's transition from espousing an orthodox leftist ideology to subscribing to indigenous thought and practices. The result has been that a master narrative has emerged in which the orthodox leftist Marcos came to Chiapas as part of a rural guerrilla *foco* belonging to the Marxist-Leninist Fuerzas de Liberación Nacional (FLN), but that during his decade-long interaction with indigenous campesinos this ideology clashed with the latter's thought and practices, and was so "badly dented" by it that "something new ... emerged ..." The present work, I am quick to stress, does not aim, as others have done,[11] at challenging the authenticity of this well-worn version of events that has been promoted by Marcos, and which has been widely accepted, adopted, and disseminated by commentators, but rather seeks to see past Marcos' dazzling Damascene conversion, to examine his political-philosophical formation, and by supplying this missing piece of the picture, to help elucidate why the Subcommander, unlike so many of Latin America's left-wing would-be revolutionary guerrillas, allowed the ideology he came to Chiapas with to be so severely "dented" by indigenous reality. In doing so, I adopt a stance that differs from that of, for example, Yvon Le Bot (1997b, p. 30), the author of a book-length interview with Marcos, who, when himself asked by an interviewer: "Does it not seem significant to you to know that they [the EZLN] were Marxist-Leninists?," replied:

> It is interesting to learn of that origin, but for me it is more interesting to see how these ultra-left traditional militants were transformed throughout their years of culture clash with the indigenous communities and to analyze the results of that evolution, of that creation of themselves by themselves precisely in that context of confrontation with others. Obviously I know that the self-creation of zapatismo takes place within a political context that must be taken into account.

— Introduction —

For my part, I maintain that both the very fact that Marcos and the other Marxist-Leninist EZLN guerrillas allowed themselves to be *transformed*, and also the way in which they were *transformed*, were determined predominantly by how, initially, they were *formed*. In short, in my opinion, the best way to fully comprehend this *transformation* is by understanding the process of *formation*—its nature and especially its profundity—that preceded it.

In addition to providing a fuller portrait of the Subcommander, I also hope to raise, and address, certain crucial points of interest that hitherto have been eclipsed by a concentration on the clash of Marxist-Leninist ideology with indigenous peoples' thought and practices, and the denting of the former at the hands of the latter. One might like to know, for example: just how "orthodox" was Marcos' leftism; how much Marx and Lenin had he imbibed, and to what extent did this form him; whether he was influenced by the thinking of Stalin, Trotsky, Gramsci or Mao, in addition to that of Marx and Lenin; how hardline or doctrinaire was he in his leftist thinking prior to arriving in Chiapas; what role, if any, did *castroism* and *guevarism*, or even Vietnamese Marxism, play in his formation; and, perhaps most significantly, were there any competing influences that may have tempered his Marxist-Leninism thereby easing his readiness to accept the ideological surrender to indigenous reality that he has several times narrated? Finally, of course, looking forward there remain the following questions posed by Dan La Botz (2007): "Today, thirteen years since the uprising, we all want to know many things about Marcos: Did he ever really give up Marxist-Leninist (i.e. Stalinist or Guevarist) politics? ... Does he really eschew the taking of state power (doubtful, or some would say dumb) ...?" Indeed, the extent to which Marcos' political-philosophical formation, including but not limited to his Marxist-Leninism, persisted in the Subcommander's discourse is a question that I treat repeatedly and at length in each of the chapters that follow.[12]

Interestingly, this latter aspect especially is one that commentators have tended to shy away from addressing. Indeed, the fullest treatment of this issue that I have been able to unearth is that of Daniela Di Piramo (2010, p. 30), who notes that "...the revolutionary Marxist tradition ... shaped Marcos' early intellectual formulation,"[13] presenting this as "the most serious legacy that Marcos has to confront" due to "the continuing vehement presence of Marxist ideas in his discourse and the simultaneous attempts he makes to distance himself from this legacy." Beyond this, and my own work on the

Subcommander's discourse on Mexico's intellectual class,[14] very little of substance has been written on Marcos' political-philosophical formation or the persistence of its influence on his discourse following his confrontation with indigenous reality.

This tendency has arisen, I would urge, for two reasons. The first derives from a comparative lack of source material available for the period of Marcos' life prior to his embarking for Chiapas. For while the Subcommander has been prepared to discuss his literary formation, especially in interviews with literary figures such as Juan Gelman and Gabriel García Márquez, he has, by contrast, proved very reticent about his political-philosophical formation. Moreover, his graduation thesis, our major source regarding this formation, has until recently been extremely difficult to consult.

The second reason concerns a desperate desire on the part of commentators to avoid being of service to the Right or being labeled reactionaries. They fear that, by revealing that the Subcommander has clearly been influenced by his reading of Marx and Lenin, as well as his having been schooled in structural Marxist philosophers such as Althusser and Poulantzas, they would be serving to discredit the Zapatista cause by emphasizing Marcos' Marxist contribution to Zapatismo's formulation.[15] Although I understand the logic of these commentators, I do not share it. Such considerations, noble as they are, should not be allowed to hinder our understanding of Marcos, and such an understanding entails building a complete profile of the Subcommander, one which does not focus solely on discussion of transformation to the exclusion of continuity, but which examines his formative years as key to understanding the man. I for one do not hold that discovering that the Subcommander brought with him to Zapatismo an understanding of the current world, and a critique of it, that was influenced by both structural Marxist, and post-structuralist, post-Marxist, thought is in any way problematic. I would thus urge that instead of avoiding discussion of the relationship between Marx and Marcos, it proves far more constructive to try and ascertain both the degree and the nature of the Marxism that he was exposed to due during his formative years, and to gauge how persistent these were in him following his ideological "denting" at the hands of indigenous thinking and practices.

Needless to say, this issue of persistence necessarily has implications concerning Zapatismo, the Zapatistas' political philosophy.[16] For, while in no way wishing to be seeming to equate Marcos' political philosophy with Zapatismo or to suggest that the two are synonymous, thereby privileging the contribution of a single, mestizo Subcommander over that of the thousands of indigenous who constitute the rank-and-file of the Zapatista army and its support bases—such a stance would not only be counterintuitive but would also run counter to the evidence, for it is undeniable that the indigenous Chiapanecans contributed to Zapatismo certain core political-philosophical concepts and practices, including dignity,[17] community-based radical (i.e. direct) democracy,[18] and *mandar obedeciendo* ("to command obeying")[19] and *preguntando caminamos* ("asking we walk")[20]—equally it would be a mistake to focus on the indigenous contribution to Zapatismo to the exclusion of all else.[21] Marcos himself, for example, has gone on record as stating that:

> Zapatismo was not Marxist-Leninist, but it was also Marxist-Leninist. It was not university Marxism, it was not the Marxism of concrete analysis, it was not the history of Mexico, it was not the fundamentalist and millenarian indigenous thought and it was not the indigenous resistance. *It was a mixture of all of this*, a cocktail which was mixed in the mountain and crystallized in the combat force of the EZLN… (my emphasis)[22]

Moreover, it further needs to be emphasized that Zapatismo's discourse and Marcos' discourse are largely inseparable given that the Subcommander is the author of the vast majority of the Zapatistas' communiqués and documents,[23] and that these tend to garner far greater attention, and enjoy a more privileged circulation, in comparison to those not penned by him.[24] Thus, while it is true that Marcos may not occupy the paramount position in Zapatismo in the same way that, say, Mao does for Maoism or Che does for Guevarism, it is nonetheless the case that the Subcommander's own political philosophy represents one of the threads in the tapestry that is Zapatismo. Hence, Madhu Suri Prakash and Gustavo Esteva (2008, p. 121) write that "Subcomandante Marcos … clearly contributed to a collective process that we now know as *zapatismo*. The outcome does not belong to him. But neither is he irrelevant;" while Jorge Lora Cam (2003, p. 258) cautions against underestimating the importance of Marcos' role in this respect, writing of

> his great influence. His knowledge of western culture, its forms of reasoning and theoretical analysis, its codes of conduct, its daily life and common sense, its symbolic language and its codes are tools that allow him to make valuations, to draft documents, to systematize information and to glimpse

>the possible responses of the enemies of Zapatismo, in order to design strategies. (my translation)

These "tools" were ones that the Subcommander had no doubt acquired during his formation, and which were subsequently re-fashioned during his prolonged contact and interaction with Chiapas' indigenous. As Marcos related to Yvon Le Bot (1997a, p. 151):

> We went through a process of re-education, of re-modeling ... As if they had dismantled all the tools we had—Marxism, Leninism, socialism, urban culture, poetry, literature—everything that was a part of ourselves, and also that we did not know we had. They dismantled us and put us together again, but in a different configuration.[25]

Ultimately, such tools enabled Marcos to contribute a crucial component to Zapatismo: namely, its devastating critique of current conditions in Chiapas, Mexico, and the world at large (and thus, by implication, the urging of a fundamental need for the construction of an alternative). In short, the Subcommander's searing indictment of the prevailing situation, and the way in which he has elected to articulate this, is a key element in Zapatismo, and one which was, I maintain, influenced by, and retains residual traces of, the literary and political-philosophical traditions—the latter including (but not limited to) Marxism—that Marcos was exposed to during his formative years.[26]

A) *The Approach and Organization of the Book*

In terms of approach, the book seeks to blend literary and political theory in order to produce a portrait of the Zapatista Subcommander's political-philosophical formation. It does so by, first, charting Marcos' literary formation, an enterprise that is pivotal when it comes to analyzing the Subcommander's subsequent discourse. Next, it draws on existing scholarship that details the socio-political context of the Dirty War in Mexico in the 1970s, within which the Forces of National Liberation (Fuerzas de Liberación Nacional or FLN)—the precursor of the Zapatista Army of National Liberation (Ejército Zapatista de Liberación Nacional or EZLN)—arose, so as to ascertain the degree of the Marxist-Leninist origins and nature of the clandestine guerrilla organization that spawned the Subcommander. This is then followed by the conducting of a close textual analysis of the graduation thesis of Ra-

— Introduction —

fael Guillén (Marcos' pre-guerrilla incarnation), with the resultant findings being compared and contrasted with those gained from having carried out a discourse analysis of the Subcommander's writings, speeches, and interviews. Put simply, aspects of literary theory and criticism are deployed alongside the tracing of the contours of Marxist, structuralist, and post-structuralist political thought in order to assess the structural Marxist (i.e. Althusserian and Poulantzian), post-Structural (i.e. Foucauldian), and absent (i.e. Gramscian) influences at work upon the Subcommander, an undertaking which allows the establishment of to what extent and in which ways Marcos' political-philosophical formation impacted on the formulation of Zapatismo.

Turning to the organization of the book, Chapter 1 examines Marcos' experience and practice of reading during his formative years, focusing in particular on his exposure to literature and poetry. This is carried out through: an extensive survey of interviews with both the Subcommander, some of them conducted by eminent men of letters themselves, and with the father of Rafael Guillén; consultation of Guillén's graduation thesis, complete with bibliography; scrutiny of a list of books discovered in Marcos' personal library when the Mexican military raided the Subcommander's guerrilla camp during its February 1995 offensive; and close examination of several hundreds of Marcos' communiqués and dozens of his speeches. What is revealed is the massive influence that his reading of world literature, including poetry, had on Marcos' political-philosophical formation, it both providing him with the primary (in terms of chronology and primacy) frame through which he views and interprets the world, and continuing to form and inform his thought and discourse.

Chapter 2 attempts to ascertain the nature and extent of Marcos' Marxist and Leninist formation (i.e. his exposure to the texts of Marx, Engels, and Lenin) as experienced through two more or less concurrent processes: his immersion in the clandestine world of the Marxist-Leninist Fuerzas de Liberación Nacional (FLN), and his university studies in political philosophy, both of which took place during his early twenties. I begin by drawing on several recent major studies of the FLN, all of which point to this clandestine organization having been considerably less orthodox Marxist-Leninist than its own statutes suggest. I then turn to conducting a textual analysis of Guillén's graduation thesis, seeking to determine the extent of its indebtedness to, specifically, the classical texts of Marx, Engels, and Lenin, as opposed to subsequent, more contemporary Marxist thinkers. The chapter ends with a discussion of whether traces of the writings of Marx, Engels, and Lenin can be detected in the Subcommander's discourse.

Chapter 3 looks at the influence of structural Marxist thought on the Subcommander. It commences with a sweeping survey of Guillén's graduation thesis that highlights the main influences at work upon it. This reveals that the work drew significantly on the thinking of, on the one hand, Althusser and his disciples, most notable among them Nicos Poulantzas, and on the other, Michel Foucault. An attempt is then made to elucidate both the reasons why, and the ways in which, Guillén chose to attempt to reconcile, and thereby synthesize, the thinking of Althusser, Poulantzas, and Foucault.

After identifying certain key Althusserian preoccupations that were taken over by the young Guillén and incorporated into his graduation thesis, I then turn to examining the Subcommander's discourse and actions in order to gauge the degree to which Althusser's concepts continued to influence Marcos. I end this subsection by noting how the Zapatistas represent a social movement that conforms very much to those that Althusser, in his final years, envisaged coming into effect; it also notes how the Zapatistas put into practice certain proposals that resemble those advocated by the French philosopher.

Next, I turn to addressing Guillén's acquaintance with Poulantzas' thought, performing a textual analysis of the former's thesis alongside key texts by the latter. I move on to attempt to ascertain whether or not, in respect to Poulantzas' thinking, there appears any conceptual continuity between Guillén's thesis and the Subcommander's discourse. In the process of doing so, I identify certain of what I term "latent legacies"—namely key concepts that Guillén would certainly have encountered in his reading of Poulantzas' work but that do not reveal themselves in his thesis, and so can be said to have lain dormant in him, only to surface years later in the Subcommander's discourse. The chapter ends by drawing attention to certain terminological similarities between Poulantzas' writings and the Subcommander's discourse.

Chapter 4 largely mirrors in its approach the preceding chapter only that instead of observing the structural Marxist formation of the Subcommander, it looks at the post-structural, post-Marxist currents that he was exposed to and influenced by. In particular, this chapter singles out Michel Foucault as a philosopher whose works shaped considerably the thinking of

— Introduction —

the young Rafael Guillén. Once again a textual analysis of Guillén's thesis is undertaken with the aim of establishing its indebtedness to, in this instance, certain Foucauldian key concepts (e.g. the power of discourse and discourses of power, and in particular the concept of words as weapons). This is followed by discussion of not only whether these core elements persisted in the Subcommander's discourse, but also to what extent in the case of Foucault too we can unearth certain "latent legacies" that surface in Marcos' thought and actions. The chapter ends by looking at points of convergence concerning the lives and core values of Foucault and Marcos.

Chapter 5 completes our picture of the Subcommander's political-philosophical formation by drawing attention to notable absences in Marcos' Marxist grounding. Chief among those Marxist authors whom one might reasonably expect to encounter in Guillén's thesis and Marcos' discourse is Antonio Gramsci; and yet the Italian fails to make an appearance, as do other Marxist luminaries. The chapter sets out to postulate reasons why Marcos may have chosen not to engage with the thinking and writings of such an influential Marxist thinker as Gramsci (as well as others) before proceeding to note how this sets him apart from other contemporary Latin American guerrillas.

The conclusion summarizes the book's findings, distilling these so as to produce a full and nuanced profile of the Subcommander's political-philosophical formation. I then utilize this to assess Marcos' role in and contribution to the formulation of Zapatismo as a political philosophy.

Finally, the appendices consist of translations into English, for the first time, of two sections from Guillén's thesis, the first of which reveals his indebtedness to Althusser, while the second illustrates his combining of Althusserian and Foucauldian thought, and also of Subcommander Marcos' highly revealing and much-commented-on *Letter to Adolfo Gilly*.

Notes

1. Gustavo Esteva (2004, p. 136) asks "…should we accept the view that he [i.e. Marcos] really is the timely saviour that the world was waiting for; an icon that globaphobics can now use to express their dissent; the new flag for rebellion in these desperate times?"
2. Regis Debray (1995).

3. To provide just a few examples, see: the biographies of Marcos by César Jacobo Romero (1994), Bertrand de la Grange and Maite Rico (1998), and Nick Henck (2007), coupled with the book-length study of the Subcommander by Daniela Di Piramo (2010), the edited collection of pieces on him by Anne Huffschmid (1995), and the curious biographical-novel by Guillermo Samperio (2011); the encyclopaedia entries of Cornelia Graebner (2011) and Nick Henck (2015); the book-length interviews with Marcos by Yvon Le Bot (1997a), Manuel Vázquez Montalbán (2000), Laura Castellanos (2008), and El Kilombo (2007); the chapters devoted to him by Andrés Oppenheimer (1996/1998), Enrique Krauze (2011), and Jorge Castañeda (2011/2012); and articles too numerous to list written by journalists, academics, and literary authors.
4. Retrieved from http://www.rebelion.org/noticia.php?id=44487.
5. In Autonomedia (1994, p. 294) and Alma Guillermoprieto (1995, p. 39) respectively.
6. See too, Marcos' comments, made during the First International Encuentro for Humanity and Against Neoliberalism (summer 1996), on the origins of the EZLN, which, he tells us, was "formed by a group that comes with the whole tradition of Latin American guerrillas of the 1970s, a vanguard group, Marxist-Leninist ideology, fighting for the transformation of the world by trying to achieve power in a dictatorship of the proletariat;" quoted and translated in Cynthia Steele (2002, p. 249).
7. In Autonomedia (1994, p. 294).
8. Marcos in Le Bot (1997a, pp. 338-339); my translation.
9. See below, Appendix III for a full translation of this *Carta*.
10. Quoted and translated in Madhu Suri Prakash and Gustavo Esteva (2008, p. 48).
11. See, for example, in this regard, the sceptical—one might even say cynical—stances of Andrés Oppenheimer (1996/1998, pp. 45 & 47), Bertrand de la Grange and Maite Rico (1998, pp. 35 & 298), Pedro Pitarch (2004, pp. 302-303), and Carlos Alberto Montaner (2001).
12. See Adolfo Gilly (1998, p. 298), who points out that: "Marcos at least also brought [to the ideas of the EZLN] his earlier formation in the academy, a philosophical and historical education that would later appear with clarity in his writings."
13. Di Piramo reiterates this on p. 138, writing: "...we can (and indeed must) locate Marcos ... in the tradition of revolutionary Marxism ... given that this tradition shaped his early intellectual formation."
14. Nick Henck (2012).
15. See Luis Lorenzano (1998, p. 128), who states: "Any attempt to understand—or sanitize—the EZLN as a mere extension of the [Marxist] guerrilla movements of the 1960s and 1970s would be not only useless but sterile and ill-intentioned or even reactionary .... It is also the attitude assumed by intellectuals close to

neo-liberalism … and by certain would-be ex-radicals who regret their past. See too, Walter D. Mignolo and Freya Schiwy (2003, p. 14), who write negatively of "… the temptation to underscore Guillen's [sic] vita instead of the significance of the transformation of Guillen [sic] into Marcos…"

16. Zapatismo is, of course, much more than a political philosophy. Richard Stahler-Sholk (2007, pp. 187-188) notes how: "There are, in effect, at least three Zapatismos: One is the armed insurgency.… A second is the project of autonomous government being constructed in Zapatista 'support base communities'.… The third is the (national and) international network of solidarity inspired by Zapatista ideology and discourse." When employing the term Zapatismo in the pages that follow however, I am referring explicitly (and exclusively) to a fourth Zapatismo, that of the political philosophy of the Zapatista movement.

17. On Dignity as "a central principle" of Zapatismo, see John Holloway (1998, pp. 159-198), esp. at (160): "dignity is the core of the Zapatista revolution." Note too Holloway's (1998, p. 164) assertion that "Dignity was presumably not part of the conceptual baggage of the revolutionaries who went into the jungle. It is not a word that appears very much in the literature of the Marxist tradition." See too, Gutiérrez Ivonne Carlin (1996, pp. 130-131) subsection headed "Aportación y motor del movimiento: la dignidad." NB Jeff Conant (2010, p. 182) notes how "In *Los Hombres Verdaderos* … Carlos Lenkersdorf looks at the Tojolabal language and finds the concept of dignity built into the very structures of the syntax, into the fabric of speaking … the Tojolabal language is predicated, Lenkersdorf suggests, on the notion of dignity—a concept central to Tojolabal culture." Cf however, Michael Löwy (1973/2007, p. 24) who writes of *dignity* [italics in the original]: "This word…constantly recurs in the writings of Che, Fidel, and other Cuban revolutionaries," adding "The theme of dignity doubtless has deep roots in Spanish-American civilization."

18. As Marcos himself, in John Ross and Frank Bardacke (1995, p. 46), has noted: "Collective work, democratic thought, and majority rule are more than just a tradition among indigenous people; they have been the only way to survive, to resist, to be proud, and to rebel." For a useful discussion of "Maya democracy" as advocated by the Zapatistas, see Enrique Dussel (1995a, pp. 51-53). NB, however, that Neil Harvey (1994, p. 30) states that it was the Maoist organization, Línea Proletaria, which had implanted itself in Chiapas in order to promote popular organization, that "revive[d] a traditional element of indigenous democracy, the division of community assemblies into 'small assemblies' or *asambleas chicas*."

19. See, Khasnabish (2010, p. 70): "In the canyons and Lacandón Jungle of Chiapas, the Chol, Tzeltal, Tzotzil and Tojolabal Mayan migrants … had been practising communal decision-making in a directly democratic way through community assemblies…. This relationship exemplifies the key Zapatista democratic notion of 'commanding obeying,' as all authority and legitimacy in this case reside in

the community and in the assembly…" Mihalis Mentinis (2006, p. 159) expresses a slightly different take on this, arguing that "what the Zapatistas often call the principle of 'command obeying', is precisely the product of the fusion between the imported project of autonomy in the form of a revolutionary discourse and the conception of humans as equal agents found in local languages and practices."

20. For further discussion of this concept and practice, see Patricia King and Francisco Javier Villanueva (1998, p. 164f) and Scott Schaffer (2004, pp. 11-12, 225 & 239ff).
21. Enrique Dussel (1995a, pp. 51, 52 & 55, respectively) appears to come dangerously close to doing just this, writing: "The [Zapatista] texts we will read are not inspired on the political, 'democracy' writings of Aristotle, Rousseau, or Bobbio. These texts are Maya, the creation of a millennial cultural experience. … The EZLN's political, theoretical frame of reference is quite theirs. There is no imitation here"; "the Maya political system … owes nothing to contemporary political science…"; and "In other words, native populations speak from their own traditions, without eurocentric imitations."
22. In Le Bot (1997, p. 197). Later on in the same interview (p. 350), Marcos points out that the language of Zapatismo was "invented … with the indigenous cultural contributions *and with* the contributions from the urban culture" (my emphasis). (The translation here is that of Cynthia Steele (2002, p. 250); for a slightly alternative but fundamentally similar translation, see Nicholas P. Higgins (2004, p. 167).) See too the Subcommander's interview with Manuel Vázquez Montalbán (2002, p. 476):

> "The EZLN was not born from approaches that arrived from the city. *But neither was it an approach deriving exclusively from the Indigenous communities.* It was created out of a mixture, a (Molotov) cocktail, out of a culture shock which went on to produce a new discourse … (emphasis mine)"

23. See Kathleen Bruhn (1999, p. 30): "In the EZLN's case, most documents are the intellectual product of a single author, Subcomandante Marcos…;" and again (p. 42): "Subcomandante Marcos is … the primary author of virtually all communiqués;" and accompanying endnote (9) on p. 52: "In addition to the stylistic unity of EZLN documents, Marcos bolsters this view in his own statements, arguing that a single spokesperson provides greater internal consistency in the public positions of a movement and that 'in a movement of this type, coherence is very important' (Le Bot 1997a, p. 365)." See too, Cynthia Steele (2002, p. 248): "…Marcos has made it quite clear that he is the one who actually writes the communiqués for the all-Mayan governing body of the EZLN, the CCRI…;" and Christopher Domínguez Michael (1999): "The three volumes of *Documentos y comunicados del EZLN*, and the recent collection *Cuentos para una soledad desvelada*, are essentially the work of one author."
24. As proof of this, see: Marcos' communiqué "Putting Out the Fire with Gasoline

(postscript to the cartoon)" dated January 11, 2013; retrieved from http://enlacezapatista.ezln.org.mx/2013/01/16/putting-out-the-fire-with-gasoline-postscript-to-the-cartoon/:

> P.S. THAT GIVES LESSONS ON RACISM IN COMMUNICATION—I read in various places "EZLN yes, Marcos, no" and that they want to hear the indigenous Zapatistas, not the egomaniacal Sup. Okay, here goes… For example, the August 15, 2012 denunciation of the Junta de Buen Gobierno of La Realidad was the principal article on the Zapatista web page for 24 straight days and got 1080 visitors/readers… Number of visits to the Sup's cartoon that so offended the enlightened ones: more than five thousand visits in less than 48 hours…

25. The translation here is that of Walter D. Mignolo and Freya Schiwy (2003, p. 13).
26. Thus there is truth in the assertion of Di Piramo (2010, p. 159), who states that "the political ideas of the Zapatista Movement cannot be completely removed from the Marxist tradition." See too, James Petras (1999, p. 36), who writes of the Zapatistas' "blend of Marxist analysis and Indian practices" and Todd Wolfson (2014, p. 33) who writes of the EZLN's "synthesis of traditional Mayan culture and Marxist praxis."

1
Literary Formation[1]

It may strike the reader as being curious that a work that sets out to explore the political-philosophical formation of a Latin-American left-wing guerrilla should begin with a chapter that discusses literature, especially fiction and poetry; however, as we shall see, the rationale for doing so rests upon solid foundations.

In an interview with Gabriel García Márquez and Roberto Pombo (2001, p. 77), the Subcommander tells us of his exposure to literature from an early age, relating how "my parents introduced us to García Márquez, Carlos Fuentes, Monsiváis, Vargas Llosa ... to mention only a few," and giving as examples of specific works: *A Hundred Years of Solitude*, *The Death of Artemio Cruz*, *Días de guardar* (*Days of Remembrance* in English), and *The Time of the Hero* (*La ciudad y los perros*). In fact, much attests to Marcos having grown up in a household conducive to reading. For example, in an early interview the Subcommander told *Vanity Fair* reporter Ann Louise Bardach:

> I learned to read in my house, not at school. So when I went to school I had a great advantage because I was already well-read. I read Shakespeare and Cervantes, Neruda, Fuentes, many books by Latin-American writers. (1994, pp. 67-68)

The testimony of Alfonso Guillén, father of Rafael Guillén (the Subcommander's pre-guerrilla incarnation), both corroborates and elaborates on Marcos' childhood experiences of reading. Alfonso, who himself "began to devour books from when he was small," proudly recounts how "his children ... grew up surrounded with books."[2] We also know that Alfonso's favourite authors were Chesterton and Balzac, but that he also liked Jaime Torres Bodet, Pablo Neruda, and Octavio Paz, and that he taught Rafael, at the age of five (and before he could read), to recite from memory the long poem "El Sembrador," by the Spanish poet Rafael Blanco Belmonte.[3] Thus, it is evident that Subcommander Marcos' family was one in which reading was actively encouraged and literature never far.

The result of this upbringing, Marcos informs us, was that he was "already, as the orthodox would say, very corrupted by the time we got to … revolutionary literature. So that when we got into Marx and Engels we were thoroughly spoilt by literature; its irony and humour."[4] This admittance, I would urge, represents a crucial revelation since it not only reveals that Marcos had been exposed to literature prior to encountering Marxism, but also that this exposure had a profound impact on him—one which influenced the way he would subsequently engage with revolutionary writings. Furthermore, in the same interview the Subcommander informs us that his early childhood exposure to literature "marked" him since because of it he "didn't look out at the world through a news-wire but through a novel, an essay or a poem …. That was the prism through which my parents wanted me to view the world, as others might choose the prism of the media" (p. 78). Thus, for Marcos, his subsequent encounter with and experience of Marxism (and later, one should add, indigenous thought and practices) would be in large part mediated through the prism of the literature that he read.

As we shall witness, the Subcommander's love of literature would remain with him throughout his teenage years, his university student days, his guerrilla days in the jungle, and for the rest of his life.

At sixth form, according to friends and classmates, Rafael always went around book-in-hand.[5] These books in all likelihood comprised literature, since we know from one interview with the Subcommander that "as a youth Marcos read Neruda, León Felipe, Antonio Machado, Vallejo," and that "he read Ernesto Cardenal and Borges later, as well as the Mexicans Efraín Huerta, Rosario Castellanos, Sabines, Montes de Oca…[and] Paz's poetic essays."[6] However, it would appear that his reading was not confined purely to poetry and novels. Marcos told Bardach (1994, p. 68) that "In high school I read about Hitler, Marx, Lenin, Mussolini—history and political science in general …" Furthermore, according to his father, "Rafael had always liked philosophy, and this is what he wanted to study."[7] Hence, in 1977 Rafael Guillén enrolled in the School of Philosophy and Arts (Filosofía y Letras) at The National Autonomous University of Mexico (UNAM).

Concurrent with writing his graduation thesis, Guillén entered the clandestine, revolutionary Marxist-Leninist Fuerzas de Liberación Nacional (FLN), a self-avowed "political-military organization whose end is the taking of political power for the campesinos and the workers of the Mexican Republic, to establish a popular republic with a socialist system."[8] Years later, having become Subcommander, Marcos would relate how

> When we joined the organization we had to be serious, respectful, boring … if the books you carried were not *Materialism and Empirical Criticism* and were for instance [Julio Cortázar's] *Historias de cronopios y de famas* or Benedetti's love poems, they stared at you in a strange way. (1995a)

Not long after graduating, Guillén departed for Chiapas to embark on a new life as a rural guerrilla, first employing the pseudonym "Zacarías" but soon afterwards adopting the *nom de guerre* "Marcos." He nonetheless managed to take with him a few treasured tomes, as Marcos (1995b, p. 72) recalls:

> Of the twelve books that I carried with me to the jungle, one was Pablo Neruda's *Canto general*; another was a selection of poems by Miguel Hernández; also poems by León Felipe; Cortázar's *Historias de cronopios y [de] famas*; the *Memoirs* of Francisco Villa; *Don Quixote* … I did not plan this or reflect on it much before taking them … I grabbed those books which came to hand, the ones that I read most often or consulted most.

These precious volumes, numbering "about 15, some five or ten kilos,"[9] Marcos (1994, p. 201) tells us, proved cumbersome in the short-run:

> I used to carry books around in the mountains, and was scolded for it: why was I carrying them around? It was really suicide … the load of ammunition, food and everything else is divided equally, and on top of that you're carrying books …

Over time, Marcos' comrades gradually began to appreciate his having brought books to the mountains, until there came a point when, as the Subcommander recalls, "every time I left a book behind, someone would offer to carry it for me …. 'A story is going to come out of that,' they would say."[10] In another interview, Marcos (1995b, p. 82) talks at some length about the importance that books, and the way they can be read and related, took on for him and the recruited cadres who accompanied him during the guerrilla column's early years of ranging throughout the mountains and canyons of Chiapas:

> A book in those circumstances is something that you take a lot of care of, you read and re-read it, and "chew it over," and among troops who were largely illiterate at that time[11] ... you impart the book, they read the book through you, and it could be the same book but one always had to find another way to relate it or discuss it, and finally many books were extracted from the one.

In addition, Marcos, in his interview with Gelman (1996), relates that during this stage of the guerrilla he read, recited, and even wrote poetry:

> I wrote poetry during the time in the mountain ... especially in the first years, 1984/1985 ... poetry which tried to be political ...[12]

> The poetry we visited was that which is considered social or engaged. Which is the kind we liked because that is what we were into. Or the most distant of the classics like Shakespeare, that, yes. But of contemporary poetry, only that which had social content. That which didn't seemed useless to us, it was counterrevolutionary, petit bourgeois, etcetera ...

Crucially here Gelman follows up on this statement, asking the Subcommander, "Do you think the same thing now?," to which Marcos replies, "Obviously not," before providing the following vivid and illuminating insight:

> We now realize what those elements—the non-schematic, the non-traditional as regards that culture of the left in which we were trained, especially in the clandestine left, that of the underground—were those which opened windows for us. What saved us as a social program, as a political program and, above all, as human beings, were those open windows, those supposed "marks" for an inflexible revolution, those which led us to jokingly say that for being inflexible [square] revolutionaries we were rather round ...

> That culture, that literature, has its place, it has its space and it cannot be categorized according to the molds they taught us, that poetry is only the poetry of "Patria or death, we will be victorious" or that which describes a social situation. There is poetry which works on the language itself and it does not matter so much what it says but on the use of the language. There is poetry which expresses everyday experiential sentiments or questions. There are many kinds of poetry.

— Literary formation —

How to say it? The political scheme we grew up with had its referent or equivalent in a cultural scheme, in an ideological scheme and even in a moral scheme which specified what was good and what was bad: good is everything which served the revolution, bad is everything that goes against the revolution. And that is not the problem with the good and the bad, in that way it is only being eluded. And that happened not only with literature, also with music, or, what we should listen to or which we should like, because that is what it is about. Once again, it has to be music with social content or revolutionary music, as we say.

And the other, there was music that is dehumanizing, alienating, etcetera. Even though we liked it, we had to be quiet and say that good music was that with social content. This concept even influenced the talks in the collective group. The mountain collective is a very solitary group, subject to very harsh conditions, which tended to close itself off, making itself strong in order to be able to resist, helping each other. Then, nostalgia was prohibited, or, in any event, exhibiting it was. Not that there was a law, but when symptoms of demoralization were noted in a compañero, he had to be helped, for example, by explaining that the proletariat, for an historic decision, was going to assume its objectives, etcetera.

Marcos also tells Gelman (1996) that later, he turned away from writing poetry for a while and "returned once again to the story and to short narratives like 'Instructions for Changing the World' and 'Instructions for Falling Down and Getting Up,' all of that much influenced by Cortázar …", before once more revisiting "poetry when we began to make contact with the indigenous communities." Elaborating on this Marcos explains:

> The way they [i.e. the indigenous] use language, the description of reality, of their world, has many poetical elements. That is how the normal or traditional cultural path I brought was altered, and that mixture began being produced which appeared in the EZLN communiqués of 1994. It was a bit like debating between the indigenous roots of a movement and the urban element …

Moving forward chronologically, Marcos, now elevated to the rank of Subcommander, established a permanent base camp which in turn allowed for both the housing of a substantial cache of books and the more sedentary life necessary to read them.[13] By now he was also interacting much more with

Chiapas' indigenous peoples, both training the indigenous recruits under his command and moving among the indigenous communities whence they were recruited. In fact, it is precisely during this period that we can witness the coming together of the "two large aspects to Marcos ... that of the orthodox left, and later the one which resulted from the process of digestion and modification which the indigenous communities provided" that the Subcommander describes in his interview with Raymundo Reynoso (2007) and with which I opened my introduction.

Over the course of almost a decade Marcos spent his time blending classical, socially engaged, and indigenous poetics, until we arrive, in 1994, at "the third element" of Marcos, "which is the contact with ... the people from the outside," whereby, the Subcommander informed Reynoso, "Marcos ... went through that process of digestion throughout all those years of contact with you, with the people from outside, with civil society ..." When the Zapatista uprising burst forth in January 1994, Marcos suddenly came into contact with the outside world, and more especially both prevailing intellectual and cultural currents, and a host of eminent public intellectuals, both national and international. Concerning the former, in his interview with Gelman (1996) the Subcommander tells us that "We did not know more recent poetry until we came down.... We discovered Pessoa when we came down from the mountain, from 1994 on, in books they gave us." As for the latter, leading writers and cultural figures such as John Berger, Carlos Fuentes, Eduardo Galeano, Adolfo Gilly, Eric Jauffret, and Luis Villoro, have engaged in epistolary exchanges with the Subcommander; while others even sat down to talk with Marcos face to face. For instance, we have already witnessed above the Subcommander being interviewed by Argentine poet Juan Gelman and Colombian Nobel Laureate Gabriel García Márquez, but other literary and intellectual luminaries, among them Guadalupe Loaeza, Carlos Monsiváis, Elena Poniatowska, Ignacio Ramonet, and Manuel Vázquez Montalbán, have done so also. Furthermore, not a few interviewers, intellectuals and journalists alike, have engaged the Subcommander specifically on the matter of his reading. As an example, note the following exchange between Gelman (1996) and Marcos:

> J.G.: *Are you still reading poetry?*
>
> S.M.: Yes, why not. In some of the communiqués I relate the story of a girl who died, Paticha ... In reality, that came from reading a poem by an

Argentinean who was talking about a girl … I found it in an anthology of Latin American poetry, along with another text of yours. I don't remember what it is called, but it talks about a girl who, forced by social conditions, commits a crime.

J.G.: *Could it be "Maria the servant"?*

S.M.: Go on, that was it. Its structure inspired the literary form of the story of Paticha. The story is real, but its presentation was quite close to "Maria the servant."

There is also Marcos' interview with journalist Raymundo Reynoso (2007):

R.R.: *Marcos … you have accumulated much reading, past, present. What are you reading now?*

S.M.: Well, I read the classics above all. The last one I was reading is Bertolt Brecht … as to literature, especially the theater, Brecht's works, novels and classics like Cervantes…

However, undoubtedly the most enlightening exchange took place between the Subcommander and journalist and author Laura Castellanos (2008, p. 96):

L.C.: *You have said that the literature of the Latin American boom and the classics of universal literature, among them Quixote of La Mancha, were formative for you. Throughout these 14 years what other literary and philosophical sources have nourished you?—I have in mind your contact with a stellar group of national and foreign artists and intellectuals.*

S.M.: Basically, the same ones, although now I read more indigenous literature, poetry, legends … But a fundamental classic is *La visión de los vencidos* [*The Broken Spears: The Aztec Account of the Conquest of Mexico*] by Miguel León Portilla, that book was added to the nightstand.

As the interview unfolds, Marcos continues, listing Juan Rulfo as an author he is fond of, as well as singling out James Joyce's *Ulysses* and the *Sonnets* of Shakespeare. He adds that *Don Quixote*, and anthologies of Miguel Hernández and Pablo Neruda, especially *Canto general*, are ones which always stay with him. In terms of (then) living writers, Marcos comments effusively on the Uruguayans, Mario Benedetti[14] and Eduardo Galeano, informing Castellanos (2008, pp. 97, 102 & 105) that

> The Latin American literary figure whom I most admire is not García Márquez nor Vargas Llosa but Eduardo Galeano, along with Mario Benedetti. Galeano even more than Benedetti ... I always admire people who can express a big idea in a few words, and Galeano is capable of expressing complete and complex feelings in small paragraphs. And I'm not referring to the book *Open Veins in Latin America*, but to *Memories of Fire*, the three volumes of which are a gem of literature and one of the most beautiful history lessons of Latin America that I have read ...

It is clear from the above then that Marcos' love of literature, acquired at a young age, not only pre-dated his exposure to Marxist-Leninism, but also continued to play a part in his formation during his years as a university student, then as a rural guerrilla, and finally as the Zapatista subcommander and spokesperson we all know today. However, our observations are not limited to this: we can go much further.

I would urge, for example, that the Subcommander's literary formation had a profound impact on his discourse, both in terms of determining his points of reference and in his choice of the vehicle by which to convey his message. Concerning the former, it is significant to note that Marcos' writings reveal a familiarity with a vast number of literary authors, including (but not limited to): Mario Benedetti, John Berger, Ray Bradbury, Berthold Brecht, Hector Aguilar Camín, Lewis Carroll, Miguel de Cervantes, G. K. Chesterton, Julio Cortázar, Roque Dalton, Dante Alighieri, Daniel Defoe, Eliseo Diego, Conan Doyle, Umberto Eco, Paul Éluard, León Felipe, Carlos Fuentes, Darío Fo, Adolfo Gilly, Ermilo Abreu Gómez, Miguel Hernández, Eric Jauffret, C. S. Lewis, Mario Vargas Llosa, Federico García Lorca, Antonio Machado, Hermann Melville, Manuel Vázquez Montalbán, Pablo Neruda, Cesare Pavese, Fernando Pessoa, Edmond Rostand, Juan Rulfo, Ernesto Sábato, Pedro Salinas, José Saramago, Manuel Scorza, William Shakespeare, Jonathan Swift, and Walt Whitman etc. The overwhelmingly literary nature of these references in Marcos' corpus of communiqués lies in sharp contrast to the dearth of authors who can be categorized as writers of political philosophy: notably absent from the Subcommander's communiqués are references to twentieth-century philosophers and political theorists such as Adorno, Althusser, Badiou, Balibar, Baudrillard, Chomsky (by some indices the most cited person alive[15]), Deleuze, Derrida, Fanon, Gramsci, Guattari, Habermas, Hardt, Heidegger, Horkheimer, Lacan, Laclau, Lévi-Strauss, Mao, Marcuse,

Mouffe, Negri, Pêcheux, Poulantzas, and Trotsky, all of whom fail to make their way into the Subcommander's missives. Even the name of Foucault, one of the twentieth century's leading intellectual luminaries, only appears twice in all of Marcos' several hundred communiqués, and one of these times is in a citation of Umberto Eco's novel *Foucault's Pendulum*, and so has nothing to do with the French philosopher. Interestingly, Kathleen Bruhn (1999, p. 42), after a fairly comprehensive examination of Zapatista communiqués dating from 1994-1997, concludes that "Sherlock Holmes's sidekick, Dr. Watson, appears more often than Mexican union leader Fidel Velázquez, communist icon Vladimir Lenin, or Mexico's only indigenous president, Benito Juárez." Also based on a reading of Marcos' correspondence, Carlos Fuentes (1994/1997, p. 93), claimed "that Subcommander *Marcos*, the Zapatista leader, has read more Carlos Monsiváis than he has Carlos Marx." Similarly, Michael Taussig (1999, p. 258), drawing attention to Marcos' views as expressed in a postscript from a July 10, 1994 communiqué[16] discussing Julio Cortázar, concludes that these are "… hardly the sentiments of a social scientist, let alone an attitude congenial to a Marxist Determinism."

I would add to these observations several of my own. First is that Marcos has claimed that:

> *Don Quixote* is the best book of political theory, followed by *Hamlet* and *Macbeth*. There is no better way to understand the Mexican political system, in its tragic and comic aspects: *Hamlet, Macbeth* and *Don Quixote*.[17]

Marcos would repeat his assertion concerning Cervantes' masterpiece in a later interview with Raymundo Reynoso (2007), where he calls *Don Quixote* "The best book of political theory," before adding "I remember that when the Italian Fausto Bertinotti, of the Communist Refundacion party, arrived, I told him I was going to give him a Political Science manual, and I gave him Quixote…Read it, I told him, and you are going to see that everything happening right now, all the parts that are at play, are there, in Quixote." Moreover, elsewhere, when discussing neoliberalism, which he dubs "The Catastrophic Political Management of Catastrophe," Marcos does not draw on his extensive reading of Marxist texts to explain his assertion that "The foundation of neoliberalism is a contradiction: in order to maintain itself it must devour itself and, therefore, destroy itself.… What keeps the system going is what will bring it down"; instead, his point of reference is G. K. Chesterton's *The Three Horsemen of the Apocalypse*.[18] Finally, there is Marcos' missive recollecting a conversation he had with the famous Spanish crime novelist, poet, and essayist Manuel Vázquez Montalbán, during which the two men "… had to agree on the fact that, many times, the best texts of political analysis are [to be found] in universal literature …"[19]

Interestingly, even when asked directly about his reading of works of a political and/or philosophical nature, Marcos proves reticent. For example, in an interview with Marcos (1994, p. 201), when discussion turned to the "many political books" the Subcommander has read, the interviewers note how "he doesn't go into details about [them]," other than to mention "his favorites of *Los agachados* and *Los supermachos* by [Mexican political cartoonist] Rius." More telling still, it is significant to note that in her interview with Marcos, although Laura Castellanos prompts the Subcommander for "literary *and philosophical* sources" (my emphasis), he provides only literary examples; or, if we acknowledge a philosophical element to the "indigenous literature, poetry, legends" which he mentions, then there is at least a lack of authors and works belonging to the canon of what could be called formal Western political philosophy. Especially notable by their absence are any references to Marx, to subsequent Marxist philosophers such as Althusser, Gramsci, or Poulantzas—or, in fact, any figures pertaining to the so-called "New Left"—or to more recent left-wing political philosophers such as Ernesto Laclau, Antonio Negri, or Michael Hardt.

Moreover, in addition to Marcos' own testimony regarding his reading of political-philosophical works, we have the accounts of two journalists who reported on the Mexican Federal Army's seizure of the Subcommander's camp, including, significantly, his personal library, during a February 1995 offensive. These are worthy of attention since they represent our only external source on the Subcommander's reading with which we can compare Marcos' own statements on the subject. José Luis Ruiz (1995, p. 12), reporting for the newspaper *El Universal*, writes of the discovery of a "mountain of books and texts … books of all types, from social and political works to ideological ones," with *Reforma*'s Juan Manuel Alvarado (1995, p. 10A) putting the total at "more than seventy books." Between them, these two journalists inform us that among the works discovered were: Fidel Castro's *History Will Absolve Me*; *The Chinese I-Ching* or *Book of Changes*; *Filosofía y marxismo*, an interview with Louis Althusser by Fernanda Navarro; Manuel López Gallo's *Economía y política de la historia de México*; Elena Poniatowska's *La noche de Tlatelolco*;

El espartaquismo en México by Paulina Fernández Christlieb; José Luis Calva's two books *La disputa por la tierra* and *El modelo neoliberal mexicano*; *Revolutionary Works* by Che Guevara; Jorge Aguilar Mora's book of essays entitled *Una muerte sencilla, justa, eterna: cultura y guerra durante la Revolución Mexicana*; Hermann Broch's modernist novel *The Death of Virgil*; Julio Cortázar's *Los autonautas de la cosmopista*; *El Prinosaurio* by Manú Dornbierer; John Le Carré's *Smiley's People*; and Hakim Bey's *The Temporary Autonomous Zone*; as well as such works as *Mujeres en tiempo de guerra* and el *Boletín del Archivo Histórico Diocesano*, and pieces by Mexican political cartoonist Bulmaro Castellanos Loza (alias "Magú"). In terms of poetry, Marcos' library contained Silvia Tomasa Rivera's *Vuelo de sombras*, Justo Sierra's *Antología del centenario*, Antón Makarenko's *The Pedagogical Poem*, and three books of love poems by Ernesto Zúñiga. Again what is striking here is both the relative lack of works of a Marxist nature—only the aforementioned works by Fidel Castro, Louis Althusser, and Che Guevara could be classified under this heading—and the wealth of works of a literary nature.

All of this brings us to another important observation concerning the Subcommander's literary formation, and the effect of this upon his writings and his Marxism; namely, that Marcos conforms very much to the tradition in Latin America of literary authors contributing more to the dissemination and acceptance of a left-wing, or even Marxist, worldview than political philosophers or theorists. For example, Roger Burbach and Orlando Núñez (1986/1987, p. 100) conclude that: "It is no exaggeration to say that poets and novelists in Latin America have played a much more important role than social scientists in raising the political consciousness of the masses against authoritarian regimes and imperialism."[20] Moreover, turning specifically to Mexico and not just its masses but all those on the left of the political spectrum, Enrique Krauze (2011, pp. 440 & 441) states that "Given the degree to which the Mexican left (even up to the present day) has been more cultural than social and more social than political, the discourse and symbols of Marcos had a truly revolutionary impact." All of which has led Christopher Domínguez Michael (1999, p. 68) to conclude that: "The novelty of the political literature of Marcos would be that, as seldom in the history of intellectual engagement, it is a cultural politics."[21]

Looking more closely at the literary nature of the Subcommander's discourse, given what we have witnessed in the preceding pages it is perhaps of little surprise that poetry makes its presence felt forcefully. Needless to say, several authors have pointed to the Subcommander's acquaintance with poetry—for example, Enrique Krauze (2011, p. 441) notes how Marcos' "use of quotations, especially from poetry, seemed natural and effortless"; while Jorge Volpi (2004, p. 300) notes that "he is undoubtedly a good reader of Latin American poetry"; and Luis Hernández Navarro (2007, p. 100) even goes so far as to claim that "Subcomandante Marcos ... is in actual fact a poet." However, of greater significance than his poetic ability is the fact that the Subcommander has elected to deploy poetic forms as part of his discursive arsenal. Marcos (1998, p. 169) makes this point explicitly in his communiqué entitled "To resist using Poetry," in which he responds to Comandante *Arturo* of Mexico's other main contemporary guerrilla group, the EPR, who during an interview had made a sly dig at the Zapatistas by remarking that "poetry cannot be the continuation of politics by other means."[22] The Subcommander countered:

> When Roque Dalton wrote that it was possible to arrive at "the revolution through poetry," the leadership of the Salvadoran ERP was planning the assassination of the guerrilla poet for "deviations" and being an "enemy agent." Today, the old and "revolutionary" leadership of the ERP is making alliances with the criminal Salvadoran right, and, from the grave, Roque continues cursing the Power and moving towards the revolution through poetry . ... In addition, I believe that for just being some poets, we have given the Power plenty of problems, no?[23]

This use of poetry as a vehicle for revolution is something made much of by Nicholas P. Higgins (2004, pp. 156-157), who writes that Marcos' "telling choice of poetry as a favored form of expression should not be acknowledged simply on the grounds of literary merit, but instead, it should be recognized as a conscious and political statement concerned with just how, and by whom, the realm of experience can best be communicated." Similarly, John Holloway (2005, pp. 175-76), urges that:

> The poetry of the Zapatista uprising ... is not peripheral to their movement ... but central to their whole struggle.... This is not just a question of pretty words or of Marcos's undoubted literary skills. It is above all that they offer a different way of seeing the world, a vision that breaks with the dominant logic of there-is-no-alternative ...

In this, Holloway echoes Laura Hernández Martínez (2002, pp. 104-106), who has argued that "the most outstanding characteristic of Marcos' discourse is its poetic quality," which "appears much closer to the poetical than the political, [b]ut not because it pertains to this literary genre," but because it "renounces certainty ... not only in the discourse which it opposes but also in its own discourse." Finally, after noting "the irrationality of the certainty of the dominant ideology," Hernández Martínez concludes: "this poetic quality underscores how the [Zapatista] discourse does not intend to postulate that its ideology is more rational than the discourse which opposes it, but rather that the postulation of certainty itself is irrational."[24]

Arguably the most important result of Marcos' poetical discourse, which combined poetic forms and influences derived from both world literature and also indigenous literature (as well as indigenous Chiapanecan linguistic practices),[25] was the new political language which emerged from it. Daniela Di Piramo (2010, pp. 124-125), has commented that "Marcos' most effective prose ... is totally different to traditional political literature ... presenting serious political issues in a colourful and appealing manner that avoids the staidness of formal political rhetoric." Similarly, Gustavo Esteva (2004, p. 138) notes how "Instead of a cold, abstract ideology, frozen in seductive slogans, Marcos uses images, stories, metaphors, and characters like Durito and old Antonio." Others go even further, with Jorge Volpi (2003) stating that: "In formulating a deeply literary revolution, Marcos not only took charge of renewing the language of the left, but he granted it the power of 'doing things with words' to use the expression of John Austin"; and Luis Hernández Navarro (2007, p. 104) claiming that "the Zapatista discourse reformulates not only the function of the left on the political spectrum but also renovates its language."[26] It is the historian Lorenzo Meyer (1994, pp. 1, 10, 36), however, who perhaps offers the fullest and most incisive comments on this subject. He begins by noting that "the discourse of the new Zapatistas is simple, comprehensible, and has a clear moral foundation. It is, therefore, the antithesis of the governmental language,"[27] while at the same emphasizing that "The discourse is also quite distinct from the stilted and esoteric language which has been used for a long time by the Mexican left."[28] Meyer proceeds:

> One of the elements of the surprising political success of the EZLN in general, and of Subcomandante Marcos in particular, is that both ... have reintroduced direct and simple—but not simplistic—discourse into Mexican

politics, and have even allowed themselves some poetic license. It is, therefore, a discourse in which words seek to recuperate their original meaning, and for this reason they have become anti-authoritarian and liberating.

Thus, Marcos' political language appears heavily indebted not to the somewhat jargon-laden and convoluted Marxist-Leninist prose he read during his university and clandestine guerrilla days, but to the literary language of the works of world literature that have accompanied him throughout his life, coupled with the linguistic forms of the indigenous peoples he encountered and lived alongside in Chiapas. In short, we are faced with the rather curious and surprising fact that Marcos, although the Subcommander of a Latin American left-wing guerrilla movement, should have been formed profoundly and enduringly through his reading of world and indigenous literature, and that it was these that provided him with his primary frame of reference, with the result that his discourse appears to be far more indebted to these literary traditions than the tradition of Marxism-Leninism.

Of course, a more cynical interpretation than the one afforded above is also possible. The portrait of the Subcommander that I have painted admittedly relies heavily on the testimony of Marcos himself, and so is open to being treated with a degree of skepticism—one which would open up the possibility that the savvy Zapatista spokesperson, ever adept at cultivating a charismatic media persona, downplays the influence that his reading of Marxist texts had on him, preferring instead to emphasize the role that his exposure to world literature played in his formation. According to this scenario, Marcos is masking what he has read in order to project a more palatable public image of himself as a man whose formation owes more to his reading of Monsiváis than Marx, and whose principal weapon in the struggle is irony not ideology.[29] However, without denying the possibility that there may be an element of truth to the above, I would point out the following. First, Marcos has never denied his Marxist roots; on the contrary, he has frequently acknowledged these.[30] Second, although references by Marcos to Marxist literature are few and far between, they nonetheless exist. (One thinks, for example, of his *Letter to Adolfo Gilly*[31] in which he makes specific reference to, and demonstrates acquaintance with, Lenin's writings.[32])

It is not then, I would urge, that the Subcommander wishes to suppress or obscure his reading of Marxist political philosophy, rather it is simply that Marxist-Leninism is not the primary (either in terms of chronology or perhaps even of importance) tradition which formed him and his discourse—hence Marcos' claim that by the time he "got into Marx and Engels" he was already "thoroughly spoilt by literature; its irony and humour"—nor is it the predominant frame through which he views and interprets the world—hence Marcos' assertion that from youth he learned to "look out at the world through … the prism [of] … a novel, an essay or a poem …"[33] It is perhaps not surprising therefore that as a consequence Marcos formulates his discourse (both written and spoken) in relation to such a literary framework. Certainly those who have conducted literary analyses of the Subcommander's texts have emphasized the influence of Spanish literature on Marcos' writings, in particular the poetry of León Felipe, Miguel Hernández and Frederico García Lorca,[34] and, of course, the canonical Quixote.[35] So pronounced, in fact, is the indebtedness of Marcos' writings to literature (as opposed to political philosophy) that Kristine Vanden Berghe (2009, pp. 67-68) has urged that whereas "traditional works of engaged literature in Latin America … sometimes … politicized literary genres, Marcos 'literalized' the political genre of the guerrilla communiqué."

Naturally, some may well argue that Marcos' decision to express his political thought using literary and poetic forms, as opposed to turgid and staid political tracts, was a calculated strategy designed to maximize the appeal of the Zapatistas' message in a post-communist (or at least post-Soviet Union) world. Certainly it is the case that Marcos' role within the Zapatista movement is both to articulate its program and to garner broad (even global) public support for it, and that in the post-Soviet Union era it is highly doubtful that these two aims could have been successfully achieved through adoption of an intensely technical Marxist discourse. In this sense, an interview given only two days after Marcos wrote his *Letter to Adolfo Gilly* (October 22, 1994), is telling since in it the Subcommander talks of "the absurdities that we had been taught; of imperialism, social crisis, the correlation of forces and their coming together, things that nobody understands …"[36] In reality, it is not that Marcos does not understand such terms—indeed, in an interview with Sergio Rodríguez Lascano (2006) he discussed the correlation of forces at some length in connection with intellectuals—it is rather that this is not the framework through which he formulates his thought and, furthermore, he knows that the employment of specialist Marxist technical jargon is not the best way to reach the mass of humanity. (In the same way, George Orwell, although undoubtedly a socialist who had read Marxist works, chose to articulate his anti-imperialist, anti-authoritarian, left-wing thinking through novels, essays and poems, and not through overtly political treatises laden with Marxist terminology.) Indeed, as Marcos explains in his interview with Yvon Le Bot (1997a, p. 356): "We are not saying that we want to create a sentimental discourse, one that's apolitical, or atheoretical, or anti-theoretical; but what we want is to bring theory down to the level of the human being, to what is lived..."[37] In short, it was his reading of literature as a child that first engaged Marcos and which has had an enduring effect on him, determining the way he chooses to express himself and articulate his political-philosophical thought; moreover, and most importantly, it is through literature that he believes he can best perform his duty as spokesperson communicating to the wider world the Zapatistas' experience and message.

Ultimately, if the preceding portrait of Marcos proves an accurate likeness, we can concur with Jorge Volpi's (2004, p. 362) portrayal of the Subcommander as one who

> belongs to the last generation of enthusiastic readers of Marx, Althusser, Martha Harnecker, Pablo González Casanova and Eduardo Galeano—the forgers of the Latin American left's discourse—and to the first who read with the same interest Borges, Ibargüengoitia, the narrators of the "Wave" and, *but of course*, Carlos Monsiváis.

Notes

1. The overwhelming majority of the material in this chapter is taken from my longer journal article: Nick Henck (2014, June), "Subcomandante Marcos: The Latest Reader," *The Latin Americanist* 58(2), 49–73, which, drawing on Ricardo Piglia's essay "Ernesto Guevara: the last reader," seeks to draw comparisons between the Argentine revolutionary and Subcommander Marcos as readers.
2. These two quotations are from Bertrand de la Grange and Maite Rico (1998, pp. 68 & 70); the rest of the information in this paragraph derives from both de la Grange and Rico (1998) and Fernando Ortega Pizarro (1995a, p. 22).
3. NB too, that when journalist Gabriela Hernández (1999, p. 62) interviewed Alfonso, she commented that he could quote Balzac and Tolstoy from memory.
4. García Márquez and Roberto Pombo (2001, p. 78).
5. De la Grange and Rico (1998, p. 73).
6. Marcos (1994, p. 201).

7. In de la Grange and Rico (1998, p. 75).
8. In FLN (1980/2003, p. 5).
9. Marcos quoted in Guiomar Rovira (1994, p. 52) and Michael McCaughan (2002, p. 72).
10. In McCaughan (2002, p. 72).
11. Elsewhere, Marcos (1995a) elaborates on the subject of illiteracy among recruits and how this was remedied: "we taught literacy with Juan Gelman's poems and *The Open Veins of Latin America* was a grammar text," adding, "Mario Benedetti played a key role for our troops: his love poems were textually transcribed to seduce 'compañeras.'"
12. An example of one of Marcos' political poems from around this period can be found translated in Nicholas P. Higgins (2004, p. 159ff).
13. According to José Luis Ruiz (1995, p. 12), when the Mexican army discovered the Subcommander's camp during its February 1995 offensive, they unearthed a "mountain of books and texts" with Juan Manuel Alvarado (1995, p. 10A) putting the total at "more than seventy books."
14. Benedetti died on May 17, 2009.
15. See Chomsky Is Citation Champ. MIT News (1992, April 15). Retrieved from http://web.mit.edu/newsoffice/1992/citation-0415.html:
    > his [Chomsky's] 3,874 citations in the Arts and Humanities Citation Index between 1980 and 1992 make him the most cited living person in that period and the eighth most cited source overall—just behind famed psychiatrist Sigmund Freud and just ahead of philosopher Georg Hegel.... But that isn't all. From 1972 to 1992, Professor Chomsky was cited 7,449 times in the Social Science Citation Index—likely the greatest number of times for a living person there as well ...
16. Communiqué retrieved from http://palabra.ezln.org.mx/comunicados/1994/1994_07_10_b.htm.
17. In his interview with Gabriel García Márquez and Roberto Pombo (2001, pp. 77 & 78).
18. In Autonomedia (2005, p. 110).
19. This correspondence is retrieved from http://www.jornada.unam.mx/2004/11/29/06an1cul.php; the translation is that of my own.
20. The same is perhaps also true in the Anglo-Saxon world; one thinks, for example, of the influence of George Orwell.
21. See too, Julio Moguel (1998, pp. 31-32), who downplays "the influence of Leninists or Maoists" on Marcos, preferring instead to emphasize that of "that generation of thinkers who, in Mexico, have Monsiváis as one of their most recognized representatives [and who] live and think of politics as culture..."
22. (1996, August 11) *Proceso* (1032). Retrieved from http://www.tmcrew.org/chiapas/epr.htm; the translation here is that of Bill Weinberg (2000, p. 299).
23. Communiqué retrieved from http://palabra.ezln.org.mx/comunica-

dos/1996/1996_08_31.htm; published in Subcommander Marcos (1998, p. 169).

24. In fact, the Zapatistas' unwillingness to indulge in an irrational assertion of certainty, as evinced by their reluctance to impose on the world a blueprint for its transformation, has been highlighted by Fiona Jeffries (2001, p. 132), Simon Tormey (2006, p. 150), and Alex Khasnabish (2010, p. 172).

25. Marcos told Gelman (1996) that the culture clash that arose from contact with indigenous communities was "noteworthy" in terms of the resultant "use of language in relation to the political …" On the influence that the Popol Vuh had on Marcos' writing, see Juan Pellicer (1996, pp. 206-208) and (2001, pp. 123-124), Kristine Vanden Berghe (2005, pp. 120-121), Nelson González Ortega (2006), and Conant (2010, pp. 92-97).

26. See too, Rebecca Solnit (2004/2006, p. 36), who states that Marcos "is the composer of a new kind of political discourse," and Daniela Di Piramo (2011, p. 204), who claims that the Subcommander "understands that a new way of doing politics requires a new discursive approach."

27. Meyer elaborates:
    The language of the Mexican political class, especially of those in power, has been, almost since its beginning, a murky language which has multiple meanings and which conceals more than it uncovers. That political discourse is basically an instrument of disinformation, of systematic lies raised to an art form, whose central objective is the defense of illegitimate interests.

28. See too, Luis Hernández Navarro (2007, p. 103), who comments that "If the troglodyte Left was accustomed to beginning each and every one of its public statements by announcing the crisis of the capitalist system and the irredeemably reactionary character of the Mexican State, then the Zapatistas' communiqués introduced irony and humour, recuperating the exemplary anecdote as a pedagogical instrument …"; and more recently, Cornelia Graebner (2011, p. 2), who writes that the Zapatistas' "tone and language differed from the discourse previously employed by Mexican and Central American guerrilla groups: the EZLN preferred literary devices, storytelling, and indigenous mythology over an ideologically based discourse."

29. On Marcos' use of irony, see: Juan Pellicer (1996, pp. 203-205) and (2001, pp. 117 & 119-122), Laura Hernández Martínez (2002), Thomas Olesen (2007), and Daniela Di Piramo (2011).

30. Indeed, Marcos has frequently asserted that he first came to Chiapas as a classic Marxist guerrilla. Nick Henck (2007, pp. 94-5 & 134-5) collects and explores these assertions.

31. In EZLN (1995, pp. 104-110). Retrieved from http://www.razonyrevolucion.org/textos/revryr/intelectuales/ryr2Marcos.pdf, and at http://palabra.ezln.org.mx/comunicados/1994/1994_10_22.htm.

32. See too, Marcos in Autonomedia (1994, p. 294):
    Now, today, I believe there are many theories in crisis. Who would have thought that it would be the Indigenous peoples who would provoke all of this? Not even in the Leninist conception of the weakest link was it thought that it might be the Indigenous people, right?
33. Marcos clearly rejects, for example, two of the central tenets of Leninism—the seizure of power and the dictatorship of the proletariat.
34. Concerning the influence of the poems of León Felipe and Miguel Hernández on the Subcommander, see Juan Pellicer (1996, pp. 200, 206 & 208) and (2001, pp. 117 & 123-124), while Kristine Vanden Berghe (2005, pp. 174-180) draws attention to Frederico García Lorca's impact on Marcos' writing.
35. See Juan Pellicer (1996, p. 203), who writes: "the spirit of Cervantes's work will be a constant presence in the writings of Marcos ..." (Correa-Díaz, trans. (2001, p. 211)). Similarly, see too, Juan Pellicer (1996, p. 203ff), (2001, pp. 120-122), (2006) and (2011, pp. 169-171); Luis Correa-Díaz (2000) and (2001); Valeria Wagner and Alejandro Moreira (2003, p. 200f); Kristine Vanden Berghe (2005) and (2009); and Jeff Conant (2010, pp. 63ff, 170ff, 211-212 & 223-225).
36. The interview is published in Adolfo Gilly (1995, pp. 129-142; this quotation is at 137); the English translation here is that of Nicholas P. Higgins (2004, p. 159).
37. The translation here is that of Nicholas P. Higgins (2004, p. 170), who, after citing this quotation, writes: "It is precisely this appeal to the human—a humanness not articulated in any theory, ideology, or doctrine but reflected within the literature and speeches of Zapatismo ... that makes the Zapatistas unique" (p. 171).

2
Marxist (and) Leninist Formation[1]

Rafael Guillén's Marxist and Leninist formation (i.e. his exposure to the texts of Marx, Engels, and Lenin) would have taken place through two processes that ran more or less concurrently: namely, his immersion during the late 1970s in the clandestine world of the Marxist-Leninist FLN[2]; and his studies at university, and especially the research he conducted for the writing of his graduation thesis which he submitted in October 1980. This chapter examines the nature of both the FLN and Rafael's thesis in an attempt at ascertaining the nature and extent of his Marxist and Leninist formation.

A) *The Fuerzas de Liberación Nacional (FLN)*

The Fuerzas de Liberación Nacional enjoys a relatively long, complex history and has recently been the subject of several major studies.[3] In this chapter, I shall be concentrating however, purely on one aspect of the organization; namely, its ideological composition and outlook during the period Rafael Guillén was enrolled within its ranks. This clandestine organization was a self-avowedly Marxist-Leninist one, describing itself as a "political-military organization whose end is the taking of political power for the campesinos and the workers of the Mexican Republic, to establish a popular republic with a socialist system."[4] It is certain then that Rafael would have received considerable exposure to the thinking and writings of Marx and Lenin during his time in the FLN.

During the period that interests us here (i.e. 1979), Marcos tells us, "The majority of the members … were from the middle class; university professors, professionals, engineers, medics," adding that "It was a very, very small group: I am talking of ten or so, perhaps twenty people."[5] Its leadership comprised older, more orthodox and doctrinaire figures who were both very much a product of the left of the 1960s and veterans of the dirty war unleashed by the government and its extra-judicial security forces in the 1970s.[6] Indeed, *Germán*, the top of the FLN, had lost his brother in a shoot-out with security forces (his body was never recovered), and had himself been tortured by the police. He, and the FLN's number two, *Rodrigo*, maintained a firm Marxist-Leninist stance, adopting an accompanying quintessentially Marxist rhetoric.[7] Article 5 of the FLN's statutes, drawn-up in 1980, i.e. a year after Rafael enrolled in its ranks, states the organization's goal as being "to install a Socialist system … in order *to exercise the dictatorship of the proletariat* [and] to form a single political party based on the principles of Marxism-Leninism."[8] Similarly, the FLN's "Insurgent Rules," drafted in 1985, state that

> the EZLN was created in order to conquer, by means of armed struggle, national liberation and our second independence, and not to suspend the struggle until we have installed in our country a political, economic and social regime of the Socialist type.[9]

Even as late as 1993, FLN documents stated that:

> The objectives of the Party are to organize, lead and to place itself at the head of the revolutionary struggle of the working classes in order to take power away from the bourgeoisie, free our country from foreign domination and install a proletarian dictatorship, understood as a government of workers that prevent a counter-revolution and begin to build socialism in Mexico.[10]

Meanwhile, the "Insurrectionary Rule," an oath that all recruits swore on entering the EZLN's ranks, read:

> I swear before the memory of the heroes and martyrs of our people and the international proletariat that I will defend the revolutionary principles of Marxist-Leninism and their application to national reality . ... I swear that I will fight, to the death if necessary, the enemies of my motherland and for socialism. To live for the motherland or to die for freedom.[11]

Not surprisingly, much has been made of the Marxist-Leninist nature of the FLN, especially by detractors of the Subcommander who wish to portray his pro-indigenous rights stance as a politically expedient ruse designed to disguise his continued orthodox leftism and garner far-reaching support.[12]

Two recent, fairly comprehensive studies on the FLN have looked beyond the rhetoric of its official documents however, and, relying also on interviews with former FLN members, paint a picture of a considerably less doctrinaire Marxist-Leninist organization. For example, Adela Cedillo (2012, p. 163, n. 25) has pointed out that "The group's documents do not reflect rich theoretical discussions, but afforded a pragmatic and empiricist view of the revolutionary process." Elaborating on this, Cedillo (2012, p. 152) urges that "In their discourse the FLN adhered to Castro-Guevarism but their ideology was eclectic, incorporating tenets from Leninism, Maoism, Vietnamese Marxism, and the leftist revolutionary nationalism embraced by the MLN [National Liberation Movement]."[13] She continues (2012, p. 152):

> What was quite unique about the FLN was that they did not seek to begin the revolution, but rather to prepare for its imminent coming according to the historical laws propounded by Marxism. Another distinguishing feature was that they did not believe the revolutionary subject belonged to a single social class, instead it would emerge from an alliance between workers, *campesinos*, students and/or progressive petty bourgeoisie.[14]

Elsewhere Cedillo (2010, p. 11) identifies the FLN "as one of the most original within the political spectrum of the Latin American armed left ... [and which] unlike most, had an eclectic ideology, although it tended to be dominated by Castro-Guevarism" (my translation). Such an eclecticism, I would urge, certainly sets the FLN apart from, say, its contemporary, the September 23rd Communist League, which tended to be far more dogmatically Marxist-Leninist.[15] Indeed, this is a point made also by Christopher Gunderson in his recent study of the FLN, which, like Cedillo's work, similarly draws on the personal testimony of former FLN members. Gunderson (2013, p. 401) writes of a "superficial orthodoxy ... on the part of the FLN that gave the group a non-dogmatic and non-sectarian cast, at least in comparison with other contemporaneous guerrilla groups."[16] He continues (2013, pp. 402-3), maintaining that the FLN was "considerably less enamoured with the power of the perfectly worked out theoretical formulation than, for example, the Liga Comunista 23 de Septiembre, which was notorious for the impenetrability of its theoretical proclamations," adding that "[a]n eventual consequence of this would be an acceptance within the FLNs ranks of an unusual degree of ideological heterogeneity." Indeed, this comparative "ideological heterogeneity" is something on which Gunderson (2013, p. 432) places much emphasis, writing also that:

> Even if the resulting discourse remained firmly within the boundaries of the FLN's Marxist-Leninist and revolutionary nationalist orthodoxies, the stated commitment to livelier debate and the actual proliferation of voices in the organization's internal publications created an internal intellectual atmosphere that would prove attractive to a more heterodox cohort of new recruits.

As a consequence, he notes (2013, pp. 434-5):

> The late 1970s thus saw the FLN grow significantly in size ... [and t]he growth of the organization brought into its ranks a layer of more theoretically sophisticated young members. It also gave the organization the means to support processes of political investigation and internal discussion that had previously been impossible.

It was precisely at this point, in 1979 more specifically, that a young (i.e. in his early twenties) Rafael Guillén joined the organization's ranks.

There are, perhaps, other indications that the FLN was not as ideologically dogmatic and doctrinaire as one may at first suppose on reading its internal documents. A possible hint is that the FLN Statutes, although written in 1980, explicitly mention the indigenous twice in their "Chapter 4: on the goals of the movement,"[17] something rather unusual among Marxist-Leninist revolutionary groups, and which reflects the organization's first, failed attempt at establishing a guerrilla *foco* in Chiapas in the 1970s. Furthermore, its leadership may not have been as dogmatic as some would have us believe. *Germán*, for one, while no doubt a hardliner, shows signs of drawing political inspiration from outside the canon of Marxism-Leninism. For example, when he gave the young, newly recruited Rafael a birthday present, a statue of Che, he had it inscribed, not with words of Marx, Lenin, Castro or even Guevara himself, but of José Martí.[18] (Of course, Martí had been appropriated by the Castro regime in Cuba, of which *Germán* was an ardent admirer; however, one might expect a die-hard Marxist-Leninist to have selected words from a more orthodox source as the only ones to adorn a statue given to a new recruit.[19]) For his part, the FLN's number two appears to have softened his stance by the early 1990s, with former-subcommander-turned-defector *Daniel*, informing us that "*Rodrigo* was considering the idea that the FLN should transform itself into a political party and abandon the armed struggle."²⁰ As for the "more theoretically sophisticated young members" mentioned above by Gunderson, which would have included the future Marcos, it is important to stress that because of their experiences (or, in some instances, the absence of certain of these) their leftist formation would have been considerably different from that of, say, *Germán* and *Rodrigo*: quite simply, their point of reference regarding revolution was not Cuba in 1959 but Nicaragua in 1979; they were not veterans of the 1960s' struggles, and were not shaped by the massacre at Tlatelolco in particular; nor had they suffered the dirty wars of the 1970s; finally, the Marxist texts they devoured, quoted, and debated were every bit as much (and perhaps even more so) those of Althusser and Poulantzas as Marx and Lenin. The ultimate consequence of all this was, as Gunderson puts it, a "more heterodox cohort of new recruits," something Marcos himself would later testify to when he told Yvon Le Bot (1997a, p. 197) of the heterogeneous nature of the FLN's Chiapas wing, the EZLN:

> There were compañeros who were for orthodox Marxism, others who were for a Marxism which was closer to Trotskyism, others who were for a Marxism closer to Gramsci, for Euro-communism, others who were not Marxists but rather Social Democrats. (my translation)

In the event, as Gunderson (2013, p. 473) notes, "More than most of the other mestizos, Marcos was apparently able to both see the limitations of the FLNs orthodoxy and to adapt to the indigenous life." Hence, when Marcos is given the freedom to write the EZLN's Declaration of War, entirely independently of the FLN's leadership, he makes no mention whatsoever of Marxism, Leninism, or Socialism; in fact, the document, as Mike Tangeman (1995, p. 89) observes, is "devoid of much of the leftist rhetorical baggage usually accompanying Latin American guerrilla movements."²¹ So too, Marcos ended his opening speech from the balcony of San Cristóbal's town hall on the first day of the Zapatista uprising, not by extolling the virtues of Marxist-Leninism, nor by advocating Socialism, calling for the establishment of a dictatorship of the proletariat, or declaring "workers of the world unite!," but by shouting vigorously "Don't forget this: This is an ethnic movement!"

What then, can we ascertain, did Rafael's years in the FLN contribute to his formation, and did these influences persist within him? As noted above, undoubtedly this process would have involved considerable exposure to the thinking of Marx and Lenin (although, as we have also seen, not exclusively these). In addition, we know that the organization, and especially its leadership, were heavily inspired by the Cuban revolution and especially the figure of Che Guevara.[22] I will postpone discussion of Marx and Lenin until the next section, since although the FLN certainly played a highly significant part in Rafael's Marxist-Leninist formation, unlike in the case of his thesis, we cannot tell precisely which aspects in particular influenced him most, let alone which persisted in him as Subcommander. Suffice to say here however, by the mid-1990s Marcos has come to reject certain key tenets of Marxism-Leninism: for example, Fernando Matamoros Ponce (2009, p. 273) argues "that neozapatismo is distinguished from pure Leninism. For the zapatistas it is not about, in the framework of their own evolution, building the party of the vanguard in order to take power;" while Antonio García de León (2005, p. 519) notes how for some observers "the EZLN … discard[s] the two main features of Leninism—the seizure of power and the dictatorship of the proletariat". For now then, let us end this section by turning to address the influence of Che, himself a self-declared Marxist-Leninist[23], on Rafael and the persistence of this in the discourse of Marcos.

I have noted elsewhere the importance of Guevara for Marcos.[24] There, I noted how Marcos had hero-worshipped Che from youth, and so we cannot attribute any Guevaran influence exclusively to the FLN—indeed, the example of Che was no doubt a factor in Rafael Guillén's decision to join the FLN. That having been said, the following point is worthy of note. Up until the Saninista Revolution of 1979, the FLN had adopted a predominantly Guevaran line, meaning not only that Che's writings would have been widely circulated, studied, and discussed within the organization, but also that the *foco* strategy was advocated and pursued. As Cedillo (2012, p. 157) observes:

> It was not until the Sandinista victory in Nicaragua that the FLN proposed to abandon *foquismo* and adopt the strategy of a people's war of national liberation inspired by the Maoist and Vietnamese experiences. In contrast with *foquismo*, which advocated the formation of a vanguard of exemplary combatants, the strategy of people's war prioritized the preparation of the popular army's bases.[25]

Turning specifically to the FLN's Chiapas wing, the EZLN, in which Rafael would rise to the rank of Subcommander, Ramón Máiz (2010, p. 269) notes that even its short first stage ... was not a mere prolongation of the focalism of the classical Marxist-Leninist Latin American guerrilla movement, as has sometimes been stated. Rather, it was a complex admixture of diverse ideas and principles emerging from the disintegration of a focalist perspective.

This having been said however, Guevara certainly influenced the EZLN in other ways. Hence, Andrés Aubry (2005, p. 188) claims that Zapatismo experienced three phases, there being an initial "guevarist Zapatismo"; while Michael Löwy (1973/2007, p. xxix) declares that "A Guevaran element is clearly present in the origins of the group that formed the EZLN ..." Moreover, elsewhere Löwy (1998) identifies five "threads" that constitute the Zapatistas' political philosophy, listing "*Guevarism*" as the first.[26] With regard to the Subcommander specifically, it is worthwhile to note that Marcos has acknowledged the influence on his formation that his reading of Che's writings had:

> I knew of Che from when I was very young, I was left with a very earthly image of him as a hero, with the writings, with his *Episodes of the Cuban Revolutionary War*. I was very impressed with his honesty in saying, 'I ran, this happened to me.' He was not someone who elevated himself, but rather he described events .... He was a man like that, upright, honest, noble, but, at the end of the day, a man. He was not a god, nor was he a leader. And if there were anything I would want to be, it is that, an honest and upright man, with defects and all of that, but without being made into a god or seen as an idol or as a celebrity.[27]

It is, however, when we turn to the Subcommander's interview with Yvon Le Bot (1997a, pp. 266-267) that Marcos reveals in most detail the ways in which he was and was not influenced by Che. Responding to Le Bot's observation that the Zapatistas' claim of not aiming to seize power was inconsistent with Guevara's strategy of seizing power through armed means, the Subcommander replied:

> That is one aspect of Che, but for the Zapatista Army of National Liberation the reference is the Che who left Cuba and went to Bolivia. The Che who continued fighting, who chose to continue being a rebel, the one who decided to abandon everything and to begin anew, in another place, with all the difficulties which this represented and the failures and errors which were committed. Our reference is more the human side, the side of resistance, of rebellion, the similarity of "for everyone, everything, nothing for

us" which we find in Guevara's proposal, more than his political proposal or his manual for taking power. Our recognition of Che is old, dating from the 10 years in the mountains, it was our historical referent. Not as regards the guerrilla method, the Guevarist *foco*, we moved towards the regular army. Not afterwards either, when zapatismo emerged as that mixture which is neozapatismo. Anyway, that is not the part zapatismo reclaimed from Guevara, but rather the human part, the sense of sacrifice, the devotion to a cause and, above all, the consistency, the convictions. He was a man who lived according to what he believed. And that is hard to find. Regardless of whether their ideas are correct or erroneous, it is difficult to find people, including those with erroneous ideas, who are consistent. And I am not referring only to famous people, they can even be everyday citizens. One way or another they represent those mirrors which zapatismo finds in the rest of the world, and one of them is Guevara, who is the most well known and who has, with us, the similarity of being a guerrillero who went on, with everything against him, to raise a dream, a utopia.

Furthermore, when Le Bot then points out that Che's venture "ended badly," Marcos responds:

> Yes, that is the problem. That revolutionary movements in the world have ended badly. It would be hard to say that there is one which has been successful. In that case, Guevara's failure was his death, October 9, 1967, which is where he failed definitively. But we have a more ethical, more moral interpretation than in terms of political effectiveness. We do not value Guevara for his political successes, nor even for his military successes, of which there are many—the taking of Santa Clara is a masterpiece of a military operation with a reduced number of forces. What we admire is that ethical and moral values which are assumed to be destined to remain in a book, in a religious doctrine, are made reality in human beings and kept consistently.
>
> For the zapatistas it is not the model of political practice, the *realpolitik*, if you like, which is the fundamental reference, but rather the ethical values. The zapatistas' options have always made them lose opportunities from the point of view of *realpolitik*, because they place greater value on moral applications.

In sum, the part played by Che in Marcos' formation does not lie in Che's Marxism-Leninism (e.g. the violent seizure of power and the establishment of a dictatorship of the proletariat), but in his moral and ethical example.

B) Rafael Guillén's Thesis

I have already discussed at some length elsewhere Rafael Guillén's time studying at the prestigious National Autonomous University of Mexico (UNAM) and the part this played in his formation.[28] Here, I wish to concentrate solely on his award-winning graduation thesis for the Faculty of Philosophy and Letters at the UNAM, and in particular its indebtedness to Marx (and Engels) and Lenin.[29] Before doing so however, it is worth noting that although Rafael's thesis is undoubtedly an extremely important text for those wishing to gain an insight into Marcos' university formation, there has to date been very little discussion of it.[30] Andrés Oppenheimer (1996/1998, p. 251) dismisses the thesis as "a mixture of radical arguments for class struggle and somewhat adolescent calls for rebellion against what he saw as the primary source of capitalist oppression—the family"; while Bertrand de La Grange and Maite Rico (1998, p. 89ff) present inaccurate information about it in their brief treatment of this work.[31] This is to be regretted since our insight into which strands of political philosophy influenced the student-who-turned-subcommander comes almost exclusively from consultation of his thesis.[32]

Marcos tells us that it was while "[i]n high school I read about Hitler, Marx, Lenin, Mussolini—history and political science in general",[33] and so he had clearly encountered Marx prior to embarking on his university studies. Furthermore, he would also have been exposed to a considerable dose of Marxism whilst enrolled in the ranks of the FLN. Regrettably, however, the relative paucity of our information concerning Rafael's schooling and the secrecy that surrounded his experience in the Marxist-Leninist FLN means that what follows cannot pretend to represent in any way a comprehensive survey of Rafael's exposure to Marxism; rather, it merely constitutes an attempt to identify what Rafael took specifically from Marx (as opposed to other Marxist thinkers), to gauge the extent of his acquaintance with his writings, and to ascertain whether or not the spectre of Marx haunts Subcommander Marcos' discourse.

In Chapters 3 and 4 we will be conducting a detailed analysis of Rafael's thesis in relation to the structural Marxist and post-structural, post-Marxist tendencies it displays. Suffice it to say here, this work, entitled *Filosofía y educación, prácticas discursivas y prácticas ideológicas. Sujeto y cambio históricos en libros de texto oficiales para la educación primaria en México*, can probably be said to borrow almost as much from structuralism as it does Marxism, and exhibits a considerable degree of eclecticism in terms of the authors it draws upon. In it Rafael seeks to marry the thoughts of Marxists (e.g. Marx, Engels, Althusser, and Poulantzas, to name but a few), non-Marxists (especially the linguists, Noam Chomsky,[34] Jerrold J. Katz, and Jerry A. Fodor), and post-Marxists (most notably, Foucault), so as to produce a concrete analysis of the way in which Mexican primary school textbooks, being part of the state education system and therefore constituting one facet of the Ideological State Apparatus, articulate discursive practices (i.e. form practices of subjection through language) and interpellate pupils as subjects of a necessary and benevolent State.[35]

The thesis, as the above brief overview suggests, is Marxist to its core, although, it is important to emphasize, not exclusively so. A worldview that is heavily indebted to Marxism informs the entire work—thus we are confronted with a picture of capitalist society as being a class-based social system in which the bourgeoisie exploit the proletariat based on their privileged relationship to the means of production, and the history of which is the history of class struggle—while Marxist terminology peppers its pages. Moreover, it is distinctly Marxist analytical tools that are employed and deployed to analyse the Mexican state education system. Much of the more nuanced discussion and detailed argument to be found in the thesis, however, owes itself not to the classical texts of Marx or Engels (or Lenin either, for that matter) but to more contemporary Marxists such as Louis Althusser and his disciples.

What then is there in the thesis that is specific to Marx, as opposed to the Marxist tradition in general, or certain modern, predominantly French Marxists in particular? The first thing to point out is that although the bibliography lists *Capital* and *The German Ideology*, it is only the former of these works, and in particular Volume One, Part II ("The Transformation of Money into Capital"), Chapter 6 ("The Buying and Selling of Labour-Power"), and Part VI ("Wages"), Chapter 19 ("The Transformation of the Value (and Respective Price) of Labour-Power into Wages"), that are quoted from.[36] Rafael quotes from these two chapters of *Capital* eight times within quick succession, in the middle of his thesis, in "Part III: El mecanismo ideológico dominante y el proceso de trabajo," which contains two subsections, headed 1) "Salario y compra-venta de la fuerza de trabajo" (pp. 59-65), and 2) "'Libertad,' explotación y discurso jurídico-político" (pp. 66-71).[37] As its title suggests, the function of Part III is to make explicit the connection between the capitalist mode of production as outlined in Marx's theory of political economy and dominant bourgeois ideology. Indeed, Rafael (1980, pp. 64-65) concludes the first subsection on "Salary and the buying and selling of Labour power" by writing:

> The bourgeois conception of profit is based on considering it as compensation for the risk run by the capitalist during the process of [commodity] circulation …
>
> From pure profit it is impossible to ascertain the share of exploitation, since there is no distinction between the elements of capital. This is how the ruling class articulates its discourse that lends a "naturalness" to its regime of exploitation; the capitalist is someone who had the "audacity" to risk their capital and therefore deserves compensation for that risk: high profit margins.
>
> Thus, in the Profit-Salary nexus we can detect how it is that certain linguistic practices are possible and others not, how it is that a domination in production corresponds to a domination in expression.

As for the concluding paragraph to the second subsection, on "'Liberty,' exploitation and juridical-political discourse," which draws heavily on Renée Balibar and Dominique Laporte's *Burguesía y lengua nacional*, it reads:

> This is to say that the social exchanges of the capitalist mode of production involve language exchanges, and they are all clad in the relations of capitalist exploitation.
>
> In summary, for the buying and selling of the workforce, the axis of capitalist exploitation, a linguistic practice that ensures the domination of the bourgeoisie is required. (p. 71)

Perhaps unsurprisingly, nowhere in the Subcommander's discourse can we find him displaying a similar acquaintance with the intricacies of Marx's political economy. In fact, in my view it is impossible to detect anything in it that one could pinpoint as being specific to Marx's writings, as opposed to pertaining to the general Marxist tradition. Notably, even if we turn to addressing the latter, very few commentators have treated in any detail what Daniela Di Piramo (2010, p. 30) refers to—but regrettably does not elaborate on—as "the continuing vehement presence of Marxist ideas in his discourse …" The fullest treatment of this to date remains Ramón Máiz's (2010) article tracing "the evolution of the political discourse of the EZLN in Mexico (1993–2009)." In it, Máiz surveys the EZLN's communiqués and declarations—the most important of which, he notes (p. 246), Marcos authored—and notes (p. 256) how from 2005 the EZLN enters a "new stage of … strategic history" in which "the underlying malady is now 'capitalist barbarity', 'unbridled capitalism', both in Mexico ('the capitalist system in Mexico is waging war throughout the land') and worldwide ('neoliberal globalization')," concluding that "[s]trikingly, for the first time since 1993, the problem is formulated in fundamentally economic terms: 'the economic model', 'exploitation', 'capitalist property'."[38] Máiz here is drawing predominantly on "The Sixth Declaration of the Lacandon Jungle" (2005), "The (Impossible) Geometry of Power" (2005), and "Zapatistas and the Other: The Pedestrians of History" (2006), which he believes exhibit: "terminology … so typically Marxist," a "Marxist framework," a "Marxist turn," and "[c]onventional Marxist vocabulary."[39] Certainly it is true that these documents are vehemently and explicitly anti-capitalist, and as such I would like to reproduce key sections from two of them. The first appears in "Zapatistas and the Other: The Pedestrians of History," under the subsection heading "Anti-capitalist and from the Left," and reads

> the principal conclusion to which we arrived in our evaluation [is that] responsible for our pain, for the injustice, the *desprecio*, the *despojo* and the blows with which we live, is an economic, political, social, and ideological system, capitalism. The next step neozapatismo would take would have to point clearly to this source, not only of the negation of indigenous rights and culture, but to the negation of the rights and the exploitation of the great majority of the Mexican population. That is, it would have to be an anti-systemic initiative. With this in mind, although all of the initiatives

of the EZLN have been anti-systemic, this wasn't always made explicit .... And defining capitalism as the culprit and the enemy brought with it another conclusion: we needed to go beyond the indigenous struggle. Not only in declarations and propositions, but in organization.[40]

The second is an extract from the third section of the Sixth Declaration, which is headed "How We See the World:"

> Now we are going to explain to you how we, the Zapatistas, see what is going on in the world. We see that capitalism is the strongest right now. Capitalism is a social system, a way in which a society goes about organizing things and people, and who has and who has not, and who gives orders and who obeys. In capitalism, there are some people who have money, or capital, and factories and stores and fields and many things, and there are others who have nothing but their strength and knowledge in order to work. In capitalism, those who have money and things give the orders, and those who only have their ability to work obey.
>
> Then capitalism means that there are a few who have great wealth, but they did not win a prize, or find a treasure, or inherit it from a parent. They obtained that wealth, rather, by exploiting the work of the many. So capitalism is based on the exploitation of the workers, which means they exploit the workers and take out all the profits they can. This is done unjustly, because they do not pay the worker what his work is worth. Instead they give him a salary that barely allows him to eat a little and to rest for a bit, and the next day he goes back to work in exploitation, whether in the countryside or in the city.
>
> And capitalism also makes its wealth from plunder, or theft, because they take what they want from others, land, for example, and natural resources. So capitalism is a system where the robbers are free and they are admired and used as examples.
>
> And, in addition to exploiting and plundering, capitalism represses because it imprisons and kills those who rebel against injustice.
>
> Capitalism is most interested in merchandise, because when it is bought or sold, profits are made. And then capitalism turns everything into merchandise, it makes merchandise of people, of nature, of culture, of history, of conscience. According to capitalism, everything must be able to be bought

and sold. And it hides everything behind the merchandise, so we don't see the exploitation that exists. And then the merchandise is bought and sold in a market. And the market, in addition to being used for buying and selling, is also used to hide the exploitation of the workers. In the market, for example, we see coffee in its little package or its pretty little jar, but we do not see the campesino who suffered in order to harvest the coffee, and we do not see the coyote who paid him so cheaply for his work, and we do not see the workers in the large company working their hearts out to package the coffee …

So we see merchandise in the market, but we do not see the exploitation with which it was made. And then capitalism needs many markets … or a very large market, a world market.

And so the capitalism of today is not the same as before, when the rich were content with exploiting the workers in their own countries, but now they are on a path which is called Neoliberal Globalization. This globalization means that they no longer control the workers in one or several countries, but the capitalists are trying to dominate everything all over the world …

So neoliberalism is like the theory, the plan, of capitalist globalization …

Then, in neoliberal globalization, the great capitalists who live in the countries which are powerful, like the United States, want the entire world to be made into a big business where merchandise is produced like a great market. A world market for buying and selling the entire world and for hiding all the exploitation from the world. Then the global capitalists insert themselves everywhere, in all the countries, in order to do their big business, their great exploitation . … And they also insert their ideas, with the capitalist culture which is the culture of merchandise, of profits, of the market.

Then, in short, the capitalism of global neoliberalism is based on exploitation, plunder, contempt and repression of those who refuse. The same as before, but now globalized, worldwide.[41]

What we have here are perhaps the most blatantly and explicitly anti-capitalist passages that have to date been produced by the Subcommander. However, this is precisely what they are, and what Marcos himself labels them: that is, "anti-capitalist." They are not, I would urge, specifically and exclusively Marxist; for example, many anarchists or other groups (such as, for instance, those comprising the Occupy Wall Street movement) would find nothing to object to, and much to agree with, in the above paragraphs. Nor, I would urge, do they display much in the way of specifically Marxist vocabulary or terminology; indeed, although they mention capitalism, profit, and exploitation—words that are hardly the sole preserve of Marxists—they are bereft of core Marxist phrases such as "the proletariat" (let alone "the dictatorship" thereof), "the bourgeoisie" (or indeed any "class" except for "the political class"), "socialism," "the means of production," "mode of production," "commodification," "surplus value," and so on. Furthermore, even if we concede a Marxist inspiration behind these passages, the most one could say is that here we have a massively (over)simplified Marxian analysis that has been stripped of nearly all Marxist terminology.[42] In any event, certainly there is no display of the Subcommander's intimate and intricate knowledge of Marxist political economy which we know from Rafael Guillén's thesis he was fully acquainted with.

This brings us to a final point regarding Marcos' Marxism, one that is concerned with what it means to be a Marxist in the twenty-first century. This is too vast a topic to address here, but it is worth noting that it is perhaps not so straightforward to attach the label "Marxist" to people. There are, for example, many who wholeheartedly concur with Marx's analysis of how capitalism functions, but who do not share all or any of his predictions (e.g. that the contradictions inherent in capitalism will ultimately cause its demise, that the class struggle will result in the dictatorship of the proletariat, or that capitalism will be followed by socialism and ultimately communism)—can such people be termed Marxists? Or put another way, is speaking of capitalism, profit, exploitation, and the commodification of absolutely everything, as Marcos does in the passages above, sufficient to qualify one as a Marxist? It is in this context then, and with such thoughts in mind, that I would like to end this section by quoting what Marcos himself proffered regarding his own Marxism in the following exchange with Maurice Najman and Yvon Le Bot:

> MN: With these concepts: nation, humanity and others, we are now quite far from orthodox Marxism...
>
> Marcos: Yes, what I am saying is that that began developing some time ago, in this process of translation from the university Marxist-Leninist culture to the indigenous culture. This translation was more of a transformation...

YLB: And the former philosophy professor of one Rafael Guillén, says that Marcos is no longer a Marxist at all, at least an Althusserian Marxist, that now he is not at all a revolutionary.[43] What do you think Marcos, in that regard?

Marcos: Yes, perhaps Marcos is no longer a Marxist, but I don't know if that's bad. I don't know if that's something that has to be reproached or to be recognized. I think that Marcos, the character once again, has known up until now how to be an instrument for the communities, and he has served to present their problems and to go about negotiating this complicated crossing which the war of '94 turned into ... I believe a transformation process has taken place. I'm not referring to Marcos, but rather to the thinking of the left. I'm not saying that being Marxist is a sin, but if being a leftist, revolutionary, is to be in motion, to be continually renewing oneself, zapatismo is revolutionary and consistent. I don't know what it can be called, whether it is Marxism, anti-Marxism, revisionism or reformism as Castañeda says.[44]

Regardless of whether or not we choose to accept the Subcommander's response at face value, ultimately, I believe, Marcos' Marxism was tempered by his literary formation, and so there may be some truth in Carlos Fuentes' (1994/1997, p. 93) statement "that Subcommander *Marcos*, the Zapatista leader, has read more Carlos Monsiváis than Carlos Marx," and even more to Julio Moguel's (1998, pp. 31-32) assertion that:

Marcos—and the EZLN—did not come to the world of war through the influence of Leninists or Maoists, or through the influence of those who were educated in the now much questioned science of politics-politics, but rather by that generation of thinkers who, in Mexico, have Monsiváis as one of their most recognized representatives. They live and think of politics as culture, as a process in which they build and rebuild, on a daily basis, positive and diverse identities, plural in their comprehensive capacities, open in their ability to confront themselves with the most varied foreign discourses.

Turning next very briefly to Engels, there is no listing of any of his works in Rafael's bibliography. However, we do encounter his "Prologue" of 1885 to Book II of *Capital* being cited and quoted from on three consecutive pages of the thesis (pp. 62-64), in "Part III: El mecanismo ideológico dominante y el proceso de trabajo," subsection "1) Salario y compra-venta de la fuerza de trabajo," which we have just looked at above in our discussion of Marx. The three quotations utilized by Rafael read (in order):[45]

> It is not labour which has a value .... As soon as labour-power becomes a commodity, its value is determined by the labour embodied in this commodity as a social product. This value is equal to the labour socially necessary for the production and reproduction of this commodity.[46]

> What is M— C (= M — L) for the buyer is here, as in every other purchase, L — M (= C — M) for the seller (the laborer).[47] It is the sale of his labour-power. This is the first stage of circulation, or the first metamorphosis, of the commodity (Buch I, Kap. III, 2a). [English edition: Ch. III, 2a — Ed.] It is for the seller of labour a transformation of his commodity into the money-form.[48]

> True, in the act M — L the owner of money and the owner of labour-power enter only into the relation of buyer and seller, confront one another only as money-owner and commodity-owner. In this respect they enter merely into a money-relation. Yet at the same time the buyer appears also from the outset in the capacity of an owner of means of production, which are the material conditions for the productive expenditure of labour-power by its owner. In other words, these means of production are in opposition to the owner of the labour-power, being property of another.[49]

From this we can gather that Rafael had grappled, and come to terms, with the complexities of Marxist political economy, including the key concept of labour power, but we can learn little else. Moreover, we can detect nothing in Subcommander Marcos' discourse that betrays the influence of specifically Engels (as opposed to Marx).

Turning finally to Lenin, one may be forgiven for finding nothing especially surprising on discovering that Rafael had been exposed to a considerable dose of Leninism. After all, Lenin's work was highly influential in Latin America, as Sheldon B. Liss (1984, p. 23) observes:

> In the more than fifty volumes comprising his complete works, Lenin refers to Latin America only eighteen times, but his ideas concerning the subjective conditions for revolution and his belief in preparing socialists for taking power simultaneously by armed insurrection and parliamentary means have had considerable influence in the region.

Moreover, with regard to Mexico specifically, Jorge Fuentes Morúa (1999, p. 120) has noted that by the start of the 1980s Lenin's "*What Is to Be Done* had circulated profusely among the intelligentsia and Mexican militant socialists" for nearly half a century. And yet, there is some evidence to suggest that Rafael's exposure to Lenin may not have been as considerable as one might reasonably expect. For example, offsetting the testimonies of Liss and Fuentes Morúa is that of Rafael's thesis supervisor, Cesáreo Morales, who claims that while students at that time read Althusser and Foucault, "Lenin was not studied ... After Marx did not come Lenin."[50] There is also the fact that Lenin's *What Is to Be Done*, which Fuentes Morúa informs us was so influential and widely read, is not listed in Rafael's bibliography, and neither is his *The State and Revolution* for that matter.

In fact, the only work of Lenin's to appear in the bibliography is *Materialism and Empirio-Criticism*. This takes on particular significance since it is a work that the Subcommander makes reference to several times in his discourse. For example, in an interview he gave in 1995, Marcos (1995a) recalls how:

> When we joined the [guerrilla] organization we had to be serious, respectful, boring. Rock was counterrevolutionary, imperialist. Anything that wasn't "fatherland or death, we shall overcome" ("patria o muerte, venceremos") and protest songs, was bad. If you listened to classical music, they didn't shoot you but you were already under suspicion; and if the books you carried were not *Materialism and Empirical Criticism* [sic] and were for instance *Historia de cronopios y de famas*...or Benedetti's love poems, they stared at you in a strange way.

Of greater significance however is the second reference, also pertaining to autumn 1995, that Marcos makes to this work. This comes in his *Letter to Adolfo Gilly* (*Carta a Gilly*), which has attracted not inconsiderable attention (and a degree of notoriety) among commentators on Marcos. For instance Yvon Le Bot (1997a, pp. 69-70, n. 52) states that the *Carta* shows that "Marcos still proclaims the merits of historic materialism and Leninist theory," while Carlos Monsiváis censures the Subcommander, claiming that in this correspondence "Marcos relapses into sectarian illusion, defends Lenin and historic materialism, fights with the left in an extremist tone and is not exempt from anti-intellectual intentions."[51] It is, however, Pedro Pitarch (2004, p. 302) who makes the most of Marcos' *Carta*, citing the text as proof of his argument "that subcomandante Marcos had not renounced his conventional revolutionary Marxist ideology" and therefore ultimately that the Subcommander's pro-indigenous stance was mere calculated and inauthentic posturing. Given the seriousness of Pitarch's accusation, and the fact that he reproduces the section of the *Carta* that concerns us here with regard to Lenin's *Materialism and Empirio-Criticism*, he deserves quoting in full:

> In October 1994, Marcos wrote a letter of reply to the Mexican historian Adolfo Gilly, who had suggested to him that his language (that is, the language of the Indians in Marcos' texts) appeared to follow what the Italian historian Carlo Ginzburg, in a celebrated article about micro-history ("Clues: roots of an evidential paradigm") had called "evidential" or "conjectural" logic. But here Marcos, yet again "between us left-wing intellectuals" (despite it being a public letter), adopted a distinct tone to the usual one. Marcos considered Ginzburg's posture of avoiding a dichotomy between "rationalism" and "irrationalism" to be just another variation of an idealist position: "In reality, the problem in the sciences occurs in the struggle between materialism and idealism (Ah, Lenin is now censured! Ah, the forgotten *Materialism and Empiro-Criticism* [sic, Lenin's text]. Ah, Mach and Avenarius revived! Ah, the stubbornness of Vladimir Ilyich!" (Subcomandante Marcos 1995a, p. 105). Historical materialism, the science of history founded by Marx, was developed as a critique of idealism and "class position" had been deemed as the basis of an objective knowledge of history. In sum, seven or eight months after having adopted apparently ethnicist positions, along with this "Indian" language, Marcos openly and almost aggressively maintained here a principle of abstract and Marxist universalism.[52]

Elsewhere I, and before me Jérôme Baschet, have addressed and critiqued Pitarch's overall claim regarding Marcos' indigenist stance being inauthentic, and so I will not waste time and space repeating those arguments here.[53] Instead, I will restrict myself to making a few comments relating specifically to how the above connects with the question of Lenin's influence upon the Subcommander. Marcos' mention of Mach and Avenarius here is a reference to certain specific sections of Lenin's *Materialism and Empirio-Criticism*: namely, ch. 1 ("The Theory of Knowledge of Empirio-Criticism and of Dialectical Materialism"), part 6, entitled "The Solipsism of Mach and Avenarius," and ch. 4 ("The Philosophical Idealists as Comrades-In-Arms and Successors of Empirio-Criticism"), part 3, entitled "The Immanentists as Comrades-In-

Arms of Mach and Avenarius." His citing of the names of Mach and Avenarius therefore clearly reveals Marcos' intimate (and still remembered) acquaintance with this work—very probably a legacy from his reading of it for his graduation thesis. To address Pitarch's comments on historical materialism, while he writes that "the science of history founded by Marx, was developed as a critique of idealism" and that this represents "a principle of abstract and Marxist universalism," it is curious that he fails to make the connection between Lenin, whom the Subcommander specifically invokes and defends here, and the theory, not of historical materialism, but dialectical materialism, on which the Russian revolutionary expounded precisely in his *Materialism and Empirio-criticism*.

There exists another occasion on which Marcos demonstrated his acquaintance with Lenin's writings. In an interview he gave in 1994 he reflected on the fact that:

> Now, today, I believe there are many theories in crisis. Who would have thought that it would be the Indigenous peoples who would provoke all of this? Not even in the Leninist conception of the weakest link was it thought that it might be the Indigenous people, right?[54]

Significantly, however, Adela Cedillo (2012, p. 164, n. 47) points out that:

> The FLN embraced the Leninist interpretation that posited the revolution would initially take place not in countries where capitalism was fully developed, but rather in "the weakest link of imperialism," much like Russia, which had an agrarian semi-feudal system. Militants used this analogy to identify *campesinos* as the weakest link in the system.

It would appear then that Marcos, as a youthful Rafael, may well have encountered Lenin's "weakest link" theory, not in the process of researching his graduation thesis, but as an active cadre in the FLN. In support of this, and as a general point on which to conclude, an examination of the thesis reveals that with the exception of the appearance of *Materialism and Empirio-Criticism* in the bibliography, Lenin is not quoted, nor his works cited in the main text or referred to in any of the footnotes. This, however, is to speak only of direct influence, for, as we shall see in the next chapter, the extensive reading of Althusser that Rafael undertook in the course of researching his thesis would have provided him with considerable, though admittedly indirect, exposure to Lenin's thought.

Marxist (and) Leninist Formation

Finally with regard to Rafael's thesis, it is worth taking time to note that this work provides an insight into the political-philosophical influences which exerted themselves upon an entire generation of university-educated, middle-class, left-wing Mexicans. For Rafael Guillén, although exceptional in terms of his academic talents and achievements, and even more so in his going on to become the world-renowned Subcommander Marcos, was perhaps not untypical of his peers in terms of the intellectual currents which he was exposed to and influenced by.

In concluding this chapter, I would like to cite two quotations. The first is that of Enrique Krauze (2011, pp. 436-437), who, in a chapter on Marcos in his book *Redeemers: Ideas and Power in Latin America*, writes of the Subcommander:

> His intellectual training in Althusser, Foucault, and the other radical scriptures of his student years, and his youthful association with the *Frente* [sic] *de Liberación Nacional* (FLN –the National Liberation Front [sic]) predisposed him to the rigid categories of academic and revolutionary Marxism. Yet early in his life ... there were certain somewhat offbeat elements in his development ... and they would come to be very useful to him in his revolutionary career. He had a Don Quixote-like dreamer of a father, who was a reader of Balzac ... he received a strict Catholic education ... with the Jesuits ... and ... he showed strong artistic and cultural interests . ... He sang songs by the popular Catalan singer Joan Manuel Serrat and devoured the socially and morally engaged work of the Spanish poets León Felipe and Miguel Hernández.

While Krauze is correct regarding the remainder of his statement, what I hope to have demonstrated in this chapter is that Marcos' "intellectual training in Althusser, Foucault, and the other radical scriptures of his student years, and his youthful association with the *Frente* [sic] *de Liberación Nacional*" would not necessarily have "predisposed him to the rigid categories of academic and revolutionary Marxism." Instead, both the FLN and his intellectual formation at university are perhaps characterized by having been less dogmatic and more ideologically eclectic than initially supposed, with the result that Rafael himself, as Marcela Capdevila, a former student of his whom Guillén advised during the completion of her final dissertation, testifies

> never went so far as to impose his views on anyone, he was not overbearing .... He was radical in his propositions, but not so as to be inflexible. He

was radical because he had training, because he had concepts, because he had a very extensive theoretical framework .... But he was not intolerant or arbitrary in this way.[55]

Notes

1. I use the term "Marxist (and) Leninist" since in the second section, which deals with Rafael's thesis, I shall be examining the influence of Marx and Lenin in isolation, whereas in the first section, which treats the FLN, I will be treating specifically Marxism-Leninism.
2. Salvador Morales Garibay, the former Subcommander *Daniel* before he left the EZLN, told Bertrand de la Grange (1999, p. 77) that Rafael "began to have contact with the FLN when he arrived at the UAM [Universidad Autónoma Metropolitana]," which was on January 16, 1979, adding "by the end of 1979 he was already helping in the safe houses."
3. I am referring here to work of Adela Cedillo (2008), (2010) and (2012), and Christopher Gunderson (2013).
4. In FLN (1980/2003, p. 5).
5. In Le Bot (1997a, p. 124).
6. *Comandante Germán*, the FLN's leader at this time, appears to have been especially severe, uncompromising, and authoritarian, on which see Nick Henck (2007, pp. 97-98).
7. See Tello Díaz (1995/2001, p. 296, n. 40), where he quotes *Germán* as stating as late as 1987 that "the armed revolutionary struggle should be led by the working class;" and *Rodrigo* in the same year as saying "the working class should play the principal role in the Socialist revolution." In an October 1988 edition of the FLN's magazine, *Neplanta*, *Germán* affords the following, rather damning, progress report:
    > We have failed in our project of incorporating the workers into being professional revolutionaries. ... It is no use idealizing the working class, thinking that by approaching them this assures the future of the revolution. Only by employing Leninist-Marxist theory and practice will we manage to get the working class to develop a consciousness and convert itself into a class in itself, for itself. (Quoted in De la Grange and Rico (1998, p. 268).)

    Moreover, De la Grange (1998, pp. 190-191) cites a former Zapatista who attests that "*Rodrigo's* language was very tough" adding that "He spoke all the time about having to fight against imperialism and for socialism."
8. Translated in Womack (1999, pp. 192-197), (original emphasis). See too Article 29 (i), which talks of "acting militarily against North American interests or their representatives, when imperialism attacks militarily against the Socialist coun-

tries or the people that fight for their liberation."
9. Quoted in Tello Díaz (1995/2001, pp. 264 & 325, nn. 13 & 15).
10. "Declaration of Principles of the Forces of National Liberation Party," quoted in De la Grange and Rico (1998, p. 226); the translation here is that of Pedro Pitarch (2004, p. 291).
11. Quoted in De la Grange and Rico (1998, p. 228); the translation here is that of Pedro Pitarch (2004, pp. 291-292).
12. See Nick Henck (2009) for a discussion of these authors and a systematic rebuttal of the arguments they put forward.
13. Christopher Gunderson (2013, pp. 369-370) provides the following description of the MLN:

> The MLN acted as a broad umbrella formation for popular movements and progressive groups—including the PCM, a range of independent forces including Ruben Jaramillo, various parastatal formations such as the *Partido Autentico de la Revolución Mexicano* (PARM) and the *Partido Popular Socialista* (PPS), and the left-wing of the PRI represented by Cardenas—to both stand in solidarity with the Cuban Revolution and to struggle for Mexico's liberation from U.S. domination.

14. Similarly, Christopher Gunderson (2013, p. 443) writes:

> Chapter II of the statutes spells out the FLN's core politics which remained consistent with the left wing revolutionary nationalism and anti-imperialism articulated by the MLN in the early 1960s and conjoined with a strategy of protracted peoples war that aimed at an armed seizure of power and the installation of a "people's socialist republic." This was to be achieved through a multi-class "alliance of workers, peasants, and the progressive layer of the petty bourgeoisie."

See too his conclusion, where he writes of "the left-wing revolutionary nationalism and associated strategic orientation towards the construction of a broad multi-class anti-imperialist front that the FLN inherited from the MLN" (p. 539).

15. See the recent study of Romain Robinet (2012, p. 133) on the dogmatic Leninism of *The League*. He writes of: their choice "to adopt dogmatically the Leninist interpretation;" their belief both that they "held the monopoly of legitimate Marxism and thus had the right to define what was revolutionary or not" and that they were "the only authorized exegete of Marx, Engels and Lenin;" "their Marxism so reduced and dogmatic;" their decision "to avoid unorthodox theorists to maintain the purity of their warlike Marxism-Leninism;" and of their "ideological blindness" (p. 134) and their "ideological dogmatism" and "dogmatic interpretation of Marxism-Leninism" (p. 143).
16. See too Raúl Romero (2014), who writes that "While the FLN had a Marxist-Leninist ideology, the group was far from falling into dogmatism."
17. *Estatutos de las Fuerzas de Liberación Nacional* (August 6, 1980). Article 5 (b),

p. 8, states that one of the FLN's goals is "to integrate the struggles of the urban proletariat with the struggles of the peasants and indigenous in the most exploited zones of our country." Article 7 (n), p. 11, states that the FLN will fight until "the State guarantees to indigenous groups the right to recover their lands; to conceal and to conserve their cultures, dialects and customs, respecting their forms of social organization."

18. Marcos relates this in his September 2002 communiqué entitled "We are in silence—and the silence is not being broken," retrieved from http://flag.blackened.net/revolt/mexico/ezln/2002/marcos/silenceSEPT.html. The inscription read: "The true man does not look at which side lives better, but on which side duty lies." Later in the communiqué Marcos adapts the phrase, bringing it up to date so that it reads: "The Man, woman, homosexual, lesbian, child, youth, old one, that is, the true human being, does not look at which side lives better, but on which side duty lies," and claims that this represents "better than anything else what the rebel's vocation is, and…surpass[es] anything I could say to you or to anyone on the subject." In April 1992, Marcos, as Rafael Guillén, gave a talk to Tampico businessmen in which he cites this quotation toward the beginning of his speech, and claims "I was shaped according to this precept, I was raised by it, and I live by it," (my translation). This presentation can be found in *Revista Impacto*. (1995, March 19), pp. 56-57; retrieved from http://www.lahaine.org/mm_ss_mundo.php/1992_2007_los_tres_mexicos.

19. Regardless of whether one sees Martí as belonging to the communist tradition or as a capitalist libertarian / liberal capitalist who has been hijacked by the Revolution, there is nothing intrinsically or exclusively Marxist about the words of the quotation itself.

20. Quoted in De la Grange (1999, p. 81).

21. See too, Pedro Pitarch (2004, p. 292): "One of the most conspicuous aspects of the Declaration of the Lacandon Jungle is the complete disappearance of leftist, revolutionary language." The same point is made by John Womack Jr. (1999, p. 245).

22. See: Oppenheimer (1996/1998, pp. 45 & 254f), de la Grange and Maite (1998, pp. 127-138), Gunderson (2013, pp. 389ff and 400-401), and Cedillo (2010, pp. 126, n. 225): "El principal modelo político posrevolucionario de las FLN era, sin duda, Cuba."

23. That Che self-identified as a Marxist-Leninist at least as late as 1965 can be seen from his statement in *Socialism and Man in Cuba* (1965/2009, p. 22) that: "What we must create is the human being of the 21st century …. This is precisely one of the fundamental objectives of our study and our work. To the extent that we achieve concrete success on a theoretical plane … we will have made a valuable contribution to Marxism-Leninism, to the cause of humanity." See too Che's "Preface" to the book *The Marxist-Leninist Party*. Finally, see the three biographies of Che by: Jon Lee Anderson (1997, p. 505), Jorge Castañeda (1997,

p. 93) and Paco Ignacio Taibo II (1997, p. 69)
24. Nick Henck (2007, pp. 21, 27-28, 52, 75, 82, 154, 165, 288-290, and 365-366). See too, Nick Henck (2014), where I discuss the similarities between Marcos and Che in terms of their reading habits, what reading meant to these two iconic figures of the Latin American left, and the effect that their reading had upon the way they saw the world and lived their lives. For instances where the Subcommander talks at length about Che, see his: Mensaje del EZLN en la ceremonia de inauguración preparatoria americana del ENCUENTRO INTERCONTINENTAL POR LA HUMANIDAD Y CONTRA EL NEOLIBERALISMO (abril de 1996), in EZLN (1997, pp. 210-212); also posted on the Internet at: http://plumaslatinoamericanas.blogspot.co.uk/2015/09/la-memoria-de-zapata.html—an English translation can be found in Olivier Besancenot and Michael Löwy (2009, p. 119f); and his interviews with Yvon le Bot (1997a, pp. 266-267) and Raymundo Reynoso (2007).
25. See too, Gunderson (2013, pp. 382, 450 and 539-540).
26. According to Löwy, the others are: (2) the legacy of Emiliano Zapata, (3) liberation theology, (4) the Mayan culture, and (5) the democratic demands made by Mexican civil society.
27. In his interview with Raymundo Reynoso (2007).
28. Nick Henck (2007, ch. 4).
29. The thesis won Rafael the Gabino Barreda Award, which is named after the Mexican positivist and is awarded for outstanding academic work produced by students.
30. There exist two insightful discussions of the thesis: those made by Felix Hoyo (1995) and Hugo Enrique Sáez Arreceygor (2012). Unfortunately, Hoyo's piece is extremely brief, amounting to three pages, with illustrations accounting for half the text on each page; while Sáez Arreceygor's concentrates almost exclusively on a single chapter (IV) of the thesis.
31. De la Grange and Rico quote Cesáreo Morales, who supervised the thesis, as saying that it was influenced by Derrida, and they even head their subsection on the thesis with the subtitle "Althusser, Foucault, Derrida." There is, however, not a single mention of Derrida in the entire thesis: he is not quoted or referred to, nor do any of his works appear in the bibliography. Moreover, I cannot detect in the thesis the slightest hint that Rafael had read Derrida's works or been exposed to his thinking.
32. I write "almost exclusively" since we also possess a handful of comments made by Rafael's fellow students and teachers. (These are collected in Nick Henck (2007, p. 33ff), drawing on Salvador Corro (1995), Bertrand de la Grange and Maite Rico (1998, p. 83ff), and Alma Guillermoprieto (2002, pp. 210-211).) We also have the brief profile of the student Rafael provided in Hugo Enrique Sáez Arreceygor (2012). Finally, there is an academic paper that Rafael delivered during this period (see below, ch. 3, p. 130).

33. In his interview with Ann Louise Bardach (1994, p. 68).
34. See Frederick J. Newmeyer (1994a, p. 426), who argues that Chomsky was "a structuralist (in the broad sense)," even though the linguist termed himself a generativist. In a separate study, Newmeyer (1994b, p. 443) comes to the conclusion that "it is not inconsistent to hold both a Chomskyan theory of language and a Marxist theory of political economy."
35. See Appendix II, which reproduces and translates Rafael's preface to his thesis in which he outlines the object of his study.
36. Rafael quotes from this section eight times: the first seven of these quotations derive from Vol. One, Part VI, Chapter 19, with only the final quotation pertaining to Vol. One, Part II, Chapter 6.
37. I reproduce here these eight quotations, which are taken from editions of Marx posted on the www.marxists.org website with 1) – 7) appearing at https://www.marxists.org/archive/marx/works/1867-c1/ch19.htm, and 8) at https://www.marxists.org/archive/marx/works/1867-c1/ch06.htm. The number in parentheses following the quotation is the page number of Rafael's thesis that they appear on:

> 1) "On the surface of bourgeois society the wage of the labourer appears as the price of labour, a certain quantity of money that is paid for a certain quantity of labour." (p. 60)
> 2) "This question unconsciously substituted itself in Political Economy for the original one; for the search after the cost of production of labour as such turned in a circle and never left the spot. What economists therefore call value of labour, is in fact the value of labour-power, as it exists in the personality of the labourer, which is as different from its function, labour, as a machine is from the work it performs." (p. 60)
> 3) "That which comes directly face to face with the possessor of money on the market, is in fact not labour, but the labourer. What the latter sells is his labour-power." (p. 61)
> 4) "The wage form thus extinguishes every trace of the division of the working-day into necessary labour and surplus-labour, into paid and unpaid labour." (p. 61)
> 5) "Hence, we may understand the decisive importance of the transformation of value and price of labour-power into the form of wages, or into the value and price of labour itself. This phenomenal form, which makes the actual relation invisible, and, indeed, shows the direct opposite of that relation, forms the basis of all the juridical notions of both labourer and capitalist, of all the mystifications of the capitalistic mode of production, of all its illusions as to liberty, of all the apologetic shifts of the vulgar economists." (p. 62)
> 6) "Practically, therefore, the only thing that interests him [i.e. the capitalist] is the difference between the price of labour-power and the value which

its function creates. But, then, he tries to buy all commodities as cheaply as possible, and always accounts for his profit by simple cheating, by buying under, and selling over the value." (pp. 62-63)

7) "This it cannot, so long as it sticks in its bourgeois skin." (p. 63)

8) "For the conversion of his money into capital, therefore, the owner of money must meet in the market with the free labourer, free in the double sense, that as a free man he can dispose of his labour-power as his own commodity, and that on the other hand he has no other commodity for sale, is short of everything necessary for the realisation of his labour-power." (pp. 69-70)

38. He continues (256):
    The Mexican political system and its "repression of the discontented masses" are still criticized, but the criticism is incorporated in an explicative model of an economic nature, the causes diagnosed being "the capitalist system," "economic relationships as the backbone of the social system," "the ownership of the means of production."

39. All these quotations appear on p. 258 of the article. Máiz contrasts these documents with the fact that
    for most of the period examined here [i.e. 1995-2002] its [i.e. the EZLN's] anti-neoliberal pronouncements were devoid of Marxist vocabulary ... the terms "revolution" and "revolutionary" were almost from the beginning replaced by "rebellion" and "rebel;" Leninist vanguardism was avoided; the proletariat was not included among the declared targets of its communiqués; and socialist or communist tradition in regard to organization, lexicon and the structure of the State was ignored (p. 265)

40. Retrieved from http://www.elkilombo.org/documents/peatonesI.html.

41. Retrieved from http://enlacezapatista.ezln.org.mx/sdsl-en/.

42. I suggest "(over)simplified" since the assertion that "the capitalism of today is not the same as before, when the rich were content with exploiting the workers in their own countries," would be one that Marx, a contemporary and critic of the British Empire, which was based on the exploitation of colonized peoples, would have found naïve, if not wholly erroneous.

43. Le Bot is probably referring here to Alberto Híjar, Professor of Aesthetics and Art Criticism at the UNAM, and head of the adjudicating panel of Rafael Guillén's thesis. He is quoted in Bertrand de la Grange and Maite Rico (1998, p. 93) as saying that Subcommander Marcos has nothing to do with the Althusserian Rafael Guillén, and that Marcos' emphasis on civil society is "anti-Marxist" and "counter-revolutionary."

44. In Yvon Le Bot (1997a, pp. 339-340).

45. The passages of Engels that follow are taken from the www.marxists.org website at (respectively): https://www.marxists.org/archive/marx/works/1885-c2/ch00.htm; https://www.marxists.org/archive/marx/works/1885-c2/ch01.htm; and

https://www.marxists.org/archive/marx/works/1885-c2/ch01.htm
46. Guillén (1980, p. 62).
47. Where M = Money, C = commodity, and L = Labour.
48. Guillén (1980, p. 63).
49. Guillén (1980, p. 64).
50. Quoted in Salvador Corro (1995, p. 26).
51. In EZLN (1997, p. 457). On the *Carta's* alleged "anti-intellectualism," see too Jérôme Baschet (2000, p. 80): "Sometimes it appears as if the irresponsible refers not just to the individual case but rather turns into a broader critique of the Academy and its superficial fashions …"
52. Pitarch (2004, pp. 302-303).
53. See Jérôme Baschet's critique of Pitarch's argument, and Pitarch's response to this (both in *istor* No. 22 (2005), pp. 110-144). For a detailed rebuttal of Pitarch's thesis as regards Marcos' pro-indigenous discourse being inauthentic, see Nick Henck (2009).
54. Quoted and translated in Autonomedia (1994, p. 294).
55. Quoted in Avaro Delgado (1995, p. 18).

3

STRUCTURAL MARXIST FORMATION: LOUIS ALTHUSSER AND NICOS POULANTZAS

Examination of Rafael Guillén's thesis reveals that, in addition to the influence of Marx (and Engels) and to a much lesser extent Lenin, the young student who in maturity would become subcommander was heavily indebted, in terms of his political-philosophical formation,[1] to French structural Marxist, and post-structural, post-Marxist, philosophy, and more specifically to the thinking of Louis Althusser (and to a lesser extent Nicos Poulantzas) and Michel Foucault.[2]

In this, and the chapter that follows, I shall be examining in considerable detail, first the influence of Althusser and Poulantzas, and then that of Foucault, upon Rafael Guillén's graduation thesis, and ultimately upon his own political-philosophical formation, before going on to ascertain the extent (if any) to which these influences persisted in Subcommander Marcos' discourse. Prior to doing so however, I would like to make some preliminary points concerning these thinkers and their appearance in Rafael's thesis.

The first of these points concerns the fact that Guillén drew on three separate thinkers who, though connected—Foucault and Poulantzas had both been pupils of Althusser—nonetheless differed in important aspects of their thought.[3] Such intellectual eclecticism was very much in vogue at that time among Latin America's leftist intellectuals. Indeed, Richard L. Harris (1979, pp. 62-63), writing during that period, noted that

> the prevailing conditions [in Latin America] ... seemed to indicate that classical Marxism was too Euro-centric and too rigid to apply adequately to the realities of the contemporary period. This provided many Leftist intellectuals with a justification for combining, in the most eclectic fashion, ele-

ments of classical Marxism with concepts and propositions from the bourgeois social sciences, humanistic philosophy, and all manner of extraneous schools of thought, in order to produce an "original" Latin American (or Third World) interpretation of their reality.[4]

That the situation in Mexico was no exception, can be seen from the testimony of the cartoonist Rafael Barajas "El Fisgón" (2008, p. 124), who, only eighteen months Guillén's senior and a contemporary of his at the UNAM, tells us that during the 1970s on campus Marxism was "an obligatory point of reference" and that "among the active Marxist theorists at that time—whom almost everyone read—were such figures as Herbert Marcuse, Louis Althusser and Ernest Mandel" but that "also in fashion were Foucault, Lévi-Strauss, Gramsci, Walter Benjamin, among many others." Indeed, as I have previously noted, the intellectual milieu in which Rafael Guillén was immersed and formed during his university years was one that encouraged the blending of myriad schools of thought, fostering an eclectic approach to political philosophy that stayed with him throughout his life and ultimately led to the Subcommander, in contrast to a good many Latin American guerrillas, being more flexible and less doctrinaire in his political thinking.[5] Consequently, neither Guillén the student, nor Marcos the subcommander, would have viewed Althusser's, Foucault's, and Poulantzas' different philosophical-political positions as being so distinct as to make their thinking fundamentally incompatible with each other's, or indeed his own, thought.

As a general illustration of the extent of Guillén's indebtedness to these thinkers, if we take Guillén's thesis' bibliography and rank all the scholars appearing in it according to the number of their works cited, Althusser comes top with seven single-authored works plus two co-authored ones, while Foucault comes second with six single-authored works. Indeed, such was Guillén's indebtedness to Althusser that a UNAM Professor of Marxism and one-time teacher of the future Subcommander Marcos has stated "… judging by his graduation thesis, he was an orthodox Althusserian, although one possessed of a humour rare among the Althusserians."[6] Regarding Foucault, Guillén included two quotations from the French philosopher on the frontispiece of the thesis. Moreover, in the first two footnotes of the thesis Foucault is cited in the first one and quoted twice in the second. Finally, unlike with Althusser, who is referred to almost exclusively in a single, short chapter of the thesis, and who is quoted only once throughout the work,

Foucault's influence can be seen throughout much of the thesis, with him being quoted seven times in four chapters, including, significantly, in the concluding section of his thesis, headed "A Manera de Conclusiones," in which the only scholar whom Guillén quotes is Foucault, doing so twice. Finally, with regard to Poulantzas, two of his seminal works, *Political Power and Social Classes* and *State, Power, Socialism*, appear in Guillén's bibliography, and he directs his readers specifically to the former work in a footnote to the main text of the thesis.[7] Moreover, certain sections of Guillén's thesis exhibit a Poulantzian "feel," containing reference to one of the Greek Marxist's core concepts, "class fractions."[8]

Turning to specific portions of the thesis' text, we find further illustration of the extent to which Althusser and Foucault influenced Rafael. Two sections in particular are especially illustrative of this indebtedness: the thesis' preface and its final pages, entitled "Philosophical Dialogue II." Let us examine these below in order.

In his Preface, under the subheading "The Theoretical Horizon of the Analysis of Discourse," Guillén (1980, pp. 1-2) outlines the theme of his thesis and explains the reasons behind why he has chosen to pursue this topic utilizing an approach that has the appearance of a postmodern fusion, not untypical of his generational milieu, of Althusserian philosophy with Foucauldian thought. Guillén writes:

> Regarding the analysis of the various discourses constructed around the specific Objects of Discourse according to the regulations and specifications of the different Discursive Formations, the archaeology of this discursive operation (rules of formation, organization, preventive incursion of discourses, etc.) inside the School Ideological System in Mexico has yet to be carried out…

Having noted this omission in scholarship to date, he continues by setting out his aim of "establishing the broad terms which allow the analysis of how the various discursive formations inside the Mexican School System are organized among themselves and how they produce their effects-practices according to the specific situations of the process of reproduction-transformation of the relations of production." Next, after noting his intention "to focus on the

DISCOURSE-IDEOLOGY relationship insofar as it is related to Ideological Discursive-Practices," he continues:

> This is concerned with detecting the mechanisms of power which allow the philosophical, administrative, pedagogical, legal-political, etc. discourses inside the space-time situations in the Mexican ideological (educational) system. In sum, if what discursive practices are about is forming the practices of subjection, how is this carried out in the educational system? From what place is the discourse "said?" How are the questions carried out? What about the contradictions which arise in the educational system? How is it formed in partnership with the family ideological system? What is at stake in the organization established by the Discourse of Power?

Finally, and tellingly I would urge, Guillén (1980, p. 2) concludes his preface: "What's at stake is not simply an academic requirement; rather what's at stake is the possibility of a new site for the functioning of philosophy, of theory, of politics…"[9]

This preface thus reveals, at a very general level, Guillén's main preoccupation as a philosophy major; namely, ideology as disseminated and perpetuated through discourse. More concretely, in his thesis Guillén set himself the task of examining the discourse employed in Mexican state/public schools, in particular through the government-issued textbooks, as a means of inculcating in pupils certain beliefs, attitudes, and ways of thinking that were beneficial to the state. The theoretical framework and analytical tools he employed to do so were provided by: Althusser, who developed the idea of schools (in addition to other institutions) functioning along the lines of an Ideological State Apparatus; Foucault, two of whose primary interests were how power relations were constituted, confronted and collapsed through discourse and how knowledge was employed as a means of social control by societal institutions; and, to a lesser extent, Poulantzas, who drew from and built on both Althusser's theories on ISAs and Foucault's formulations on the nature of power being primarily relational.[10]

Second, moving on to Rafael's "Philosophical Dialogue II," with which he ends his thesis, we find one-and-a-half pages of text (pp. 107-109) that encapsulate this indebtedness perfectly. For instance, when discussing some of the problems related to the "theory of ideologies," Rafael claims that certain of these can be resolved or at least confronted theoretically, among them:

> Ideology as a representation of the imaginary relationship of individuals to their real conditions of existence,[11] ideological effect as an effect of structure, the ideological function of the "interpellation" of subjecting-subjected subjects, the materiality of ideology in ideological practice, the ideological class struggle, the ISAs as the sites in which subjects assume their ideological places in accordance with the discursive devices of power…

Next, Rafael moves on to note how "discourse is not as transparent as it would appear," that "internal and external mechanisms determine what is said, how it is said, who says it, and for whom it is said," and goes on to quote from Foucault's *The Discourse on Language / The Order of Discourse*:[12]

> We know perfectly well that we are not free to say just anything, that we cannot simply speak of anything, when we like or where we like; not just anyone, finally, may speak of just anything.[13]

Rafael then points out how the relationship between discourse and ideology poses diverse problems, such as:

> The relationship between discourses and the places where they are produced and where they are concerned with producing effects-practices-ideologies; the way in which ideological discourses carry out the "interpellation" of subjects; what are the specifically discursive forms of articulation of the statements; the emergence and/or disappearance and/or reinforcement of discursive objects, their rules of formation and dispersion, etc.

This is immediately followed by a quotation from Foucault's *Archaeology of Knowledge*:

> Thus a space unfolds articulated with possible discourses: a system of *real* or *primary relations*, a system of *reflexive* or *secondary relations*, and a system of relations that might properly be called *discursive*. The problem is to reveal the specificity of these discursive relations, and their interplay with the two other kinds.[14]

Before we move on to a detailed examination of Althusser's influence on Rafael Guillén, it is worth noting that subsequent scholarship has tended to view certain key elements of these three philosophers' theses as being not only non-contradictory but in fact similar or even complimentary. Of course, Poulantzas drew on and developed Althusser's theories, frequently refining (but also on occasion refuting) some elements of his teacher's thought.[15] Consequently, rather than representing contradictory or incompatible stances vis-à-vis Althusser's thought, Poulantzas' works appear far more a continuation or extension of Althusserianism. More controversial, given their ostensible incompatibility, are Althusser's and Poulantzas' relations to Foucault.

Let us begin by examining what appears, on initial inspection, to be the somewhat incompatible thinking of Althusser and Foucault. As Adam Holden and Stuart Elden (2005, p. 1) point out:

> Althusser noted that Foucault "was a pupil of mine, and 'something' from my writings has passed into his, including certain of my formulations. But … under his pen and in his thought even the meanings he gives to formulations he has borrowed from me are transformed into another, quite different meaning than my own" (Althusser 1969, p. 257). Foucault put it in a similar way: "Having been his student and owing him much, I perhaps have a tendency to claim under his influence that which he might deny, although of course I cannot speak on his behalf. But I would say to everyone: open Althusser's books" (Foucault 1994, I, 587).[16]

Indeed, examining the works of the two French thinkers, Holden and Elden (2005, p. 2) write of "Influence but not indebtedness [in] the way of evaluating the Foucault/Althusser relation…," continuing "aside from the direct references, Althusser figures as a kind of absent presence in Foucault's works. When references to repression, the state and Marxism are encountered in Foucault's work as often as not Althusser is lurking somewhere in the background."[17]

In addition, Robert Paul Resch (1989, p. 539) has emphasized Foucault's indebtedness to Althusser, writing:

> Aside from his focus upon knowledge as an ideological apparatus … all the positive, historical, and materialist attributes of Foucault's books on prisons and sexuality derive from the recognition of subjectivity as a social production—an insight taken over completely from Althusser and then impregnated with a Nietzschean vitalism.

In a subsequent work Resch (1992, p. 233) would proffer a more elaborate and nuanced assessment of the relationship between Althusser and Foucault; thus, while noting that "there were significant differences between the two men, and these differences crystallized into outright opposition in 1969-70, when Althusser introduced his concepts of interpellation and ideological apparatuses and Foucault responded with his neo-Nietzschean formulation 'knowledge/power'," he observes that nevertheless:

> Prior to 1968, Foucault seemed to be engaged in a project not dissimilar to that of Althusser, despite Foucault's admittedly non-Marxist orientation.[18] Both were obviously indebted to the same philosophy of science for their focus on knowledge as a historical problem and for their relativistic epistemology; both were pursuing a structural, explicitly anti-humanist, anti-Hegelian explanation of historical phenomena;[19] and both spoke about and against certain forms of historically structured domination that they held to be constitutive of contemporary society.[20]

Furthermore, Warren Montag (1995, p. 57) writes that both thinkers sought to question certain accepted "certitudes"—what Althusser called "obviousnesses" and Foucault called "self-evidences" and "commonplaces"—and that "common to both Althusser and Foucault ... their primary concern was to discover how certain concepts functioned in specific historical conjunctures, not from a position outside this history, but rather from within it..." Moreover, Montag (1995, p. 75) urges: "In fact, Althusser's central thesis (ideology interpellates individuals as subjects) only takes on its full meaning in relation to what we might call Foucault's reading of the materiality of ideology, a notion rewritten as the 'physical order' of the disciplines." Of significance with regard to the present study, given that Rafael Guillén's thesis was concerned deeply with the education system, discourse, power, and ideology, Montag (1995, p. 59), commenting specifically on Althusser's "Ideological State Apparatuses" and Foucault's *Discipline and Punish*, notes the two thinkers' "stubborn insistence that the individual was not given, but constituted or produced as center of initiatives, an effect, not a cause of the conflictual processes of ideology or power (a thesis central to both works)..." He thus proposes that

> the two works are not opposed and external to each other, the one an alternative to the other. Rather than feeling compelled to choose between "Ideology and Ideological State Apparatuses" and *Discipline and Punish*, and thus between Althusser and Foucault ... we may read the apparent dilemma, Althusser or Foucault, in the manner of Spinoza, as Althusser *sive* Foucault, Althusser, that is, Foucault.[21]

Montag (1995, pp. 76-77) concludes that "from the materialist positions that Althusser and Foucault occupy, there can be no total domination or total authority … [P]ower, which both Althusser and Foucault conceive in physical terms, 'is exercised rather than possessed' (*Discipline and Punish*, 26) and cannot be given or taken away."

    Finally, most recently Andrew Ryder (2013, p. 148) has urged that:

> Both Foucault and Althusser are concerned with power relations and their capacity to produce knowledge and subjects … Both Foucault and Althusser reveal thinking individuals as effects rather than causes of societal institutions, their apparent liberal freedoms only concealing the context of power and domination in which they are enmeshed.

He concludes (p. 153) by stating that: "An essential unity can be found between Althusser and Foucault in their insistence on the primacy of language and the mediation of discourse before an immediate understanding of bodily need, and following from this, the rejection of the question of 'man' as crucial to knowledge."

    Interestingly, even at the time when Guillén was writing his thesis (i.e. 1979/80) there was already a precedent for blending the theories of Foucault with those of Althusser: namely, Luis Crespo and Josep Ramoneda's *Sobre la filosofía y su no-lugar en el marxismo* (1974), which, significantly, is listed in Guillén's bibliography.[22] Nor was Guillén the last to attempt such a blending, for Philip Goldstein (2005, p. 112) notes how Pierre Machery, "adopts Althusseriam Marxism and Foucauldian poststructuralism."[23] Significantly, by the time the mid-1990s rolled round, with a decade-and-a-half having elapsed since Rafael wrote his thesis, and with the Zapatista movement, and with it Marcos, now emerging on the word stage, several eminent scholars were drawing attention to certain common ground between the works of Althusser and Foucault.[24]

    Finally, let us briefly address the points of convergence and divergence between Poulantzas' and Foucault's thought. Bob Jessop (2007, pp. 142-43), while acknowledging that "[i]n contrast to Foucault, Poulantzas never abandoned his fundamental commitment to Marxism" and that "Poulantzas rejected Foucault's general epistemological and theoretical project" which was "incompatible with Marxism,"[25] and also noting that "while Foucault had rejected the temptations of state theory, Poulantzas … eventually claimed to have completed Marx's unfinished theory of the state," nonetheless states that "Despite some obvious differences ... some fascinating and surprising convergences developed in their work over the course of the 1970s." Indeed, Jessop (2007, p. 143) identifies, and expounds upon, "eight main areas of convergence between the[se] contemporaries."[26] Significantly, taken together these convergences cover (a) how the state constitutes acting and knowing subjects and the subsequent relationship between the former and the latter, and (b) power, and resistance to power predominantly in the form of micro-revolts and rank-and-file movements—both subjects that Rafael the student and Marcos the subcommander concerned themselves deeply with.

For the remainder of this chapter, and in the one that follows, we will turn to examining in greater detail which elements of these philosophers' thought Guillén drew upon in his thesis, before going on to assess to what extent, if any, they persisted in the thought and discourse of Subcommander Marcos.

That Rafael Guillén's thesis should exhibit a considerable indebtedness to thinkers commonly labelled structural Marxists,[27] should come as no surprise given that his student years (i.e. the late 1970s) coincided with the ascendancy of Marxist Structuralism among Latin America's left-wing academics.[28] Richard L. Harris (1979, pp. 62-63), writing precisely during that period, provides the background to, an explanation for, and a useful synopsis of, the rise to prominence of this politico-philosophical current within Latin American leftist intellectual circles:

> The contemporary Western European school of "Marxist Structuralism" has influenced to a considerable degree the intellectual Left in Latin America...
>
> Today [i.e. the late 1970s] ... there has been a pronounced effort to recuperate Marxist theory and engage in a rigorous Marxist analysis of the present historical period. Having recognized the inadequacies of dependency theory and ultra-Left political positions, there was really nowhere else to go but back to "classical" Marxism (i.e. the works of Marx, Engels, and Lenin) and to renew the long-established linkage with the intellectual Left in Western Europe (particularly France). Their earlier rejection of "Euro-centric" Marxism was quickly forgotten and replaced by widespread interest in not only the "classics" but the contemporary theoretical work of Western European Marxists such as Louis Althusser, Etienne Balibar, Nicos Poulantzas, Pierre-Philippe Rey, Maurice Godelier, Emanuel Terray, etc...[29]

A)   *Louis Althusser*

When addressing specifically Althusser, Harris (1979, p. 70) writes that:
> it is safe to say that his works are well-known among a good part of the intellectual Left in Latin America. His book, *Reading Capital*, (which was translated into Spanish in 1969) is widely read by young Leftists students, and his notion of *ideological State apparatuses* is widely used in Leftist intellectual circles.

Moreover, Harris' is no voice crying out in the wilderness: Althusser's impact on the Latin American left has been remarked upon by numerous commentators, including several philosophers, among them Jacques Derrida[30] and the Argentine-Mexican Enrique Dussel (2003a, p. 24), who writes: "In Mexico … the Althusserian current … had a great influence in the seventies through the work of Martha Harnecker."[31] Indeed, Althusser's impact on Mexico in particular is also well attested to by Marxist political scientist, former editor of the renowned left-wing journal *Cuadernos Politicos* and member of UNAM's Institute for Social Research, Arnaldo Córdova[32], who writes (1987/1991, p. 162):
> In 1967, Louis Althusser's work started being published. Its dissemination was extraordinarily swift and on a massive scale, including in academic circles which had been open to New Marxism in the early seventies. The same was true of its acceptance … Althusser … was still being extremely widely disseminated in academic and militant left circles throughout a good part of the 70s.[33]

Unsurprisingly therefore, an examination of Rafael's award-winning graduation thesis from UNAM's Faculty of Philosophy and Letters reveals, very much in keeping with the times, traces of the influence of Althusser, the philosopher's former students Nicos Poulantzas and Michel Foucault, as well as of certain of Althusser's disciples (e.g. Pierre Macherey, Michel Pêcheux, Étienne Balibar, and Dominique Lecourt).[34] Significantly, as noted above, Guillén's bibliography lists seven single-authored works plus two co-authored ones by Althusser; moreover, if we include the works of Althusser's aforementioned disciples, the number of "Althusserian works" listed in Rafael's bibliography can be extended by a further eight pieces (Balibar accounting for three, Macherey for one, and Pêcheux for four). Rafael Guillén then was clearly not immune to what has been called the "Althusserian Revolution,"[35] and was even dubbed "the Althusserian Rafael Guillén" by Alberto Híjar, who presided over the adjudication panel which examined Rafael's graduation thesis and who had himself been the first professor in Mexico to promote Althusser's theories.[36] Indeed, how could he not have been given both the pervasive presence of Althusser among his milieu and also that his graduation thesis was supervised by Cesáreo Morales, who had only recently returned from studying in Paris where he had been imbued with a deep-seated predilection for contemporary French philosophy, especially Althusser (but also Foucault), and who had just written the introduction to the Mexican edition of Althusser's *¿Es sencillo ser marxista en filosofía?* (1978). Moreover, Guillén's Althusserianism persisted with him when he went to teach at Mexico City's other main university, the Metropolitan Autonomous University (Universidad Autónoma Metropolitana), where, UAM professor García Canclini (1988, p. 471) informs us, "the Althusserian vogue" was influencing a generation of Mexican students. Indeed, Mexican journalist Alma Guillermoprieto (2002, pp. 210-211) quotes a friend of hers who taught at the UAM at the same time as Guillén (i.e. the early 1980s) as saying that Rafael and the clique of which he was part "were big on Althusser ... on his theories of ideology and communication..."[37] Not only that, but we also know that Guillén set his students at the UAM the works of Althusser (and Foucault) to read.[38]

Given the above, it is perhaps unsurprising that upon consulting Rafael's thesis almost immediately we encounter, sandwiched between the contents page and the preface, unpaginated preliminary matter which both echoes Althusser's obsession with what texts do/do not and can/cannot say to us,[39] and can be interpreted as a postmodernly ironical *hommage* to the preamble of *The Communist Manifesto* in which both the "Communism" and "Communists" of the original are replaced by "non-existent Althusserianism" and "non-existent Althusserians" (respectively), and "the powers of Europe" becomes "the powers of philosophy."[40]

Having established that Guillén was very much an Althusserian, and that his thesis was very much indebted to the writings of Althusser (and his students and disciples), let us turn to examining concretely and precisely the way Althusser's thinking influenced Rafael.

At a fundamental level, we can see that Althusser's structuralist, anti-humanist outlook makes its presence felt in the thesis. For example, in his "Reply to John Lewis,"[41] Althusser (1976, pp. 63-64) states:

> If the workers are told that "it is men who make history," you do not have to be a great thinker to see that, sooner or later, that helps to disorient or disarm them. It tends to make them think that they are all-powerful as men, whereas in fact they are disarmed as workers in the face of the power which is really in command: that of the bourgeoisie, which controls the material conditions (the means of production) and the political conditions (the state) determining history. The humanist line turns the workers away from the class struggle, prevents them from making use of the only power they possess: that of their *organization as a class* and their *class organizations* (the trade unions, the party), by which they wage *their* class struggle.[42]

A similar assertion can be found in Guillén's (1980, p. 20) thesis in the following form: "In Humanism, Man is the source and motor of history. This not only signifies the negation that *the masses make history*, but even the negation of the presence of class struggle." Moreover, Guillén, after taking this idea over from Althusser, then applies it to the Mexican school textbooks which, he argues, promote among pupils what Althusser identifies as "a humanist line." Indeed, Guillén devotes a subsection (5.2b) of his thesis, entitled "Historical Subject" (pp. 95-97), to inveighing against the Mexican government's social science school textbooks' depiction of history as being made by great individuals.[43] He begins this section by pointing out that "To the question 'Who is it that makes History?,' the textbooks reply: 'great figures (*personalidades*) who possess ideas that move the world'." He then goes on to examine how the textbooks treat the Conquest of Mexico, the grandeur of the Roman Empire, the discovery of the Americas, and India's winning independence from the British Empire, by attributing these to the personal qualities of great figures: Cortés' astuteness and audacity, Caesar being a great soldier and statesman as well as a good orator and writer, Cristóbal Colón's boldness, and Gandhi being a great, intelligent and pacifistic man. Guillén counters such a depiction by adopting a more structuralist and anti-humanist approach akin to that of Althusser's, postulating that material conditions are what have led to the above historical phenomena: hence the Conquest took place thanks to "the means of production in Spain [being] more developed than in Mexico [thereby enabling] the Spaniards to produce weapons that the

Aztecs could not"; "the very structure of the Roman state favored the concentration of power in a single person"; the Discovery of the Americas was owing "to the crisis of the markets and the expansion of the means of production in Spain and the need for new markets"; and Indian independence came about through "the development of the class struggle in India." Rafael concludes this section thus: "In summary, we have [from the textbooks the idea] that historical change is owing to great ideas and the historical subject is formed by great figures who are bearers of said ideas." Interestingly, more than two decades later, in 2001 and now as Subcommander, Marcos would repeat his contesting of a humanist view of history with its emphasis on great figures, reflecting:

> And so, like when one studies history, and realizes that the great figures of history were, in reality, not them but rather a group of individuals (a collective, ultimately), a group of circumstances which made this historical situation appear to be the responsibility of an individual. But, with the passing of time, it can be seen that it was not so.[44]

Marcos (2013) would go on to express a similar sentiment twelve years later, writing:

> what makes the old wheel of history move are collectives and not individuals. Historiography thrives on individualities but history learns from a people ... when rebellion is individual it is pretty. But when it is collective and organized it is terrible and marvellous. The former is the material of biographies, the latter is what makes history.

It is, however, when his thesis turns to treating ideology that it is at its most Althusserian, and where Rafael exhibits his most profound indebtedness to Althusser. Ideology is strongly connected in Althusser's thinking to the class struggle because, as the philosopher's eminent disciple, Étienne Balibar, in his paper entitled "Althusser's object," puts it, "philosophical discourses are related to ideological practices, thus to political practices, thus in the last analysis to the class struggles that transform the world."[45] As we proceed through the pages of Rafael's thesis, we soon encounter sections and passages that echo Althusser's arguably most significant political-philosophical contribution, namely, his formulations concerning ideology, and more specifically both his thesis that individuals are interpellated as subjects by ideology, and his theory of Ideological State Apparatuses.

Immediately following the preface, at the start of Part I (entitled "Philosophical Practice") one finds a section entitled "Monologue in two voices that disguises itself as a philosophical dialogue" (pp. 4-7). The first two-and-a-quarter pages of this section are taken up with urging the need for "a theory of ideology that would have to give an account of, to explain, ideological practices…" It also sees Rafael levelling sarcasm at an overly-simplistic orthodox Marxist conception of ideology—rejected by Althusser[46]—which states

> ideology is only bourgeois ideology. Lies which the bad bourgeoisie tell the good proletariat. Omnipresent and omnipotent, without any contradiction, that is, without class struggle, ideology is a kind of "mask" that, by merely lifting it, one discovers the TRUTH (ONE, SINGLE and PROLETARIAN) that shines in all its splendour.

Next, in "Part II: General Concepts of the Theory of Ideology," section 1, entitled "Concerning General Concepts of the Theory of Ideologies" (pp. 31-39), we encounter in its initial three pages a lucid summary of numerous points pertaining to Althusser's essay on "Ideology and Ideological State Apparatuses"; indeed, we even find Rafael repeating (p. 33) Althusser's phrase that "man is an ideological animal."

It is, however, in Part Two, Chapter 4, of Rafael's thesis (pp. 54-57) that we encounter Rafael's most detailed and Althusserian discussion of the theory of ideology. Rafael leads with the following quotation from Althusser (1971/2001c, p. 109): "Ideology represents the imaginary relationship of individuals to their real conditions of existence," before going on to provide a thirteen-point summary of Althusser's theories on ideology, the first twelve of these relating to material found in Althusser's essay on the ISAs—"his single most influential text" according to Gregory Elliott (1993, p. 237)—and the final one deriving from his "Philosophy Course for Scientists." Rafael ends this section by stating (p. 57):

> In the present study we will solely concern ourselves systematically with issues related to the "interpellation" of subjects and will provide some pointers concerning the relationship between the dominant ideology and the dominated ideology, and the AIEs [Aparatos Ideológicos de Estado (Ideological State Apparatuses)] as sites of class struggle.

While reading Althusser's essay on "Ideology and Ideological State Apparatuses" Rafael would have encountered sections covering education, and more specifically schools, and it was these, presumably, that suggested the theme of his graduation thesis and also provided its theoretical underpinnings. In that work Althusser (1971/2001c, p. 103) states:

> I believe that the ideological State apparatus which has been installed in the *dominant* position in mature capitalist social formations ... is the *educational ideological apparatus* ... Hence I believe I have good reasons for thinking that behind the scenes of its political Ideological State Apparatus, which occupies the front of the stage, what the bourgeoisie has installed as its number-one, i.e. as its dominant ideological State apparatus, is the educational apparatus.

He then elaborates further (pp. 104-105):

> [O]ne Ideological State Apparatus certainly has the dominant role . ... This is the School. It takes children from every class at infant-school age, and then for years, the years in which the child is most "vulnerable," squeezed between the family State apparatus and the educational State apparatus, it drums into them, whether it uses new or old methods, a certain amount of "know-how" wrapped in the ruling ideology (French, arithmetic, natural history, the sciences, literature) or simply the ruling ideology in its pure state (ethics, civic instruction, philosophy) ....no other ideological State apparatus has the obligatory (and not least, free) audience of the totality of the children in the capitalist social formation, eight hours a day for five or six days out of seven...[47]

Having adopted Althusser's theoretical framework, Rafael subsequently, in Part Four (pp. 73-104), then applies it to provide a "concrete analysis" of both the family—another institution that forms part of the Ideological State Apparatuses according to Althusser—and the Mexican education system, and in particular the official school textbooks used in primary schools.[48] In doing so, Rafael was engaging very much with one of the major political-philosophical preoccupations of the time: certainly he was not alone in examining in more detail what Althusser had identified as "the School-Family couple" and its relation to the state.[49] In fact, in the same year that Rafael completed and submitted his thesis (i.e. 1980), Miriam E. David published her *The State, the Family and Education*, in which she acknowledged that Althusser's work on ISAs has "provided the impetus for this study" (p. 2, n.), and stated on her first page that: "My central argument is that the family and the education system are used in concert to sustain and reproduce the social and economic *status quo*" (p. 1); concluding more than 200 pages later that: "the State uses the 'family-education couple' to maintain and reinforce both class and sexual divisions and that these divisions are necessary for the reproduction of the conditions of the capitalist economy" (p. 239).

Turning to the education system as constituting one facet of the Ideological State Apparatuses, Rafael (1980, pp. 86-92) observes how the Mexican government's official philosophy is heavily Hegelian, with its stressing of the necessity of the state for resolving conflicting tendencies within society by conciliating groups and social classes under its direction and arbitration. He also notes that the Mexican state emphasizes its role of safeguarding progress in general, and links education to the project of national development in particular. In this way, Rafael (1980, p. 88) points out, "the state presents itself as an immediate and inescapable necessity." Examining the school textbooks specifically, he notes how these "are the discursive vehicle of the Mexican State in its intervention in education" (p. 92) through which is promoted a self-justificatory ideology that: fosters nationalism and forges national unity in an attempt to both paper over, and in fact, neutralize, class antagonisms between the proletariat and bourgeoisie, and draw attention away from confronting the exploitative national bourgeoisie and toward warding-off foreign imperialism (pp. 99-100); utilizes a pacifistic discourse that is aimed at deterring any would-be non-peaceful opposition to the State (pp. 100-101); bounds discussion of economic change to merely the achieving of higher standards of living, not a total rejection of capitalism with its exploitative means of production and social relations (pp. 101-102); and legitimates the institutional regime by associating poverty and exploitation with not voting, thereby suggesting that such social ills can be remedied simply through participating in elections (p. 102). Rafael, sets out precisely how the textbooks achieve the above, elaborating thus:

> Armed struggle? It is discarded by "demonstrating" the history that ... "wars never fix anything, they result in a never-ending story." In this way even thinking about armed revolutionary struggle is prevented since the child is made to think about its disadvantages ....

> With the possibility of armed struggle eliminated in the individual and in the basic cultural code, the only path possible is the peaceful one, the institutional. It is essential not to forget, since war is detrimental, that "... governments and institutions were created so that men would live in peace with their fellow men..." And so what has to be done in order to achieve a change is to participate in those institutions through peaceful means, and history has "demonstrated" that this yields good results...
>
> ...[B]y characterizing class struggle at a mere structural economic level, as the simple confrontation for higher wages and better conditions, what is done is internalizing in the working class the belief that the only thing that is necessary is to achieve better living conditions but without changing the system, without confronting the bourgeoisie and, much less, the State; that these conditions can be achieved by peaceful and institutional means...
>
> The institutional regime, which is assumed to be elected by universal vote, makes itself necessary in order to avoid exploitation and poverty. History "teaches" us that "in the majority of countries there are groups which do not participate in elections, poverty and ignorance cause many people not to vote, not to demand their rights and, therefore, they are exploited." Therefore the only thing necessary to get out of poverty is to vote and, consequently, legitimize that institutional regime.

Ultimately, Rafael (1980, p. 103) concludes by stating that

> there is a relationship between philosophy and education and this relationship takes place in the Mexican State through the textbooks whose conception of historic change and subject allows the State to create consensus about the need for its existence and for the union of all Mexicans without regard to race, creed, color or CLASS. We have also seen that this project serves to hide from the worker class consciousness and the struggle which fights against capital. (capitals in the original)

Next, let us turn now to discuss a preoccupation that Rafael would have encountered time and again in Althusser's writings: namely, the question of the relationship between theory and praxis. Of course, this is not a matter that Althusser alone has concerned himself with: rather, Marx first addressed it in his *Theses on Feuerbach* (1845), in which he advocated "'practical-critical' activity," which involves the combining of theory with practice, and he was subsequently followed by Lenin, Gramsci, and a host of other leading

Marxists in wrestling with this question. (Indeed, one wonders how it would be possible for someone to be a Marxist and not be concerned with the issue of how precisely theory and praxis related to one another.) This having been said, Althusser devotes considerable space and attention to this issue throughout his works—clearly it was a matter that preoccupied him immensely—and as a result Rafael would have been exposed to this, which, presumably, in turn contributed to the formulation of his own stance regarding the marrying of theory and praxis—something which may have shaped his decision to embark on the life of a rural guerrilla and an issue we witness him grappling with years later, as subcommander, in his discourse.

Despite his name being frequently associated with rather dense, intricate, even somewhat obtuse formulations and seemingly highly abstract theorization, Althusser saw his own work, and indeed philosophy as a discipline, as being practical, indeed highly political, something to be pursued so as to be put at the service of the proletariat in the waging of their class struggle. Nowhere is this more apparent than in his illustratively titled work "Philosophy as a Revolutionary Weapon," in which we encounter statements such as: "philosophy is fundamentally *political*," and "Philosophy represents the class struggle in theory. That is why philosophy is a struggle (*kampf*, said Kant), and basically a *political* struggle: a class struggle."[50] Moreover, it is a position Althusser reiterated seven years later in his "Is it Simple to Be a Marxist in Philosophy?," writing that "philosophy is, in the last instance, class struggle at the level of theory, as I have recently argued ... I claimed that it was necessary to get rid of the suspect division between philosophy and politics."[51] Thus, Simon Choat (2010/2012, p. 20) points out:

> Althusser read Marx not as a dry academic exercise, but for political reasons .... This attempt to revive a radicalized political Marx, free from dogma, accords with Althusser's definition of philosophy as class struggle in theory. The point for Althusser is ... to recover a political Marx who can serve practical purposes .... It is not until the mid-1960s that Althusser explicitly insists on the political nature and role of philosophy .... These claims for a politicized philosophy are nonetheless implicit, present in a latent form, in Althusser's earlier work...[52]

Naturally then, and quite expectedly for an academic and philosopher intent on advancing the class struggle, Althusser was especially concerned with the relationship between theory and practice; indeed, it is a theme that can be found in much of his oeuvre. For example, as early as 1965, in his seminal work *For Marx*, Althusser (1965/1969, p. 166) quoted Lenin's statement that "Without revolutionary theory, no revolutionary practice," before adding that "theory is essential to practice, to the forms of practice that it helps bring to birth or to grow, as well as to the practice it is the theory of." So too, in his "Theory, Theoretical Practice and Theoretical Formation: Ideology and Ideological Struggle," Althusser (1974/1990b, p. 42) warned that:

> We will fall into *idealism* pure and simple if theory is severed from practice, if theory is not given a practical existence—not only in its application, but also in the forms of organization and education that assure the passage of theory into practice and its realization in practice. We will fall into the same idealism if theory is not permitted, in its specific existence, to nourish itself from all the experiences, from all the results and real discoveries, of practice. But we will fall into another, equally grave form of idealism—*pragmatism*—if we do not recognize the irreplaceable specificity of *theoretical practice*, if we confuse theory with its application, if—not in words, but in *deeds*—we treat theory, theoretical research and theoretical formation as purely and simply auxiliary to practice, as "servants of politics", if we construe theory as pure and simple commentary on immediate political practice.

In another of his works, "On Theoretical Work: Difficulties and Resources," Althusser (1974/1990b, p. 67) would pose the question "in the theoretical practice of Marxism, as in its political practice, what conditions must be observed to assure a *correct union* of theory and practice…?" (italics in original). Finally, in his "Philosophy as a Revolutionary Weapon," Althusser (1968/2001a, p. 19) states:

> Marxist-Leninist philosophy, or dialectical materialism, represents the proletarian class struggle *in theory*. In the union of Marxist theory and the Workers' Movement (the *ultimate* reality of the union of theory and practice) philosophy ceases, as Marx said, to "interpret the world." It becomes a weapon with which "to change it": *revolution*.

That Rafael fully shared in Althusser's view that philosophy should not be an abstract exercise but rather one that is placed in the service of practical, political ends, and indeed that philosophical theory and political praxis should be united, can be readily seen from study of his thesis. First, he ends his preliminary matter, sandwiched between the title page and the table of contents, by proposing, in the words of Althusser, "a new practice of philosophy: PHILOSOPHY AS A REVOLUTIONARY WEAPON" (capitals in Rafael's original).[53] Second, Rafael concludes his preface by declaring that, with regard to his investigation, "What is at stake is not simply an academic requirement; rather, what is at stake is the possibility of a new site of operation of philosophy, of theory, of politics."[54] Third, in Part IV of the main body, which is entitled "Undertaking a Concrete Analysis" and is the longest section of his thesis, Rafael applies the Althusserian and Foucauldian theories he has been discussing to the very concrete subject of State ideology as promoted in Mexican schools, and especially in the official textbooks used in them.[55] Fourth, in the "Philosophical Dialogue II" with which his thesis ends, Rafael constructs a mock dialogue between himself and an imagined, somewhat adversarial, interlocutor,[56] in which he sums up his approach by claiming that "what has been done here is … to attempt to break with philosophical practices that deny their links with politics and revel in the academic space," and instead to "establish the relationship between philosophical practice and political practices."[57] Finally, Rafael demonstrates his concern with making philosophy serve politics, as well as an equally Althusserian preoccupation with the relationship between theory and practice, in the final sentences of his conclusion:

> I would like to end … by noting the importance of POLITICS, of assuming a political position which makes possible an "other" discursive strategy, which opens an "other" space of theoretical production, which allows an "other" philosophical work than the merely academic. And the proletarian political practice is the only one that makes this possible. We practice politics, we make theory with politics and politics with theory…[58] (capitals in the original)

Significantly, according to his thesis examiner, Alberto Híjar, it was Rafael's practical application of Althusser's theories to concrete instances that caused him to "stand out" (*destacaba*) from his peers.[59] Elaborating on this, Híjar informs us that the generation of students to which Rafael belonged in the UNAM's philosophy department were "very well-schooled in philosophical debate, especially that taking place in France, but they displayed an encyclopaedic ignorance with respect to what was occurring in Latin America and the rest of the world, especially in Mexico." Moreover, "the majority," he tells us, were the kind who could debate philosophy in general, and Al-

Structural Marxist Formation: Louis Althusser and Nicos Poulantzas

thusser's theories in particular, but exhibited "a great inability to ground these discussions in anything concrete," which, Híjar points out, was something that "went against Althusser himself." In contrast, Híjar notes, Rafael (and a few others) "sought to make concrete their talent for philosophical reflection [by applying it to] specific fields."

Interestingly, in his thesis Rafael satirized precisely the kind of students who formed the majority of his peers and are described by Híjar above, labelling them "café Marxists" and painting the following portrait of them:

> They are in the café, discussing how to make revolution. However, they have not been able to reach an agreement on the concepts of "theory" and "praxis." They have consulted various books on the subject, and their discussions abound with quotations from the texts of Marx, Engels and Lenin. And yet, although four hours have already gone by in discussion, they cannot even reach agreement on whether these coffee shop discussions themselves constitute theory or practice.
>
> The coffee-table Marxists ... are the theoretical vanguard ... Preoccupied with truly transcendental matters, such as "alienation," the philosophy of "praxis," the logical formalization of *Das Kapital*, the latest "waves" of the last Marxists, they look on political activism with Olympic disdain. They shake their heads with disapproval when presented with a pamphlet talking about the struggle in a given factory, farm workers here or peasants there. Political activism, rallies, assemblies and street protests are petty things for them. No political activity must interfere with their theoretical musings...[60]

It has been commented on that many of these coffee-table Althusserian students went on to become part of the state bureaucracy. Indeed, Félix Hoyo (1995, p. 34) writes that "the typical progression of the Althusserians of the seventies involved becoming functionaries or advisors of the Mexican government."[61] This leads Hoyo (1995, p. 34), when discussing the transformation of (the Althusserian) Guillén into (the Subcommander) Marcos to state that:

> What is surprising is the fact that an Althusserian yielded a revolutionary .... Perhaps we are able to say that if Guillén converted into Marcos it was not due to Althusser ... that is to say, Guillén converted into Marcos in spite of the academic accident of Althusserianism being in vogue during his student days.

– 95 –

However, I believe Hoyo is in error here. The student became the Subcommander *precisely because* Rafael was a *true* Althusserian (i.e. following Althusser he sought to unite philosophical theory and political practice), whereas faux-Althusserian students saw mastering Althusser's complex theories as a mere intellectual exercise, a proof of intellectual rigour and, ultimately, a form of academic credential that would allow them to enter the political or bureaucratic class and become part of the ruling elite. In short, Rafael's Althusser was the Althusser who viewed "philosophy as a revolutionary weapon;" who would several times repeat the quotation, from Marx's *XI Thesis On Feuerbach*, which stated "The philosophers have only interpreted the world in various ways; the point, however, is to change it;"[62] and who insisted point blank that:

> In order really to understand what one "reads" and studies in these theoretical, political and historical works, one must directly experience oneself the two *realities* which determine them through and through: the reality of theoretical practice (science, philosophy) in its concrete life; the reality of the *practice of revolutionary class struggle* in its concrete life, in close contact with the masses. For if theory enables us to understand the laws of history, it is not intellectuals, nor even theoreticians, it is the *masses* who make history. It is essential to learn with theory—but at the same time and crucially, it is essential to learn with the masses.[63]

Having steeped himself in Marxist theory during his years studying political philosophy at the UNAM, thereby directly experiencing "the reality of theoretical practice," Rafael set about directly experiencing the second of Althusser's two *realities*, "the *practice of revolutionary class struggle*," becoming a cadre of the Marxist-Leninist revolutionary Fuerzas de Liberación Nacional (FLN) and ultimately a rural guerrilla living, working, and learning alongside Chiapas' campesinos.[64]

We have witnessed above certain quintessentially Althusserian elements that found reflection in Rafael's thesis: namely, those related to an overall structuralist, anti-humanist outlook, and Althusser's theories regarding ideology and the relationship between theory and praxis. It now remains to discuss the extent to which this Althusserian formation persisted in Marcos and helped to shape the Subcommander's discourse.[65]

The first thing to note is that there are some who flatly deny there are similarities between Subcommander Marcos and Louis Althusser. For example, Fernando Matamoros Ponce (1996, pp. 240-241) not only rejects any suggestion of similarity but goes even further, stating:

> Marcos is in fact the opposite of Althusser, from the point of view of theory and politics. His discourse does not contain orthodox Marxist formula, but is principally a blend of ancient pre-Columbian memory, with a dash, linguistically speaking, of evangelical liberation prophecies. We are very far here from the scientific thought of orthodox French Marxism.[66]

Another example is Alberto Híjar, Professor of Aesthetics and Art Criticism at the UNAM, and head of the adjudicating panel of Rafael Guillén's thesis, who had been the first professor in Mexico to promote Althusser's theories, and who has been quoted as saying that Subcommander Marcos has nothing to do with the Althusserian Rafael Guillén.[67] Finally, Félix Hoyo (1995, p. 34) argues that

> if Guillén converted into Marcos it was not due to Althusser, but to the formulation of his sensibility that led him to an "epistemological rupture" with structural Marxism; that is to say, Guillén converted into Marcos in spite of the academic accident of Althusserianism being in vogue during his student days.

If we were to sum up the position adopted by Matamoros Ponce, Híjar, and Hoyo employing Althusserian terms, then there appears to have taken place a "rupture" separating the Althusserian political and philosophical thought of the young student Rafael from that of the more mature, guerrilla Subcommander Marcos—a "rupture" similar to that which Althusser had argued separated the "ideological" young (i.e. pre-1845) Marx from the "scientific" more mature (i.e. post-1845) Marx.[68]

At the other end of the spectrum, however, several commentators have claimed they are able discern similarities, even continuities, between Althusser and Marcos. For instance, at the stylistic level, Carlos Monsiváis, who surveys "Marcos' thinking, distributed over hundreds of pages," has declared that the Subcommander's "discourse was initially very oversimplified, with too many paeans to the unreadable translations of Althusser and Poulantzas…"[69] (For my part I would urge that both Althusser and Marcos exhibit a penchant for frequent qualifying statements, commonly taking the form of parentheticals in the writings of the former and postscripts in those of the latter). Moving away from stylistic aspects and toward conceptual ones, journalist Alma Guillermoprieto (2002, p. 211) has stated: "Marcos' preoccupation with symbolic language is certainly worthy of a student of Althusser. He has created his own dazzling image as a masked *mito genial*—his term, meaning 'an inspired act of mythmaking'." So too, José de Colina (2002, p. 366) states that the Subcommander espoused "a Marxism jumbled with subliminal citations from Foucault, Althuser [*sic*]..." Finally, Daniela Di Piramo provides the fullest discussion of the relationship between Althusser and Marcos. In her book on Marcos and charismatic authority, she writes (2010, p. 113):

> Marcos, in his thesis entitled "Philosophy and Education" had argued that discourse is not only a medium for translation or reproduction of the hegemonic system but also a medium of struggle, while ideology (a system of ideas and practices) conforms to practices that support the dominant system. Clearly inspired by Althusser and his work on ideology, Marcos sees discourse as a weapon against *ideologies* through which, as Althusser has argued, subjects interpret their relation to the real conditions of existence...[70]

It is clear from the above that the question of whether any Althusserian influence persisted within Rafael after he had become Subcommander Marcos is a contentious one. Moreover, even if Guillermoprieto, Colima, and Di Piramo are correct in rejecting the idea of Rafael having completely abandoned his Althusserianism at some point after he embarked on the life of a rural guerrilla in the jungles of Chiapas, they leave unanswered the questions of to what extent and in which ways Althusserian tendencies persisted in the Subcommander. Although no answer can be deemed definitive, I believe we can form some kind of judgment from a close examination of Marcos' discourse and actions following the Zapatista uprising on January 1, 1994.

That the Subcommander retained at least an interest in Althusser can perhaps be inferred from the following piece of (admittedly circumstantial) evidence. Journalists who reported on the Mexican Federal Army's seizure of the Subcommander's camp during a February 1995 offensive, and who wrote about the discovery in Marcos' library of a considerable stash—more than seventy—of books make mention of Fernanda Navarro's interview with the French philosopher, published as *Filosofía y marxismo: Entrevista a Louis Althusser* (México: Siglo XXI editores: 1988).[71] Of course, we do not know whether Marcos actively sought out this tome for himself, or even if he had read it; however, the presence of *Filosofía y marxismo* on the Subcommander's shelves may perhaps point to a continued interest in Althusser, one that persisted for at least eight years following the completion of Guillén's graduation thesis.

More importantly however, we can catch numerous glimpses of Althusser's reflection in the discourse and deeds of Marcos: these range from major conceptual influences, namely regarding ideology and a concern with the relationship between theory and practice, to more minor points of convergence. Let us begin then with ideology. Althusser's philosophical contribution to the field of ideology involved refining previous theories to develop a nuanced view of how ideology functions, and in particular how it interpellates people as subjects, represents the imaginary relationship of individuals to their real conditions of existence, and can be disseminated through Ideological State Apparatuses. At a very general level, Althusser showed how the dominated (but also the dominant) in society accept the status quo as something that is a natural state of affairs due to the ideology disseminated by the State through various institutions[72]; consequently, he urged the need to confront this ideology by contesting it on numerous sites of ideological struggle. This inheritance, we shall now see, is what Marcos brought to Zapatismo.

That the Subcommander's reading of Althusser did more than imbue Marcos with a keen appreciation of the importance of ideology is evident:[73] rather, it led him to wage an ideological struggle against the Mexican State, confronting and challenging its ideology on numerous battlegrounds and sites of contestation.[74] Thus Marcos set about systematically demolishing the government's key ideological underpinnings.[75] Put briefly, he savagely denounced neoliberalism; he lambasted *mestizaje*; and he fundamentally undermined the (pseudo)legitimacy that the State derived from being self-professed sole heir to, and continued upholder of the values of, the Mexican Revolution, a promoter of modernization (and ultimately a bearer of modernity), and a guarantor of the Rule of Law. Let us briefly examine Marcos' attacks on the State's ideological pillars in the order they are given above.

First, with regard to neoliberalism Marcos has observed:

> Salinas de Gortari's strategy within neoliberalism was to construct a publicity campaign, presenting abroad a stable country, a good product that he was selling … we managed to affect that publicity campaign … to … demonstrate what was really happening, what this political, economic project meant for this country, for a part of the country, for the indigenous.

He continued: "Society is beginning to march in one direction and the State, the political system, in another ... one is talking about two Mexicos: the virtual one of the political class with its great economic successes, the 7.5% Gross National Product growth and that of the rest of society which does not see economic growth anywhere."[76] In fact, after the financial debacle of late 1995, the Subcommander would proclaim: "Neoliberalism is not a theory to confront or explain the crisis. It is the crisis itself made theory and economic doctrine!"[77] Indeed, as Daniela Di Piramo (2011, p. 183) has observed, "Marcos uses irony in his discourse both in terms of content and linguistic practice to expose the dominant neo-liberal order as irrational."

The second of the State's ideological pillars was *mestizaje*. As José Rabasa (1997, p. 411) explains:

> The state-sponsored ideology of *mestizaje* after the 1910 Revolution theoretically should have extended bonds of solidarity with Indians, but its historical effect was to promote a systematic denial of Indian roots—though the pre-Columbian past was idealized—and a program of acculturation that aimed to destroy indigenous languages and cultures. Only "mestizos" were deemed by the state to be authentic Mexicans.[78]

Marcos basically exploded the myth of *mestizaje*, laying bare to *mestizo* Mexico, through his eloquence and satirical wit, its inherently racist nature and discriminatory function.[79] In particular, the Subcommander exposed the hypocrisy of an ideology which while it lauded the nation's indigenous past, often cynically exploiting Mexico's Indians as a tourist attraction, callously ignored or even expunged the indigenous present by both condemning contemporary indigenous peoples to live in a state of abject neglect and also writing them out of recent history.[80] Concerning the former, as Marcos told interviewer Medea Benjamin (1995, p. 58):

> The government ... want[s] to show the tourists the lovely Mexican culture ... the folkloric dancing, the beautiful clothing and crafts of the indigenous people. But behind this picture is the real Mexico, the Mexico of the millions of Indians who live in extreme poverty. We have helped peel off the mask to reveal the real Mexico.

Indeed, this is one of the central, underlying themes in Marcos' fictional tales: Kristine Vanden Berghe and Bart Maddens (2004, p. 139), on examining the Subcommander's stories involving Old Antonio and Don Durito, note that "Marcos appears ... to point to the gap between ... the inclusion of the indigenous peoples in official discourse about mestizaje and their exclusion in practice." Regarding the latter, the Subcommander sought to rewrite Mexico's indigenous peoples into the nation's recent history; he told Julio Scherer García (2001, p. 13): "Mexico has had almost 200 years as an independent nation, and at every point in time the indigenous have appeared as the fundamental part, but at no time has any such thing been recognized."

Next, one of the State's primary sources of legitimacy derived from its self-proclaimed status as exclusive heir to the Mexican Revolution and promoter of the values that both inspired, and subsequently arose from, it. Through his re-appropriation of the figure of Zapata in the service of the Zapatista movement, the Subcommander wrested from the government its long-held, monopolistic grip on being the Revolution's authentic heir. As Marcos explained to Yvon Le Bot (1997a, pp. 347-348):

> When the EZLN ... appeared, it had to fight the Mexican State for certain symbols of the nation's history. The terrain of symbols is an occupied terrain, above all as regards Mexican history .... In this case, that of historic symbols, the Mexican State uses them in a way which must be fought over. Zapata, for example.

Indeed, so successful was the Subcommander in this regard that the government withdrew Zapata's image from the 10 peso note and President Salinas changed the backdrop of his televised statements from a hanging portrait of Zapata to one of Carranza. As a result, George A. Collier and Elizabeth L. Quaratiello (1994/1999, p. 158) point out: "These days, no one thinks of Zapata without thinking of Chiapas and Mexico's new indigenous movement ... the ruling party has lost virtually any credible claim to Emiliano Zapata as one of its heroes."[81]

The State also sought to portray itself as a promoter of modernization, and ultimately a bearer of modernity, both substantial elements of *salinismo*, President Salinas' (1988-1994) neoliberal ideology. In an interview dated June 8, 1995, Carlos Monsiváis looked back over the preceding years, stating: "It was an incredible time. Rational, intelligent people were really in love with Salinas's ideas and Salinas's attitude ... Salinas was the image of modernity ... it was utter rubbish!"[82] In a later interview Monsiváis recalled how

> [b]efore the rebellion in Chiapas, the key word in Mexico was 'modernization,' the illusion of the First World around the corner .... 'Moderniza-

tion' took the place of nationalism, the old-time 'act' that united all sectors through festivity, mythology.[83]

Marcos immediately set about puncturing this myth of modernity: interviewed on the first day of the uprising, the Subcommander declared that "the indigenous ethnicities of Mexico … are perfectly dispensable in the modernization program of Salinas de Gortari."[84] Subsequently he would recall how "thousands of indigenous armed with truth and fire, with shame and dignity, shook the country awake from its sweet dream of modernity," and talked of "the crime that, disguised as modernity, distributes misery on a global scale."[85] He would also boast sarcastically in a 1995 communiqué that:

> History written by Power taught us that we had lost, that cynicism and profit were virtues, that honesty and sacrifice were stupid, that individualism was the new god, and hope was devalued money, without currency in the international markets, without purchasing power …. We did not learn the lesson. We were bad pupils. We did not believe what Power taught us. We skipped school when in class they taught conformism and idiocy. We failed [the subject of] modernity.[86]

The Subcommander's most eloquent statement on the subject, and the one which perhaps has elicited the most resonance, came, however, in a communiqué written on January 20, 1994:

> [B]y taking off its own mask, Mexican civil society will realize, with a stronger impact, that the image that it has sold itself is a forgery, and that reality is far more terrifying than it thought. Each of us will show our faces, but the big difference will be that "Sup Marcos" has always known what his real face looked like, and civil society will just wake up from a long and tired sleep that "modernity" has imposed at the cost of everything and everyone.[87]

Thus modernity, as with neoliberalism, *mestizaje*, and Mexico's revolutionary heritage, became an ideological battleground contested by the State on the one hand, and Marcos on the other, through their respective discourses and counter-discourses.[88] The result, as George A. Collier and Elizabeth L. Quaratiello (1994/1999, p. 155) observe, was as follows:

> At the time of the Zapatista rebellion, Mexico was synonymous with "economic modernization" …. At least for a time, the Zapatistas successfully deflected attention away from those who were pursuing modernization at any cost, and they forced a change in the public discourse over Mexico's

future.... During 1994, the Zapatista rebellion seemed to stop the steamroller of Salinas de Gortari's modernizing project in its tracks.

The final ideological lynchpin of the state that the Subcommander attacked was the rule of law (Estado de Derecho),[89] which the government frequently claimed to be upholding in a somewhat unconvincing attempt to maintain legitimacy.[90] Indeed, this is a theme that Marcos returned to several times in his communiqués. For example, in a June 1995 communiqué he writes: "No longer able to win legitimacy, incapable of struggling to achieve it, the Power dresses itself with 'legality'. The legal mantle can do anything ... including the violation of the law. That is how the mirror of Power works, with a legal although illegitimate image."[91] So too, in a September 1995 communiqué the Subcommander, describing both the government's February offensive which contravened the ceasefire it had agreed with the EZLN and the mass demonstrations that this action provoked on the part of civil society, wrote: "Trying to cover the lack of legitimacy of their actions with the thin veil of legality the evil government put the entire country at the edge of a civil war.... The so-called 'Iruegas' doctrine, the strategy that replaces legitimacy with legality, failed."[92] Later, Marcos would elaborate on this theme, exposing how the government had donned a "rule-of-law mask" in order to disguise its practice of persecuting the poor while protecting the rich:

> Lacking the legitimacy which can only be obtained by the governed, these characters [i.e. key figures in the government, including the president] from the Mexican tragedy at the end of the century supplant it with a mask made "ex profeso," that of the Rule of Law (Estado de Derecho)[93]. In the name of the "Rule of Law" they impose economic measures, they assassinate, they imprison, they rape, they destroy, they persecute, they make war...[94]
>
> On top of this ... nightmare cocktail, in addition to their poverty, millions of Mexicans will now have to take responsibility for the rescue of those other criminals, the bankers, who use the "Rule of Law" as an alibi, and who have an ever-willing accomplice and procurer in the Government.[95]

In a speech at the inauguration of the forum for the reform of the state (July 1, 1996), Marcos went even further, stating: "That which kills a person is homicidal. That which kills many [people] is genocidal. What should one call that which kills a nation? The Mexican political system calls it 'the rule of law.'"[96]

In sum then, the Mexican State's legitimacy rested on certain ideological cornerstones—i.e. being perceived as: the creator of prosperity, or at least sufficiently high economic performance to ensure the provision of social welfare through neoliberalism; a promoter of *mestizaje* as a means of fostering national unity and securing social cohesion; the exclusive heir to Mexican Revolution; an agent of modernity; and a guarantor of Rule of Law—however, Marcos severely undermined these and in doing so was able, as Althusser (1971/2001c, pp. 99, n. 11) put it, to "turn the weapon of ideology against the classes in power…" A final point needs making here in relation to Marcos' strategy. Some, no doubt aware of the considerable impact made on the Latin American left by the writings of Antonio Gramsci, may be tempted to attribute Marcos' strategy to the influence of the Italian Marxist, and in particular his writings regarding hegemony and counter-hegemony, rather than to Althusser. As will be seen in Chapter 5, however, there is considerable evidence to suggest that Rafael Guillén would have shunned Gramsci like a precipice on account of his being a Marxist humanist, and because he would have first encountered the Italian's theories, not through the latter's *Prison Notebooks*, but through both Althusser, who believed Gramsci to be irredeemably tainted with historicist tendencies, and Poulantzas (1968/1977, pp. 260–262 & 291), who accused him of "frequent conceptual confusion in his analyses" specifically regarding the concept of hegemony. In contrast, as we have seen (and will continue to do so) in this chapter, the young Marcos underwent a heavily Althusserian and Poulantzian formation.

Finally, while the Mexican government sought to dismiss Marcos' discursive attack on these ideological pillars of state legitimacy as a "propaganda war" and a "war of ink,"[97] the Subcommander preferred instead to emphasize how for the Zapatistas "Our words are weapons,"[98] and in doing so echoes Althusser (1968/2001a, p. 21), who, in his "Philosophy as a Revolutionary Weapon," urged that:

> The realities of the class struggle are "represented" by "ideas" which are "represented" by words. In … political, ideological and philosophical struggle, the words are also weapons, explosives or tranquillizers and poisons. Occasionally, the whole class struggle may be summed up in the struggle for one word against another word. Certain words … are the site of an ambiguity: the stake in a decisive but undecided battle.

Althusser concludes (1968a/2001, p. 22):

The philosophical fight over words is a part of the political fight. Marxist-Leninist philosophy can only complete its abstract, rigorous and systematic theoretical work on condition that it fights both about very "scholarly" words (concept, theory, dialectic, alienation, etc.) and about very simple words (man, masses, people, class struggle).

We have already seen above that Rafael Guillén inherited from Althusser the latter's preoccupation with the relationship between theory and practice; and, indeed, I closed the section in which I discussed this by pointing out that Rafael, having amassed a considerable body of political theory as a philosophy student, then turned to engaging in political practice through joining the Marxist-Leninist revolutionary FLN and ultimately becoming a rural guerrilla. In doing so, I urged, Rafael was attempting to experience, directly, Althusser's two "realities": "the reality of theoretical practice" and "the *practice of revolutionary class struggle.*" In the present section we shall examine to what extent and in which ways the question of the correlation between theory and practice, a matter that Althusser devoted not inconsiderable time and energy to addressing, continued to occupy Marcos.

That the Subcommander similarly concerned himself with wrestling with the exact nature of the connection between philosophical theory and political practice can be readily witnessed from examination of his discourse over the last twenty years. The first point to note is that on several occasions Marcos exhibits a tendency to critique strongly that theory which seems to him so abstract as to be totally removed from (or even in opposition to) reality. For example, in his communiqué entitled "The World: Seven Thoughts in May of 2003," Marcos (2003) writes:

> The position of theory (and of theoretical analysis) in political and social movements is usually obvious. However, everything obvious usually conceals a problem, in this case: that of the effects of a theory on practice and the theoretical "rebound" of the latter…
>
> Producing theory from within a social or political movement is not the same as producing it from within academia. And I am not speaking of "academia" in the sense of sterility or (nonexistent) scientific "objectivity," but only in order to note the place of reflection and intellectual production as being "outside" of a movement…

> We believe that a movement should produce its own theoretical reflection .... There it can incorporate what is impossible in an armchair theory, that is, the transformative practices of that movement...

Similarly, three years later, in an interview with Sergio Rodríguez Lascano (2006) in *Rebeldía* magazine, Marcos stated:

> We say that there is a problem in the intellectual sector, not in just the part you talk about but among the entire intellectual sector—including on the radical left—which is the separation or detachment of intellectual action and political action...
>
> We say that theory, in this sense, over there, above, is always going to stumble with that. Because the saying—I don't remember who said it—that the problem of theory is that praxis, fundamentally praxis, is not taken into consideration...[99]

Finally, the following year, in what has been to date the Subcommander's fullest discussion of the connection between theory and practice, Marcos (2007a) discusses at length what he calls "theory from above" ("la teoría de arriba"), meaning theory wholly removed from reality.[100] He begins by outlining the origins and modus operandi of this "white and pristine theory" ("la teoría blanca e impoluta"):

> The conceptual stone touched the surface of [the pond that is] theory, and a series of waves took place that affected and modified the different adjacent scientific and technical procedures. The consistency of the analytical and reflective thought did, and does, mean that those waves stay defined ... until a new conceptual stone falls and a new series of waves changes theoretical production. Perhaps the same density of theoretical production could explain why the waves, in most cases, do not reach the shore, that is to say, reality...

He continues:

> In this conception of theoretical work, in this meta-theory,[101] not only is the irrelevance of reality insisted on, but also, and especially, it is boasted that reality has been completely dispensed with, in an effort of isolation and sanitation, as they say, that deserves to be applauded.
>
> The image of the sterile laboratory is not limited only to the so-called "natural sciences" or to the "exact sciences," no. In the final throes of the cap-

italist world-wide system, this obsession with sanitary anti-reality reached the so-called "social sciences."[102] Among the global scientific community the following thesis then began to gain force: "if reality does not behave as theory indicates, all the worse for reality."[103]

The Subcommander's wariness concerning theory that is removed from lived reality ought not to surprise us however. Indeed, Marcos' own experiences of attempting to unite philosophical theory with political practice undoubtedly fostered such an attitude: after arriving in Chiapas intent on putting into (revolutionary) practice the considerable amount of Marxist-Leninist theory he had previously accumulated, he encountered a "reality check" in discovering that these theories did not conform to the daily lived experiences of Chiapas' indigenous peasantry. Tellingly, Marcos has related this experience thusly:

> [T]he most orthodox proposals of Marxism or Leninism, theoretical concepts or historical references—for example, that the vanguard of the revolution is the proletariat, that the taking of state power and the installation of the dictatorship of the proletariat is the aim of the revolution—were confronted by an ideological tradition that is ... somewhat magical. It is magical in one sense, but very real in another .... Now, today, I believe there are many theories in crisis. Who would have thought that it would be the Indigenous peoples who would provoke all of this? Not even in the Leninist conception of the weakest link was it thought that it might be the Indigenous people, right? ... [A]t the beginning of our work here [w]e were closed-minded, like any other orthodox leftist, like any other theoretician who believes that he knows the truth.[104]

In my biography of the Subcommander I argued that Marcos' ability to recruit Chiapas' indigenous into the ranks of the EZLN guerrilla to such an extent that (as he puts it) "our army became scandalously Indian"[105] was due fundamentally to his willingness to jettison certain doctrinaire Marxist-Leninist theories that he had mastered through years of hard study when they failed to correspond to, or even contradicted, the social realities and practices he encountered among indigenous Chiapanecan campesinos.[106] When so many on the Latin American revolutionary left had persisted in trying to bend the realities and practices they came up against in the field to conform to their theories, Marcos' novelty, not to mention ultimately his success, lay in his privileging reality over theory, and this, I would insist, explains why we find the Subcommander frequently asserting the primacy of the former over the latter in his discourse.

In addition to critiquing both theory at its most abstract, as well as armchair theoreticians, the Subcommander has, over the years, also articulated in some detail the Zapatistas' approach to theory, including the movement's stance on the question of the relationship between theory and praxis. The first point to note upon examining his discourse is that Marcos has twice asserted the need to "bring down" theory: in his interview with Le Bot (1997a, p. 356) the Subcommander insists that "We are not saying that we want to create a sentimental discourse, one that's apolitical, or atheoretical, or antitheoretical; but what we want is to bring down theory to the level of the human being, to what is lived, to share with the people the experiences that make it possible to continue living";[107] and then again, almost a decade-and-a-half later, Marcos (2011) reiterates this point in his "Third Letter to Don Luis Villoro" (July-August, 2011):

> To "bring down" theory to concrete analysis is one path. Another is to anchor it in practice. But this practice is not carried out in the epistles [between us]; at most one makes note of it. For that reason I think we should continue to insist on "anchoring" our theoretical reflections in concrete analysis...[108]

This brings us nicely to the question of the precise nature of the connection between theory and practice as elaborated in Marcos' discourse. Turning once again to Marcos' communiqué "The World: Seven Thoughts in May of 2003," the Subcommander first discusses the object of the movement's theoretical reflection:

> Our theoretical reflection as Zapatistas is not generally about ourselves, but about the reality in which we move. And its nature is approximate and limited in time, in space, in concepts and in the structure of those concepts. That is why we reject attempts at universality and eternity in what we say and do.

However, more important than theoretical reflection, he urges, is the Zapatista emphasis on practice:

> Answers to questions about Zapatismo are not in our theoretical reflections and analyses, but in our practice. And practice, in our case, carries a heavy

moral, ethical burden. That is, we try to act (not always successfully) in accordance not only with a theoretical analysis, but also, and above all, according to what we consider our duty to be. We try to be consistent, always.[109] Perhaps that is why we are not pragmatic (another way of saying "action without theory and without principles")…

Theoretical reflection on theory is called "Meta-theory." The Meta-theory of the Zapatistas is our practice.[110]

And yet, despite asserting the primacy of practice over theory, Marcos nonetheless concludes his communiqué by emphasizing the need "to … produce … a theory and a practice which does not include arrogance in its principles, but which recognizes its horizons and the tools that serve for those horizons." It would appear then that, for the Zapatistas, theory, though of secondary importance in relation to practice, is nevertheless an indispensable element of Zapatismo.

By 2007 however, it seems that Marcos' stance on the correlation between theory and praxis had undergone a degree of revision; one that brought it more in line with Althusser's endeavour to unite theory and practice, or, as Badiou in his 2013 lecture at Princeton entitled "The Althusserian Definition of Theory" phrased it, "the attempt of Althusser … to destroy the opposition between theory and practice…" In the first in a series of seven oral presentations appearing under the general heading "Neither the Center Nor the Periphery" and given at the Andrés Aubry Colloquium held in December 2007 in San Cristóbal de las Casas (Chiapas),[111] Marcos (2007a), after quoting his fictional alter-ego Don Durito as commenting ironically that "The problem with reality, is that it knows nothing of theory," declares his intention "to explain the rudimentary foundations of this [Zapatista] theory, one so different that it is practice."[112] He begins by suggesting that that "we should find a way of linking theory with love, music and dancing," adding "[p]erhaps this same theory would not manage to explain anything worthwhile, but it would be more humane, because seriousness and rigidity does not guarantee scientific rigor." However, there then follows, not so much a detailed discussion on Zapatista theory and its precise relationship to practice, as a protracted critique of how abstract and removed from reality "theory from above," which has predominated in academia in general and the (natural, exact, and social) sciences in particular, has tended to be. Thus, in place of an explicit exposition on Zapatista theory, we have the implicit implication that it is the very antithesis of "theory from above," from which Marcos' audience is left to infer that Zapatismo prefers to ground its theory in reality. Indeed, during the entire remainder of the presentation, there is but a single other reference to practice (práctica), and this comes at the end (during the thirty-third minute of a thirty-four minute speech), when he advocates the "tearing down [of the fences] of theory and to do it with practice."[113] And this, it should be noted, has a very different feel to it than his opening statement that the Zapatistas' "theory … is practice."[114]

In the seventh and final presentation in the series Marcos (2007c) first declares that "for us Zapatistas, the theoretical problem is a practical problem," before going on to assert that "theories should not only not isolate themselves from reality, but should instead find in reality the loopholes that are sometimes necessary when one comes across an alley with no conceptual way out," adding "Well-rounded theories, complete, finished, coherent, are good for presenting professional exams or to win awards, but tend to shatter upon the first gust of reality."[115] He ends his presentation by saying: "We believe, however, that that other theory, some general strokes of which have been presented here, should also break with this logic of centers and peripheries, and anchor itself in the realities that erupt, that emerge, and open up new avenues."[116]

Surprisingly, the absence in the Subcommander's discourse of any lengthy and substantial exposition definitively detailing and clarifying the precise nature of the relationship between theory and practice has not prevented this component of Zapatismo from attracting considerable attention from commentators. Hence, Daniela Di Piramo (2010, p. 156) states that for the Zapatistas "Theory is seen as the product of everyday practice rather than being derived from an external source…"; Alex Khasnabish (2010, p. 87) writes of "Zapatismo as rebel political philosophy and practice";[117] and Jeff Conant (2010, p. 46) stipulates that "when we speak of *Zapatismo*, we are speaking of two different things—the theory, or ideal of *Zapatismo*, and the ways in which it is carried out in practice," adding "Generally speaking, the theory is grounded in the structures of democratic governance that emerge from the autonomous communities, while the practice hinges largely on tactical decisions made by Marcos and the Comandancia." Most recently, Eugene Gogol (2014, p. 30) has noted how "the massive march [i.e. the March in Silence on December 21, 2012] followed by the [series of] communiqués [written by Marcos soon after and entitled "Them and Us"] was a manifestation of the unity of practice and theory that characterize the Zapatistas' work.")[118] Indeed, some have expounded at not inconsiderable length on this theme. For example, Guillermo Michel (2001b, pp. 13 & 19), in his piece entitled "No morirá la flor de la palabra. La Utopía zapatista: Teoría y Praxis," writes effusively:

> Underwritten by its actions ... the Zapatista political ethic is not merely one of the many profound meditations that spring forth from the pens of professional philosophers. In its philosophical task, in its radical critique of the System which oppresses us *all* (although millions do not realize it, or pretend not to realise it), those who we are really able to call philosophers of hope have learned to unite theory and praxis in a manner so congruous as has seldom been seen in the history of humanity...
>
> [The Zapatistas] ... propose a new political ethic in which the true word is a commitment embodied in actions congruent with this word. In this sense, zapatismo is not only an ethical theory but a daily, arduous *praxis*... (

So too, Thomas Nail, in his *Returning to Revolution: Deleuze, Guattari and Zapatismo* (2012), has recently argued that

> the Zapatistas have created a revolutionary and participatory body politic in practice. The two sides of theory and practice thus constitute the strategy I am calling revolutionary participation. Zapatismo presents an interesting case in political theory and practice because it cannot be understood by the political philosophies of liberalism or Marxism...
>
> The Zapatistas ... aim to transform the conditions for material production and distribution not just in theory but also in practice.[119]

Of all the scholars who have stressed this particular aspect of Zapatismo however, it was John Holloway who first drew attention to the Zapatistas' approach to theory and practice, and who in all likelihood has written most on the subject. After noting the Zapatistas' "rethinking of revolutionary theory and practice," Holloway quotes from an interview with Marcos in which the Subcommander points out that

> The original EZLN, the one that is formed in 1983, is a political organisation in the sense that it speaks and what it says has to be done. The indigenous communities teach it to listen, and that is what we learn. The principal

lesson that we learn from the indigenous people is that we have to learn to hear, to listen.[120]

Commenting on Marcos' statement, Holloway (1998, p. 164) argues that:
> Learning to listen meant incorporating new perspectives and new concepts into their theory. Learning to listen meant learning to talk as well, not just explaining things in a different way but thinking them in a different way.

Consequently, according to Holloway (ibid), "When the emphasis shifts to listening … [t]he whole relation between theory and practice is thrown into question: theory can no longer be seen as being brought from outside, but is obviously the product of everyday practice." Finally, after noting the "confrontation between the received ideas of revolution [of the EZLN] and the reality of the indigenous peoples of Chiapas," Holloway (1998, p. 165) again quotes the Subcommander, this time as reflecting that "I think that our only virtue as theorists was to have the humility to recognise that our theoretical scheme did not work, that it was very limited, that we had to adapt ourselves to the reality that was being imposed on us," before himself concluding that "the result was not that reality imposed itself on theory, as some argue, but that the confrontation with reality gave rise to a whole new and immensely rich theorisation of revolutionary practice."

In sum then, and by way of concluding this section, we have seen that while Marcos has not elaborated a coherent and detailed discussion of the exact nature of the relationship between theory and practice, he has been highly consistent in his opposition to theory being removed from reality, and all that this implies (i.e. the need for theoretical analysis to be grounded in concrete analysis). We have also witnessed how a succession of commentators have emphasized the Zapatistas' combining of theory and practice—certainly undeniable if we take "theory" in this instance to refer to the articulation of a transnational discourse that rejects the status quo and aims at changing power relations, and "praxis" to refer to the building of democratic autonomous rebel municipalities on the ground in Chiapas. Finally, we can say that even if the union of theory and practice as advocated by Althusser was not a constant reference point for Marcos, it may have provided the framework within which the Subcommander thought about theory and practice, and was, at the absolute least, an issue that he and Althusser alike wrestled with and devoted considerable time and mental energy to addressing.

If there is a single text that best reveals the persistence of an Althusserian influence on Marcos while at the same time exhibiting certain shared politico-philosophical preoccupations connecting him and Althusser (including ones that have a bearing on ideology and others that touch upon theory and praxis), it is undoubtedly the Subcommander's *Letter to Adolfo Gilly*. The letter was written in response to UNAM political science professor, Adolfo Gilly, having sent the Subcommander a copy of Carlo Ginzburg's (1979) essay "Clues: Roots of an Evidential Paradigm."[121] In this *Carta* the Subcommander critiques Ginzburg's arguments,[122] and in the process of doing so reveals certain elements of political philosophy that he has been exposed to and has engaged with through his reading of either Althusser or thinkers who influenced the French philosopher. Appendix III contains a complete English translation of Marcos' *Carta*—the only one in existence to the best of my knowledge—however, in the pages that follow I shall examine those Althusser-related political-philosophical elements contained within this epistle, quoting the relevant passages from this text.[123]

Prior to embarking on a detailed analysis, it is worth making a general point concerning Marcos' rejection of Ginzburg's evidential paradigm. Given what we have seen above of Guillén's Althusser-inspired structuralist approach to history, and the persistence of this perspective in Marcos, it is only to be expected that the Subcommander should have critiqued Ginzburg's thesis by challenging him precisely on its "idealist position," since as Peter Dews (1994, p. 105) observes: "The advent of structuralism was experienced both as a 'crisis of the subject' and as a 'crisis of history'." Marcos writes:

> The author [i.e. Ginzburg] tries to get out "of the predicament of the contraposition of rationalism and irrationalism." But where does that get anyone? I mean, the supposed fight between "rationalism" and "irrationalism" is just a variant of an idealist position: the subject, the individual, as the basis of knowledge. This dispute is just for resolving whether the subject is rational or irrational about knowledge.

Here, of course, the "idealist position" Marcos refers to is the German ideology of philosophical idealism which held that the subject (i.e. the individual) was the basis of knowledge, as opposed to structuralism which privileges structures over subject. The Subcommander's critique here was possibly formed by what he had encountered in Althusser, and specifically his *Essays in Self-Criticism*:

> [T]he revolutionary thesis of the primacy of the class struggle is a materialist one. When that is clear, the question of the "subject" of history disappears.... History is a process, and a *process without a subject.* The question about how "*man* makes history" disappears altogether.... And with it disappears the "necessity" of the concept of "transcendence" and of its subject, man.[124]

Turning away from the general and toward the specific, the *Carta*, as we saw in Chapter 2, invokes Lenin, and does so in what appears to be a sympathetic manner. We know that Rafael Guillén would have been exposed to the works of the Russian communist both while researching his graduation thesis, for which he read Lenin's *Materialism and Empirio-criticism*, and concurrently during his time in the Marxist-Leninist FLN; however, in addition to this, he would also have encountered the Russian revolutionary's theories extensively, though indirectly, through his exhaustive reading of Althusser.[125] The latter placed enormous emphasis on Lenin, and in particular his interpretation of Marxism, to the extent that Axel Honneth (1994, p. 73) states: "Althusser practically endorses only Lenin's brand of Marxism," while Althusser expert, Gregory Elliott (1990, p. xvi), observes that the French philosopher's "'Lenin and Philosophy' is a rereading of Lenin's *Materialism and Empirio-criticism...*"

One aspect of Lenin's thought that Althusser drew particular attention to was the former's thesis that in philosophy there is an ongoing struggle between materialism and idealism. In his essay entitled "Lenin and Philosophy," a work listed in Guillén's bibliography, Althusser (1971/2001c, p. 34) writes of the Russian revolutionary:

> In *Materialism and Empirio-criticism* ... he jettisons all the theoretical nuances, distinctions, ingenuities and subtleties with which philosophy tries to think its "object": they are nothing but sophistries, hair-splitting, professorial quibbles, accommodations and compromises whose only aim is to mask what is really at stake in the dispute to which all philosophy is committed: the basic struggle between the tendencies of materialism and idealism.[126]

Furthermore, Guillén would have encountered almost identical statements in other of Althusser's works. For example, in an interview entitled "Philosophy as a Revolutionary Weapon," Althusser (1968/2001a, p. 18) talks about "world outlooks of antagonistic tendencies: in the last instance idealist (bourgeois) and materialist (proletarian)," and declares that "The ultimate stake of philosophical struggle is the struggle *for hegemony* between the two great tendencies in world outlook (materialist and idealist)." And in fact, we find Guillén (1980, pp. 12 & 14) repeating a similar position twice in close succession in his thesis, writing that "The history of philosophy is the history of the struggle between idealism and materialism" (p. 12),[127] and "the history of philosophy is the historical struggle between materialism and idealism" (p. 14). Fourteen years later, in his *Carta*, the student-turned-Subcommander restated the assertion concerning "the struggle between materialism and idealism."

In addition, in the *Carta*, Marcos, as both Le Bot and Pitarch point out, also invokes historical materialism. Indeed, in a later section of the epistle the Subcommander writes:

> Now let's go to a paradigm in disuse. It will be necessary to go to the wastebasket, smooth out that crumpled old piece of paper which is called "The Science of History," historic materialism. Why did they throw it out? Because of the moral hangover after the collapse of the socialist camp? A tactical "retreat" in the face of the overwhelming force of the "marine boys" and neoliberalism? The "end of history?" Did it go out of fashion along with the desire to fight?

That Marcos should have invoked historical materialism in this *Carta* ought not to surprise us. He would, for example, have encountered strong advocacy of this key tenet of Marxism in his reading of Althusser. Indeed, Susan James (1985/2000, p. 143), notes that the French philosopher's work "initiated a renewed and intense debate about Marx's central doctrine of historical materialism;" while Gregory Elliott (1994, p. viii) argues that Althusser's "endeavour to salvage historical materialism as an explanatory science, both from its ossification under Stalinist auspices and its demotion or denigration at Western Marxist hands," led to an "Althusserian 'renovation' of historical materialism."[128] Moreover, of great pertinence to our understanding of the political-philosophical formation of Rafael, who not only chose to apply Althusser's theories to the concrete example of the Mexican education system but was also, at the same time he was reading the French Marxist's works, already enrolled in the revolutionary FLN, is Elliott's (1987/2006, p. 125) observation that: "Althusser sought to reconstruct historical materialism in such a way that it provided a basis for the investigation and illumination of the complexities of real history and concrete societies, thereby furnishing guidance to revolutionary politics." The result was that Guillén's university years (1977-1983), covering his time as an undergraduate at UNAM and subsequently as a teacher at UAM, witnessed historical materialism reaching its apogee, at least outside of France.[129] For example, British Marxist Perry Anderson (1983, pp. 86-87), in his *In the Tracks of Historical Materialism* published in 1983, a year prior to Guillén embarking on his new life as a rural guerrilla in Chiapas, wrote

> [T]here is only one contender as a general account of human development across the centuries from primitive societies to present forms of civilization. That is historical materialism. All other partial versions are derivations, or fragments, by contrast. Marxism alone has produced at once a sufficiently general and sufficiently differential set of analytic instruments to be able to integrate successive epochs of historical evolution, and their characteristic socio-economic structures, into an intelligible narrative. In this respect, indeed, it remains unchallenged not only within socialist, but also non-socialist culture as a whole. There is no competing story.[130]

Even if historical materialism had not been accepted by everyone, and it certainly had not, it was of such monumental import that even those outside of Marxism were forced to devote considerable energy to addressing it. For example, Anthony Giddens (1985/2000, p. 124) notes that Habermas claimed he was engaged in a "reconstruction of historical materialism." Moreover, Giddens himself devoted an entire book to analyzing this core element of Marxist thought, publishing his *A Contemporary Critique of Historical Materialism* in 1983. Giddens (1983/1995, pp. 1-2) opens this work with a blistering critique of this core Marxist theory;[131] however, immediately after having launched into his stinging indictment, he crucially (ibid, p. 2) adds the following proviso, thus leaving the door open to historical materialism:

> Only if historical materialism is regarded as embodying the more abstract elements of a theory of human *Praxis*, snippets of which can be gleaned from the diversity of Marx's writings, does it remain an indispensable contribution to social theory today.

In any event, Giddens' onslaught against historical materialism certainly did not prove fatal, at least not immediately. For instance, Alex Callinicos, to name but one accomplished scholar, posed the following question and answer in his 1987 book *Making History*: "What then remains of historical materialism? The answer is: a great deal."[132] Also writing that same year, Gregory Elliott (1987/2006, p. xxii) would similarly argue that: "historical materialism will only be superseded as a research programme when it has been improved upon; and it has not been thus improved upon." In fact, as late as 1992, i.e. just two years before Marcos penned his *Carta* to Gilly, Perry Anderson (1992, p. xiv) would predict "The come-back of historical materialism." Furthermore, even today, with historical materialism having undergone severe critique (most notably at the hands of Giddens) and considerable reform (most notably at the hands of G. A. Cohen, Perry Anderson, and Alex Callinicos[133]), and with the emergence of compelling alternatives (most notably that of Michael Mann[134]), historical materialism cannot be considered an entirely spent force, as is evidenced by the persistence of the *Journal of Historical Materialism* (1997 to the present); the holding of the Annual Historical Materialism Conference; the academic publisher Brill's decision in 2004 to create a Historical Materialism Book Series comprising reprints and revised versions of, to-date, more than twenty of the classic texts on this subject; and the continued publication of books (outside the Brill series) bearing historical materialism in their title or subtitle.[135] Little wonder then that "In a text of October 1994 Marcos still proclaims the merits of historic materialism..."[136]

Interestingly, also in his *Carta*, Marcos recollects:

> I remember having read the book by T. S. Kuhn about the structure of scientific revolutions, I think it was in an edition of the Economic Culture Fund (breviaries?). At that time there was a discussion about whether there were differences or similarities between the natural and the social sciences, the epistemological "slant," the "paradigms" and their "rupture" and the etceteras which, as always, have nothing to do with reality.[137]

That Marcos should have read Kuhn is perhaps unsurprising.[138] Barry Barnes (1985/2000, p. 85), writing in 1985, notes that Kuhn's "*The Structure of Scientific Revolutions*, published in 1962, has become a classic, a routine point of reference for discussion and debate throughout our culture generally." Even more significantly, according to the Arts & Humanities Citation Index, *The Structure of Scientific Revolutions* was the most cited work during the period 1976-1983;[139] namely, the years covering Rafael's final year at High School, through his undergraduate days at the UNAM, to his last full year of teaching at the UAM, or what we may call his formative years of formal education. There were, however, other, more specific reasons why Guillén would have deemed Kuhn's work of particular interest: namely Rafael's absorption in Althusserianism. Kuhn (1922-1996) and Althusser (1918-1990) were almost exact contemporaries who represent the foremost advocates of applying a structuralist approach—i.e. the privileging of structure over agents—to their respective fields of discipline, science and philosophy. Moreover, Althusser was himself reading Kuhn in the 1970s, and certain of the French philosopher's circle, notably Dominique Lecourt and Étienne Balibar, acknowledge a certain affinity or resemblance between Althusser's conception of the history of science and Kuhn's.[140] Finally, Kuhn's theories also shared some similarities with Michel Foucault, another thinker who influenced Rafael at this time.[141] Indeed, Quentin Skinner (1985/2000a, p. 10) observes:

> Kuhn adds that, if we wish to explain the acceptance or rejection of particular scientific hypotheses, what we need to invoke are the established customs of science as a profession, not merely the purportedly rational methods of disinterested scientists. In a fascinating parallel with Foucault's thought, the practice of science is thus depicted as a means of controlling what is permitted to count as knowledge.[142]

However, a problem arises as to ascertaining precisely when it was that Guillén/Marcos read Kuhn. In his *Carta*, Marcos refers to "an edition of the Economic Culture Fund" (una edición del Fondo de Cultura Económica) of Kuhn's *The Structure of Scientific Revolutions* (*La estructura de las revoluciones científicas*), the first edition of which was published in 1971. This was a work therefore that Guillén could easily have consulted for his thesis, and yet it nowhere appears in the main text, footnotes, nor even in the bibliography. (Indeed, the sole reference to Kuhn throughout Rafael's thesis appears in the bibliography, with the listing of Michel Pêcheux's *Bachelard-Kuhn-Popper*, and, interestingly, in this bibliographic entry Guillén (1980, p. 120) misspells Kuhn (as "Khun"), which may indicate his lack of familiarity with the U.S. philosopher of science at that time, although equally it may merely represent a typographical error.[143]) Thus we may suppose that October 1980 represents the *terminus post quem* regarding Rafael's consultation of Kuhn's *The Structure of Scientific Revolutions*, although he experienced a degree of indirect exposure to Kuhn's writings through Pêcheux's aforementioned work.

If our supposition is correct, it is to be regretted that Rafael had not read *The Structure of Scientific Revolutions* prior to writing his thesis, since Kuhn's work was of direct relevance to certain parts of it. For example, significantly Guillén and Kuhn were both concerned with the role played by textbooks in education, and in particular the way such works were susceptible to ideological influences which could distort the history of the subject treated in them, disguising the efficacy or even the very existence of revolutions, be they political (as in Rafael's case) or scientific (as in Kuhn's). For instance, Kuhn (1962/1996, pp. 136-137), when discussing textbooks as an authoritative source of information of the history of scientific revolutions, wrote that:

> I suggest that there are excellent reasons why revolutions have proved to be so nearly invisible. Both scientists and laymen take much of their image of creative scientific activity from an authoritative source that systematically disguises—partly for important functional reasons—the existence and significance of scientific revolutions. Only when the nature of that authority is recognized and analyzed can one hope to make historical example fully effective .... In short, they [textbooks] have to be rewritten in the aftermath of each scientific revolution, and, once rewritten, they inevitably disguise not only the role but the very existence of the revolutions that produced them.

This disguising of the crucial role played by revolutions, be they scientific or political, in favor of the promotion of a sanitized picture of progress that emphasizes the institutional, is something that Guillén made much of in his discussion of the role of Primary School Social Science textbooks in Mexico. In particular, in a section entitled "Institution and Change" Guillén quotes from the textbooks, arguing that they serve to justify the existence of the State and promote a pacifistic discourse aimed at heading off any would-be threat to it posed by forces that are other than peaceful and institutional. He argues (pp. 100-101) that by "demonstrating" that war is detrimental and never solves anything, by encouraging pupils to think that the only way to effect change is by participating peacefully in institutions that have been created by the government for the purpose of allowing man to live in peace with his fellow man, and by arguing that history has "shown" such participation provides good results, this ultimately eliminates the possibility of revolutionary armed struggle.[144] The result, as Guillén notes, is that:

> With the possibility of armed struggle eliminated in the individual and in the basic cultural code,[145] the only path possible is the peaceful one, the institutional…
>
> …[A]ll the discourses by the branches of the governmental machinery do nothing but sing the praises of the institutional regime which allows the continuation of the "Mexican Revolution" through peaceful means. The very name of the official party, "Institutional Revolutionary," demonstrates the importance of this discursive object ("institutionalism") in order to shape practices which prevent a revolutionary change.

Having recalled reading Kuhn's *The Structure of Scientific Revolutions*, the Subcommander proceeds:

> At that time there was a discussion about whether there were differences or similarities between the natural and the social sciences, the epistemological "slant," the "paradigms" and their "rupture" …. Now I read that this Carlo Ginzburg person trawls for signs in psychoanalysis, detective literature and the aesthetics of the late 19th century, the coincidences of a new paradigm: the evidential.

Marcos then assails Ginzburg's methodology, ultimately dismissing the "said paradigm" as "a tautology." However, while doing so Marcos launches into a critique that betrays the influence of Althusser and Kuhn. He writes:

> Fine, Ginzburg is difficult to follow. I imagine that now the intellectual fashion is this everythingology (*todología*), mixing all kinds of social "sciences" in order to make reality explicable in an incomplete theoretical framework which, in order to be complete, resorts to other theoretical frameworks, even contradictory ones. That constant leap of knowledge from "common sense" to scientific knowledge to aesthetic products is a way in which the dominant ideology dominates in the sciences. Given that "common sense" jumps to scientific knowledge, it's worth asking oneself: what is the frame of reference for "common sense?" Isn't it the dominant ideology?[146] The author manages to be sublime: the law and medicine are referred to as two "sciences." With such forceful arguments he "forgets" the central problem: how are the indicators "read?" From what class position? If you make the leap from hunters' anecdotes to the science of history, what are the "historical readings" of the collected signs? Don't you have to question the method of collecting the signs? Isn't there a class position in choosing some signs and

not others? Isn't there a relationship with a political position on "reading" those signs? Isn't, ultimately, that criteria for selecting the signs, and for reading them, a criterion of class?

This section of his *Carta* is rich with Althusserian and Kuhnian undertones. First, the Subcommander's railing against "everythingology" mirrors Althusser's (1967/1990, p. 97) dismissal of interdisciplinarity as a "myth," and his disparagement of the tendency whereby "Sociology, economics, psychology, linguistics and literary history constantly borrow notions, methods and procedures from existing disciplines, whether literary of scientific." Indeed, Althusser (1967/1990a, pp. 97 & 98) maintains that

> interdisciplinarity therefore remains a magical practice, in the service of an ideology, in which scientists (or would-be scientists) formulate an imaginary idea of the division of scientific labour, of the relations between sciences and the conditions of "discovery," to give the impression of grasping an object that escapes them. Very concretely, interdisciplinarity is usually the slogan and the practice of the spontaneous ideology of specialists: oscillating between a vague spiritualism and technocratic positivism … interdisciplinarity … is massively *ideological* in character.

Secondly, Marcos' assertion that "the dominant ideology dominates in the sciences" fits very well with Althusser's observations on science being anything but free from ideology.[147] Indeed, according to Althusser not only is science influenced by the dominant ideology, but in turn it also functions as ideology. For example, in his First Lecture in his "Philosophy and the Spontaneous Philosophy of the Scientists"[148], Althusser (1967/1990a, pp. 98-99) wrote:

> Finally, it is necessary to pose the question of questions: are the human sciences, with certain limited exceptions, what they think they are—that is, sciences? Or are they in their majority something else, namely *ideological techniques of social adaptation and readaptation*? If this is in fact what they are, they have not, as they claim, broken with their former ideological and political "cultural" function: they act through other, more "sophisticated," perfected techniques, but still in the service of the same cause …. Question: what makes up the *apparatus* that permits disciplines to function as ideological techniques? This is the question that philosophy poses… (emphasis in the original)

Althusser continues, writing of

> The existence, reality, consistency and function of what we have called theoretical or scientific *ideology*—or, better still, the spontaneous *ideology* of the practice of scientists or supposed scientists. And behind these forms of ideology, other forms—practical ideologies and the dominant ideology. (emphasis in the original)

Similarly, in his Second Lecture in the same series Althusser (1967/1990a, pp. 115-116) asserted

> that every scientist is affected by an ideology or a scientific philosophy which we propose to call by the conventional name: *the spontaneous philosophy of the scientists* (abbreviated as SPS). We say that all scientists are, unbeknownst to them, permanently affected by it ... for they see science in its normal state as a pure science, free from any SPS. (emphasis in the original)

Finally, the remainder of the Subcommander's statement is taken up with how signs are collected and how they are "read," concerns which echo the preoccupations of, respectively, Kuhn and Althusser. Marcos clearly shares Kuhn's caution regarding the criteria by which signs are selected. As Quentin Skinner (1985/2000a, p. 10) has observed, "Kuhn's most basic contention is that ... our access to the facts in the light of which we test our beliefs is always filtered by what Kuhn has called our existing 'paradigms' or frameworks of understanding ... there *are* no facts independent of our theories about them..." Indeed, Kuhn (1962/1996, pp. 16-17) himself stated that:

> No natural history can be interpreted in the absence of at least some implicit body of intertwined theoretical and methodological belief that permits selection, evaluation and criticism. If that body of belief is not already implicit in the collection of facts—in which case more than "mere facts" are at hand—it must be externally supplied, perhaps by a current metaphysic, by another science, or by personal and historical accident.

Little wonder then that Marcos questions Ginzburg's methodology involving the recognition and collection of signs. Indeed, if scientists choose paradigms based on their professional training and socialization, how sure can we be of the validity of how the historian (in this case Ginzburg) may choose his "clues"? What especially perturbs the Subcommander about Ginzburg's methodology is that, as Marcos sees it, this analysis or "search" needs a frame of reference. Something with which to compare or contrast the gathered signs. And if there isn't anything in that frame of reference against which to contrast the sign? . ... In sum, said paradigm is a tautology. Its assumption is taken as truth (the frame of reference with which the "signs" are contrasted), and, ergo, the conclusion is true (the "collection of signs" method).

Turning to the "reading" of signs, Marcos' heavy emphasis on this, down to his placing of this verb in inverted commas, is one that he inherited from Louis Althusser.[149] In his *Reading Capital*, one recalls, Althusser identifies various forms of reading: "symptomatic," "expressive," "critical," "epistemological," "scientific," "philosophical," and so on. Indeed, Margaret Majumdar (1995, pp. 52-53) points out that

> Althusser's understanding of the practice of reading is critical to any appreciation of what he was trying to do in his theoretical interventions, especially given the role which readings of other authors' texts play in his work …. He starts from the premise that there is no "innocent" reading of a text; one always reads a text from a particular point of view, addressing particular questions to it.

Crucially here given the Subcommander's insistence on the class and political position from which signs are "read," Majumdar (1995, p. 87) notes how: "Althusser proposes ... a "reading" of *Capital* in which Marxist philosophy is seen as a guide to "reading" a text, albeit from a political, proletarian class point of view…"

Finally with regard to Marcos' *Carta*, the Subcommander here again touches upon the matter of the relationship between theory and practice, and also that between theoreticians and practitioners. On a general level, in his response, Marcos deliberately chooses not to acknowledge, and even less acquiesce in, Gilly's attempts to postulate convergences between the lives and works of "theoreticians" and those of revolutionaries. Rather, he elects to emphasize the different conditions in which they live and labor by drawing attention to "a new incursion by a patrol of federal police" and the passing overhead of an observation airplane, which were intruding upon and thus interrupting his theoretical exchange with Gilly. Thus Marcos emphasizes what he perceives to be the stark dichotomy between "guerreros," who fight the revolution, and "theoreticians," who write about it. Turning to specifics,

Marcos makes the point that "for some time now, the role of the dominant social theories has been to "justify" (that is, "make just") the dominant system ... the brutal process of appropriation of wealth, conscience and history that was begun again with the end of the century..." before going on to state that under neoliberalism, which he sarcastically dubs "the 'highly original' theory of the new dividing up of the world," it is the case that "if reality does not correspond to what the theory says and orders, then a new 'reality' must be invented, the reality of the media." Finally, he turns to discussing "historical materialism," asking why so many of those formerly of the left seem to have abandoned it:

> Why did they throw it out? Because of the moral hangover after the collapse of the socialist camp? A tactical "retreat" in the face of the overwhelming force of the "marine boys" and neoliberalism? The "end of history?" Did it go out of fashion along with the desire to fight? Why, today, is a revolution quickly consigned to the place of utopias? What happened to them, Güilly[sic]? Did they get tired? Did they get bored? Did they sell out? Did they surrender? Wasn't it worth it? Isn't it worth it? *Or did that theory take them down the blind alley (for the theoreticians) of having to be consistent in practice?* What happened to them, Gilly? I see that now cynicism is the flag of the left. (my emphasis)

In short then, the *Carta* exhibits, and therefore Marcos clearly retained, an essentially "Althusserian spirit."

Prior to concluding this section on Althusser let us turn toward more superficial points of convergence between Althusser and Marcos. The first concerns shared terminology. In a communiqué dated January 6, 1994, and signed by the Subcommander, Marcos employs the phrase "the repressive State apparatuses" ("los aparatos represivos del Estado"), which closely echoes the term "the repressive state apparatus" ("el aparato represivo de Estado") coined by Althusser.[150] Similarly, in his essay entitled "The Seven Loose Pieces of the Global Jigsaw Puzzle" (June 1997), the Subcommander writes of "the repressive apparatus of the modern states" ("los aparatos represivos de los Estados Modernos").[151] The Second point consists of a reminiscence made by Marcos in a filmed interview that he gave for a documentary, and is related to education. The Subcommander, recalling his university days, mirrors Althusser's views on the education system functioning as an Ideological State Apparatus, noting how: "we did not study and were not shaped to know and to work as we wanted to, but in what society and the Power demanded that we become.... University was a large corral for the domestication of youth."[152]

Finally, by way of concluding this section, I would like to cite three leading experts on Althusser—the first commenting on his legacy, the remaining two quoting the French Marxist philosopher's words pertaining to the final years of his life—and to illustrate how their comments relate to the Subcommander. The first of these is Gregory Elliott (1987/2006, p. 316), who writes:

> The history of Althusserianism ... continues—to the undoubted benefit of Marxist and socialist culture. It has ended only to the extent that much of what is best in it ... has been assimilated into the culture, becoming part of the theoretical consciousness—or, often, unconscious—of left-wing intellectuals.

Subcommander Marcos, I would argue, represents precisely one such left-wing intellectual, and a very prominent and potent one at that.

The second scholar is Warren Montag (2003, p. 125), who quotes what he calls Althusser's "final word on Marxism" as it appears in his autobiography written during the mid-1980s:

> [A]t a time when Marxism is declared dead and buried ... on the grounds of an unbelievable theoretical eclecticism and poverty, on the pretext of a so-called postmodernity, or, yet again, on the notion that matter has disappeared, having given way to the immaterialities of communication ... I remain profoundly attached not, of course, to the letter—to which I have never adhered—but to the materialist inspiration of Marx. I am an optimist: I believe that this inspiration will cross every desert and even if it takes new forms—which is inevitable in a world so rapidly changing—it will live again.

Althusser's optimism proved prescient here, since at the same time he was penning the above, far away in Mexico, Subcommander Marcos, who, as we have seen, was also "profoundly attached ... to the materialist inspiration of Marx," was busy taking this inspiration and fashioning it into a new form: Zapatismo.

Lastly, there is Fernanda Navarro (1998, pp. 155-156), who interviewed Althusser in the winter of 1983/4 and maintained correspondence with him for several years thereafter.[153] While visiting Althusser to conduct the interview she had access to a number of the philosopher's unpublished manuscripts, and in these, she tells us:

> [T]here are some that refer to the modern spaces, or what he called interstices, that have emerged all over the world, bringing some hope with their different way of functioning and organizing, with no intention of instituting new pyramids with dominating structures. He referred to the social and popular movements and the struggles of marginalized people that are taking place all over the planet with a growing vitality and success, such as the pacifist, ecological, feminist, gay, student, and immigrant movements as well as the liberation theology movement in Latin America .... These movements, without knowing it, he added, followed the line of Rosa Luxemburg and not that of Lenin. Althusser was convinced of their priority, as opposed to those with rigid, vertical structures that make the practice of democracy difficult, if not impossible.

Navarro (1998, p. 156) adds:

> Althusser believed that these organized minorities coexist already at a microscale and are working on an alternative platform seeking a different kind of politics that may allow a different kind of human practice and human relations, one sharing a common goal: to build a more just society, free from ideological manipulation, misery, and oppression. Althusser believed that the key to their success is "organization" with a democratic conception and starting from within, in a self-governing manner .... He concluded that they should be not centralized but local, not international but regional. Their unity should be given by objective intersecting lines, by communitarian forms with transversal relations.

The Zapatistas would come to epitomize precisely the sort of movement that is outlined in the first quotation, while their autonomous civil councils and Juntas de Buen Gobierno, employing non-hierarchical communitarian democratic practices, conform broadly to the description of organizing that is advocated in the second quotation.

Finally, Navarro (p. 156) also notes that Althusser "conceive[d] of a Center for International Liberation whose main task would be that of providing information, not direction ... an open Centre where active revolutionary groups and alternative movements might meet and exchange experiences and strategies for transforming society." He also came up with the idea, she observes, of forming an "International Liberation Movement" comprising "former Communists, Trotskyists, anarchists, ultra-leftists, members of alternative groups, veterans of the Résistance, believers, young people and old..."[154] Allowing for certain minor modifications, we can see that Marcos harbored similar notions. For example, he built "Aguascalientes," a convention center comprising an amphitheater large enough to seat 8000, twenty buildings to house visitors and to act as canteens, fourteen roasting pits, latrines, tanks of drinking water, and parking for 100 vehicles,[155] and where, from August 6-9, 1994, he convoked the National Democratic Convention, convening attendees from Mexican civil society. So too, the Subcommander proposed something not entirely different from Althusser's International Liberation Movement: namely, the formation initially of a National Liberation Movement, and subsequently an "International of Hope" which involved convening gatherings, the most notable of which being the summer 1996 *Intercontinental Encuentro for Humanity and against Neoliberalism* which proved to be a space where, as Marcos put it, "Some of the best rebels from the five continents arrived ... brought their ideas, their hearts, their worlds ... [and] ... came ... to find themselves among other ideas, other reasons, other worlds...,"[156] and which was attended by

> representatives from fifty-five nations ... ideologues from the European left parties—the Italian "Communist Refoundation," the Spanish trade unionist, Basque independence fighters, Greens, German anarchist posses—intermeshed with the Brazilian Party of Labor, retired guerrilla leaders like Douglas Bravo (Venezuela) and Hugo Blanco (Peru), the *Sem Terras* (sometimes called Brazil's Zapatistas), [and] even a very formal Cuban delegation.[157]

B) Nicos Poulantzas

Although Poulantzas was born in Athens to Greek parents, he undertook his PhD in France and subsequently lived and taught there for the remainder of his life; he was chiefly influenced by French thinkers, especially Sartre in the early days, later becoming a core member of the "Althusser" group, which consisted of Balibar, Macherey, Rancière, and Debray, while also engaging closely with Foucault's thinking, especially on power; and he also wrote all his major works in French. He was then, very much part of the French structural Marxist milieu.

That Guillén should have been influenced also by Poulantzas, whom Bob Jessop (1991, p. 75) has described as "the single most important Marxist political theorist of the postwar period,"[158] is hardly surprising. Indeed, as Richard L. Harris (1979, p. 66), publishing a year prior to Rafael's completion and submission of his thesis, noted: "…Poulantzas' theoretical works have exercised a considerable degree of influence on Marxist analyses of the contemporary political scene … in Latin America." Such an influence is clearly reflected in certain parts of Guillén's thesis. Richard L. Harris (1979, p. 66) also writes that:

> His [Poulantzas'] concepts of *power bloc, hegemonic class* or *hegemonic class fraction, social categories* and *social forces* have been widely employed in analysis of the class composition of the State and the power structure of the contemporary Latin American societies.

He adds, "Poulantzas' concepts of *power bloc, class fraction*, and *hegemonic class* or *hegemonic class fraction* have perhaps been employed with greatest frequency…" And it is precisely these concepts, and certainly this terminology, we can witness in the section of Rafael's thesis that is undoubtedly most heavily indebted to Poulantzas: namely, the first section of "Part II: General Concepts of the Theory of Ideology: Concerning General Concepts of the Theory of Ideologies" (pp. 31-39), and more specifically the last five pages of that section (i.e. pp. 35-39). Throughout these pages Rafael employs the quintessentially Poulantzian terminology we have seen above, including phrases such as "power bloc," "social forces," and class "fractions."[159]

Moreover, on inspecting this section more closely we see that Rafael (p. 36, fn. 1) directs his reader to Poulantzas' *Poder político y clases sociales en el estado capitalista* (*Political Power and Social Classes*). And, although he does not stipulate which sections of Poulantzas' almost 500-page work the reader should consult, the context in which this footnote appears perhaps permits us to identify the pages in Poulantzas that he had in mind: given that the footnote appears in a subsection in which Rafael writes of alliances, the power bloc and supporting classes, and that it is attached to the end of a sentence that reads: "The power bloc must consider the interests of the supporting classes and grant them political and economic privileges," Rafael most probably intends his reader to go to Section III.4.iii entitled "Bloque en el poder.

Alianzas. Clases-apoyos" ("Power bloc, alliances, supporting classes") in Poulantzas' aforementioned work.¹⁶⁰

Rafael's text is at its most Poulantzian however, where he discusses the relationship between economic crises and political crises, and specifically how the latter are related to ideological crises and ultimately the crisis of the State. In a two-page portion of text, from midway down page 35 to the midpoint of page 37, Rafael begins by echoing Poulantzas' statements that "The generic elements of crises are always [contained] within the process of the extended reproduction of capital"; that "crises are a concentration of contradictions in capitalism"; and that "Political crisis should not be considered as a mere 'dysfunction' of the State and its apparatus…" He subsequently proceeds (pp. 37-39) to identify a series of nine "elements" related to the State, including (1) the relationship between political crises and the crisis of the State, (2) the State's "relative separation" from the economy, (3) its promotion of a juridical-political ideology, (4 & 7) its organization of the ruling class and representation of the bourgeoisie's interests, (5) its appearance as "regulator" of the economy despite both taking over certain economic sectors (e.g. those to do with public services, such as social security, housing, education, transportation, etc) and participating in the extraction of surplus value, (6) its intervening to raise the rate of profit and surplus value, and (8 & 9) state apparatuses.

These, of course, are all subjects to which Poulantzas devoted considerable attention in his works, and in particular those Rafael lists in his bibliography: *Political Power and Social Classes* and *State, Power, Socialism*. However, it is the first of these nine elements, on crises, that proves most Poulantzian. In this element, which is divided into subsections (1, 1.1, 1.2, 1.3, 1.4, and 1.5), Rafael starts by discussing the relationship between economic crises and political crisis, before moving on to deal with that between political crises and the crisis of the State, finally ending with that between political crises and ideological crises. Here, not only the subject matter and content of this first element, but also the terminology employed, reveal it to be heavily indebted to Poulantzas' article "The Political Crisis and the Crisis of the State" (1976/2008).¹⁶¹ Indeed, examples of shared terminology include: "bloque en el poder," "alianzas," "nuevas fuerzas sociales," "las formas de organización-representación," "coyuntura," "posición de clase," "relación de dominación–subordinación," "clases-apoyo," "las relaciones de fuerza," and "las relaciones ideológicas."¹⁶² It is perplexing to note that this particular work by Poulantzas, in contrast to his *Political Power and Social Classes* and *State, Power, Socialism*, is not cited anywhere in Guillén's thesis, nor is it listed in his bibliography. That being said, however, we will witness below (p. 202, n. 10) an instance whereby Rafael consulted a work—i.e. Foucault's *Microfísica del poder*, which he even quotes from—that is absent in his bibliography: the same thing may well have taken place here concerning Poulantzas' essay "The Political Crisis and the Crisis of the State." Moreover, we can be certain that Guillén would have encountered a reference to Poulantzas' *La Crisis del Estado*, which contained his essay "Las transformaciones actuales del Estado, la crisis política y la crisis del Estado," in the pages of *State, Power, Socialism*.¹⁶³

In addition to this section of his thesis, there is at least one other in which we can detect Poulantzas' influence on Rafael. In a subsequent subsection on "The Mexican State and Official Education," Guillén (p. 87), after writing that it is the bourgeoisie that the Mexican State serves, qualifies this statement using Poulantzian terminology, adding in parentheses, "although it would have to be established which factions of this class are in the power block, how they achieve their alliances and support, etc."¹⁶⁴

Finally, we have a copy of a paper Guillén published in 1980 entitled "Elements for an Analysis of Political Discourse: Legality and Class Project,"¹⁶⁵ in which he (p. 4, n.1) reproduces the following quotation from Poulantzas' *Poder político y clase sociales en el estado capitalista* (*Political Power and Social Classes*), which states that a characteristic of the dominant bourgeois ideology is that: "*Toda huella de dominio de clase está sistemáticamente ausente en su lenguaje propio*" ("*all trace of class domination is systematically absent from its language*").¹⁶⁶

From reading Rafael's thesis, and especially from what we have observed above, it is evident that what Rafael took from Poulantzas was: a deep theoretical understanding of capitalist modes of production and the class contradictions inherent in capitalism; a profound knowledge concerning the role of the state, its intervention in and relation to the economy, and its ideology and ideological apparatuses; a firm grasp of crises, political, economic, and ideological, and how these relate to the crisis of the state as well as to one another; the concept of class fractions, how the power bloc itself was made up of these, and how these formed alliances and garnered support; the realization that the dominant bourgeois ideology masks its inherently class-based exploitative nature even, or perhaps especially, in its discourse; as well as a not inconsiderable dose of Poulantzian terminology.

What is interesting to note here, however, is that, as we shall now see, it is not crises (economic, political, ideological, or of the State), nor which class factions form the power bloc of the Mexican bourgeoisie (and how they achieve their alliances and support), nor even dominant bourgeois ideology's attempt to conceal class exploitation (and the absence of "*all trace of class domination ... from its language*"), but rather other Poulantzian preoccupations that emerge in the discourse of Subcommander Marcos.

A cursory inspection of Marcos' writings reveals, in places, certain stylistic tendencies and terminological traits indicative of a Poulantzian influence. We have already witnessed (above, p. 97) Carlos Monsiváis' observation that the Subcommander's discourse, initially at least, contained "many paeans to ... Althusser and Poulantzas." For my part, I would note that an isolated remnant of quintessentially Poulantzian terminology can be seen in the *Second Declaration of the Lacandon Jungle* (June 12, 1995). In this document, which calls for "a transition to democracy" and proposes the holding of a "National Democratic Convention" to "demand free and democratic elections ... [and] the right to decide, freely and democratically, what form the government will take," we encounter the following statement:

> We aren't proposing a new world, but something preceding a new world: an antechamber looking into the new Mexico. In this sense, this revolution will not end in a new class, *fraction of a class (fracción de clase)*, or group in power. It will end in a free and democratic space for political struggle. (my emphasis)

If we turn away from matters of style and terminology, and instead search for evidence of Marcos being indebted conceptually to the Greco-Franco Marxist, then, unlike in the cases of Althusser and Foucault, where we can perceive at least a degree of continuity between the Althusserian and Foucauldian influences on display in Rafael Guillén's thesis and those exhibited in the subsequent discourse of the Subcommander, the same cannot be said regarding Poulantzas. Instead, what we find in Poulantzas' case is not so much a persistence in the Subcommander's discourse of those Poulantzian preoccupations that we unearthed in Rafael's thesis (i.e. a concern with crises and class fractions) but rather the emergence of two latent legacies of Poulantzas: namely, the emphasis placed on democracy, one so strong that it took precedence over the pursuit of revolution which had hitherto been deemed by the Marxist-Leninist Left to be the preeminent path to be taken toward socialism[167]; and the importance attributed to social movements, again marking a significant break with the attitude prevailing among the orthodox hard-line Left.

Let us begin by looking at the first of these latent legacies that emerges in Marcos' discourse: an emphasis on democracy, and his insistence on what form this should take. As already noted, Poulantzas' writings were widely disseminated in Latin America, where they exerted not inconsiderable influence.[168] In fact, his works coincided with, and, at the theoretical level, contributed to, a continental shift in emphasis among the Latin American left in favour of privileging democracy as the defining issue (replacing that of revolution) of the time.[169] (Simultaneously, at the practical level, certain political experiences and circumstances, such as living in the shadow of the Cuban and Sandinista revolutions on the one hand and authoritarian rule and military regimes on the other, similarly contributed to this trend.) That Mexico was no exception to this continental paradigm shift can clearly be observed. For instance, UNAM professor and one of Mexico's most prolific left-wing intellectuals, Roger Bartra, published an essay in 1982 in which he described the present "difficult search for a new living space for the Left ... a space whose organizing axis is the struggle for democracy..."[170] (Interestingly, in the same piece Bartra declared that "the one thing that is truly revolutionary about socialism ... [is] its fusion with democracy."[171]) Nor was this new privileging of democracy limited to Mexico's political theorists: in the world of practical politics, for example, Barry Carr (1985, p. 219) notes how delegates at the Mexican Communist Party's 19th Congress (March 1981) "voted by a narrow margin to abandon the term 'dictatorship of the proletariat' and to replace it with 'democratic workers' power' (*poder obrero democrático*)."

Crucially concerning the focus of this study, this new-found, invigorated emphasis on democracy took place precisely in the period spanning Rafael Guillén's formative years. Indeed, if Norbert Lechner (1985, p. 64) is correct in his pinpointing of the dominant paradigm shift as taking place "around 1980, and especially from the worsening economic crisis in 1982…," this period covered precisely those years spanning Guillén's writing and completion of his thesis, his graduation from the UNAM and his teaching at the UAM, and his immersion in the clandestine world of the FLN guerrilla. It is surely highly probable then that the youthful Rafael Guillén, who at the UNAM was an avid reader of classical and contemporary left-wing political philosophy and himself the author of a quintessentially leftist thesis, would have found himself exposed to, and influenced by, this intellectual current. Furthermore, in addition to general exposure to the trend of privileging democracy, Guillén would also have encountered a strong emphasis on democracy specifically through his reading of Poulantzas.

A note of caution needs to be introduced here however in order to avoid painting an overly simplistic picture, both of the Latin American left's transition from promoting revolution to advocating democracy, and of Rafael Guillén's personal trajectory. First, this transition, as with any other major paradigm shift, was a process, not an event, and one which lasted several years and was not accepted by all. Indeed, in an article published in 1980, Mexican sociologist and former rector of the UNAM, Pablo González Casanova (1980, p. 66), depicts a complex and antagonistic situation:

> One of the most significant debates is that which distinguishes two large sectors engaged in the struggle for socialism in Latin America: one large sector holds that it is necessary to carry out the struggle for democracy in order to move towards the struggle for socialism, while the other holds that it is necessary to put forth the struggle for socialism directly, to march directly toward the socialist revolution. In this bitter debate, the groups that support taking the direct road go so far as to say that the position of the other group is basically bourgeois.... The other forces answer that it is necessary to carry out the struggle for democracy on its own as part of a long and complex battle for the new society, for socialism. To elucidate this problem is one of the most necessary tasks of political thought and of the social sciences in Latin America.

Significantly, Casanova had begun the article by stating that: "Today in Latin America we are witnessing a new movement of struggle for democracy ... the struggle for democracy is in the last instance a struggle for socialism...," and concluded it by referring to what he saw as the "long and complex historical process that leads in the final instance to socialism and to democracy in socialism."[172]

Turning to Guillén's personal and political development, one needs to keep in mind that in 1979 he joined a revolutionary armed guerrilla, the FLN, which declared in its *Reglamento insurgente* ("Insurgent Rules") drafted in 1985, that its fledgling organization, which Rafael would later become Subcommander of, the EZLN, "was created in order to conquer, by means of armed struggle, national liberation and our second independence, and not to suspend the struggle until we have installed in our country a political, economic and social regime of the Socialist type."[173] Thus Guillén, at least at this stage in his life, clearly belonged to the former "sector" as identified by Casanova, one which comprised those who opted "to put forth the struggle for socialism directly, to march directly toward the socialist revolution." What I am suggesting here then is that over the subsequent decade-and-a-half, Guillén, like many fellow left-wing Latin Americans, underwent a transformation, eventually becoming a member of that sector which "holds that it is necessary to carry out the struggle for democracy in order to move towards the struggle for socialism." In Guillén's case, this transformation perhaps resulted from a combination of experiences, direct and indirect. For example, his confidence in the viability, and perhaps even desirability, of a socialist revolution was no doubt shaken by El Salvador's FMLN, Colombia's M-19, and Ecuador's "Alfaro Lives, Dammit!" guerrillas all entering into peace negotiations with their governments (in 1989, 1990, and 1991, respectively), and by the democratic ousting from power of the Sandinista National Liberation Front in Nicaragua's 1990 general election—a huge blow for Marcos, who had been an ardent admirer of Nicaragua's Socialist revolution as a young man. Moreover, Colombia's M-19 (April 19) movement's subsequent gains in the 1991 general election, after it had converted into a political party, may have led him to question his faith in the pre-eminence of revolution over democracy as the preferred path to Socialism. His own failed attempt at instigating insurrection in January 1994 when the Mexican people did not heed his call to take up arms and march on the capital to oust the dubiously elected government of Salinas di Gortari no doubt also played a part in this transformation. Finally, the Subcommander's decision to turn away from the revolutionary road to socialism and toward a democratic one may have been facilitated by his witnessing, first-hand and over many years, consensus-built, communitarian democracy as exercised by Chiapas' indigenous communities, with their emphasis on communal assemblies and *mandar obedeciendo* ("to command obeying"), which resonated with his reading years earlier of Poulantzas, who emphasised the role "direct, rank-and-file democracy" and "self-management networks" can play in the democratic transition to democratic socialism.[174]

Let us briefly inspect then the emphasis on, and conceptualization of, democracy that Rafael Guillén would have encountered in his reading of Poulantzas' works, before turning to examine whether traces of this persisted in the political philosophy of Subcommander Marcos.

According to Ted Benton (1984, p. 160), "Both Althusser and Poulantzas ... are quite explicit that a democratic road to socialism is possible (indeed, as Poulantzas points out, 'socialism will either be democratic or it will not be at all')..." He continues (1984, p. 161) however, "Poulantzas is more explicit than Althusser in arguing that this combination of diverse sites and forms of struggle will involve, in particular, a combination of both direct and representative democratic forms, both as a means of struggle, and as actually constitutive of socialist democracy." Indeed, a major significance of Poulantzas lies in his break from the Leninist stance which dismissed representative democracy by means of the following equation: "representative democracy = bourgeois democracy = dictatorship of the bourgeoisie."[175] Instead, as Poulantzas makes clear in his "Towards a Democratic Socialism,"[176] the institutions of representative democracy "were ... a conquest of the popular masses"[177] and what is required "is a real permanence and continuity of the institutions of representative democracy—not as unfortunate relics to be tolerated for as long as necessary, but as an essential condition of democratic socialism."[178] At the same time however, Poulantzas asserts that "the democratic road to socialism is ... not simply a parliamentary or electoral road,"[179] and in his eyes therefore representative democracy is a necessary but far from sufficient precondition for achieving a democratic socialism.[180]

Linked to the above is another important Poulantzian prescription, one which concerns the "popular struggle" or the "struggle of the popular masses ... to modify the relationship of forces within the State."[181] Poulantzas is adamant that such a "struggle must always express itself in the development of popular movements, the mushrooming of democratic organs at the base, and the rise of centres of self-management...," adding "The question of *who* is in power *to do what* cannot be isolated from these struggles for self-management or direct democracy..."[182]

The Zapatistas, of course, have been widely hailed as a movement that places strong emphasis on democracy as well as having contributed considerably to a deepening of the democratization process in Mexico.[183] Significantly, they have also emphasized the importance of both representative and direct democracy, as can be evidenced from their communiqués,[184] but also from the agenda put forward for the Second Table of the San Andres dialogue (February 1996), entitled "Democracy and Justice," in which the first of the proposed sub-themes up for discussion was "electoral democracy" and the second was "direct democracy."[185] Such emphases led the Peruvian ex-guerrilla, Hugo Blanco, while attending the Zapatistas' August 1996 Intercontinental Encuentro, to reflect and declare poignantly:

> The Zapatistas deserve our recognition .... They are radical democrats. Something we, in the Left, never learned. It is said that the Left made mistakes. No! We simply were defeated. A defeat is all my generation has to offer. And the main cause is that we did not know how to be democratic.[186]

Indeed, in February 1995 the Subcommander himself asked rhetorically:

> What other guerrilla force has appealed, not to the proletariat as the historical vanguard, but to the civic society that struggles for democracy? What other guerrilla force has stepped aside in order not to interfere in the electoral process? What other guerrilla force has convened a national democratic movement, civic and peaceful, so that armed struggle becomes useless? What other guerrilla force asks its bases of support about what it should do before doing it? What other guerrilla force has struggled to achieve a democratic space and not take power?[187]

Turning to the Subcommander specifically, several commentators have stressed his commitment to democracy, with Alain Touraine dubbing Marcos "an armed democrat."[188] Enrique Krauze, for instance, has written that "Marcos and his movement have been enormously helpful to Mexico in helping to accelerate political and democratic reform," elsewhere stating that, "Beginning with their first communiqués, Marcos and the Zapatistas have constantly reiterated their adherence to democracy. Almost all their statements end with the phrase 'democracy, justice, liberty.'"[189] So too, Jorge Lora Cam (2003, p. 264) has maintained that "Marcos focuses on stimulating the political participation of civil society which neoliberal individualism seeks to enclose within the sphere of private life; he calls for democratic participation in the direction of the country"; and Jorge Volpi (2003) has declared that "In effect, the words of the *Subcomandante* produced demonstrable effects: without a doubt, his voice ... contributed to the democratization of the country..."[190] Indeed, even if we leave to one side the numerous Zapatista communiqués penned by the Subcommander which address democracy,[191] Marcos has talked extensively in interviews about democracy, the need for it, and what it means to him and the Zapatista movement.[192] In this way, Marcos can be said to echo Poulantzas in his repeated emphasis on democracy.

Perhaps of greater significance however, Marcos also echoes Poulantzas concerning the road to democracy; namely, as Poulantzas put it, one which involves "combining the transformation of representative democracy with the development of forms of direct, rank-and-file democracy or the movement for self-management."[193] Indeed, in this respect let us compare Poulantzas' statement with some of the Subcommander's utterances. In his interview with Yvon Le Bot (1997a, pp. 281-283), Marcos declared:

> The EZLN's proposal is that democracy cannot be only electoral. It can also be electoral, but not only that.[194] The concept of democracy should include many aspects of the democratic life of the country. One is the electoral, which needs many resources, and, I would say, a reform, a true revolution which would open the electoral space. But it also must be recognized that other types of non-representative democracies exist, but ... [t]he Mexican legal apparatus does not recognize this form of government of the communities, communitarian democracy. We say there are other kinds of democracy which are practiced in unions, student organizations, in neighborhoods, in rural communities . ... We say that representative democracy functions on certain levels, or it can function if it exists effectively. But communitarian democracy or direct democracy or social democracy functions in others.

In addition, in an interview with Marta Durán de Huerta and Nicholas Higgins (1999, pp. 271-272), Marcos stated:

> We believe that the practice of direct democracy can achieve this recognition for certain aspects of the social life of the communities. When I say communities I'm not referring only to indigenous communities but also to villages, city neighbourhoods and agricultural collectives (*ejidos*). This is to suggest that people can discuss and take decisions about how to resolve their own problems, and to suggest that these decisions will be infinitely better than the decisions that are normally taken from the centre...

> By democracy, though, we do not simply mean elections. For while the struggle for democracy in Mexico is a fight for clean, transparent and fair

elections, it also goes further. It is not a struggle that can be limited to the electoral aspect of democracy only.

We fight for a democracy that will create a new relationship between those who govern and those who are governed, what we have called "command-obeying." Until now, and in the best of cases, representative democracy or electoral democracy has referred simply to the citizen participating in an electoral process, choosing a candidate on the basis of programmes or policies, and then proceeding to delegate the taking of political decisions to that person or that party. From that moment on, or at least until the next election, that delegate, being either a person or a party, and supposedly with the backing of the majority, commands. In the new relationship that we are proposing, representative democracy would be more balanced. It would enrich itself with direct democracy, with the continual participation of the citizens, not only as electors or as consumers of electoral proposals, but also as political actors.

It would appear then that Subcommander Marcos has concerned himself deeply with the same question that Nicos Poulantzas wrestled with, namely: *"how is it possible radically to transform the State in such a manner that the extension and deepening of political freedoms and the institutions of representative democracy ... are combined with the unfurling of forms of direct democracy and the mushrooming of self-management bodies?"*[195] Moreover, it seems that Marcos sees in the communitarian democracy practiced by Chiapas' indigenous one form of direct democracy and self-management of the kind Poulantzas thought to be so crucial.

Inextricably linked with the new emphasis being placed on democracy from about 1980 onwards was the growing phenomenon of social movements (e.g. Church-based entities, environmentalists, women's groups, indigenous organizations, and so on) as agents of substantial transformations of society.[196] As Evelina Dagnino (1998, p. 47) observes in the Latin American context:

[S]ocial movements have advanced a conception of democracy that transcends the limits both of political institutions as traditionally conceived and of "actually existing democracy." The distinctive feature of this conception, which points toward the extension and deepening of democracy, is the fact that it has as a basic reference not the democratization of the *political regime* but of society as a whole, including therefore the cultural practices embodied in social relations of exclusion and inequality.

Again, as in the case of democracy, the significance of Poulantzas lies in his break from the traditional Marxist-Leninist stance which tended to dismiss social movements or, at best, relegate them to being of secondary importance (i.e. taking a backseat to political actors). Indeed, as Arthur Hirsh (1982, p. 192) observed at the time:

> [H]e [Poulantzas] argued that the new social movements (feminism, ecology, etc.) should be taken seriously by marxists as new forms of popular revolt and not be considered as secondary to the workers' movement. Thus, the later Poulantzas appears to have undergone a decisive intellectual and political evolution away from orthodox structural marxism toward an open, flexible neo-marxism which has incorporated new left themes.

In fact, in an interview he gave in 1979, Poulantzas (1979, p. 201) asked: "What is the feminist movement, what is the ecological movement, what are the other types of social movements?," only to answer: "These are not mere secondary movements in relation to the working class movement or to the party. Otherwise, everything becomes secondary. This question of primary and secondary relations must be rethought." This interview does not appear in Rafael Guillén's bibliography, and so we do not know if he encountered this statement; however, we do know that the young student read Poulantzas' *State, Power, Socialism*, published the previous year, in which the Greco-Franco Marxist wrote that, in order to forestall the bourgeoisie from "boycotting an experience of democratic socialism and of brutally intervening to cut it short," what is required is an "active reliance on a broad, popular movement … [and] … [i]n order to arouse [a] broad movement, the Left must equip itself with the necessary means, taking up especially new popular demands on fronts that used to be wrongly called 'secondary' (women's struggles, the ecological movement, and so on)."[197] Interestingly, we find an echo of Poulantzas' thoughts on the non-secondary significance of social movements in a presentation that Subcommander Marcos gave in 2007:

> Us maintaining that the core of capitalist domination lies in ownership of the means of production does not mean that we ignore or are unaware of other spaces of domination. It is clear to us that transformations must not focus only on material conditions. That is why for us there is no hierarchy

of spheres; we do not maintain that the fight for land has priority over the gender struggle, nor that the gender struggle is more important than the fight to recognize and respect difference.[198]

In sum, Marcos' transition from advocating revolution over democracy to privileging the latter over the former, i.e. his transformation from a Marxist-Leninist would-be revolutionary to "an armed democrat," not to mention his steering of the Zapatistas through their transition from a guerrilla army to an armed social movement (as acknowledged in his declaration that "more than an army, the EZLN is a social movement"[199]), as well as his attempts at reaching out to and forging links with other social movements, perhaps owe something to, or at least resonate with, the passages of Poulantzas that he had read as a student.

Notes

1. I specify "political-philosophical formation" here since Rafael's thesis was influenced in terms of linguistic philosophy by Noam Chomsky—a chapter of the thesis dealing predominantly with syntax and syntactical structures is heavily indebted to the North-American linguist.
2. Valentín Galván (2010, pp. 278 & 279) writes, regarding Guillén's thesis, "His research is imbued with the work of Althusser and Foucault" and represents a "Foucauldian reading garnished with Althusserian principles." Yvon Le Bot (1997a, p. 16), also commenting on the thesis, writes that in it we can "perceive the influence of Althusser and Poulantzas, sprinkled with some Foucault…" See too, Félix Hoyo (1995, p. 34) and Hugo Enrique Sáez Arreceygor (2012).
3. The constraints of time and space preclude discussion of all the differences that exist between these philosophers' thinking. To provide but a cursory and rather superficial illustration of the fundamental nature of some of the differences that separated them: Foucault was never a Marxist, let alone a structuralist one like both Althusser and Poulantzas; Poulantzas was far more embracing of Gramsci than Althusser; and Foucault and Poulantzas differed significantly on the role and nature of the state. For further discussion of these differences (as well as certain convergences), see Bob Jessop (2007, p. 142ff) and (2014).
4. See too, Evelina Dagnino (1998, p. 40):
    An emphasis on pluralism, diversity, and flexibility … [the] … blending … [of] … Marxist and non-Marxist authors. From Foucault to Cornelius Castoriadis and Agnes Heller, from Claude Leffort to Jürgen Habermas, Norberto Bobbio, Tocqueville, and Hannah Arendt, the renovation of the Left opened itself to an antiauthoritarian eclecticism that makes it difficult

to single out particular influences.
5. Nick Henck (2013, p. 453).
6. In "Entrevista a Adolfo Sánchez Vázquez (segunda parte)," publicado en https://pensamientofilosoficoenmexico.wordpress.com/category/adolfo-sanchez-vazquez/ el 18 noviembre, 2008, and retrieved from https://pensamientofilosoficoenmexico.wordpress.com/2008/11/18/entrevista-a-adolfo-sanchez-vazquez-segunda-parte/
7. See above, p. 128.
8. See Guillén (1980, pp. 35-39 & 87).
9. See Appendix II for a translation of the complete text of Guillén's preface.
10. Félix Hoyo (1995, p. 34) writes concerning Guillén's thesis: "On opening the first pages and reading the epigraphs we encounter another surprise: Michel Foucault and Louis Althusser are the fundamental sources which support Guillén in formulating a theoretical framework." See too, Hugo Enrique Sáez Arreceygor (2012).
11. Compare Rafael's statement ("la ideología como representación de la relación imaginaria de los individuos con sus condiciones reales de la existencia"), with that of Althusser's subheading in his paper on ISAs ("La ideología es una 'representación' de la relación imaginaria de los individuos con sus condiciones reales de existencia").
12. Confusingly, this work of Foucault, entitled *L'Ordre du discours* in French and *El Orden del Discurso* in Spanish, has appeared under two different titles in English: "The Order of Discourse" (trans. Ian McLeod) and "The Discourse on Language" (trans. A. M. Sheridan Smith). I have generally preferred the translation provided by Sheridan Smith; however, when translating scholars writing in Spanish who refer to this work I have employed McLeod's title "The Order of Discourse" so as not to jar with the Spanish (i.e. *El Orden del Discurso*).
13. Foucault (1970/1972, p. 216).
14. Foucault (1969/1972, p. 50).
15. See Robert Paul Resch (1992, p. 319): "…the central insight on which his [i.e. Poulantzas'] entire body of work is built, is a creative application of Althusser's concepts of structural causality, overdetermination, dominance, and economic determination in the last instance, reformulated by Poulantzas…;" and (p. 385, n. 1): "Poulantzas found in Althusser's concept of structural causality the key to the problems of political power and hegemony raised by Lenin, Gramsci, and Weber. Take away Althusser's problematic and Poulantzas' entire work becomes incomprehensible." See too, Arthur Hirsh (1982, pp. 183-184), Bob Jessop (1985, pp. 317-18, 326 & 328), and James Martin (2008a, pp. 6-11).
16. The references to Althusser and Foucault here are to (respectively): *For Marx*. (B. Brewster, trans.). London: Allen Lane; and D. Defert and F. Ewald (Eds.). *Dits et écrits 1954-1988* (Vols. 1-4). Paris: Gallimard.
17. Looking specifically at Althusser's and Foucault's treatments of Machiavelli,

they (2005, p. 48) conclude that
> for all the marked differences of emphasis and interpretation, Althusser's reading of Machiavelli provides an insight into the absent presence of Foucault in his work. Of course, Althusser renews and reinforces those terms—ideology and state apparatus—that Foucault found so problematic. But Althusser's concern with how a change in political rule might take shape, namely how a relation of duration between people and Prince as a form of political subjectification might emerge, has much that speaks to Foucault.

18. For a useful discussion of Foucault's relationship with Marx and Marxism, see Simon Choat (2010/2012, ch. 4), who also provides (n. 1, p. 185) a brief but helpful survey of those who have commented on this relationship. In brief, Choat (p. 101) urges that:
> In no way can Foucault's attitude be labelled "anti-Marx": he is clearly influenced by Marx and in many places explicitly praises him. There is certainly an ambiguity in Foucault's attitude towards Marx—but this tension discloses the complexity of the relationship rather than revealing a fundamental hostility.

Furthermore, Choat (p. 171) urges:
> In detailing the links between the organization of men and the accumulation of capital, between the development of disciplinary power and the rise of a capitalist economy, Foucault's work (especially *Discipline and Punish*) can at times seem like an addendum to [Marx's] *Capital*.

See too, Andrew Ryder (2013, pp. 136 & 148):
> *The Archaeology of Knowledge*, takes note of Althusser's insights. As a result, he develops a new understanding of Marx as a founder of discursivity who has allowed new truths to become possible. This encounter leads to the possibility of a "Foucauldian Marxism"…
>
> In *The Archaeology of Knowledge*, Foucault first concedes the continuing significance of Althusser's Marx. This willingness to advocate an anti-humanist Marx is the necessary precondition for his reception of Marxist ideas in *Discipline and Punish*.

19. See too, Adam Holden and Stuart Elden (2005, p. 47), who write: "As is well known, Althusser shares with Foucault an anti-humanist conception of political strategy and a critique of the subject." They (2005, p. 2) also point up Althusser's and Foucault's "works' relation to Bachelard and Canguilhem in terms of questions of history and epistemology."

20. Resch (1992, pp. 233-34) immediately follows this statement with an elaboration of what separated Althusser's and Foucault's projects:
> The differences between Althusser and Foucault center on the problem of historical thinking generally and, more specifically, on historical materialism as a scientific discourse…. Althusser's project was, as we have seen, to revive Marxism as a theoretical perspective, to establish its claims as a science of

history within a modernist reworking of the ideas of science and historical discourse, and to elaborate a form of historical causality that would do justice to the complexity of social formations and human subjectivity within a framework of economic determination. Foucault, by contrast, was never persuaded by Althusser's attempt to overcome the limitations of Marxism … Foucault's project was to investigate the structures of human knowledge in relation to their conceptual conditions of existence and to their institutional forms without recourse to any theory of historical determination.

21. Montag (1995, p. 56). He continues (56-57):
Perhaps it is now (that is, from a certain historical distance) possible to regard Althusser and Foucault (understood as proper names that denote bodies of work) as reciprocal immanent causes, dynamic and inseparable, no longer as creators of systems that must be accepted or rejected *in toto*, but rather as philosophers who sought to problematize certain concepts and notions that many in their time and ours felt could not be questioned.

22. On this work, see Valentín Galván (2010, p. 279), and below, pp. 161-162.

23. Goldstein devotes an entire chapter (ch. 5) to elaborating on precisely how Machery drew on both of these philosophers' works. He also notes (2005, pp. 67-68 and 111) that Judith Butler claims that "Althusser's notion of interpellation and Foucault's theory of subjugation justify her belief that the heterosexual norms imposed by power govern the construction of gender."

24. See, for example, Robert Paul Resch (1992, pp. 229, 233, 247), Peter Dews (1994, p. 121), and Warren Montag (1995 esp. at pp. 56-59, 69-71 and 75-77).

25. Poulantzas himself clearly did not view all of Foucault's analyses as being "incompatible with Marxism." Indeed, in his *State, Power and Socialism* (1978, p. 68), Poulantzas would write that "[s]everal of his [i.e. Foucault's] analyses are not only compatible with Marxism: they can be understood only if it is taken as their starting-point."

26. The eight convergences discussed by Jessop (2007, pp. 143-145) are: (1) "Each denied the existence of subjects endowed with free will and both examined the mechanisms in and through which acting and knowing subjects were constituted;" (2) "Each explored the relations between sovereignty and individual citizenship and its impact on political relations;" (3) "Each adopted a relational approach to power and explored the links between power and strategies;" (4) "Each insisted that power is always correlated with resistance;" (5) "They agreed in treating power as productive and positive rather than simply repressive and negative;" (6) "While Foucault is widely and rightly celebrated for his analysis of the mutual implication of power and knowledge, Poulantzas noted how political and ideological class domination was reproduced in part through the mental-manual division of labour and its consequences for the exclusion of the working class and other subaltern elements…;" (7) "Both were staunch

critics of Fascism and Stalinism but also noted the continuities between liberal democracy and fascist and Stalinist forms of totalitarianism grounded in the matrix of statehood…;" and (8) "Following May 1968 and the development of new forms of struggle, both thinkers became interested in 'micro-revolts,' rank-and-file movements, and what Poulantzas termed 'struggles at a distance from the state'."

27. Althusser is commonly regarded as a (Marxist) structuralist, and I too, for the sake of convenience, shall also employ this label throughout this work. However, it is as well to heed the caveats of three experts on Althusser concerning this label: Warren Montag (2003, pp. 11, 13, 151, & 153) repeatedly questions the depiction of Althusser as a structuralist, citing Althusser's (1976, p. 131) own statement in his *Essays in Self-Criticism* that "we were never structuralists;" Gregory Elliott (1987/2006, pp. 158-165 & 346-347) describes Althusser's as "a most unusual structuralism," employing this phrase as the subheading to his section dealing precisely with Althusser's relation to structuralism, and quotes Althusser at times distancing himself from structuralism; finally, Simon Choat (2010/2012, p. 19) argues that Althusser can be seen to have been "as much a contemporary as a precursor to the poststructuralists" and that "in his later work it is possible to see evidence of the influence of post-structuralism upon Althusser."

28. Rafael Guillén enrolled at the UNAM in 1977, aged 20, and submitted his graduation thesis in October 1980, aged 23.

29. Harris (1979, p. 63) adds: "The theoretical formulations of the so-called Marxist Structuralists have influenced the thinking of Leftist intellectuals in Latin America on a wide range of questions…"

30. See Derrida (1993, p. 210): "Althusserianism was a model for many theoreticians abroad, notably in Latin America…"

31. For a useful discussion of the dissemination of Althusser in three leading academic journals in Mexico during the 1970s, see Jaime Ortega Reyna (2015).

32. Interestingly, Rafael lists two of Córdova's books (*La formación del poder político en México* and *La ideología de la revolución mexicana*) in his thesis' bibliography, and quotes from the second one on p. 89.

33. My translation. Unless otherwise stated, all the translations that appear in the pages that follow are those of the author.

34. The first four footnotes (accompanying pages 8-11) of Rafael's thesis cite, in the following order: both Pêcheux and Foucault (in the first footnote), Foucault (quoted twice in the second footnote), Pêcheux (in the third footnote), and Macherey (in the fourth footnote). Although absent in the thesis' footnotes, two of Dominique Lecourt's books appear in Rafael's bibliography.

35. For this phrase, see Ernesto Laclau (1977/1979, p. 51) and Frederic Jameson (1981, pp. 23-58, esp. at 37).

36. Quoted in Salvador Corro (1995, 23, & 26). On Guillén's exposure to Althuss-

er's works while at the UNAM, see Salvador Corro (1995), Nick Henck (2007, pp. 33-37, 44, and accompanying notes at 377 & 379), and Hugo Enrique Sáez Arreceygor (2012).

37. For Althusser's impact on Guillén, and in particular the testimony of the latter's peers, teachers, and colleagues concerning this influence, see Salvador Corro (1995) and Nick Henck (2007, pp. 33-37, 44, and accompanying notes at 377 & 379). See too, Fernanda Navarro (1998, p. 158) who notes that following the identification of Marcos as Guillén she came across "the following clipping: 'Rafael Sebastian Guillén: An Althusserian Philosopher.'"

38. See Alvaro Delgado (1995, pp. 13 & 17).

39. See Althusser's concept of a "symptomatic" reading in his *Reading Capital*. As Resch (1992, p. 177) points out "a symptomatic reading reveals the unconscious infrastructure of a text by investigating what it does not, or rather cannot, say as well as what it actually does say."

40. The text of this preamble appears, translated for the first time into English, in Appendix I.

41. This work is contained in the book *Para una crítica de la práctica teórica*, which is listed in Guillén's bibliography.

42. Similarly, see too, Althusser (1968a/2001, p. 9):

> However, the whole Marxist tradition has refused to say that it is "*man*" who makes history. Why? Because practically, i.e. in *the facts*, this expression is exploited by bourgeois ideology which uses it to fight, i.e. to kill another, true, expression, one vital for the proletariat: *it is the masses who make history*. (italics in original)

This assertion is repeated in Althusser (1967/1990, p. 163) and (1968b/2001, p. 42). It is significant to note that all three of these works by Althusser are listed in Guillén's bibliography.

43. Section 5 of Part IV of the thesis, headed "The State: Knowledge and Power" (pp. 90-104), contains a subsection (5.2) headed "Subject and Change in Official History" (pp. 93-97); "Historical Subject" (pp. 95-97) represents a subsection within this.

44. In an interview that he granted to Uruguay's Radio *El Espectador* (March 15, 2001); retrieved from http://riie.com.mx/?a=23100.

45. Quoted in William S. Lewis (2005, p. 194). Lewis himself observes (p. 190) how "Althusser's ... goals were to articulate Marx's real philosophy and to defend Marxism as a science that produces objective knowledge of the world, knowledge that, in its resistance to ideology, provides real direction for political action."

46. See Robert Young (1981, p. 79): "The importance of Althusser's essay ["On Ideology and Ideological State Apparatuses"] lay in the fact that it broke with the 'essentialist' concept of ideology which sees ideology in terms of 'illusion' versus 'reality,' a system of (false) ideas masking the 'real' material structure."

See too, Philip Goldstein (2005, p. 25): "Althusser endowed ideology with a positive role …. Ideology does not represent falsehood or misrepresentation; ideology explains the subject's role in a society's socioeconomic structure, what Althusser calls the subject's relation to the relations of production."

47. See too, Althusser (1971/2001, p. 89):
[C]hildren at school also learn the "rules" of good behaviour, i.e. the attitude that should be observed by every agent in the division of labour, according to the job he is "destined" for … which actually means rules of respect for the socio-technical division of labour and ultimately the rules of the order established by class domination …. In other words, the school … teaches "know-how," but in forms which ensure *subjection to the ruling ideology* or the mastery of its "practice" (italics in original).

48. See Hugo Enrique Sáez Arreceygor (2012) for a brief but fruitful discussion of the Althusserian aspects of this section (i.e. Part IV) of Rafael's thesis.

49. In his "Ideology and Ideological State Apparatuses," Althusser (1971/2001, p. 104) notes how: "the School-Family couple has replaced the Church-Family couple," concluding (106): "the School (and the School Family couple) constitutes the dominant Ideological State Apparatus."

50. Althusser (1968a/2001, pp. 12 & 18, respectively). See too Althusser (1976, p. 37): "…*philosophy is, in the last instance, class struggle in the field of theory*" (italics in original); and Althusser (1974/1990, p. 265), where he writes of a "new practice of philosophy [which] serves the proletarian class struggle…"

51. In Althusser (1976, pp. 167-168).

52. Choat (2010/2012, p. 24) also draws attention to "Althusser's call for an explicitly political and practical Marx…" (p. 36).

53. We have seen above Althusser's (1968a/2001, p. 19) work entitled "Philosophy as a Revolutionary Weapon"; for his use of the phrase a "new practice of philosophy," see Althusser (1974/1990, p. 265).

54. Rafael Guillén (1980, p. 2).

55. See Choat (2010/2012, p. 24), who observes that "Althusser … is fond of quoting Lenin on … '*the soul of Marxism is the concrete analysis of a concrete situation*'…" In this section of his thesis Rafael provides a very concrete analysis of the concrete situation that existed at that time in Mexico's schools.

56. Interestingly, this discursive technique of constructing an imagined verbal exchange with an interlocutor is one that the Subcommander would deploy in certain of his communiqués, most notably one published in *La Jornada* (October 29, 1999) entitled "La P.D. toma la Cámara … de video" in which he imagined a dialogue between himself and Carlos Monsiváis; retrieved from http://www.jornada.unam.mx/1999/10/29/comunicado.html, and http://palabra.ezln.org.mx/comunicados/1999/1999_10_08_b.htm.

57. Guillén (1980, pp. 106 & 107).

58. Guillén (1980, p. 110).

59. The information and quotations which follow all derive from Salvador Corro (1995, p. 23); the translations are my own.
60. Rafael Guillén (1980, pp. 17-18); my translation.

    Poignantly, over a quarter of a century later, Subcommander Marcos would express similar concerns to Sergio Rodríguez Lascano (2006) regarding intellectuals maintaining their distance from concrete political struggles: "We say that there is a problem in the intellectual sector ... among the entire intellectual sector—including on the radical left—which is the separation or detachment of intellectual action and political action ... [P]raxis is not teaching a class. It is not writing an article. It is connecting yourself directly with a social or political movement..."

    See too Marcos' (2003) criticisms of "armchair" analysts and theoreticians.
61. One eminent example of this phenomenon is Raúl Olmedo, who had studied under Althusser in Paris in the 1970s and then returned to Mexico where he wrote a series of Althusserian academic articles in the journal *Historia y sociedad. Revista latinoamericana de pensamiento marxista*. He subsequently joined the ranks of the governing PRI party in the early 1980s. These details concerning Olmedo's career derive from Jaime Ortega Reyna (2015, p. 145).
62. Althusser (1968a/2001, p. 19) and (1968b/2001, pp. 36 & 67).
63. Althusser (1968a/2001, p. 20); italics in the original.
64. Or, as René Rodriguez (1996, p. 131) puts it: "Four years later, Marcos fulfils that which he had announced as Guillén in the conclusion of his philosophical dissertation: he dedicates himself entirely to politics..."
65. Despite what its title ("La tesis de filosofía del sub Marcos: una lectura de Althusser") suggests, Hugo Enrique Sáez Arreceygor's (2012) article, while providing a short but useful discussion of Rafael Guillén's exposure to, and influence by, Althusser, conversely has comparatively little to say about the French philosopher's influence on Subcommander Marcos. Moreover, although Sáez Arreceygor is clearly interested in the question of "what incidence of continuity and rupture exist between the university student [Rafael Guillén] and Subcommander Marcos," he points to very few similarities between the two, these being limited to their writings on the one hand exhibiting a flamboyant, irreverent, and caustic wit, but on the other depicting Mexican society in a way that lacks both profundity and nuance. Indeed, Sáez Arreceygor states "that it is fair to assume a paradigm shift [took place] between the University campus and the rainforest of Chiapas."
66. This is a position that Matamoros Ponce (2009, p. 281) restated more recently:
    If we compare Althusserian thought with that of Marcos, we can observe multiple differences. Marcos is the opposite of Althusser, from a theoretical as well as a political point of view. His language does not use orthodox Marxist prescriptions. He incorporates into the Marxism of his political discourse the sense of the negation of the shout of *Ya basta*, the symbolic

dimension of the thousand-year old Pre-Columbian memory with a tone of *evangelical liberation prophecy*. (emphasis in the original)
67. Quoted in Salvador Corro (1995, pp. 23 & 26): "I believe that in this sense Subcommander Marcos has nothing in common with the Althusserian Rafael Guillén;" reiterated again three pages later: "Subcommander Marcos has nothing in common with the student of Althusser, Rafael Guillén, of the 1970s."
68. It is perhaps interesting to note the words of Rafael's thesis supervisor, Cesáreo Morales, concerning Rafael's decision to become a guerrilla: "I believe that it was a very personal decision, not linked to his being at the university. I don't know if he experienced a *rupture* in his personality or [if] he remains the same, I don't know what his evolution was..." (my emphasis); quoted in Bertrand de la Grange and Maite Rico (1998, p. 93).
69. In EZLN (2003, p. 22).
70. In an article she published the following year, Di Piramo (2011, pp. 178-179) repeats this assertion, slightly rewording it.
71. See Juan Manuel Alvarado (1995, p. 10A), Jose Luis Ruiz (1995, p. 12), and Bertrand de la Grange (1995).
72. See Althusser (1965/1990, p. 28) and (1976/1990, p. 257), respectively:
    ...The "beautiful lie" of ideology thus has a double usage: it works on the consciousness of the exploited to make them accept their condition as "natural"; it also works on the consciousness of members of the dominant class to allow them to exercise their exploitation and domination as "natural"...
    To preserve its power ... the dominant class must transform its power from one based upon violence to one based upon consent. By means of the free and habitual consent of its subjects, such a dominant class needs to elicit an obedience that could not be maintained by force alone ... This is what, following Gramsci, I have called the system of the Ideological State Apparatuses, by which is meant the set of ideological, religious, moral, familial, legal, political, aesthetic, etc., institutions via which the class in power, at the same time as unifying itself, succeeds in imposing its particular ideology upon the exploited masses, as their own ideology. Once this occurs the mass of the people, steeped in the truth of the ideology of the dominant class, endorses its values (thus giving its consent to the existing order), and the requisite violence can either be dispensed with or utilized as a last resort.
73. On the importance of not underestimating the significance of ideology, see Phil Hearse (2007, p. 36):
    Underestimating ideology leads to a lack of understanding of the ideological apparatuses of modern capitalism, which are massively powerful in generating and reiterating fetishised, pro-capitalist views. A possible consequence of this, logically, is a lack of understanding of the centrality of ideological struggle, of the necessity for a ceaseless fight—in propaganda and agitation as well as "theory"—and against the "false" ideas pumped out

by the pro-capitalist media (and academy) on a daily basis.
74. I have deliberately chosen here to eschew employing Gramscian terminology (i.e. the waging of a "war of position") to describe the Subcommander's strategy in the hope of disabusing the reader of the impression that Marcos was directly influenced by the Italian Marxist—an hypothesis that has been much touted but for which, I argue in Chapter 5, there is no evidence.
75. I use the terms Mexican "State" and "government" interchangeably for stylistic reasons (i.e. to avoid the monotonous repetition of the former)—this terminological "looseness" is made more forgivable, I feel, by the fact that until the year 2000 the same government (i.e. the PRI Party) had held the state reins for more than seven decades.
76. In Yvon Le Bot (1997a, pp. 212 & 298 respectively).
77. In Autonomedia (2005, p. 54).
78. See too, Josefina Saldaña-Portillo (2001, p. 409) who writes that prior to the Zapatista uprising there prevailed "a hegemonic consciousness in which indigenous identity is always in a subordinate position to the dominant mestizo identity ... for hegemonic mestizo consciousness, this translated into a veneration of noble Indian ancestors, but a general amnesia about the living Indian peoples of Mexico."
79. Again, see Saldaña-Portillo (2001, pp. 405 & 407):
   The Zapatista uprising has brought the Mexican nationalist project to crisis and has challenged mestizaje as its dominant trope for citizenship...
   The Zapatista movement insists that the current ideology of mestizaje, like its nineteenth century counterpart, has incorporated the historical figure of the Indian in the consolidation of a nationalist identity in order to effectively exclude contemporary Indians from modernization.
   She goes on to elaborate (ibid): "This process of exclusion is not exterior to mestizaje; in other words, it is not a simple oversight or a misinterpretation of mestizaje in the application of governmental policy. Rather, the erasure of the indigenous is interior to the logic of mestizaje..."
80. On this, see the following observation of Carlos Fuentes (1994, p. 54):
   We have always congratulated ourselves in Mexico on our extraordinary Indian culture which we display in museums and through imposing monuments along our boulevards. We say we are proud of being the descendants of that culture .... In actual practice, however, we have treated the Indians with more cruelty, perhaps, than Cortez .... The events of Chiapas have reminded us that Mexico is a multiethnic, multicultural country.
81. See too, Kristine Vanden and Bart Maddens (2004, p. 127):
   What renders the Zapatista effort unique is that it has ... deprived the Mexican elite of its discursive monopoly with regard to the Mexican Revolution in general and Zapata in particular, something Carlos Monsiváis (1996) has described as "an exceptional feat."

82. In Claire Brewster (2005, p. 150).
83. In David Thelen (1999, pp. 613-14).
84. In Tom Hayden (2002, p. 216).
85. In, respectively, Žiga Vodovnik (2004, p. 61) and Autonomedia (2005, p. 119).
86. Marcos in Juliana Ponce de León (2001, p. 173); here I have very slightly modified in places the translation provided there.
87. In Autonomedia (1994, p. 116). See too Marcos' blistering attack on Mexican modernity in his communiqué entitled "Above and below: masks and silences," dated July 1998 in Žiga Vodovnik (2004, pp. 319-341, esp. 321ff).
88. Josh Bahn (2009, pp. 541–560, at 541 & 552) goes even further, arguing that the Zapatistas' discourse challenged the very concept of modernity.
89. On the Rule of Law in Mexico, see Manuel González Oropeza (1996). Commenting specifically on President Zedillo (1994-2000), González Oropeza (1996, p. 64) observes:

    [I]n one of his first presidential acts, he decided to "pack" the Supreme Court, by retiring all the 25 judges through an extensive constitutional reform. (For twenty days there was simply no Supreme Court in Mexico.)

90. Or, as Marcos himself—in Vodovnik (2004, p. 321)—put it in a February 1998 communiqué, "The Mexican State (and not just the government) ... supplant[s] its lack of legitimacy with legality." See too, Marcos, in Ponce de León (2001, p. 122) where he writes that "Despotism is consecrated as the 'rule of law'."
91. In Vodovnik (2004, p. 155).
92. In Vodovnik (2004, pp. 184-185).
93. In the translation in Vodovnik, "Estado de Derecho" is rendered rather literally but awkwardly "State of Law"; I have preferred to substitute it here with the more natural "Rule of Law."
94. See too Marcos' communiqué, in Vodovnik (2004, p. 355) and Ponce de León (2001, p. 141): "Don Jacinto died a few weeks ago, after being brutally beaten in one of those attacks of the 'Rule of Law' against the indigenous autonomous municipalities;" and *The Fifth Declaration of The Lacandon Jungle*, in Vodovnik (2004, p. 672), where Marcos, when talking about the government, writes of unmasking "the assassins ... who were hiding behind the robes that they call the "Rule of Law". (NB In all three translations "Estado de Derecho" is translated as "State of Law," which I have again here substituted with "Rule of Law".)
95. In Vodovnik (2004, pp. 321 & 325). See too, Marcos' October 1998 communiqué—in Vodovnik (2004, p. 351)—in which he writes of "the legal victories of usury (ah, the state of law (el estado de derecho)!!! So far from justice and so close to crime!!)..."
96. In EZLN (1997, p. 287).
97. The first phrase was that of President Ernesto Zedillo, as reported in *La Jornada* (April 18, 1998); the latter was coined by Secretary of Foreign Affairs José An-

gel Gurría, as reported in *La Reforma* (April 26, 1995).
98. In his interview with Gabriel García Márquez and Roberto Pombo (2001, p. 77). See too, Marcos' October 1999 communiqué, in Juliana Ponce de León (2001, p. 168): "We have other arms. For example, the arm of the word." For further instances of Marcos employing this motif of words being weapons, see below, Chapter 4, subsection A).
99. Marcos in his interview with Sergio Rodríguez Lascano (2006).
100. For further discussion of this important but neglected presentation, see above, pp. 109-110.
101. Later on in the same presentation, Marcos continues his discussion of Meta-theory by expounding on what he sees as its origins: "As reality was not the reference to determine the truth or falsity of a theory, then philosophy came to fulfil that role. Thus appeared the 'philosophy of science', i.e. the theory of theory, the Meta-theory."
NB Rafael, in his thesis (p. 6), briefly mentions "theory of theory (teoría de la teoría)," which he derides as "mental masturbation that never arrives at orgasm."
102. Marcos appears to hold the social sciences in poor regard; see too Marcos (2003) where he talks of those who "can discover things that those who add and subtract in the armchairs of the social sciences cannot manage to see."
103. At present there exists no translation of this oral presentation; the above then is my own.
104. In Autonomedia (1994, p. 294). Similarly, see Marcos' *Letter to Adolfo Gilly* (in Adolfo Gilly, 1995, p. 22):

Our rigid conception of the world and of revolution was left rather dented in the confrontation with the indigenous Chiapan reality. Something new (which doesn't mean "good") came out of the blows, what is now known as "neozapatismo."

105. Quoted in A. Guillermoprieto (1995, p. 39).
106. See Nick Henck (2007, p. 134f).
107. The translation here is that of Nicholas P. Higgins (2004, p. 170).
108. NB in his 1996 interview with Yvon Le Bot (1997a, p. 199), Marcos tells us that "the Marxism of concrete analysis" formed part of the "cocktail" that is Zapatismo.
109. In this, Marcos can be said to resemble Che Guevara, since Michael Löwy (1973/2007, p. xxxii) writes of something "profound that illuminates Che's life and gives it its true meaning: *the rigorous, total, and monolithic coherence between theory and practice, words and deeds.*" [italics in the original] Significantly, Marcos himself drew attention to this aspect of Che in his interview with Yvon Le Bot (1997a, p. 266), where he states "the part zapatismo reclaimed from Guevara ... [is] ... the human part, the sense of sacrifice, the devotion to a cause and, above all, the consistency, the convictions. He was a man who lived

according to what he believed."

110. Curiously, this last sentence is absent from the English translation produced by Irlandesa and distributed variously on the Internet; it appears in the Spanish-language original however.
111. The title of this first presentation is: "Arriba, pensar el blanco. La geografía y el calendario de la teoría." A convenient document containing the transcript of all seven presentations can be retrieved from http://www.nodo50.org/cubasigloXXI/taller/marcos_301207.pdf.
112. Oscar García Agustín (2009, p. 293) notes how: "When Marcos refers to a theory 'so different that is practice' he refers to theoretical reflection that is based on zapatista practice—where the subject which acts, and that which reflects, coincide." García Agustín (2009) affords a useful discussion of Marcos' thinking on the subject of theory and practice, during which he analyzes this particular presentation as a component in the Subcommander's discourse.
113. In the Spanish original: "Habría, creemos nosotros, nosotras, que desalambrar la teoría, y hacerlo con la práctica." The verb "desalambrar" typically means "to remove the wires" or "go wireless," but here, as seems apparent from the next sentence, Marcos is probably thinking of the title of the Daniel Viglietti song "A desalambrar" about tearing down fences that landlords have erected in Uruguay in an attempt at enclosure.
114. Interestingly, this opening statement echoes Foucault's (1977, p. 208) declaration that "theory does not express, translate, or serve to apply practice: it is practice."
115. The translation here is from http://www.naomiklein.org/shock-doctrine/communique-english.
116. For this sentence I prefer to offer my own translation.
117. Later in the same work Khasnabish (p. 203) reiterates this, writing of "…Zapatismo as political philosophy and practice…"
118. See too, Gogol (2014, pp. 13-14, 26 and 54-60) for further discussion of the Zapatistas' conception of theory and practice (or "organization," as Gogol sometimes refers to Zapatista practice).
119. Nail (2012, pp. 137 & 179, n. 7, respectively).
120. Holloway (1998, pp. 162 & 163, respectively).
121. See Stephanie Jed (2001, p. 378ff) for a useful discussion of Marcos' *Carta* and Gilly's response to it.
122. Serna and Pons (2000, p. 148) dismiss Marcos' comments as "perfectly forgettable," but I would urge that the *Carta* is more important for what it reveals about the Subcommander's political thinking than it is for contributing to the debate on the merits of Ginzburg's essay. See Edward Muir (1991, p. 124) for an insightful review of Ginzburg's essay, which he notes "has previously been badly misunderstood and severely criticized" and which he dubs "masterful."
123. The Spanish original of this text can be found in EZLN (1995, pp. 104-110);

and is retrieved from http://www.razonyrevolucion.org/textos/revryr/intelectuales/ryr2Marcos.pdf, and on the http://palabra.ezln.org.mx/ webpage in the "Cartas y Comunicados" section dated October 22, 1994.
124. Althusser (1976, p. 51); italics in original.
125. It must be conceded that attempting to ascertain which of Lenin's theories Guillén/Marcos was exposed to directly, and which he encountered through his reading of Althusser, is frequently impossible. For example, when the Subcommander refers in one interview to "the Leninist conception of the weakest link"—in Autonomedia (1994, p. 294)—he may have read this in Lenin's own works, or have been exposed to it indirectly through reading the section entitled "Contradiction and Overdetermination" in *For Marx* where Althusser discusses it.
126. Earlier in the same essay Althusser (1971/2001, p, 32) writes:
    Here, too, Lenin is taking up a classical thesis expounded by Engels in *Ludwig Feuerbach and the End of Classical German Philosophy*, but he gives it an unprecedented scope. This thesis concerns the history of philosophy conceived as the history of an age-old struggle between two tendencies: idealism and materialism.
127. The accompanying footnote directs the reader to "La historia de la filosofía como la historia de la lucha de tendencias," by Pierre Machery, a former student of Althusser.
128. Similarly, see Elliott (1987/2006, pp. 178 and 311 respectively): "Althusser's writings from 1967 to 1974 are largely taken up with producing a new definition of Marxist philosophy and a revised account of the relations between it and historical materialism;" and "Althusser's conceptual clarifications and constructions effected a certain recommencement of historical materialism…"
129. Ironically, historical materialism died quickest of all in Althusser's homeland, murdered by his countrymen. See Elliott (1987/2006, p. 262), who talks of "the major, if largely implicit challenge that had been mounted to historical materialism in such works as Deleuze and Guattari's *Anti-Oedipus* (1972) and Foucault's *Discipline and Punish* (1975)," concluding that: "By 1977, historical materialism was generally regarded as theoretically and politically discredited in France."
130. Later in the book Anderson (1983, p. 105) reiterates the significance and enduring relevance of historical materialism:
    Where does this leave historical materialism, in the 80's? … [H]istorical materialism remains the only intellectual paradigm capacious enough to be able to link the ideal horizon of a socialism to come with the practical contradictions and movements of the present, and their descent from structures of the past, in a theory of the distinctive dynamics of social development as a whole … [L]ike any other such paradigm, it will not be replaced so long as there is no superior candidate for comparable overall advance in knowledge.

There is no sign of that yet…
131. Giddens writes:
> Let me try to put the facts of the matter as bluntly as possible. If by "historical materialism" we mean the conception that the history of human societies can be understood in terms of the progressive augmentation of the forces of production, then it is based on false premises, and the time has come finally to abandon it. If historical materialism means that "the history of all hitherto existing society is the history of class struggles," it is so patently erroneous that it is difficult to see why so many have felt obliged to take it seriously. If, finally, historical materialism means that Marx's scheme of the evolution of societies … provides a defensible basis for analyzing world history, then it is also to be rejected.

132. *Op. cit.*, p. 102.
133. In their *Karl Marx's Theory of History: A Defense* (1978), *In the Tracks of Historical Materialism* (1983), and *Making History: Agency, Structure, and Change in Social Theory* (1987), respectively.
134. *The Sources of Social Power* (1986). Mann (1986, p. 369) rejected what he called the "false opposition" and "sterile dualism" of the ranging of idealism and materialism in antithesis to one another that had hitherto defined theories of social development.
135. See, for example, to name but a few: Ellen Meiksins Wood, *Democracy against Capitalism: Renewing Historical Materialism* (1995); Jonathan Hughes, *Ecology and Historical Materialism* (2000); Paul Blackledge and Graeme Kirkpatrick (eds.), *Historical Materialism and Social Evolution* (2002), and Mark Rupert (ed.), *Historical Materialism and Globalisation: Essays on Continuity and Change* (2002).
136. Le Bot (1997a, pp. 69-70, n. 52).
137. See Oscar García Agustín (2009, pp. 294 & accompanying n. 6 on p. 314) who, in examining Marcos' series of presentations entitled "Ni el centro ni la periferia," comments on the Subcommander's shared vocabulary with Kuhn, including "paradigmas científicos," "comunidad científica," and "revoluciones científicas." See too Marcos' March 1995 communiqué—in Ponce de León (2001, p. 253)—where he writes of "an epistemological breakthrough (ruptura epistemológica) and the birth of a new scientific paradigm," before adding "By the way, speaking of T. Kuhn and of *The [Structure of] Scientific Revolutions*, I once wrote a letter to Güilly [sic]…"
138. See too, Marcos (2007a), where he again shows his acquaintance with Kuhn's work through his discussion of "scientific paradigms" and reference to "scientific revolutions."
139. See Eugene Garfield (1987, p. 103).
140. I am very grateful to Warren Montag for bringing this information to my attention during an e-mail correspondence (October 13, 2008).

141. Althusser, Foucault and Kuhn, all of whom appear to have influenced Guillén/Marcos, were themselves in turn all influenced by the French philosopher of science, Gaston Bachelard, and especially his notion of epistemological rupture. See Hubert L. Dreyfus and Paul Rabinow (1982, pp. 76, 197, and 199, respectively) on: Foucault "introduc[ing] a new notion, similar to a Kuhnian paradigm"; the "striking similarity between Kuhn's account of normal science and Foucault's account of normalizing society"; and "the analytic dimension Foucault's work shares with Kuhn."
142. See too Robert Nola (2003, p. 368), who draws "a number of comparisons … between the Kuhn of paradigm incommensurabilities and the Foucault of ruptures and discontinuities," and who, whilst acknowledging that "there are differences to be noted" between these two thinkers, nonetheless observes that "there are a number of quite fruitful similarities to note amid the differences."
143. Interestingly, in a communiqué entitled "La luna tiene ganas" (March 24, 1995) in which Marcos specifically refers to Kuhn's [*La estructura de*] *las revoluciones científicas*, he cites its author as being "T. Kuhn o Khum," again revealing a lack of certainty regarding the spelling of Kuhn's name. (The communiqué is retrieved from http://palabra.ezln.org.mx/comunicados/1995/1995_03_24_a.htm.)
144. Guillén writes:
    Armed struggle? It is discarded by "demonstrating" the history that … "wars never fix anything, they result in a never-ending story." In this way even thinking about armed revolutionary struggle is prevented since the child is made to think about its disadvantages…
145. This term, "El código básico de cultura" in the Spanish original, which Guillén employed several times in his thesis (twice on p. 15, once on p. 73, and three times in close succession on p. 76), appears, almost verbatim (i.e. "El código básico cultural"), in Marcos' February 1998 communiqué entitled "Un periscopio invertido (o la memoria, una llave enterrada)," retrieved from http://palabra.ezln.org.mx/comunicados/1998/1998_02_a.htm and translated into English in Vodovnik (2004, p. 314).
146. Similarly, see Althusser (1976, p. 94), where he talks of "the 'evidence' of common sense, that is (Gramsci) of the dominant ideology…"
147. As Robert Paul Resch (1992, p. 227) observes: "Althusser is quite aware that ideology invades theoretical practice through the 'spontaneous philosophy' of scientists and he insists that science, being historical and social in nature, always exists in a certain relation to ideology and power."
148. This work not only appears in Guillén's bibliography (as *Curso de Filosofía Marxista para Científicos*), but is also referred to on p. 55, fn. 1, of the thesis.
149. Significantly, Althusser (who "read" Marx) and also Foucault (who "read" Nietzsche), were both part of a tradition of scholars, which also included Jean Hyppolite (who "read" Hegel) and Jacques Lacan (who "read" Freud) writing

in the mid-twentieth century who produced stimulating contributions in their field from "reading" predecessors' works.
150. The original is published in EZLN (1994, pp. 72-78, at 75); an English translation can be found in John Ross and Frank Bardacke (1995, p. 58).
151. In EZLN (2003, pp. 47-72, at 64), and translated in Vodovnik (2004, pp. 257-278, at 271). Also related to commonalities concerning terminology, interestingly, though admittedly an argumentum ex silentio, one notes that Althusser railed against the term "alienation," including it in a list of "bourgeois ideological notions" which "are anti-scientific and anti-Marxist: built to fight revolutionaries," and that over the course of five volumes of communiqués (totalling over 1900 pages), and hundreds more of speeches and interviews, Marcos, a champion of the underdog and vehement critic of capitalism, fails to employ the word *alienación* once.
152. This interview appears as a bonus feature in the DVD edition of *Zapatista* (Big Noise Films: 1998).
153. It is interesting to note that a copy of Navarro's interview with Althusser, *Filosofía y Marxismo: Entrevista a Louis Althusser* (México: Siglo XXI editores: 1988), was discovered on Marcos' shelves when the Mexican Federal Army seized the Subcommander's camp during its February 1995 offensive.
154. See Althusser (2006, p. 249, n. 29).
155. See Nick Henck (2007, p. 258f) on this structure.
156. In Ponce de León (2001, p. 113). See too, Marcos' (1996) speech at the 1st roundtable of the International Encuentro:
   [T]his Encuentro, is ... an encuentro of pockets of resistances who are looking for their similarities and recognizing their differences ... an encuentro at the international level about how possible it is to ... [build] a world where all worlds fit, as many worlds as necessary so that every man and woman has a dignified world where they are ... So that everyone lives with dignity, that is the world we Zapatistas want.
157. John Ross (2000, p. 191).
158. Bob Jessop (1991, p. 75).
159. See too Richard L. Harris (1979, p. 67):
   Poulantzas' concepts of *social categories*, *social forces*, and *state apparatuses* (repressive, ideological and economic) have also been employed increasingly by Latin American Marxist intellectuals in their analyses of the contemporary political and ideological suprastructure of their societies.
160. This section occupies pages 311-317 in the version Rafael would have used, and pages 240-245 in Timothy O'Hagan's English translation for NLB.
161. The English translation referred to here and in the following pages can be found in James Martin (2008b, pp. 294-322). The Spanish version no doubt utilized by Rafael can be found in the 1977 book *La crisis del Estado* (Barcelona: Editorial Fontanella) edited by Nicos Poulantzas under the title "Las transforma-

ciones actuales del Estado, la crisis política y la crisis del Estado," pp. 33-76.
162. One sentence in particular is especially indicative of this shared terminology:
En tanto que parte de *las relaciones de fuerza* de *las clases* en lucha, *las relaciones ideológicas* determinan en forma muy inmediata *las formas de representación-organización* de las *clases* y *las alianzas* entre esas mismas clases. (Guillén, 1980, p. 37)
… *las relaciones ideológicas* toman parte directamente de *las relaciones de fuerza* entre *las clases*, en la configuración de *las alianzas*, en *las formas de organización-representación* que estas_clases se dan… (Poulantzas, 1977, p. 44, emphasis in original)
163. In Part IV, entitled "The Decline of Democracy: Authoritarian Statism," section 1, headed "Authoritarian Statism and Totalitarianism."
164. Guillén (1980, p. 87).
165. Originally published in (1980) *Teoría: anuario de filosofía 1*(1), 299-306; reprinted in (1996, June) *Comunicación Media 3* (20), 3-7.
166. Although Guillén does not cite the page number, it is from p. 275 in the version he would have used, and in the original Poulantzas italicizes this statement for emphasis. The full quotation reads: "En efecto, uno de los caracteres particulares de la ideología burguesa dominante consiste en que oculta de una manera totalmente específica la explotación de clase, *en la medida en que toda huella de dominio de clase está sistemáticamente ausente de su lenguaje propio.*" (In Timothy O'Hagan's English translation for the NLB this appears on p. 214 and is translated as follows: "One of the particular characteristics of dominant bourgeois ideology is, in fact, that it conceals class exploitation in a specific manner, *to the extent that all trace of class domination is systematically absent from its language.*")
167. See Bob Jessop (2007/2014): "in *State, Power, Socialism*, Poulantzas … cautioned strongly against regarding violent onslaught on the state as a genuine alternative to a democratic transition to democratic socialism."
168. See Bob Jessop (1985, p. 5):
[I]t is no exaggeration to claim that Poulantzas remains the single most important and influential Marxist theorist of the state and politics in the postwar period. This becomes especially clear when we consider his influence outside the anglophone world in such areas as Latin America and Scandinavia and in countries such as France, Portugal, Spain, and Greece.
169. Numerous contemporary Latin American scholars attested to this intellectual sea-change: for example, Norbert Lechner (1985, p. 58), Robert Barros (1986, p. 52), and Tomás A. Vasconi (1990, p. 25). Echoing these contemporary Latin American scholars, see, more recently, Gideon Baker (2002, p. 63) and Barrett, Chavez, and Rodríguez-Garavito (2008, p. 28).
170. Reprinted and translated into English in Roger Bartra (2002, p. 201).
171. Bartra (2002, p. 198).
172. González Casanova (1980, pp. 64, 65, & 69, respectively).

173. Quoted in Tello Díaz (1995/2001, pp. 264 & 325, nn. 13 & 15).
174. See Poulantzas, *State, Power, Socialism*, pp. 153 & 261.
175. *State, Power, Socialism*, p. 252. See too Marta Harnecker (2007, pp. 93-4), herself, like Poulantzas, a one-time student of Althusser: "the Marxist Left … didn't sufficiently value democracy because it associated the word 'democracy' with bourgeois representative democracy…" Barrett, Chávez, and Rodríguez-Garavito (2008 p. 28) paint a more nuanced picture:
    > On the one hand, the confluence of ideas drawn from Marx, Gramsci and Luxemburg had contributed to the formation of a radical democratic tradition in Latin America that inspired agendas of free and egalitarian participation, in both the political and economic spheres. On the other hand, the widespread acceptance of Leninist vanguardism and the demonstration effect of the Stalinist experience had given rise to a rejection of so-called "bourgeois democracy" or "strictly formal democracy" by influential sectors of the old left.
176. "Towards a Democratic Socialism" constitutes Part 5 of Poulantzas' *State, Power, Socialism*.
177. *State, Power, Socialism*, p. 256.
178. *State, Power, Socialism*, p. 261.
179. *State, Power, Socialism*, p. 259.
180. Ted Benton (1984, p. 161) succinctly summarizes Poulantzas' stance:
    > Struggles to extend these representative institutions and transform the other state apparatuses are not incompatible with, but are, in fact, a *condition of possibility* of the simultaneous flourishing of forms of direct democracy and self management…. [D]irect democracy is indispensable to democratic socialism, but direct democracy is itself dependent for its democratic character upon the preservation and extension of the political liberties established in the form of representative democracy.
181. *State, Power, Socialism*, p. 259.
182. *State, Power, Socialism*, p. 260.
183. See, for example: Alan Riding (1994); Neil Harvey (1998, p. 12); Gustavo Esteva (1999); Josée Johnston (2000, p. 478ff); Chris Gilbreth and Gerardo Otero (2001, pp. 7 & 25); Jeffrey Rubin (2002, *passim*); Iain Watson (2002, p. 123ff); Valeria Wagner and Alejandro Moreira (2003, p. 190); Elizabeth (Betita) Martínez and Arnoldo García (2004, p. 214); Scott Schaffer (2004, pp. 12 & 221); Kristine Vanden Berghe and Bart Maddens (2004, p. 126); Pablo González Casanova (2005, p. 81ff); George A. Collier and Jane F. Collier (2005, p. 450); Montesano Montessori (2009, pp. 267-269); Analisa Taylor (2009, p. 56); Jeff Conant (2010, p. 272ff); Daniela Di Piramo (2010, p. 109), Alex Khasnabish (2010, p. 88f); Ramón Máiz (2010, p. 263); and Pablo González Casanova (1994/1996, p. 287). Cf, however, Pedro Pitarch (2004, pp. 301 & 308), who writes:

At the end of the day, from a distance it was difficult to work out whether the Zapatistas really constituted a democratic movement … the EZLN's policy in Chiapas had demonstrated their open rejection of elections and political parties: in the 2000 elections, the Zapatistas abstained and the previous elections were boycotted and even ballot boxes were burnt.

184. To provide but one, though highly illustrative, example, see the communiqué entitled "Of bombs, firefighters and light bulbs," dated to November 1998: "Our wind pushes the boat of the struggles for direct democracy and for representative democracy …. The direct participation by the governed in those issues which concern them (that is, in all of them), and obligating the elected representatives to 'govern obeying,' are path and season in the transition to democracy." For the Spanish original, see EZLN (2003, p. 258); the English translation is retrieved from http://flag.blackened.net/revolt/mexico/ezln/1998/ccri_bombs_cs_nov98.html.
185. For a list of these sub-themes and their proposed contents, see EZLN (1997, pp. 161-164).
186. Quoted in Fernanda Navarro (1998, p. 161).
187. In Julia Ponce de León (2001, p. 232).
188. Quoted in Jean Meyer (2002, p. 368).
189. Enrique Krauze (2001, pp. 32-33) and (2011, p. 445), respectively.
190. Cf, however, Pedro Pitarch (2004, p. 308), who writes "subcomandante Marcos was not a supporter of democratic elections, although his declarations on this issue were characteristically vague ('those rule in a democracy, should do so through obeying')…" So too, Andrés Oppenheimer (1996/1998, pp. 44 & 46) also expresses doubt concerning the Subcommander's democratic credentials.
191. See, especially: communiqués dated January 6 & 10, 1994 (entitled "Responses to Government Lies" and "Letter from Subcommander Marcos to the Press," respectively); Marcos' communiqué entitled "The Story of the Words" (December 30, 1994); *The Second Declaration of the Lacandon Jungle* (June 1995); *The Fourth Declaration of the Lacandon Jungle* (January 1996); communiqué entitled "The Government Delegation is Responsible for the absence of Agreement" (August 12, 1996); communiqué entitled "Of bombs, firefighters and light bulbs" (November 1998); and Marcos' message before the July 2, 2000 Elections (June 19, 2000).
192. See, for example, Marcos' interviews with: René Báez (1996, pp. 76-77), Le Bot (1997a, pp. 281-283, 298), Marta Duran de Huerta and Nicholas Higgins (1999, pp. 271-272), Jorge Ramos (2006, pp. 77-80), and Sergio Rodríguez Lascano (May 31, 2006, n.p.).
193. *State, Power, Socialism*, p. 260.
194. Similarly, see the EZLN's communiqué entitled "Sobre el próximo proceso electoral," (June 19, 2000):
For the Zapatistas, democracy is much more than the electoral contest or

alternation in power . ... Today, facing the current electoral process, the Zapatistas reaffirm our struggle for democracy, not *only* for electoral democracy, but *also* for electoral democracy.

Quoted and translated in Richard Stahler-Sholk (2001, p. 497). For a full version of this communiqué and an alternative translation, see http://www.narconews.com/Issue41/marcos1.html. For the original Spanish version, see http://palabra.ezln.org.mx/comunicados/2000/2000_06_19_b.htm.

195. Poulantzas, *State, Power, Socialism*, p. 256 (italics in the original).
196. See Alvarez, Dagnino, and Escobar (1998b, pp. 1-29).
197. *State, Power, Socialism*, pp. 263-264. See too, p. 211, where Poulantzas writes of "a new popular awareness concerning questions that are now no longer 'secondary' fronts—witness, in this regard, the student movement, the women's liberation movement and the ecological movement."
198. Marcos (2007b); the translation here is that of Henry Gales.
199. Quoted in Carlos Monsiváis (2009/2011, p. 389).

4

Post-Structural, Post-Marxist Formation: Michel Foucault

Let us now turn to Foucault, himself a former student of Althusser.[1] Cesáreo Morales, who supervised Rafael's thesis, informs us that although Althusserian interpretations were popular among the students of Guillén's generation, so too were Foucauldian ones.[2] What we encounter in Rafael's thesis is the combining of certain of Althusser's theories, and in particular that which saw the education system as functioning as part of the Ideological State Apparatus, with a concrete analysis of the workings of that system in its institutional form which was the hallmark of the majority of Foucault's work.[3]

It is important to note that the blending of Althusserian and Foucauldian interpretations and approaches was not the norm among the Marxist Left during the last years of the 1970s and the first year of the 1980s, when Rafael was writing his thesis. Rather, at that time Foucault tended to be either studiously ignored or, worse still, scathingly critiqued by orthodox Marxists: an illustrative instance of the latter being the Althusserian Marxist, Dominique Lecourt, whose *Pour une critique de l'épistémologie (Bachelard, Canguilhem, Foucault)*, which Rafael lists in his bibliography, was highly dismissive of Foucault's *The Archaeology of Knowledge*.[4] And yet, while certainly not typical among the Marxist-Leninist Left at that time, attempts at simultaneously harnessing Althusserian and Foucauldian theories were not unheard of, and so Rafael's endeavour to do precisely this was not unprecedented. As briefly mentioned in Chapter 3, Luis Crespo and Jose Ramoneda Molins' *Sobre la filosofía y su no-lugar en el marxismo* (Laia, 1974) adopted just such an approach. Indeed, in their "Nota bibliográfica general," with which they end their work, Crespo and Molins (1974, p. 96, entry no. 4) write:

> In our attempt to integrate categories of the philosophy of Michel Foucault into Marxist philosophy, we basically start from the *Archaeology of Knowledge* (Siglo XX) and the *Order of Discourse* (Tusquets). But many suggestions derive from his previous works: *The History of Madness in the Classical Period* (Siglo XX) and from the classes taught at the Collège de France during 1972-1973.[5]

Significantly given that the focus of our interest lies in Rafael Guillén and his thesis, Valentín Galván (2010, p. 279), commenting on Crespo and Molins' work, writes "In this work the Althusserians sought to integrate categories from the works of Foucault, especially from *The Archaeology of the Knowledge* and *The Order of Discourse*, with Marxist-Leninist philosophy",[6] crucially adding "And this was also the intention of Rafael Guillén, as can be established from his constant references to the two aforementioned texts." I certainly would not contest the general thrust of Galván's assertion here, although I would point out that Rafael's thesis technically does not contain "constant references" to the *Archaeology of Knowledge* and *The Order of Discourse*; rather, in its 111 pages it deploys three quotations from the former book, and four from the latter, and otherwise makes only one specific reference to Foucault's *Archaeology of Knowledge* (and that in a footnote which merely directs the reader to consult the work[7]): consequently, it would probably be more accurate to write that Guillén's thesis at times echoes Foucault's two works.

It would thus appear that Rafael, in contrast to more orthodox Althusserian Marxists such as Dominique Lecourt, saw no problem in yoking Foucault's theories as laid out in the *Archaeology of Knowledge* to Althusser's Marxism. That he was able to do so, I would argue, both exemplifies Rafael's flexibility of mind and foreshadows a lack of dogmatism—emphasized much in my biography of Marcos[8]—so characteristic of the Subcommander.

If we extend our gaze beyond the *Archaeology of Knowledge* to take in Foucault's general thought, we can readily discern key aspects of his thinking and approach that would have resonated with Rafael. The following, lengthy quotation from Foucault during his debate with Noam Chomsky in 1971, for example, displays a political-philosophical perspective highly compatible with Rafael's own thinking on the subjects of power, state apparatuses, the education system and the dominant class, although it must be stressed that there is no indication that Guillén encountered this particular passage in his reading:

[I]t is the custom, at least in European society, to consider that power is localized in the hands of the government and that it is exercised through a certain number of particular institutions, such as the administration, the police, the army, and the apparatus of the state .... But I believe that political power also exercises itself through the mediation of a certain number of institutions which look as if they have nothing in common with the political power, and as if they are independent of it, while they are not.

One knows this in relation to the family; and one knows that the university, and in a general way, all teaching systems, which appear simply to disseminate knowledge, are made to maintain a certain social class in power; and to exclude the instruments of power of another social class...

It seems to me that the real political task in a society such as ours is to criticize the workings of institutions, which appear to be both neutral and independent; to criticize and attack them in such a manner that the political violence which has always exercised itself obscurely through them will be unmasked, so that one can fight against them.

This critique and this fight seem essential to me for different reasons: firstly, because political power goes much deeper than one suspects; there are centers and invisible little-known points of support; its true resistance, its true solidity is perhaps where one doesn't expect it. Probably it's insufficient to say that behind the governments, behind the apparatus of the State, there is a dominant class; one must locate the point of activity, the places and forms in which its domination is exercised. And ... this domination is not simply the expression in political terms of economic exploitation .... Well, if one fails to recognize these points of support of class power, one risks allowing them to continue to exist and to see this class power reconstitute itself even after an apparent revolutionary process.[9]

Let us now proceed with a close examination of Rafael's thesis which will reveal it to have been extremely heavily indebted to Foucault. First, Rafael lists six single-authored works by Foucault in his bibliography.[10] Moreover, he places two quotations from the French post-structuralist on the frontispiece of the thesis. They read as follows:

[I]f power is properly speaking a way in which relations of forces are deployed and given concrete expression, rather than analysing it in terms of cession, contract or alienation, or functionally in terms of its maintenance

> of the relations of production, should we not analyse it primarily in terms of *struggle*, *conflict* and *war*?[11] (emphasis in both Rafael and in Foucault's original)

And

> speech is no mere verbalisation of conflicts and systems of domination, but that it is the very object of man's conflicts.[12]

Furthermore, unlike with Althusser, who is referred to almost exclusively in a single, short chapter of the thesis, and who is quoted only once, Foucault's influence can be seen throughout much of the work, with the philosopher being quoted a total of eight times (twice in the frontispiece and six times spread over four chapters).

We have already seen above (Ch. 3) how Rafael's preface exhibits a glimpse of the extent of his thesis' indebtedness to Foucault through the terminology it employs: indeed, that one-and-a-half page preliminary section is replete with Foucauldian terms, including: "objects of discourse," "discursive formations," "discursive practice," "rules of formation," "the discourse of power," and the use of the word "archaeology." However, we can also see Rafael drawing on Foucault in Part One, Chapter Two of his thesis, entitled "The Space of Production of Philosophical Discourse", in which he again refers to "discursive formations." Indeed, Guillén (1980, pp. 9-10) includes two long quotations from Foucault's *Archaeology of Knowledge* in his second footnote accompanying this section:

> Whenever one can describe, between a number of statements, such a system of dispersion, whenever, between objects, types of statement, concepts, or thematic choices, one can define a regularity (an order, correlations, positions and functionings, transformations), we will say, for the sake of convenience, that we are dealing with a *discursive formation*…

> One might say, then, that a discursive formation is defined (as far as its objects are concerned, at least) if one can establish such a group; if one can show how any particular object of discourse finds in it its place and law of emergence; if one can show that it may give birth simultaneously or successively to mutually exclusive objects, without having to modify itself.[13]

Rafael's indebtedness to Foucault can also be witnessed in Part Four of the thesis, entitled "Towards a Concrete Analysis." There, in Chapter Two, headed "The Second Image—School, Knowledge, Power," while analysing the education system in Mexico, he includes (p. 78) the following quotation from Foucault (1970/1972, p. 227):

> What is an educational system, after all, if not a ritualisation of the word; if not a qualification of some fixing of roles for speakers; if not the constitution of a (diffuse) doctrinal group; if not distribution and an appropriation of discourse, with all its learning and its powers?

Five pages later (p. 83), Rafael heads his Chapter Four, entitled "Interval—Some considerations concerning the schooling apparatus in Mexico," with another quotation from Foucault:

> Education may well be, as a right, the instrument whereby every individual, in a society like our own, can gain access to any kind of discourse. But we well know that in its distribution, in what it permits and in what it prevents, it follows the well-trodden battle-lines of social conflict. *Every educational system is a political means of maintaining or of modifying the appropriation of discourse, with the knowledge and the powers it carries with it.*[14]

The appearance of these two Foucauldian quotations in a section that deals with educational institutions, and more specifically schools, and how these articulate a discourse of power by means of which individuals are interpellated as subjects, is perhaps only to be expected however given that, as Michael Hardt (2000, p. 163) has observed:

> Michel Foucault's work has made clear that the institutions and *enfermements* or enclosures of civil society—the church, the school, the prison, the family, the union, the party, etc.—constitute the paradigmatic terrain for the disciplinary deployments of power in modern society, producing normalized subjects[15] and thus exerting hegemony through consent in a way that is perhaps more subtle but no less authoritarian than the exertion of dictatorship through coercion.

Finally, in the concluding section of his thesis (headed "By way of Concluding"), the only scholar whom Rafael quotes is Foucault, and he does so twice, both in the main body of his text: the first time (p. 108) from *The Discourse on Language / The Order of Discourse*: "We know perfectly well that we are not free to say just anything, that we cannot simply speak of anything, when we like or where we like; not just anyone, finally, may speak of just anything"[16]; and the second (pp. 108-109) from *The Archaeology of Knowledge*, Chapter 3, which is headed "The Formation of Objects":

Thus a space unfolds articulated with possible discourses: a system of *real* or *primary relations,* a system of *reflexive or secondary relations,* and a system of relations that might properly be called *discursive.* The problem is to reveal the specificity of these discursive relations, and their interplay with the other two kinds. (emphasis in original)[17]

In the final pages of his thesis Rafael constructs a mock dialogue between himself and an imagined, somewhat adversarial interlocutor, which he uses to anticipate potential criticisms of his thesis and head them off, a format and technique utilized by Foucault in the conclusion to his *The Archaeology of Knowledge*. We have already seen above that this section of his thesis (pp. 108 & 109) contains two quotations from Foucault, however, it is in the final page-and-a-half of his conclusion, in which Rafael anticipates potential criticisms of his thesis, that he is at his most Foucauldian:

- Well, finally you accept something. But I would also like to point out that the part which deals with the concrete analysis is too focused on what the dominant ideology is and on its discourse, and seems to forget what is happening with the discourse and ideology of the exploited classes.

- The initial purpose of the work envisioned, in addition to the analysis we conducted, the discursive forms of "resistance" and "combat" of the dominated ideology compared to the discourses which had been imposed on them. The final result omits this last part, but we can say that the general notes in the theoretical part can "function" equally for the analysis of these dominated forms of practical ideologies.

- It remains to be seen.

- I believe that in the analysis, rather, in the aim at concrete analysis, the discourse mechanisms of power-knowledge by which the Mexican State operates in order to implement its class project, in order to impose its CODE, were fully established. It can be seen how the State ORDERS history and its learning, how it ORDERS the assimilation of the need of itself, "I am, therefore I am necessary" the State tells us. Also established is a characterization of the space where this discourse produces effects, the school and its coordination with the family.[18]

Judging from the quotations that he includes in his thesis, as well as some of his own more Foucauldian passages, it is clear that Rafael was influenced by certain of Foucault's thoughts on education systems, and that he also took over from Foucault the latter's theories concerning both what one may call, following the title of Rafael's thesis supervisor Cesáreo Morales' article on Foucault, the power of discourse and the discourse of power,[19] and also, linked to this, discursive formations and relations. Indeed, it is worth emphasizing that seven of the eight quotations from Foucault deployed by Rafael in his thesis derive from *The Archaeology of Knowledge* (1969) and *The Order of Discourse* (1970),[20] and also to note with what these works are concerned. The former raises and treats what Colin Gordon (1980, p. 233) calls the "Archaeological question," namely: "how can the production in our societies of sanctioned forms of rational discourse be analysed according to their material, historical conditions of possibility and their governing systems of order, appropriation and exclusion;" whereas the latter, Gordon (1980, p. 245) observes:

> [S]hows how the rules of formation of discourses are linked to the operation of a particular kind of social power. Discourses not only exhibit immanent principles of regularity, they are also bound by regulations enforced through social practices of appropriation, control and "policing." Discourse is a political commodity.

Having demonstrated the ways in which Foucault influenced Rafael, we will next turn to ascertaining whether these preoccupations persisted in Marcos. I would like to close this section, however, by quoting Adolfo Gilly (1998, p. 313), who, following a discussion of the importance and merits of Subcommander Marcos, and after noting that Rafael cites, at the beginning of his thesis, Foucault on discourse being not the verbalization of struggle but the actual object of human conflict,[21] writes:

> The Indian rebels' dispute with the national state started with the occupation of a *physical space*. It wound up growing into a dispute conducted in multiple spaces: *political* spaces, *symbolic* spaces, and *discursive* spaces, inside and outside Mexican territory.

A singular perceptiveness, that of the student.

That Foucault's influence on Rafael Guillén persisted palpably in the discourse (and practice) of Subcommander Marcos is undeniable. John Womack Jr (1999, p. 44) has stated that "*Marcos*' communiqués and interviews were … Foucaultian…," a verdict seconded by José de Colina (2002, p.

366), who believes that he can detect in the Subcommander's prose "subliminal citations from Foucault…" Turning to specific resemblances and points of convergence, Carlos Antonio Aguirre Rojas (2011, p. 45) sees similarities between Foucault's Lecture of January 7, 1976 (which, significantly, Rafael had quoted from in the frontispiece to his thesis[22]) and Marcos' first letter to Luis Villoro, headed "Notes on wars" (January-February 2011).[23] Analysing the Subcommander's epistle, Aguirre Rojas (2011, p. 45) notes that:

> Reading the reflections contained in the text "Notes on wars," the thesis postulated by Michel Foucault, which inverts the classic dictum of Carl von Clausewitz in his book *On War* to affirm that "politics is the continuation of war by other means," immediately comes to mind.[24]

Aguirre Rojas then goes on to argue that "capitalist politics" are the continuation of class war in capitalist societies, thus connecting Marcos' essay, with its theme of war for profit and its argument "that war is inherent to capitalism," with Foucault's inversion of Clausewitz's dictum, provided presumably that the latter be slightly modified to read "[capitalist] politics is the continuation of [class] war by other means."[25]

A)   *Discourse as War or Words as Weapons*

Let us turn to examining more deeply Foucault's influence on Marcos. It will be remembered that the French thinker's main impact on the student Rafael concerned what could be termed the power of discourse and the discourse of power. As we saw above in Chapter 3, and in particular the section on his undermining the Mexican State's ideological underpinnings, the Subcommander has exhibited a keen appreciation of the potency of discourse, deploying a counter-hegemonic discourse to challenge successfully the dominant discourse, or discourse of power, employed by the government. Interestingly, for Gustavo Esteva (2004, p. 157) this evidently conjures-up associations with Foucault, since when commenting on it he employs distinctly Foucauldian phraseology:

> Words always enfleshed in their behavior have been the main weapon of the Zapatistas. Using brilliantly and effectively their words, they have been dismantling the dominant discourse. They continually undermine the institutional system of production of the dominant statements, of the established

"truth." They thus shake, peacefully and democratically, the very foundation of the existing Power/Knowledge system. While this system hides within spectacular shows of strength its increasing fragility, the Zapatistas exploit for their struggle its profound cracks, denounce it as a structure of domination and control, and begin the construction of an alternative.

That Marcos in particular clearly views his discourse as fulfilling a combative function is abundantly evident. For example, in an interview with Gabriel García Márquez and Roberto Pombo (2001, p. 77), Marcos declared that "our weapons are words," while in another interview he talked of "the basic weapon which we have, the word".[26] Moreover in a succession of communiqués that he wrote in 1999, the Subcommander had foreshadowed this sentiment: "our most powerful and feared (by our enemies) weapon: the word"; "even writing is combat"; and "the Zapatistas have a very powerful and indestructible weapon: the word".[27] Elsewhere Marcos talks about the Zapatistas "transforming their poverty into a weapon—the weapon of resistance," adding that "we have other arms. For example, we have the arm of the word"; while in the *Fifth Declaration of the Lacandon Jungle* he relates how: "we discovered the weapon of words after the combat in January of 1994."[28]

Moreover, numerous commentators have emphasized the potency, rhetorical but also (concerning us most here) political, of the Subcommander's discourse.[29] Hence, Illan Stavans (2002, p. 387) has urged that Marcos "is a *guerrillero* for the 1990s who understands, better than most people, the power of word and image"; Ignacio Corona and Beth E. Jörgensen (2002, p. 244) have written that "Marcos's discourse certainly renews hopes for the power of words as political action…"; Kristine Vanden Berghe (2005, p. 95) has affirmed that "Marcos … believes that the written word constitutes an effective weapon in political and social struggles…. Furthermore … he appears to attribute to narrative fiction a central role in the formation and transformation of power relations"[30]; and Jorge Volpi (2003) has stated that:

> Without a doubt, a good part of the fascination which Marcos provokes lies in his willingness to transform reality through words…. It is enough to read any of his communiqués in order to realize that the *Subcomandante's* unbridled prose, full of lyrical, humorous and sentimental effusions, is not simple boasting in order to confuse the enemy, but rather a careful strategy of combat … his fight against injustice and discrimination and in favor of indigenous rights is based in large measure in his rhetorical skills.

Most recently Daniela Di Piramo (2011, p. 204) has asserted that the Subcommander

> understands that a new way of doing politics requires a new discursive approach. His narrative aims to … differentiate itself from conventional discourse, by appealing to the imagination of the readers and by adopting both fantasy and irony as linguistic devices to "unmask" existing power relations…[31]

It is, however, the historian Lorenzo Meyer (1994, pp. 1, 10, 36), who has proffered the fullest and most incisive comments on this subject. In a newspaper article entitled "The Murky Language of Power," he contrasts Marcos' and the Zapatistas' language with that of the government's, writing "the discourse of the new Zapatistas is simple, comprehensible and has a clear moral foundation. It is, therefore, the antithesis of the governmental language."[32] (At the same, Meyer also emphasizes that Marcos' "discourse is also quite distinct from the stilted and esoteric language which has been used for a long time by the Mexican left."[33]) Meyer (1994, p. 36) continues:

> One of the elements of the surprising political success of the EZLN in general, and of Subcomandante Marcos in particular, is that both, with great consistency between words and action, have reintroduced direct and simple—but not simplistic—discourse into Mexican politics, and have even allowed themselves some poetic license. It is, therefore, a discourse in which words seek to recuperate their original meaning, and for this reason they have become anti-authoritarian and liberating.

Finally, in keeping with Marcos' own view that sees his words as weapons, Meyer (1994, p. 36) urges that "In effect, the discourse of the EZLN is the 'Big Bertha' of its artillery, its heavy-caliber and long-range weapon."

It is perhaps unsurprising then that Luis De la Peña Martínez (2004), in a piece that connects Foucault with Zapatismo on precisely the issue of the power of discourse, should have observed that:

> It is possible to fight, as Foucault warns us, through discourse. The discursive rebellion which has been carried out by the Zapatista movement in Mexico … is an example of this. The power of the word … of the Chiapas indigenous represents through its various forms of resistance, a series of strategies and "possible inventions" (the term is Foucault's), answers and creative responses that oppose a particular type of power relationship.

Foucault's emphasis on the interconnectedness between discourse and power, as expressed in (among other works) his *The History of Sexuality. Volume 1: An Introduction*,[34] a book that Rafael Guillén had read, leads us to an examination of the convergences between the French thinker and the Subcommander's thought concerning what form(s) power takes and how it can be resisted.

B)   Power and Resistance

For Foucault (1978/2006, p. 208), "Power is not a substance.[35] Neither is it a mysterious property whose origin must be delved into. Power is only a certain type of relation between individuals." In the first volume of his *The History of Sexuality* he elaborates further, writing:

> Power's condition of possibility, or in any case the viewpoint which permits one to understand its exercise ... and which also makes it possible to use its mechanisms as a grid of intelligibility of the social order, must not be sought in the primary existence of a central point, in a unique source of sovereignty from which secondary and descendent forms would emanate; it is the moving substrate of force relations which, by virtue of their inequality, constantly engender states of power, but the latter are always local and unstable. The omnipresence of power: not because it has the privilege of consolidating everything under its invincible unity, but because it is produced from one moment to the next, at every point, or rather in every relation from one point to another. Power is everywhere; not because it embraces everything, but because it comes from everywhere ... power is not an institution, and not a structure; neither is it a certain strength we are endowed with; it is the name that one attributes to a complex strategical situation in a particular society...
>
> Power is not something that is acquired, seized, or shared, something that one holds on to or allows to slip away; power is exercised from innumerable points, in the interplay of nonegalitarian and mobile relations...[36]

That Marcos, like Foucault, wrestled with the concept of power can be readily discerned. We have, for example, several statements made by the Subcommander in connection with the Zapatistas' Intercontinental Encounter for Humanity and Against Neoliberalism (1996). Indeed, in a communiqué penned in May 1996 inviting people to attend this *encuentro*, Marcos wrote: "It is necessary to construct a new political culture. This new political culture can arise from a new way of looking at Power. This is not about taking Power, this is about revolutionizing its relationship with those who have it and those who suffer its consequences."[37] Moreover, in a speech given during the first roundtable of the gathering on June 30, 1996, the Subcommander explained:

> [W]e believe that the problem of power must be redefined, not repeating the formula that in order to change the world it is necessary to take power and, once in power, then we are going to organize things in the best interest of the world, that is, in my own best interest since I am in power. We have thought that if we were to conceive of a change of premise in looking at power, the problem of power, explaining that we did not want to seize it, this was going to produce another form of politics and another kind of politician. Other human beings who engage in politics differently from the politicians we suffer from today throughout the entire political spectrum…[38]

Furthermore, that Marcos shares a conception of power that closely approximates that of Foucault's is evidenced from a systematic examination of his discourse.[39] First, the Subcommander follows the French thinker in perceiving power to be something other than an entity that can be seized. For instance, there is the following comment, made by Marcos in his interview with Ignacio Ramonet (2001, p. 17): "The problem is not to conquer power, we know that the site of power is henceforth empty. What we need, in the time of globalization, is to build a new relationship between power and citizens." We also have his August 29, 1996, communiqué to the *Ejército Popular Revolucionario* (EPR) guerrillas,[40] in which Marcos explains that "What we seek, what we need and want is … not to take power, but to exercise it."[41] Significantly, this last statement of Marcos' on exercising, rather than taking, power is quoted by Shannon Speed and Alvaro Reyes (2008, p. 301), who, in an accompanying note, briefly comment on what they perceive to be "the striking similarity between Subcomandante Marcos's statements and those made by Michel Foucault (1980) in his famous 'Two Lectures'…"[42] Indeed, Marcos has frequently gone on record as rejecting the taking of state power,[43] and, as is clear from his interview with Gabriel García Márquez and Roberto Pombo (2001, p. 70), has done so due to his belief that merely overthrowing those in power and replacing them with others does nothing to alter the fundamental power structure:

> The worst that could happen to it [the EZLN], apart from that, would be to come to power and install itself there as a revolutionary army. For us it would be a failure. What would be a success for the politico-military organizations of the sixties or seventies which emerged with the national liberation movements would be a fiasco for us. We have seen that such victories proved in the end to be failures, or defeats, hidden behind the mask of success. That what always remained unresolved was the role of people, of civil society, in what became ultimately a dispute between two hegemonies. There is an oppressor power which decides on behalf of society from above, and a group of visionaries which decides to lead the country on the correct path and ousts the other group from power, seizes power and then also decides on behalf of society. For us that is a struggle between hegemonies, in which the winners are good and the losers bad, but for the rest of society things don't basically change.[44]

Indeed, so adamant in this belief is the Subcommander that in an interview with Julio Scherer García (2001, pp. 14-15) he rejected the label revolutionary, proposing instead that of "social rebel," and drawing the distinction on the grounds that

> a revolutionary proposes fundamentally to transform things from above, not from below, the opposite to a social rebel. The revolutionary appears: We are going to form a movement, I will take power and from above will transform things. But not so the social rebel. The social rebel organizes the masses and from below, transforming things without the question of the seizure of power having to be raised.[45]

It is far from inconceivable that the Subcommander derived such a belief not just from having observed historical examples of various revolutions betrayed, but also, in part, from his reading of Foucault, who, it will be remembered, stated that:

> [P]olitical power goes much deeper than one suspects; there are centres and invisible, little-known points of support …. Well, if one fails to recognise these points of support of class power, one risks allowing them to continue to exist; and to see this class power reconstitute itself even after an apparent revolutionary process.[46]

And who also declared:
> I would say that the state consists in the codification of a whole number of power relations that render its functioning possible, and that Revolution is a different type of codification of the same relations. This implies that ... one can perfectly well conceive of revolutions that leave essentially untouched the power relations that form the basis for the functioning of the State.[47]

Perhaps unsurprisingly, Marcos' conceptualization of power as something other than an entity to be seized constitutes an aspect of Zapatismo that has attracted the attention of numerous commentators.[48] The observations of two in particular, however, are deserving of singling out here, the first on account of its pertinence to the focus of this chapter, and the second due to its perceptiveness and the fact that it leads on naturally to discussion of our next topic (i.e. resistance). Luis de la Peña Martínez (2004), in a piece that specifically identifies points of convergence between the Zapatistas and Foucault, writes:

> And here the way in which zapatismo has raised the problem of power should be emphasized: throughout its experience, this social and political movement ... in conjunction with so-called national and international civil society, has sought and created alternatives to the usual ways of exercising power. Their struggle is not limited to the taking of political power ... but, first and foremost, is aimed at transforming our ideas about power itself...

Second, Jeff Conant (2010, p. 15) reiterates the point about Marcos and the Zapatistas rejecting the seizing of state power, while making the following perceptive point concerning attempts to alter the existing power structure through effecting a transformation in social relations:

> ...the strength of the Zapatista struggle, and its broad appeal, is that it does not seek to take state power, but to "open a space for democracy," to transform social relations. What this effort at transformation implies is that power does not reside merely in the authority of the state, or in the hand of the market, visible or invisible...[49]

This brings us to our next observation: Marcos appears to follow Foucault not only in his conceptualization of what power is *not* (i.e. a thing to be seized), but also of what it *is*: namely, a network of relations.[50] Indeed, in the first volume of his *The History of Sexuality*, a work that Marcos had read as a student, Foucault (1976/1978, p. 92) declares that "power must be understood in the first instance as the multiplicity of force relations,"[51] before elaborating at length on these:

> Relations of power are not in a position of exteriority with respect to other types of relationships (economic processes, knowledge relationships, sexual relations), but are immanent in the latter; they are the immediate effects of the divisions, inequalities, and disequilibriums which occur in the latter, and conversely they are the internal conditions of these differentiations…

> …the manifold relationships of force that take shape and come into play in the machinery of production, in families, limited groups, and institutions, are the basis for wide-ranging effects of cleavage that run through the social body as a whole.[52]

This conceptualization of power as relational, which Hwa Yol Jung (1987, p. 28) heralds as "[t]he most seminal insight of Foucault," appears to be shared by Marcos, who sought, in true Foucauldian fashion, by means of discourse,[53] both to unmask existing power relations through the formulation and articulation of a "counter-discourse" to the Mexican State's dominant discourse, and to transform the prevailing power structure through the promotion of changes in social relations.[54]

Marcos in fact makes frequent reference to the need to change social relations. To provide but a few examples, in chronological order: in a February 1995 communiqué he wrote that "a new political, economic and social relation has to be created among all Mexicans, and later on, among all human beings…"[55]; in a June 1995 communiqué he maintained that "There can be no change without a rupture. A profound and radical change of all the social relations in today's Mexico is necessary. A REVOLUTION IS NECESSARY, a new revolution;"[56] in an interview with Julio Scherer García (2001, p. 12) he stated that "That's what's at stake: chances of creating other types of relations, even in the marketplace, that don't represent the savage capitalism of dog-eat-dog"; and, finally, he told Jesús Quintero (2007, p. 86) that

> we think that society, and the world, should be transformed from below. We think we also have to transform ourselves: in our personal relations, in culture, in art, in communication … and create another kind of society, in such a way that power, or he who has power, comes to have another relationship with society…

Naturally given such statements, and the Zapatistas' practice of establishing concretely the means of transforming these relations (more of which below), a host of observers have emphasized this element of Zapatismo. To cite but a handful, Sergio Rodríguez Lascano (2002) has written that "Zapatismo reminds us that power is a social relation, not a thing or a palace that can be taken, won electorally or assaulted"; Valeria Wagner and Alejandro Moreira (2003, p. 205, n. 38) claim that "Their [i.e. the Zapatistas'] empowerment here stems from their newly gained grasp of their social relations, which grasp cannot be dissociated from the process of conceiving and instituting as real other power relations"; Mariana Mora (2003, p. 19) asserts that "a fundamental element of *Zapatismo* ... [is that] ... the movement is not about usurping state power so much as about transforming power relations through the creation of democratic spaces for collective discussions that allow people to take part in decisions that affect their lives"; Scott Schaffer (2004, p. 225) maintains that by "[m]oving from the vertical, hierarchized conception of power present in Western societies to a more horizontal form of social relations ... [and] ... [b]y structuring the Zapatista forms of social organization in such a way that there is continual interrogation of both the policies and the organizational forms themselves ... the EZLN has modeled a significant change in the form of power relations"; Kara Zugman Dellacioppa (2012. pp. 2 & 7) urges that the Zapatistas "believed that by changing relations of power at the micro level, eventually the state would have to respect the 'dignity' of their struggle and to 'mandar obedeciendo' (rule by obeying)," adding "power for the EZLN is a relation, rather than an object or thing";[57] and, perhaps most fully, Alex Khasnabish (2010, p. 84) writes that "What distinguishes the discourse of Zapatismo ... is precisely its radical critique of power ... and ... the belief that if one begins with answers and seeks to impose solutions, systems of power and domination are merely reproduced...," adding that "The challenge of creating a new world rooted in social relations that are not power relations and that emerge out of the mutual recognition of dignity is something the Zapatistas have undertaken most seriously."[58]

An example of the Zapatistas' deep concern regarding the promotion of more equal social relations so as to change existing power structures can be found in the Subcommander's (2004) "Reading a Video (Part II): Two Flaws,"[59] in which he acknowledges the persistence of glaring gender inequalities within the autonomous civil councils and *Juntas de Buen Gobierno*

[JBGs], and the tendency of the EZLN's military structure to contaminate, and in the worst cases interfere in the workings of, these institutions.[60] It is important to note here, as Thomas Nail (2012, p. 67) does, that "These are two mistakes/dangers that have been historically neglected by revolutionary movements, in part because they are more supple non-state kinds of social power ignored by dialectical and insurrectionist theories of history." This brings us to a key point concerning Marcos' conception of power, and the influence Foucault had in forming this. All too often previous traditional Marxist-Leninist guerrilla groups had concentrated on State power to the exclusion of other force relations. Indeed, one would find among their writings and utterances comparatively few elaborations on power that equal in nuance and sophistication those we have seen above in the Subcommander's discourse, or merely even his observation, made during the first few months of the uprising, that: "It is better to speak about Power [rather than the State], because there are places in which the action of the State is not perfectly definable as such, and it makes more sense to speak of Power—in this case, the Power of a dominant class that spreads to other areas—culture for example."[61] In Marcos' case, one could perhaps argue that had he been influenced exclusively by Althusser (with his emphasis on State Apparatuses) and Poulantzas (who, although interested in, and to some degree sympathetic toward, Foucault's conception of power, nonetheless holds that "power is pre-eminently concentrated and materialized by the State which is thus the central site of the exercise of power"[62]), and not at all by Foucault,[63] the result would have been an emphasis on political power, and especially State power, and a relative neglect (or, at least, underplaying) of social relations, that is characteristic of many of the Subcommander's Marxist-Leninist revolutionary guerrilla predecessors.

In addition, the Zapatistas' focus on social relations, and in particular the building of democratic, non-hierarchical relations based on human dignity within their network of autonomous indigenous communities, has important ramifications in terms of current political philosophy since it provides a possible alternative to "classical Marxism and liberalism," which, Richard J. F. Day (2005, p. 14) observes, "share a belief that there can be no 'freedom' without the state form (Leviathan or dictatorship of the proletariat), and therefore also share a commitment to political (state-based) rather than social (community-based) modes of social change."⁶⁴ Significantly, Day (2005, p. 9) notes how

> poststructuralist theorists such as Foucault, Deleuze and Guattari, and to some extent Derrida have worked intensively on the question of how we might continue to struggle against oppression without reproducing the modern fantasy of a final event of totalizing change (the revolution), or falling back into the abyss of liberal pluralism.

Marcos' name, I would urge, could justifiably be added to that of the French thinkers cited above by Day, although it would perhaps be more accurate in his case to replace the labels "post-structuralist" with "postmodern" and "theorist" with "practitioner," since he too has wrestled with this question and in doing so has helped the Zapatistas to navigate a path between the Charybdis of Marxist revolution on the one hand and the Scylla of Liberal reform on the other.⁶⁵

Finally with regard to power, there remains to be discussed the issue of resistance, another matter on which Marcos and Foucault display significant convergences, and one of particular significance for a rebel spokesperson and subcommander. Foucault's (1980, p. 142) fundamental stance on the issue of resistance is that "there are no relations of power without resistance,"⁶⁶ since "in power relations there is necessarily the possibility of resistance because if there was no possibility of resistance (of violent resistance, flight, deception, strategies capable of reversing the situation), there would be no power relations at all."⁶⁷ The Subcommander, for his part, has gone on record as stating that "the only virtue of Power is that, in the end, it inevitably produces a revolution against itself."⁶⁸

Furthermore, from Foucault's conceptualization of power as being a series of relations exercised in local situations, it naturally follows that resistance too will emerge to confront power at each site where power is trying to impose itself.⁶⁹ Hence Foucault (1977, p. 214) states: "Each struggle develops around a particular source of power (any of the countless, tiny sources—a small-time boss, the manager of H.L.M. [a housing project], a prison warden, a judge, a union representative, the editor-in-chief of a newspaper)." Again we find faint Foucauldian echoes to this effect made by Marcos, who explains:

> What exists is a global power that produces local dominations in different places …. In that sense we can say that it is a world war, not only in Chiapas, but in the streets, in the universities, the factories, in the fields of the

world. Where each one of us reproduces this battle, fights it, and wins it or loses it.⁷⁰

Moreover, in the same work, Foucault (1977, p. 216) elaborates on local points of resistance, detailing which groups typically wage these:

[I]f the fight is directed against power, then all those on whom power is exercised to their detriment, all who find it intolerable, can begin the struggle on their own terrain and on the basis of their proper activity (or passivity). In engaging in a struggle that concerns their own interests, whose objectives they clearly understand and whose methods only they can determine, they enter into a revolutionary process .... Women, prisoners, conscripted soldiers, hospital patients, and homosexuals have now begun a specific struggle against the particularised power, the constraints and controls, that are exerted over them.

Importantly, we can detect an echo of these statements in the Subcommander's discourse. For example, in a February 1998 communiqué, "An Inverted Periscope or Memory, A Buried Key," Marcos writes:

New forms of struggle are creating their own masks .... Little by little the honorable mask of resistance grows and multiplies .... Behind the same mask of anonymity, the indigenous, workers, campesinos, housewives, neighbors, unionists, students, teachers, Christians, retired persons, disabled persons, drivers, shopkeepers, activists from political and social organizations, women, youth, children and old persons, all those who discover each other day by day, who resist...⁷¹

So too, in the *Sixth Declaration of the Lacandon Jungle* (June 2005), the Subcommander explains that:

[T]he exploited of each country become discontented, and ... they rebel ... And that is why we see, all over the world, those who are being screwed over making resistances ... in other words, they rebel, and not just in one country but wherever they abound...

And it is not just the workers of the countryside and of the city who appear in this globalization of rebellion, but others also appear who are much persecuted and despised for the same reason, for not letting themselves be dominated, like women, young people, the indigenous, homosexuals, lesbians, transsexual persons, migrants and many other groups who exist all over the world...⁷²

Finally regarding resistance, Foucault's description of power relations, and resistance to them, as a "net" or "network,"[73] (as exemplified in his statement that "Just as the network of power relations ends by forming a dense web that passes through apparatuses and institutions, without being exactly localized in them, so too the swarm of points of resistance traverses social stratifications and individual unities"),[74] and his urging that "like power, resistance is multiple and can be integrated in global strategies,"[75] also find resonance in the Subcommander's discourse. Indeed, nowhere is this better demonstrated than in Marcos' words at the closing ceremony of the Zapatistas' First Intercontinental Encuentro for Humanity and Against Neoliberalism (August 3, 1996) and in the *Second Declaration of La Realidad for Humanity and Against Neoliberalism* that emerged from this meeting.[76] In the first of these, in which the Subcommander talks of the *encuentro* as representing "A world of all the worlds that rebel and resist Power," he urges that the meeting produce an echo, continuing

> Let it be an echo of our own smallness, of the local and particular, which reverberates in an echo of our own greatness, the intercontinental and galactic…
>
> Let it be a network of voices that resist the war the Power wages on them…
>
> A network of voices that not only speak, but also … that are born resisting, reproducing their resistance in other quiet and solitary voices.
>
> A network that covers the five continents and helps to resist the death that Power promises us…
>
> The multiplication of resistances—the "I am not resigned," the "I am a rebel"—continues…
>
> The human and rebel voice, consulted on the five continents in order to become a network of voices and resistance, continues…[77]

So too, in the *Second Declaration of La Realidad*, we find similarly Foucauldian articulations:

> [W]e will make a collective network of all our particular struggles and resistances, an intercontinental network of resistance against neoliberalism, an intercontinental network of resistance for humanity.
>
> This intercontinental network of resistance, recognizing differences and acknowledging similarities, will strive to find itself in other resistances around

the world. This intercontinental network of resistance will be the medium in which distinct resistances may support one another .... We are the network, all of us who resist...

We propose that this Intercontinental *Consulta* for Humanity and against Neoliberalism be realized on all five continents, during the first two weeks of December, 1996...

The Intercontinental *Consulta* is part of the resistance we are organizing and one way of making contacts and encounters with other resistances. Part of a new way of doing political work in the world—that is what the Intercontinental *Consulta* wants to be.[78]

Unsurprisingly, this emphasis on forming networks or webs of resistance on the part of Marcos, and through him the Zapatistas, has not gone unnoticed by commentators; hence, to cite but two examples, Ana Esther Ceceña (2004, p. 368) writes that "in *Zapatismo* ... [t]he revolution is conceived of as a process in which the networks of power are unraveled and deconstructed to permit the creation of resistance networks...," while Laura Carlsen (2007, p. 20) observes that "The zapatista movement proved the power of language to weave global webs of resistance at the same time that it rejected the language of power." Similarly, the Foucauldian notion, clearly shared by the Subcommander, that local resistances can be integrated in global strategies, is also something that observers have been keen to stress. Thus Gustavo Esteva and Madhu Suri Prakash (1998, p. 35) explain that: "Global forces, in their local incarnation, were challenged by the Zapatistas. Local initiatives spread that challenge around the globe, forging resistance against other local incarnations of those global forces, forcing the latter to take the first step back"; while Ulrich Brand and Joachim Hirsch (2004, p. 376) argue that "the *Zapatistas* are a good example of how local processes of learning and organizing can spread and stimulate further struggles in their own specific contexts. To this extent one could speak here in an exemplary fashion of *glocal* resistance."[79]

To conclude this subsection, statements such as those made by the Subcommander and reproduced above go a long way to support Iain Watson's (2002, p. 115) observation that "...the EZLN approaches the nature and meaning of political resistance and political power in ways that resemble the kind of political resistance envisaged by Michel Foucault."

C) Genealogy

Another of Foucault's major contributions to twentieth-century thought concerned what he called genealogy,[80] an approach he pursued and perfected in his two works *Discipline and Punish* and *The History of Sexuality*. Foucault (1980, p. 83) himself later provided "a provisional definition" of this "union of erudite knowledge and local memories which allows us to establish a historical knowledge of struggles and to make use of this knowledge tactically today," elaborating on this approach as follows:

> [I]n the case of the erudite as in that of the disqualified knowledges ... with what in fact were these buried, subjugated knowledges really concerned? They were concerned with a *historical knowledge of struggles*. In the specialised areas of erudition as in the disqualified, popular knowledge there lay the memory of hostile encounters which even up to this day have been confined to the margins of knowledge. What emerges out of this is something one might call a genealogy, or rather a multiplicity of genealogical researches, a painstaking rediscovery of struggles together with the rude memory of their conflicts. And these genealogies, that are the combined product of an erudite knowledge and a popular knowledge, were not possible and could not even have been attempted except on one condition, namely that the tyranny of globalising discourses with their hierarchy and all their privileges of a theoretical *avant-garde* was eliminated.

Crucially, this approach was not one of purely academic abstraction but rather one which, as several commentators have been keen to stress, could be put to highly practical use in aiding those who resist power. Indeed, Mark Philp (1985, p. 76) writes of genealogy that "It aims to unmask the operation of power in order to enable those who suffer from it to resist,"[81] adding that through it Foucault's

> support is lent to those who resist the subjugating effects of power: those who ... resist ethnic, social, religious, sexual or economic domination or exploitation; and those who resist the identities imposed upon them by others—as women have begun to resist their subjection to men ... and as sections of the population have resisted interferences in their lives and environment by central and local authorities. These struggles are immediate responses to local and specific situations .... Foucault's works are intended

as a stimulant to ... recalcitrance—they attempt to offer new spaces for the emergence of subjugated knowledge and for the organisation of resistance.

Similarly, Simon Choat (2010/2012, p. 107) in discussing "Foucault's historical work," by which he means that dealing with genealogy, declares that:

> [I]t is politically committed, acknowledging its own place in history and actively engaging in present struggles: it does this by demonstrating the fragility and contingency of existing customs and institutions and by "an insurrection of subjugated knowledges," a recovery of buried struggles and local memories against "the tyranny of globalising discourses" (Foucault, 1980, pp. 81 & 83).

Naturally, the relevance of such an approach to the subcommander and spokesperson of an indigenous movement that rose up against what it saw as 500 years of oppression to wage a "war against oblivion"[82] and declare its resistance to neoliberal globalization, is obvious. In fact, in a very real sense, we can witness in Marcos' discourse a determined effort to: resurrect "buried, subjugated knowledges"; promote "a historical knowledge of struggles"; jog "the memory of hostile encounters which even up to this day have been confined to the margins of knowledge"; and foster "a painstaking rediscovery of struggles together with the rude memory of their conflicts." For example, in his interview with Julio Scherer García (2001, p. 13), Marcos points out that "Mexico has had almost 200 years as an independent nation, and at every point in time the indigenous have appeared as the fundamental part, but at no time has any such thing been recognized." Interestingly, it is evident that prior to his embarking for Chiapas to begin a new life as a rural guerrilla, Marcos, and his fellow mestizo EZLN guerrilleros, had similarly failed to recognize the role played by Mexico's indigenous peoples throughout the nation's history. Having arrived in Chiapas with a certain amount of Marxist-Leninist baggage, it is evident from the Subcommander himself that it was only through sustained contact with indigenous communities that he and his urban, university-educated compañeros consequently underwent

> a process of cultural contamination, in the sense of seeing the world, one that obliged us to reconsider our politics and the way in which we viewed our own historical process and the historical process of the nation.[83]

Nicholas P. Higgins (2004, pp. 162-63), drawing largely on the Subcommander's own testimony, elaborates on this process:

> As they sat round the fire at night, the Indians' stories ... became ... the primary means through which the mestizos became aware of the cultural richness and otherness of the Indians of southeast Mexico...
>
> [U]nsettled by the seeming confusion of temporalities that littered the indigenous histories, the mestizos found it difficult to understand the legitimacy and respect with which such stories and the elders who told them were held. Slowly, however, they came to recognize that outside of the schoolroom and the university, this was how history worked.
>
> It was this experience of history, and the constant invocation of inherited oral history, that provided the basis upon which the language of Zapatismo was constructed. By listening to the Indians' own history of exploitation, of humiliation and racism, the Zapatistas found the keystones upon which to build a new politics. The local history revealed just how partial were non-Indian claims to a national history, and to a large extent the Zapatistas learned first-hand what it meant to be erased from the history books.

Here, an important question arises: If Higgins' account is accurate—and there is little reason to suspect otherwise—and Marcos' discourse relating to indigenous history owed its impetus to his protracted exposure to the indigenous campesinos who constituted his cadres and potential recruit base, is there any reason to posit a correlation between this element in the Subcommander's discourse and Foucault's genealogical approach? My own view is that, while I certainly do not believe that prior to, or even upon, his arrival in Chiapas Marcos made the mental connection between Foucault's genealogical approach and the clandestine and subversive oral history of the indigenous he hoped to recruit, it may well have been the case that the Subcommander's reading of Foucault years earlier, as the student Rafael Guillén, perhaps paved the way for, thereby facilitating, Marcos' subsequent assimilation of indigenous (approaches to) history—an accomplishment that sets him apart from so many of his Latin American left-wing guerrilla predecessors.

Moreover, it should be further noted that Marcos does not limit his exposing of subjugated historical knowledge of struggles to solely those derived from indigenous oral history. Rather, he resurrects other examples of those who have struggled to resist subjugation but who have similarly been excluded from history; in a communiqué written in response to the Mexican government's February 1995 attempt to discredit the EZLN by publicizing the fact that it had originated as a politico-military Leninist-Marxist guerrilla group called the FLN, the Subcommander wrote:

> To the name of the "Forces of National Liberation," the government should add as the antecedents of the EZLN those of all the guerrilla organisations of the 70s and 80s, Arturo Gamiz, Lucio Cabanas, Genaro Vazquez Rojas, Emiliano Zapata, Francisco Villa, Vicente Guerrero, Jose María Morelos y Pavón, Miguel Hidalgo y Costilla, Benito Juárez and many others whom they have already erased from the history books because a people with memory is a rebel people.[84]

Indeed, if, as Michael Payne (1997, pp. 17-18) urges, "genealogy turns to what history has despised or neglected … priz[ing] sentiments and instincts which have been neglected by history, but also significant absences and silences in the records of the past," then examination of Marcos' discourse spanning more than two decades reveals several key texts that display aspects or elements that are entirely in keeping with Foucault's "genealogical researches."

Surveying these texts in chronological order, we first encounter his essay, "A Storm and a Prophecy," which was written in 1992 but not made public until January 1994.[85] Jeff Conant (2010, p. 69), commenting on this essay, does well to point out that it represents "Marcos's first attempt to give the Zapatista uprising historical context," adding that "[t]his context has several dimensions," which Conant identifies as:

> the indigenous history of the region, a history characterized by uprisings and resistance, as native peoples sought to free themselves from colonial oppression … [t]he history of the Mexican Revolution and the Institutional Revolutionary Party (PRI) … whose trajectory toward political monopoly led ultimately to the marginalization, exclusion, and oppression of large segments of the Mexican population … [a]nd … the history of the outgrowth of corporate capitalism.

In the fourth and final section of this essay, headed "The Second Wind: the Wind from Below," Marcos first identifies indigenous Chiapanecans as "the product of the Annexation act of 1824 … of a long chain of … rebellions … [f]rom the time when cassocks and armor conquered this land."[86] He then continues:

> It has mistakenly been said that the Chiapas rebellion has no counterpart,

that it is outside the national experience. This is a lie. The exploited Chiapaneco's specialty is the same as that of exploited people from Durango, Veracruz, or the plateau of northern Mexico: to fight and to lose. If the voices of those who write history speak exclusively, it is because the voice of the oppressed does not speak ... not yet.[87]

The Subcommander adds that "There is no historic, national or region calendar that has documented each and every rebellion against this system that is imposed and maintained with blood and fire throughout the national territory. In Chiapas, this rebel voice is only heard when it shakes the world of the landowners and business people," before going on to list six recent acts of resistance by indigenous and peasant Chiapanecans.

Next comes the *First Declaration of the Lacandon Jungle*, which is the first text issued publicly by the Zapatistas and so the document through which the world gained its introduction to the movement.[88] From the outset this text both situates the Zapatistas within a historical context of resistance and demonstrates the movement's "historical knowledge of struggles":

> We are a product of five hundred years of struggle: first, led by insurgents against slavery during the War of Independence with Spain; then to avoid being absorbed by North American Imperialism; then to proclaim our constitution and expel the French empire from our soil; later when the people rebelled against Porfirio Díaz's dictatorship, which denied us the just application of the Reform Laws, and leaders like Villa and Zapata emerged, poor men just like us...

Walter D. Mignolo (2005, p. 14), after reproducing these lines, along with those that constitute the remainder of the Declaration's initial paragraph, argues that this text has significant historiographical implications:

> The declaration, then, outlines the direction of a project to rewrite the colonial history of modernity from the perspective of coloniality (instead of writing the history of coloniality from the perspective of modernity) .... Professional historians could argue that there is little historical rigor in this "pamphlet" and that what we need is serious and rigorous histories of how things "really" happened. Again, that argument assumes that the events carry in themselves their own truth and the job of the historian is to discover them. The problem is that "rigorous historiography" is more often than not complicitous with modernity ... the argument for disciplinary rigor turns

out to be a maneuver that perpetuates the myth of modernity as something separate from coloniality.

Moving forward through the corpus of Marcos' discourse, Enrique Krauze (2011, p. 442) observes that: "Since his [i.e. Marcos'] first communiqué from the Lacandon Jungle on January 2, 1994, his historical references had been constant: the comandantes are 'insurgents,' they are like Hildago and Morelos, the leaders of the independence movement and the country's founding fathers," while Valeria Wagner and Alejandro Moreira (2003, p. 209) note how:

> Subsequent communications show that the Zapatistas invoke their ancestors not simply to authorize their use of weapons but to redeem them from "their senseless deaths" and, more crucially, to bring them back "to die again but this time to live" (EZLN I, 90). To give the ancestors' deaths a sense is, of course, to recall them from oblivion and inscribe them in the history rewritten by the oppressed.

In addition, Kristine Vanden Berghe and Bart Maddens (2004, p. 141), in their analysis of the Subcommander's tales, observe that those which involve

> Marcos's rewriting of the Popol Vuh and the history of Zapata serve the same purpose: to rehabilitate the indigenous peoples in national history and historiography. Both rewritings advocate change, urging that the indigenous people be recognized as having played an important part in Mexican history.

Turning once again to specific communiqués, 1998 in particular witnessed the release of two that "establish a historical knowledge of struggles and … make use of this knowledge tactically today." The first appeared in February and was entitled "An Inverted Periscope or Memory, A Buried Key." In it the Subcommander writes of

> Mexican indigenous, those who first populated these lands, those who resisted the war of conquest, those who gave birth to the Nation fighting with Miguel Hidalgo, Jose María Morelos, Vicente Guerrero, those who fought against the gringos in 1847, those who fought by Juárez's side against the French invasion, those who gave flesh, blood and cries for justice in the revolution of Villa and Zapata, those who refused to be liquidated by a model, the neoliberal model, which makes a war of extermination against them through all means and in all forms.[89]

However, it is in Marcos' July communiqué, "Above and Below: Masks and Silences," that we encounter an articulation that best resonates with Foucault's genealogies:

> In order to supplant its lack of legitimacy with legality, the Mexican State (and not just the government) must carry out a complex surgical operation on the entire social order. That is, to eradicate the historical memory from the governed. And they try to do this by substituting the true history (in lower case), with the Official History (in upper case)...[90]

> As is evident, all attempts to "bring" the past into the present is subversion of the "peace and tranquility," it is illegal, ultimately something to be combated. There you have, for example, those Indians who "bring" Zapata to these times of modern globalization and they have him speak and make history . ... How well off we were with that Zapata in his grave, in the museum, in the book that was never opened! Therefore, those who "bring" Zapata are illegal and subversive, that Zapata is illegal and subversive because of the nightmares he provokes, and, ergo, history is illegal and subversive—not just because it questions today, but also because it makes one believe (and struggle for!) that another today is possible.[91]

Five years later, in 2003, the Subcommander released a series of communiqués comprising thirteen *stelai* which, given that each one was devoted to a particular month and state in the Mexican Union, lent the corpus the appearance of a calendar and road tour combined. Communiqué by communiqué the Subcommander related the indigenous peoples (and some of their myths) which pertained to each locale, preceded to give examples of prior injustices recently committed against local underdogs and the latters' struggles against these, and finally cited current instances of oppression and resistance to it. In doing so, Cornelia Graebner (2011, p. 5) observes, "Marcos has ... produced ... an alternative history of Mexico ... organized through steles ... referencing indigenous conceptions of history and adapting them to the contemporary situation." Moreover, in a communiqué entitled "The World: Seven Thoughts in May" (May, 2003) that dates from this period but which lies outside the *stelai* corpus, the Subcommander notes the implications of such a project: "A tour, even if it is merely expository, of the different resistances in a nation or on the planet, is not just an inventory. There one can divine, even more than the present, the future."[92] Significantly, the initial communiqué in the *stelai* corpus, entitled "Another Calendar: That of Resistance" and dated January 2003, contains several passages that express sentiments consistent with Foucault's formulations regarding genealogy.[93] For example, early on in the communiqué Marcos writes of

> the city of Oaxaca, the capital of this province which, like all of them in Mexico, only makes the news when it experiences the passing of hurricanes, earthquakes and false governors, or when oppressive poverty follows the path of armed rebellion.
>
> As if history only counts when it narrates the defeats, desperation and misery of those who are below, and it forgets the fundamental: resistance.

Later in the text the Subcommander continues

> Since ancient times, the governing elites have been fashioning calendars according to the political world, which is nothing but the world which excludes the majority. And the disparity between those calendars and those of lives below, is what provokes the earthquakes in which our history abounds.
>
> For every stele which the power sculpts in its palaces, another stele rises from below. And, if those stelai are not visible, it is because they are not made of stone, but of flesh, blood and bone, and, being the color of the earth...

Marcos then provides a litany of recent, local acts of oppression, and the resistance put up against these, among them the following example:

> One year later, in 2002, Governor Murat took a step towards realizing Salinas de Gortari's dream: the Monte Albán XXI project, privatizing ejidal lands in the areas surrounding the archeological complex and repressing those who were opposed to this commercialization of history. The resistance, however, was maintained, even though it was banished from the media.

Finally, toward the end of the stele we find the following:

> [T]hose below ... know that history is nothing more than a jigsaw puzzle which excludes them as primary actor, reserving for them only the role of victim.
>
> The piece which is missing in national history is the one which ... includes everyone in its true reach: the constant struggle between those who are attempting the end of times, and those who know that the last word will be

> built through resistance, sometimes in silence, far from the media and the centers of Power.
>
> Only in that way is it possible to understand that the current world is neither the best nor the only one possible, nor that other worlds are not merely possible, but, above all, that those new worlds are better and are necessary. As long as that does not happen, history will remain nothing but an anarchic collection of dates, places and different colored vanities.

In this way, Marcos adopts the kind of genealogical approach advocated by Foucault, laying bare "buried, subjugated knowledges" and reviving "local memories ... of hostile encounters..."

Finally, we arrive at *La Otra Campaña* of 2006. Although obviously not a discourse in and of itself but rather a tour lasting more than six months, the Other Campaign generated a great deal of discourse: more importantly however, by traversing the length and breadth of Mexico listening to those participating in frequently neglected local struggles and while doing so identifying common sites and sources of oppression, Marcos undertook what was, framed in Foucauldian terms, "a painstaking ... discovery of struggles," through his seeking out and engaging with "local," "disqualified, popular knowledge ... of hostile encounters" which were currently being "confined to the margins of knowledge." Indeed, as Patrick T. Hiller (2009, p. 274) points out:

> The Zapatistas represent individuals or groups who are systematically oppressed ... these individuals and groups share a similar fate of being excluded from the dominant societal discourse determining history and history-making. *La Otra Campaña* (the Other Campaign), initiated in 2006, is the Zapatistas' manifest attempt to unify struggles and visualize all these "invisible histories"[94] and give voice to the voiceless.[95]

Needless to say, much has been written on Marcos and the Zapatistas' emphasis on the indigenous peoples' role in Mexican history and the challenges mounted by Zapatismo to the State's exclusionary and self-justifying "official history."[96] And yet, in my research I have been unable to discover a single commentator who has explicitly associated specifically Marcos', or even more generally the Zapatistas', approach to history with Foucault's genealogical approach, despite the obvious parallels provided above. Jeff Conant, at least in the phrasing he employs, perhaps comes closest to doing so, writing:

> Marcos understands well the importance of creating an alternative discourse, of allowing a diversity of voices to speak .... It is this ... diversity of voices and visions, that is the real history, because it is the history of everyone at once...
>
> Once we accept the fact that the making of history, both in terms of enacting historical events and in terms of the recording, classifying, and subsequent restructuring of these events, is not the privileged activity of the dominant culture and its scholars, and has in it nothing of truth per se, we can look at the activities of Marcos as a historical mover, mythmaker, and rewriter of histories in a fresh context ... of one writer or speaker creating histories to defeat and derail and debunk others' histories.[97]

Nevertheless, despite Conant's (2010, p. 236) noting that Rafael Guillén began his thesis with the quotation from Foucault's "The Order of Discourse" that we discussed above (p. 164), and even reproducing this quotation, he draws no explicit connection between Marcos (or the Zapatistas) and Foucault concerning their approaches to history. His failure to do so is perhaps curious given that in addition to depicting Marcos' approach to history in terms reminiscent of Foucault, Conant makes a very important point concerning the Subcommander's penchant for utilizing specifically stories (as opposed to other forms of discourse) as a means of challenging the State's monopoly on national history. For after pointing out that given "history is not events that happened, but stories about events that might have happened or not," Conant (2010, pp. 57 & 58) urges that

> Marcos's fictions often come in the form of actual fables ... while the "official version" masks itself as historical fact. One of the hallmarks of totalitarian history is that it vigorously presents itself as the one truth, the one story, while the history of the "subaltern" ... is more like a collection of stories reflecting a diversity of voices...

Moreover, a few pages later Conant (2010, p. 62) adds:

> Indigenous history is fundamentally different from occidental history[98]; the difference between these two histories is largely the ground of struggle. The fables, jokes, anecdotes, epistles, diatribes and manifestos written by Subcomandante Marcos tell the story—one of the stories, some of the stories—of the place between these two histories...

Given the strong connection between the act of story-telling and genealogy, especially when the stories involved originate among those oppressed by power, Conant's above comments on Marcos' "fictions" and "stories" can be said to evoke the spirit of Foucault. It will be recalled, after all, that Foucault (1980, p. 193) famously stated that:

> [T]he problem of fiction ... seems to me to be a very important one. I am well aware that I have never written anything but fictions. I do not mean to say, however, that truth is therefore absent. It seems to me that the possibility exists for fiction to function in truth, for a fictional discourse to induce effects of truth, and for bringing it about that a true discourse engenders or "manufactures" something that does not as yet exist, that is, "fictions" it. One "fictions" history on the basis of a political reality that makes it true, one "fictions" a politics not yet in existence on the basis of a historical truth.[99]

Moreover, in the introduction to *The Order of Things*, Foucault (1966/2002, p. xvi) acknowledges that the book drew inspiration from Jorge Luis Borges' fictional story about a Chinese encyclopaedia,[100] the "Celestial Emporium of Benevolent Knowledge," that codifies the natural world:

> In the wonderment of this taxonomy, the thing we apprehend in one great leap, the thing that, by means of the fable, is demonstrated as the exotic charm of another system of thought, is the limitation of our own, the stark impossibility of thinking *that*.[101]

Significantly, Foucault has also been quoted as saying that *The Order of Things* was "a 'fiction' pure and simple; it's a novel, but I didn't make it up."[102]

In this connection, and all the while keeping Marcos in mind, it is worth noting the comments of two Foucault scholars regarding the French thinker's relation to fiction. The first, of obvious pertinence regarding the Subcommander of an armed movement of hitherto criminally neglected indigenous peoples, is Clare O' Farrell's (2005, p. 86) observation that "Foucault's works may indeed be described as fictions, but they are fictions which are generated ... with an aim of drawing attention to forgotten people and forgotten forms of knowledge or those otherwise deemed to be of no importance." The second concerns Mark Philp's (1985, p. 79) verdict that

> Foucault's philosophy is rooted in story-telling.... His histories, he says, are fictions which seek to forge connections, establish relationships and trans-

gress the established order and unity of discourse. His intention is to throw our assumptions and certainties into question...

Here too, the similarities between Foucault and the Subcommander are striking. That Marcos' philosophy too is grounded in story-telling can hardly be doubted.[103] For example, Cornelia Graebner (2011, p. 5) writes that "Through the combination of political critique with storytelling, and of scholarship with literary imagination, Marcos articulates a metaphorical reflection on knowledge, on its contingency in the context of its production, and on the ways in which it is conveyed."[104] Kristine Vanden Berghe (2005), who produced a book-length study of the Subcommander's *relatos* (stories), subsequently analyzed and plotted the changes and continuities taking place in Marcos' discourse from his early stories involving Old Antonio and Don Durito to his 2005 novel *Muertos incómodos (falta lo que falta)*, noting how the latter work articulates a pro-ecology, pro-democracy, anti-discriminatory (racial, gender and sexual orientation), anti-neoliberal globalization and anti-capitalist philosophy.[105] Finally, Conant (2010, p. 87) points out concerning Marcos' tale "The Story of the Questions" that: "The story illustrates the value of questioning, of cooperation and of duality, of a world made up of many worlds." Regarding the Subcommander's Foucauldian ability "to forge connections" and "establish relationships," Marcos' success in reaching out to, and forming bonds with, Mexican civil society, and beyond, is amply attested,[106] as is his penchant for transgressing "the established order and unity of discourse"—a tendency that has earned him the label of "first post-modern guerrilla."[107] Finally, we have witnessed in this subsection and in the preceding chapter on Althusser how the Subcommander has sought to "throw our assumptions and certainties into question" through his challenging and subverting conventionally held beliefs relating to Mexican history, modernity, *mestizaje*, the Mexican government being both the exclusive, legitimate heir of the Mexican Revolution and the upholder of the Rule of Law, and the desirability of neoliberal globalization.

Ultimately then, in light of the preceding pages, there is much to suggest that when, in a recent presentation, Marcos (2015) made mention of "the genealogy of Zapatista resistance. Its history, how it became what it is...," his choice of the word "genealogía" and the frame of reference underlying it may owe something to the continued influence of Foucault upon his thinking.

D) Grand Narratives

Finally, and obviously linked to the topic of genealogy discussed above, let us turn to discussion of the Subcommander's attitude toward grand narratives, a matter which, over the past decade, several commentators have drawn attention to. Foucault, it will be remembered, rejects grand narratives,[108] while Marcos, for his part, has been found on occasion to call them into question through his use of parody. For example, in Chapter Five, Section Four, entitled "la burla de los grandes relatos" ("mocking grand narratives"), of her book *Narrativa de la rebelión zapatista*, Kristine Vanden Berghe (2005, pp. 180-188), in examining the Subcommander's tales involving Old Antonio and Don Durito, writes that "The texts on Durito not only parody the narrative of post-revolutionary Mexican modernity but Marcos is also skeptical toward various 'grand narratives' that circulate on a broader scale in the so-called western world," before concluding that "Marcos' practice consists in parodying and undermining grand narratives."[109] Moreover, in this section of her work Vanden Berghe identifies a series of targets that Marcos takes satirical aim at, including: "the great stories of Mexican history…" (p. 182); "the essentialist and dogmatic way in which concepts relating to revolutionary ideology have sometimes been used" (p. 183)[110]; "the vanguards of the Left…" (p. 183); "…The petrified and solemn images of the guerrillas displayed as a vanguard" (p. 184); and "the myth of the guerrilla fighter" (p. 185). Elsewhere, Vanden Berghe had already noted how Marcos' "tales of *Don Durito de la Lacandona* … contribute to the deconstruction of the grand narrative of revolutionary nationalism as well as to the subversion of the grandiloquent use that has been made of the symbols derived from this narrative."[111]

Nor is Vanden Berghe a voice crying out in the desert. In his book-length study entitled *A Poetics of Resistance: The Revolutionary Public Relations of the Zapatista Insurgency*, Jeff Conant (2010, p. 326), also examining the Subcommander's tales involving Don Durito, similarly points out that

> the stories of Don Durito, by making a mockery of the Western canon, act to undermine grand narratives of History (like that, with a capital H) … the effort to dismantle grand narratives allows space for living history to emerge … Don Durito is an anti-hero, breaking down grand narratives and

fragmenting and fracturing and decomposing them (a job certainly fit for a beetle)...[112]

Moreover, when turning his attention to the specific Durito tale entitled "The Story of the Bay Horse," Conant (2010, p. 254) states that here "Marcos engages in one of his literary-political games, which is the calling into question of narrative itself, especially grand narratives." Conant (2010, p. 254), however, does not limit his discussion to Marcos' stories but also cites an example of the Subcommander's parodying of grand narratives from outside that genre:

> Marxism, one of modernity's grand historical narratives, and one that weighs especially heavy on the international left as it struggles to construct an emancipatory vision, received parodic treatment by Marcos at the Festival de la Digna Rabia in early 2009 when Marcos told a story of a woman quoting "Carla Marx." "I believe it's Carlos Marx," the Subcomandante told her, to which she replied, "That's only because it's always men who talk about these things."

As Conant (ibid) points out

> The joke makes the point that, for those who've been silenced for too long by dominating voices ... the effort to dismantle the grand narratives has a practical function beyond merely tearing at the fabric of the overdetermined world of modernity; it makes space for the stories, myths, and foundational beliefs of marginalized peoples. It makes way for living history.

Finally, and most recently, Daniela Di Piramo (2011, pp. 177-205) has devoted an entire article, entitled "Beyond Modernity: Irony, Fantasy, and the Challenge to Grand Narratives in Subcomandante Marcos's Tales," to addressing this issue. There, after noting how "Subcomandante Marcos challenges the necessity for a grand narrative and a mighty narrator" and that "he *attempts* to dismantle the grand narratives and thereby pave the way for individuals and civil societies to find their own voices,"[113] she sets about explaining why the Subcommander elects to do so and the tactics he employs. Concerning his motivation, after asking "why Marcos attempts to escape or move beyond modernity and grand narratives," she postulates:

> The answer to this question has important implications for political theory: master narratives inevitably become obstacles to political change or obstruct effective challenges to the status quo.[114]

A little later, elaborating:

> Marcos's political discourse … suggests that the particular might, one day, be able to conquer master narratives and that collective entities might master unbridled self-interest and isolating individualism … this position constitutes a substantial challenge to the tyranny of grand narratives and the historical elitism of political struggle.[115]

Regarding the Subcommander's tactics, Di Piramo (2011, p. 192) identifies "two mechanisms through which Marcos challenges the official political system and proposes something new":

> First, he employs irony as a form of wit to "disarm" the opposition and to undermine its credibility. Second, he uses a language of fantasy through which he proposes a different pathway to political life, one that attempts to make a definitive break with grand narratives and other defining features of modernity.[116]

In doing so, Di Piramo (2011, p. 197) notes, "Marcos is striving to offer an alternative to yet another grand narrative—the Mexican government's official version of history that constructs the mestizo as a vital aspect of the Mexican Revolution."

As can readily be seen from the above then, Marcos clearly shared with Foucault a postmodern skepticism toward grand narratives.

E) A Miscellany

I would like to end this chapter with a miscellany or mélange in which appear glimpses of derivation, or sometimes merely similarity, in the thinking, works and lives of Marcos and Foucault. In terms of derivation, we can detect traces of Foucault's influence on the Subcommander in the latter's *Letter to Adolfo Gilly* in which Marcos critiques an essay written by Carlo Ginzburg thus:

> For example, the author says that "relationships between the doctor and the patient … have not changed much since the times of Hippocrates." Relationships between doctor and patient? No! It's something more complicated: the institutional medical-body relationships and all those "scientific" concepts such as "normalcy."[117]

This final sentence is quintessential Foucault. First, it echoes the French thinker's preoccupations with human science, both in terms of its being rooted in non-rational origins[118] and its function as a disciplinary discourse of power. Foucault (1980, p. 84), one recalls, posited his genealogies in opposition "to the effects of the centralising powers which are linked to the institution and functioning of an organised scientific discourse within a society such as ours," adding that "it is really against the effects of the power of a discourse that is considered to be scientific that the genealogy must wage its struggle." He also described "the human sciences" as "discourse and practices that belong to the disciplinary realm."[119] Second, it reflects Foucault's focus on the role of institutions in defining what is normal/abnormal. Foucault (1980, pp. 61 & 62) describes his own studies thus:

> I have attempted to analyze how, at the initial stages of industrial societies, a particular punitive apparatus was set up together with a system for separating the normal and the abnormal .... The archaeology of the human sciences ... enables us to rediscover one of the conditions of the emergence of the human sciences: the great nineteenth-century effort in discipline and normalization...[120]
>
> Naturally it's medicine which has played the basic role .... It was in the name of medicine ... that people ... classified individuals as insane, criminal, or sick.

Turning away from derivation and toward similarities, I would urge that Foucault and Marcos combine within themselves the dual qualities of militant and intellectual, though in different measure. Foucault's credentials as an intellectual are glaringly evident, while several commentators have emphasized the actions and deeds that readily qualify him also as a militant,[121] with Didier Eribon (1989/1991, p. 210) even dubbing him "the militant intellectual." As for Marcos, his credentials as a militant (i.e. "A person who strongly espouses a cause, esp. one who is aggressively active in pursuing a political or social cause")[122] are impeccable, while I have argued elsewhere for his status as an intellectual,[123] and so the Subcommander, in my view, is deserving of the epithet "the intellectual militant."

This similarity, the embodying of the qualities of intellect and militancy that Foucault and Marcos shared, owes itself to the fact that these two men, like Althusser, are thinkers in the same vein, who, in the spirit (and adhering to the letter) of Marx, sought not merely to interpret the world but to change it. In the process of doing so, Marcos and Althusser (as we have seen), concerned themselves considerably with the relationship between theory and practice; so too, Foucault.[124] Indeed, the latter writes:

> A new mode of the "connection between theory and practice" has been established. Intellectuals have got used to working ... at the precise points where their own conditions of life or work situate them (housing, the hospital, the asylum, the laboratory, the university, family and sexual relations). This has undoubtedly given them a much more immediate and concrete awareness of struggles .... And ... I believe intellectuals have actually been drawn closer to the proletariat and the masses, for two reasons. Firstly, because it has been a question of real, material, everyday struggles, and secondly because they have often been confronted, albeit in a different form, by the same adversary as the proletariat, namely the multinational corporations, the judicial and police apparatuses, the property speculators, etc.[125]

(Important to recall, Marcos' "conditions of life" situated him in direct and daily contact with the "real, material, everyday struggles" of the indigenous peasants of Chiapas, in the course of which he "confronted ... the same adversary" as them: neoliberal globalization of capital, "the judiciary and police apparatuses," the local state and national government, local landowners and so on.) Elsewhere, Foucault (1969/1996, p. 55), in response to being asked to define his position "in regard to action and politics," felt the need to address the accusation that his (and others') highly theoretical studies were in antithesis to existentialism which fostered action and engagement:

> [T]he idea that to devote oneself as we are doing now to properly theoretical and speculative activities is to turn away from politics strikes me as completely false. It's not because we are turning away from politics that we are occupied with such strictly and meticulously defined theoretical problems, but rather because we realize that every form of political action can only be articulated in the strictest way with a rigorous theoretical reflection...
>
> ...the difference is not that we have separated politics from theory, but rather to the contrary ... we bring theory and politics more closely together...

There is, additionally, a further similarity, one somewhat related to the above, that the Subcommander and the French philosopher share, one that concerns both the rejecting of dominant social norms regarding homosexuality and the promotion of gay rights. Foucault, as is well-known, challenged mainstream society's view of homosexuality in his writings,[126] while he pushed for gay rights through his actions.[127] As for the Subcommander, in June 1999 he wrote a communiqué "To the Committee of Sexual Diversity; To the lesbian, gay, transsexual and bisexual community," in which he began by stating "We are grateful that you have allowed us the opportunity to say our word on this, the 21st March of Lesbian, Gay, Transsexual and Bisexual Pride, which has convened some of the best of sexual diversity in Mexico," before going on to express admiration, respect and solidarity with the movement, and declaring:

> For a very long time, homosexuals, lesbians, transsexuals and bisexuals have had to ... bear having their humanness reduced for the simple fact of not being in accord with a nonexistent sexual norm .... From all social sectors, from all corners of the country, from all workplaces, from studies, from struggles, from life: a human demand is raised: respect and recognition for the rights of the lesbian, gay, transsexual and bisexual community.[128]

By 2002 Cynthia Steele (2002, p. 248) was already writing that Marcos "increasingly includes discussions of feminist and gay struggles in his chronicles." However, this tendency would intensify in 2005 and 2006, first with the publication of the Subcommander's and Paco Ignacio Taibo II's joint novel, *Muertos incómodos* (*The Uncomfortable Dead* or *The Inconvenient Dead* in English), and then with the advent of the Other Campaign. The detective novel features as significant characters a transsexual called Margarita, a homosexual Filipino mechanic named Juli@, and a lesbian German motorbike pizza deliverer. Indeed, Kristine Vanden Berghe (2007), who compares and contrasts Marcos' earlier tales involving Old Antonio and Don Durito with the *Muertos incómodos*, detects a discernible shift from the subaltern being characterized according to their ethnicity in the stories, to their being distinguished based on the criteria of gender in the novel.[129] Less than six months later, the Zapatistas' *Sixth Declaration of the Lacandon Jungle* listed among those Mexicans who resist neoliberalism:

> [H]omosexuals, lesbians, transsexuals ... who do not put up with being ridiculed, despised, mistreated and even killed for having another way which is different, with being treated like they are abnormal or criminals, but who make their own organizations in order to defend their right to be different.[130]

Furthermore, *La Otra Campaña* launched in 2006 by the Zapatistas, and headed by Marcos, saw the Subcommander reach out to the LGBTQ community. As Mark Swier (2006) observes:

> On his "Other Campaign" ... Subcomandante Marcos regularly invites the participation of workers, farmers, indigenous peoples, women, youth and elders in constructing a national anti-capitalist campaign, "from below and to the left." But perhaps alone among nationally-recognized political leaders he adds gays and lesbians—what he frequently refers to as the community of "other loves"—to the list of people who fight for a new Mexico and who the Zapatistas seek to ally with in a larger struggle. He has been met along the campaign trail by a broad spectrum of the Lesbian, Gay, Bisexual, Transgender and Queer (LGBTQ) community...[131]

Indeed, on the evening of February 9, in the main plaza of the town of Oaxaca, when the Subcommander addressed a crowd of several thousand people (the author among them) who had come to hear him speak, he was accompanied on the bandstand by Leonardo Tlahui, who, Swiers (2006) tells us, is a "queer artist, writer and organizer who had been active throughout the planning process for the Other Campaign in Oaxaca City, and is one of the founders of the Nancy Cardenas Sexual Diversity Collective in Oaxaca." Tlahui had delivered a speech immediately before Marcos spoke in which he related a history of queer struggle and asked the Subcommander that "whenever he speaks of struggles that he be inclusive," adding admonishingly, "In this tour you have been on you have forgotten about us a little. Here we are, and we are also of rebel spirit."[132] When the Subcommander took-up the microphone, Swier's (2006) relates, "Marcos responded directly to Tlahui's message, affirming publicly a commitment to the continued struggle against homophobia and alongside movements for sexual and gender liberation..."

There remains, finally, a point of convergence between Marcos and Foucault, one which concerns politics and ethics, or perhaps rather, politics as ethics. In one interview, Foucault (1984, p. 375) declared: "in fact what interests me is much more morals than politics or, in any case, politics as an ethics." The Subcommander, for his part, has also given an interview in which he talked of

> The idea of a more just world, everything that was socialism in broad brushstrokes, but redirected, enriched with humanitarian elements, ethics, mor-

als, more than simply indigenous. Suddenly the revolution transformed itself into something essentially moral. Ethical.[133]

He has also been quoted as saying that

> it is hope which obliges ... [us] to seek new forms of struggle, new ways of being political, of doing politics. A new politics, a new political ethic is not just a wish, it is the only way to advance...[134]

Finally, in recent years the Subcommander engaged in a series of epistolary exchanges with Mexican philosopher Luis Villoro, one of whose many books was entitled *El poder y el valor. Fundamentos de una ética política*: the agreed theme under discussion was "Politics and Ethics," and in this correspondence, Marcos reflects, "theory, politics, and ethics are interwoven in ways that are not obvious."[135]

Notes

1. See above, p. 80. That this influence was not of a one-way nature, is shown by Montag (2003, p. 44), who points out that Althusser took the significant phrase *absences d'oeuvres* ("absence of works") "from the preface to the first edition of Foucault's *Madness and Civilization* (1961), a work that Althusser lectured on and of which he was particularly fond." Moreover, Althusser (1970/1997, p. 16, n.1) himself acknowledged the "debts which bind us to our masters in reading learned works, once Gaston Bachelard and Jean Cavaillès and now Georges Canguilhem and Michel Foucault."
2. He is quoted in Corro (1995, p. 26) as saying: "Althusserianism began to become attractive to the students. But there were others, such as Foucault .... Fundamentally, Marx, Foucault provided the way of thinking." That this was part of a continental trend can be seen from Norbert Lechner (1985, p. 62), who notes "the massive reception of Gramsci in the middle of the 70s, [and] of Foucault subsequently..."
3. NB Alan Sheridan (1980, p. 213): "*L'archéologie du savoir* reverses Foucault's usual practice: it is his only full-length book devoted primarily to theoretical and methodological problems—though even here, in the way it extends the concrete analysis of the previous book, it is not a matter of *pure* theory."
4. On orthodox Marxism's general reaction to Foucault, as well as more specifically the response of Lecourt, see Sheridan (1980, pp. 209-212 & 214-217 respectively).
5. See too the book's blurb, printed on the verso facing the title page, which states: "In this book converge philosophical paths that are shaped by epistolary ex-

changes and meetings with Louis Althusser, and discussions and courses at the Collège de France of Michel Foucault."
6. Earlier in his book, Galván (2010, p. 50) had commented that Crespo and Ramoneda Molins' "Foucauldian vocabulary was obviously intended to align Althusserian antihumanism, implicit in the scientific rereading of the [*Economic and Philosophic*] *Manuscripts* [*of 1844*] and *Capital*, with the archaeology of science and knowledge that involved the death of man in Foucault."
7. Rafael Guillén (1980, p. 8, n. 1).
8. On the Subcommander not being a doctrinaire Marxist or rigid in his thinking, see Nick Henck (2007, pp. 4-5, 67, 130, 134, 137, 161, 224, 231, & 361).
9. In Chomsky and Foucault (1971/2006, pp. 40-41).
10. I.e. his paper entitled "Nietzsche, Freud, Marx," and the following books: *The Order of Discourse* (also known as *The Discourse on Language*), *Discipline and Punish*, *The Order of Things*, *The Archaeology of Knowledge*, and *The History of Sexuality: Vol. 1, The Will to Knowledge*. Not included in his bibliography, but quoted from on Rafael's frontispiece and cited in the accompanying footnote, is a collection of works by Foucault, appearing under the title *Microfísica del poder*.
11. Translated in Foucault (1980, p. 90).
12. Translated in Foucault (1970/1972, p. 216).
13. Foucault (1969/1972, pp. 38 & 44, respectively).
14. Foucault (1970/1972, p. 227); emphasis added by Guillén.
15. See Guillén (1980, pp. 75, 76 & 77) who notes, echoing Foucault, the way in which schools produce normalized subjects.
16. Foucault (1970/1972, p. 216).
17. Foucault (1969/1972, p. 50).
18. Rafael Guillén (1980, pp. 109-110); emphasis in the original.
19. NB Cesáreo Morales' piece, entitled "Poder del discurso o discurso del poder," in (1975) *Historia y Sociedad* (segunda época) 8, pp. 38-48, appears in Rafael's bibliography, and the reader is also directed to it on p. 15, n. 1, of the thesis. Commenting on Morales' paper, Héctor Mario Cavallari (1994, p. 222, n. 3) writes: "Although primarily concerned with *Discipline and Punish*, Mr. Morales offers a very useful, informative review of Foucault's theorizations around the concept of power in its relation with discourse."
20. The remaining (i.e. eighth) quotation is from Foucault's Lecture of January 7, 1976; the Spanish version utilized by Rafael derives from *Microfísica del poder* (Genealogía del Poder No.1, 1979), (Madrid: Ediciones de la Piqueta), pp. 125-137, quotation at p. 135; an English translation can be found in Foucault (1980, pp. 78-92), quotation at p. 90.
21. NB Gilly provides Foucault's quotation, but employs the translation of Ian McLeod found in Robert Young (1981, pp. 52-53), instead of that of Sheridan Smith, which I employed above.

22. For this quotation, see above, p. 164; Rafael cites the source of this quotation as being the *Microfísica del poder*, which contains this lecture on pp. 125-137. This book is not listed in Rafael's bibliography however.
23. Printed in (2011, March 18) *Rebeldía 76*, 29-44, and retrieved from http://revistarebeldia.org/revistas/numero76/06carta_villoro.pdf; an English translation can be found at: http://www.elkilombo.org/letter-from-subcomandante-insurgente-marcos-to-luis-villoro-on-war/.
24. The full quotation reads: "This reversal of Clausewitz's assertion that war is politics continued by other means has a triple significance..." Foucault (1980, p. 90). Similarly, see too, Foucault (1976/1978, p. 93):
> Should we turn the expression around, then, and say that politics is war pursued by other means? If we still wish to maintain a separation between war and politics, perhaps we should postulate that this multiplicity of force relations can be coded ... either in the form of "war," or in the form of "politics"...

Interestingly, a sentence from the same paragraph in which Foucault reverses Clausewitz's assertion concerning war and politics is employed as one of two quotations from Foucault that form the frontispiece of Rafael Guillén's thesis.
25. See Foucault (1980, p. 280), where he poses the question: "Is civil society riven by class struggle to be seen as a war continued by other means?"
26. Interview dated November 16, 1998; translated into English and retrieved from http://flag.blackened.net/revolt/mexico/ezln/1998/inter_marcos_nov98.html.
27. In Vodovnik (2004, pp. 361, 406 & 461, respectively).
28. In Ponce de Leon (2001, p. 168) and Vodovnik (2004, p. 671), respectively.
29. Eugene Gogol (2014, pp. 58 & 79) notes that as early as February 1995 the following observation had been written by students on the walls of the UNAM: "The true arms of the Zapatistas is the pen of Marcos."
30. Vanden Berghe (2006, pp. 147 & 148) reproduces this statement almost verbatim.
31. Elsewhere Di Piramo (2010, pp. 124-125) has similarly commented that "Marcos' most effective prose ... is totally different to traditional political literature ... presenting serious political issues in a colourful and appealing manner that avoids the staidness of formal political rhetoric."
32. Meyer (1994, pp. 10 & 36) writes of the government's discourse thusly:
> In the politics of Mexican power, the dominant language serves for various things, but rarely for what it is assumed it should serve: in order to clearly express the ideas and feelings of those who use it. The language of the Mexican political class, especially of those in power, has been, almost since its beginning, a murky language which has multiple meanings and which conceals more than it uncovers. That political discourse is basically an instrument of disinformation, of systematic lies raised to an art form, whose central objective is the defense of illegitimate interests.

33. Similarly, Luis Hernández Navarro (2007, p. 103) comments that "If the troglodyte Left was accustomed to beginning each and every one of its public statements by announcing the crisis of the capitalist system and the irredeemably reactionary character of the Mexican State, then the Zapatistas' communiqués introduced irony and humour, recuperating the exemplary anecdote as a pedagogical instrument..." See too, Ann Carrigan (2001, p. 417), who writes that the Zapatistas' "pronouncements disclosed a dramatic break with the dogmas and romantic machismo of all previous Latin American Guerrillas..." Most recently, Cornelia Graebner (2011, p. 2) has written that the Zapatistas' "tone and language differed from the discourse previously employed by Mexican and Central American guerrilla groups: the EZLN preferred literary devices, storytelling, and indigenous mythology over an ideologically based discourse."
34. See Foucault (1976/1978, p. 101):
    [D]iscourse can be both an instrument and an effect of power, but also a hindrance, a stumbling-block, a point of resistance and a starting point for an opposing strategy. Discourse transmits and produces power; it reinforces it, but also undermines and exposes it, renders it fragile and makes it possible to thwart it...
35. See too, similarly, Foucault (1980, p. 98): "Power ... is never localized here or there, never appropriated as a commodity or piece of wealth."
36. Foucault (1976/1978, pp. 93-94). In fact, Foucault (1976/1978, pp. 93-96) contains an elaborate and fairly extensive treatise relating to power, power relations and resistance to power, and this will form the basis of much of what follows in our discussion of Marcos' attitude toward power and resistance.
37. Marcos' "Invitation to the Intercontinental Encounter for Humanity and Against Neoliberalism," in EZLN (1997, p. 258); the English translation here is retrieved from http://www.cacim.net/bareader/pages/Beyond%20Bamako5.html.
38. The text of the original, Spanish version of this speech can be found here: http://palabra.ezln.org.mx/comunicados/1996/1996_07_30.htm. An English translation is provided by Gustavo Esteva (2004, pp. 25-26); however, here I have preferred to provide my own.
39. Given this approximation, and James Martin's (2008a, p. 20) observation that the Greco-French Marxist's "...*State, Power, Socialism* ... demonstrated Poulantzas' ... interest in Foucault's 'anti-essentialist' conception of power," we can see that Foucault, Poulantzas, and Marcos converge to some extent in their conception of power. Cf., however, Resch (1992, pp. 257-58) and Jessop (2007, pp. 147-148) point out several important divergences between Foucault and Poulantzas concerning the relationship between power and the State.
40. This translation of the communiqué is retrieved from http://struggle.ws/mexico/ezln/ezln_epr_se96.html.
41. See Foucault (1976/1978, p. 94): "Power is not something that is acquired,

seized, or shared, something that one holds on to or allows to slip away; power is exercised from innumerable points, in the interplay of nonegalitarian and mobile relations."

42. Shannon Speed and Alvaro Reyes (2008, p. 304, n. 23). The two lectures to which they refer can be found in Foucault (1980, pp. 78-109).

43. In addition to the quotations above, see Marcos' comments in interviews with: Radio El Espectador de Uruguay (2001): "zapatismo is ... revolutionizing political power. And I am not referring to the taking of power, imposing its will by arms, but rather that the form of doing politics is what is changing fundamentally"; and Jesús Quintero (2007, p. 86): "The problem with being revolutionary is that the taking of power must be considered and one must think that things can be transformed from above. We do not think that: we think that society, and the world, should be transformed from below." (These translations are my own.)

44. See too, Marcos' communiqué of June 1995: "We just point out that a revolution which is imposed, without the support of the majority, eventually turns against itself," retrieved from http://flag.blackened.net/revolt/mexico/ezln/marcos_durito_state_jun95.html.

45. See too Marcos' parable concerning rebellion and chairs of power in Autonomedia (2005, p. 309), in which he contrasts the Revolutionary, who "throws off whomever is sitting on the chair [of power] with one shot, sits down and ... [t]here he remains until another Revolutionary ... comes by, throws him off and history ... repeats itself...," with "the rebel [who] runs into the Seat of Power..., looks at it carefully, analyzes it, but instead of sitting there he goes and gets a fingernail file and, with heroic patience, he begins sawing at the legs until they are so fragile that they break when someone sits down, which happens almost immediately."

46. In Noam Chomsky and Michel Foucault (1971/2006, p. 41).

47. The quotation is from Foucault's (1980, pp. 122-23) "Power and Truth," a piece Rafael Guillén would have encountered in his reading of *Micofísica del poder* (ch. 12, p. 175ff), a collection of Foucault's works from which he quotes in the frontispiece to his thesis. See too Foucault's (1980, pp. 60 & 61) piece "Body/Power," which again Guillén would have come across in his reading of *Micofísica del poder* (ch. 6, p. 103ff): "...nothing in society will be changed if the mechanisms of power that function outside, below and alongside the State apparatuses, on a much more minute and everyday level, are not also changed."

48. In addition to the two examples which follow, see too: Fernanda Navarro (1998, pp. 161-62):

> There is one key concept that stands out in the Zapatistas' thought: the reformulation of their conception of power.... What did they mean when they said "no" to the seizure of power? ... They mean a different way of relating to power.... In short, their conception of power is closer to the verb

than to the noun ... that is, a faculty, a strength that you conjugate in the plural, collectively, not that heavy weight of an unalterable noun: Power, imposing, appalling, domineering.

And Gustavo Esteva (1999, p. 173):

[T]he Zapatistas practice a political style that is not focused in seizing the State power .... Their struggles are oriented towards a civil society that becomes political, displacing the political question to another field, in which the most important is the very exercise of power.

49. Later in the same work Conant (2010, p. 231) similarly notes:

In its explicit rejection of the goal of state power, the Zapatista project carries with it a notion that there is, perhaps, another locus of power rarely taken into account either by the state or by the traditional leftist opposition. In reviving national symbols, rebirthing native beliefs, reinhabiting a narrative of history that includes a future as yet unwritten, and galvanizing civil society not at the voting booth but in the streets and schools and fields and factories and prisons, *Zapatismo* affirms that power—and especially the transformative power that guides the *realpolitik* of social change at the grassroots—lives not in the halls of government but in the fabric of culture.

50. See Foucault (1980, p. 198): "...In reality power means relations, a more-or-less organised, hierarchical, co-ordinated cluster of relations."

51. The full quotation reads:

It seems to me that power must be understood in the first instance as the multiplicity of force relations immanent in the sphere in which they operate and which constitute their own organization; as the process which, through ceaseless struggles and confrontations, transforms, strengthens, or reverses them; as the support which these force relations find in one another, thus forming a chain or a system, or on the contrary, the disjunctions and contradictions which isolate them from one another; and lastly, as the strategies in which they take effect, whose general design or institutional crystallization is embodied in the state apparatus, in the formulation of the law, in the various social hegemonies.

52. Foucault (1976/1978, p. 93).

53. Foucault (1980, p. 93): "relations of power cannot themselves be established, consolidated nor implemented without the production, accumulation, circulation and functioning of a discourse."

54. See Foucault (1976/1978, p. 86): "power is tolerable only on condition that it mask a substantial part of itself. Its success is proportional to its ability to hide its own mechanisms..." Foucault (1977, p. 209) employs the term "counter-discourse." Kara Zugman (2008, p. 352) writes that "The long-standing objective for the EZLN ... is to reconfigure power relations by delegitimizing the government..."

55. In Vodovnik (2004, p. 94).

56. In Vodovnik (2004, p. 163).
57. She is perhaps here recalling Marcos' own musings—in Vodovnik (2004, p. 217)—in his letter to Carlos Monsiváis entitled "Of Trees, Criminals, and Odontology," (September-November 1995):
    > Should political morality be defined always in relationship with the issue of power? Alright, but that is not the same as saying "in relationship to the taking of power." Perhaps, the new political morality is constructed in a new space which will not be the taking or retention of power, but the counterweight and opposition which contains and obliges the power to "rule by obeying," for example.
58. Khasnabish (ibid.) continues: "This refusal to claim a 'power over' and simultaneously the affirmation of a 'power to' create a world rooted in dignity, democracy, justice and liberty can thus be seen as embodying what Subcomandante Marcos means when he calls Zapatismo an 'intuition'."
59. Retrieved from http://alainet.org/active/6725&lang=es.
60. Marcos (2004) states: "one flaw which we have been dragging along with us for some time has to do with the place of women. The participation of women in the work of the organizational management is still small, and it is practically nonexistent in the autonomous councils and the JBGs"; and "The fact that the EZLN is a political-military and clandestine organization still corrupts processes that should and must be democratic."
61. In Autonomedia (1994, p. 291).
62. Poulantzas (1978/2014, p. 44). See Bob Jessop (2007, p. 142ff) for a nuanced treatment of the convergences and divergences between Foucault and Poulantzas on the matter of State power. In particular, points 1, 3 and 7 of what Jessop identifies as "eight main areas of theoretical convergence" (pp. 143-145) highlight their similarities connected to the State; conversely, pp. 147-148 emphasize their divergence: "Whereas Poulantzas devoted his life to a critique of the capitalist state, Foucault had an antipathy to state theory," and "In developing this analytics of power, Foucault rejected attempts to develop any general theory about state power..."
63. See Foucault (1980, p. 122):
    > I don't want to say that the State isn't important; what I want to say is that relations of power, and hence the analysis that must be made of them, necessarily extend beyond the limits of the State. In two senses: first of all because the State, for all the omnipotence of its apparatuses, is far from being able to occupy the whole field of actual power relations, and further because the State can only operate on the basis of other, already existing power relations. The State is superstructural in relation to a whole series of power networks that invest the body, sexuality, the family, kinship, knowledge, technology and so forth.
64. Day (ibid) continues: "The paradoxical belief that state domination is necessary

to achieve 'freedom' is perhaps *the* defining characteristic of the hegemony of hegemony, in both its marxist and liberal variants," with Day (2005, p. 8) having defined "hegemony of hegemony" as "the assumption that effective social change can only be achieved simultaneously and en masse, across an entire national or supranational space."

65. Likewise, Pablo González Casanova (2003/2005, p. 83) observes how the Zapatistas similarly shunned two other political-philosophical extremes:

> The [Zapatista] project, moreover, is not built on the logic of "state power" which entrapped previous revolutionary or reformist groups, leaving the main protagonist—be it the working class, the nation or the citizenry—bereft of autonomy. Nor is it built on the logic of creating a society without power—a logic which prevailed among anarchist and libertarian groups, surviving in such infelicitous expressions as "anti-power" (which even its authors do not understand)…

66. This quotation is from Foucault's "Power and Strategies," a piece Rafael Guillén would have encountered when reading the *Microfísica del Poder* (ch. 11, p. 163ff). See too, Foucault (1976/1978, p. 95), another work which we know Guillén read while a student: "Where there is power, there is resistance, and yet, or rather consequently, this resistance is never in a position of exteriority in relation to power…" Indeed, this page in *The History of Sexuality*, and the one that follows it, contains Foucault's most detailed exposition on the relationship between power and resistance, although, see too Foucault (1982, pp. 208-226).

67. Foucault (1984/1997, p. 292).

68. Quoted in Fernanda Navarro (1998, p. 161).

69. Foucault (1976/1978, p. 95) writes of "…a multiplicity of points of resistance … [which] are present everywhere in the power network. Hence there is … a plurality of resistances, each of them a special case…"

70. From an interview with Marcos that appears in the bonus material/feature section in the documentary DVD *Zapatista* (Big Noise Films: 1998).

71. In Vodovnik (2004, p. 333).

72. Retrieved from http://enlacezapatista.ezln.org.mx/sdsl-en/. Later on in the same Declaration, Marcos goes on to list those in Mexico who have resisted (including various indigenous peoples, campesinos, urban workers, students, women, youth, homosexuals, lesbians, transsexuals, priests, nuns, laypeople, and social activists), and specific nations (such as Cuba and Venezuela) and movements in Latin America (e.g. the Mapuche in Chile, the indigenous in Ecuador and Bolivia, the *piqueteros* in Argentina, the *sin tierra* in Brazil, and so on), as well as taking note of the resistance to neoliberalism that is taking place elsewhere on the globe, including in Europe, North America, Africa, Asia, and Oceania.

73. See, for example, Foucault (1980), where he states: "Power is employed and exercised through a net-like organisation," (p. 98); "power establishes a network

through which it freely circulates" (p. 99). He also talks of "the web of power" (p. 116), "a network ... of bio-power" (p. 186), and "networks of power" (p. 138). See too, Foucault (1976/1978, p. 95), where he writes of "the entire network of power that functions in a society," going on to state that "...points of resistance are present everywhere in the power network."

74. Foucault (1976/1978, p. 96). He continues: "And it is doubtless the strategic codification of these points of resistance that makes a revolution possible, somewhat similar to the way in which the state relies on the institutional integration of power relationships."

75. Foucault (1980, p. 142).

76. Whereas Marcos' closing remarks at the *Primer Intercontinental Encuentro* are clearly his own, technically the *Second Declaration of La Realidad* is signed by "The Indigenous Revolutionary Clandestine Committee⊠General Command of the Zapatista Army of National Liberation" (and not by the Subcommander), although I would urge that this document's style betrays Marcos' authorship. On Marcos being the author of the vast majority of EZLN communiqués, see: Kathleen Bruhn (1999, p. 30), Christopher Domínguez Michael (1999), and Cynthia Steele (2002, p. 248).

77. In Ponce de León (2001, pp. 113-114).

78. In Ponce de León (2001, pp. 117-118).

79. See too, Richard Gilman-Opalsky (2008, p. 299) who talks of "Zapatismo [being] very plug-in-able all over the globe to fight local struggles," and who produces a highly theorized discussion of this phenomenon (p. 263ff) within his chapter headed "The Zapatistas' Transgressive Public Sphere."

80. See John Foran (1997, p. 205):
    Pushing beyond the boundaries of French structuralism he pioneered ... a radically new way of writing history that attempted to unearth and map what he called the "genealogies" of how power intersects with discourse to produce institutions such as the modern prison, asylum, and hospital clinics or ways of thinking about sexuality, academic disciplines, and other discursive formations.
    See Foucault (1980, p. 85), where he describes genealogy as "the tactics whereby, on the basis of the descriptions of these local discursivities, the subjected knowledges which were thus released would be brought into play."

81. Similarly, see Alan Sheridan (1980, p. 221): "The Foucauldian genealogy is an unmasking of power for the use of those who suffer it. It is also directed against those who would seize power in their name."

82. Marcos—in Juliana Ponce de León (2001, p. 86)—employs this phrase in his January 1996 "Closing Words to the National Indigenous Forum." See too, Marcos' communiqué—in Vodovnik (2004, p. 284)—on "The table at San Andrés" (March 1998), where he talks of "a struggle between oblivion against memory," in which "On the side of oblivion are the multiple forces of the Mar-

ket," and "On the side of memory is the solitary reason of History."
83. In Adolfo Gilly (1995, p. 138); quoted and translated in Nicholas P. Higgins (2004, p. 162).
84. In *La Jornada*, February 13, 1995; quoted and translated in John Holloway (1998, p. 190, n. 10).
85. This essay can be found translated in Ponce de León (2001, pp. 23-37).
86. In Ponce de León (2001, p. 33).
87. Ibid. See too Marcos' July 1999 communiqué entitled "The Democratic Teachers and the Zapatista Dream," in Ponce de León (2001, pp. 275-76), where the Subcommander talks about "true history" and how "if it does not appear in the primary school textbooks, that is because history is still being written by those above, even though it is made by those below."
88. This Declaration can be found translated in Ponce de León (2001, pp. 13-16) and Vodovnik (2004, pp. 643-45).
89. In Vodovnik (2004, p. 328).
90. In Vodovnik (2004, pp. 321-22). Marcos adds: "And this Official History is not learned in books, rather it was created in the mental laboratories of postgraduates in foreign universities. Harvard, Oxford, Yale, and the MIT are the modern 'Founding Fathers' of the current Mexican leaders."
91. In Vodovnik (2004, pp. 323-24). See Lynn Stephen (1997, p. 43): "All the discourses on Zapata and the Mexican Revolution—state, local, and Zapatista—draw on what [Raymond] Williams calls 'selective tradition': 'an intentionally selective version of a shaping past and pre-shaped present…' (1994, p. 601)." Stephen (ibid) adds: "Each discourse seeks to capture the past and connect it to a particular version of the present."
92. Marcos continues, "rewriting (and erasing) national history … the last Mexican governments have managed, through various means, to make this country less and less ours, and less and less a country."
93. This communiqué is retrieved from http://flag.blackened.net/revolt/mexico/ezln/2003/marcos/resistance1.html.
94. The phrase is from J. P. Linstroth (2005). Hiller (p. 273) elaborates on the nature of "invisible histories," quoting from Linstroth:
> Here I want to refer to Linstroth's (2005) notion of "invisible histories" that are "not histories about élites and biographies of the well-to-do but those which emphasize collective discord and collective suffering, individual histories of non-famous peoples, histories of the weak, histories of the voiceless, histories of the developing world and the fourth world, those social and political histories which are the undercurrents of our times" (Linstroth, 2005, p. 14).
95. On the preceding page, Hiller (2009, p. 273) wrote similarly that "the Zapatistas do not only provide a different interpretation of history but … are actively and consciously participating in the task of an alternative-history making …

The Zapatistas achieved to make invisible histories visible to a global audience."

96. E.g., limiting myself solely to the inclusion of instances dating from the last ten years (i.e. 2004-2014), see: Ana Esther Ceceña (2004, p. 363) on how "In *Zapatismo*, the recovery and recreation of history, as a sphere of resistance, becomes crucially important…"; Mihalis Mentinis (2006, pp. 126-27) on the Zapatista strategy "to appropriate … combative national history from its deployment and manipulation by the Mexican state … [and] … to incorporate the excluded indigenous populations within Mexican history as well as to expropriate the Mexican state's privileged use of nation and its symbols"; Josh Bahn (2009, pp. 541 & 557) on Zapatismo "constitut[ing] an alternative philosophy of history that is articulated to political practice, an alternative way of locating ourselves in time and space," and his conclusion (557) that for the Zapatistas "history is an ongoing process of articulating 'the screwed' to the political present"; Patrick T. Hiller (2009, p. 268) on how "The Zapatistas use their interpretation of history to contest dominant state ideologies," concluding (p. 275) that "Based on the discussion of the emerged reinterpretation of indigenous history … the Zapatista movement can be considered the embodiment of a new form of Mexican historiography…"; and Kara Zugman Dellacioppa (2009, pp. 38 & 168) on the Zapatistas' "awakening of historical memory." It is undoubtedly Jeff Conant (2010, pp. 27-28, 57-58, 60, 67, 111 & 232), however, who in recent years has had most to say on the Zapatistas' approach to history.

97. In the final section of his book Conant (2010, pp. 315-316) concludes that: "Marcos's hybrid insurgent narrative, aims to change the common interpretation of history, and to reveal undetected patterns of internal colonialism, in order to once and for all undermine the imperial and arbitrary basis of state authority."

98. Conant (2010, p. 114) similarly notes how: "the Zapatistas define their movement as a … redefinition of the relation of indigenous history to occidental history."

99. See David Macey (1993, p. 480), who quotes Foucault as saying that "…in my books I do like to make fictional use of the materials I assemble or put together, and I deliberately make fictional constructions with authentic elements."

100. Foucault writes:
    This book first arose out of a passage in Borges, out of the laughter that shattered, as I read the passage, all the familiar landmarks of thought— *our* thought, the thought that bears the stamp of our age and our geography—breaking up all the ordered surfaces and all the planes with which we are accustomed to tame the wild profusion of existing things and continuing long afterwards to disturb and threaten with collapse our age-old definitions between the Same and the Other.

101. It is interesting to note that in his communiqués Marcos quotes from various of Borges' stories. On this, and the Subcommander's attitude toward the Argen-

tine author, see Kristine Vanden Berghe (2005, p. 174).
102. In David Macey (1993, p. 480).
103. An important point needs emphasizing however in this connection. No doubt some, noting the importance that storytelling plays among many indigenous peoples, would attribute Marcos' use of this medium to his immersion in indigenous society and culture. Such a scenario is, of course, entirely plausible. All I would say in response is that we need not assume an "either/or" equation here: the reality, as is so often the case, may be significantly more nuanced. It is possible, for example, that the Subcommander's encountering of an indigenous storytelling tradition reinforced in his mind the importance and utility of a practice which he had first come across in Foucault: in short, its resonance with what he had encountered in Foucault may have made the indigenous practice of using stories as a vehicle for conveying their thought appear less alien and therefore easier to accept, adopt, and deploy himself.
104. Graebner (2011, pp. 3-5) then provides an extremely useful, succinct survey of the various categories of Marcos' stories—those involving Old Antonio, others featuring the beetle Don Durito, still more depicting interactions with and among children from the indigenous community of Guadalupe Tepeyac—as well as his co-authored novel *Muertos incómodos* (*The Uncomfortable Dead*), and the political-philosophical, epistemological, and ethical themes they treat.
105. In Vanden Berghe (2007).
106. For the Zapatistas' reaching out to civil society, see Ana Carrigan (1998), Ana Esther Ceceña (2001), Chris Gilbreth and Gerardo Otero (2001), María Elena Martínez-Torres (2001), Gideon Baker (2003), Josée Johnston (2003), and Nick Henck (2007); for discussion of Zapatismo's international reach, see Thomas Olesen (2005) and Alex Khasnabish (2008).
107. The label is that of Tim Golden (1994). See too, Manuel Vázquez Montalbán (2000, p. 209), who has extolled the Subcommander as "a master in the postmodern literary game of utilizing *collage*s and the intertextuality of two literary cultures, the indigenous and the Latin American." On Marcos' writings comprising a sort of postmodern pastiche, see Jeff Conant (2010, p. 33):

> [W]e find in Marcos' communiqués ... a literature that escapes the bounds of literature ... they are a hybrid form: neither poetry nor testimony, neither fiction nor nonfiction, neither essay nor journalism, they are an apparently unceasing cascade of "*relatos*," meaning stories, "*cuentos*," meaning fables, "*cronicas*," meaning reportage, and "*communicados*," meaning, in the military language of the guerrilla, communiqués, but in a more literal sense simply meaning "communications."

Conant (2010, p. 250) later adds: "Considered as literature, the communiqués do not fit any clear genre ... the writing is a hybrid of forms that places it squarely outside all literary canons." Vanden Berghe (2005, pp. 163-168 & 188-193) surveys the arguments in the debate over the extent to which the

Zapatistas can be accurately labelled "postmodern."
108. See Gary Gutting (2005, p. 46): "Foucault was sceptical of grand teleological narratives…" See too, Gutting (2011, p. 99) where he writes of Foucault's "fear of slipping into … 'grand narratives'" and his "delineat[ing] a topology of the *historical ground* that leaves no room for Hegelian, Marxist, or other unifying grand narratives." Similarly, Mark Philp (1985, p. 68), Thomas Flynn (2003, p. 44), and Jana Sawicki (1991, pp. 51-53) all note Foucault's rejection of grand theories.
109. Vanden Berghe (2005, pp. 182-83 & 184, respectively). See too p. 190, where she writes of Marcos' "subversive parodying of grand narratives … in his texts involving Durito."
110. See too, Adam David Morton (2000, p. 267), who writes that "the [Zapatista] rebels … defy grand-theorized strategies of revolutionary thought…"
111. Kristine Vanden Berghe and Bart Maddens (2004, p. 140).
112. Conant (ibid) continues, extending his discussion to the Durito tales in general:
[B]y pushing "revolution" with a small "r," by directing timeless "mythic" stories of the time-before-time to six-year-olds with corncob dolls, and by alternating such stories with tales of chocolate bunny rabbits and cat-and-mouse cartoons, the communiqués serve to undermine the kind of totalizing theories of history known to sociology as "metanarratives."
113. Di Piramo (2011, pp. 177 & 183, respectively).
114. Di Piramo (2011, p. 182).
115. Di Piramo (2011, p. 184).
116. Note the interesting observation of Fred Halliday (2003, p. 303) who, discussing "the fundamental case for revolution, from 1789 to 1989…," points out that "Revolution fulfilled, rather than opposed, the economic, social, and political project of modernity," whereas, in contrast, "Today this is, in many ways, contested. Modernity itself as a goal, and as a grand historical narrative, is in question."
117. Interestingly, Marcos immediately continues:
Examples? AIDS, wasn't it a curiosity while it was limited to affecting homosexuals? Didn't the "real" concern about AIDS start when it began affecting heterosexuals? Didn't interest increase when it began "striking" distinguished persons?
One cannot help wondering here, given that these sentences follow on immediately from such an obviously Foucauldian formulation, whether the Subcommander, either consciously or at the subconscious level, did not have Foucault in mind when he wrote the phrase "distinguished persons."
118. John Sturrock (1979, p. 98) notes:
The Order of Things is about the use and abuse of the "authority" of the "human sciences." In it Foucault wishes to show that the disciplines which deal with man as a social and cultural being are as little "scientific" as those

conceptions of the "body" which have successively informed medical practice from the sixteenth century to our own day.

See too, Alan Sheridan (1980, p. 138), writing on the position adopted by Foucault in *Discipline and Punish*:

The provenance, the *Herkunft*, of the human sciences is not a pure, disinterested search for knowledge, the fruits of which were then passed on in the "humanization" of "carceral" institutions. It is rather that those "sciences" have a common origin with those institutions. The forms of power at work in such institutions and, increasingly, in society at large are imbued with social and psychological knowledge, but, equally, those forms of knowledge are permeated by power relations.

119. Foucault (1980, p. 108).
120. See too p. 107, where Foucault notes "the procedures of normalisation" and "disciplinary normalisations" which characterize contemporary society as a "*society of normalisation.*"
121. See, for example, David Macey (1993, pp. 290-322), who, in a chapter entitled "the professor militant," devotes over thirty pages to discussion of Foucault's militancy. See too, Michael Payne (1997, p. 15):

Foucault was an active, eager, and inspiring model of the engaged intellectual, often literally putting his body at risk for those who were mentally and physically ill and for those imprisoned for crimes or for challenging the power of the state…

As James Miller (1993/2000, p. 438, n. 3) points out: "'Militant and professor at the Collège de France' is the by-line Foucault used for his first articles in *Libéracion*…" Claude Mauriac (1976) provides numerous instances of Foucault's militancy. Finally, and most recently, Clare O' Farrell (2005, p. 116) has noted "Foucault's extensive militant activity in support of various oppressed and marginal groups after 1970…"

122. Militant. (2014, December.) In *Oxford English Dictionary Online*. Oxford University Press.
123. See: Nick Henck (2011, p. 332), where I note others who have deemed the Subcommander to be an intellectual; Henck (2012, pp. 64-67), where I do the same and argue myself that Marcos constitutes an intellectual; and Henck (2013, pp. 429, fn. 3 & 446), where I discuss those scholars who view Marcos as an organic intellectual.
124. See Foucault (1977, p. 208): "theory does not express, translate, or serve to apply practice: it is practice." NB however, Foucault's (1977, p. 231) interview entitled "Revolutionary Action: 'Until Now'," in which he advocates that we should "reject theory …. This need for theory is still part of the system we reject." Hubert L. Dreyfus and Paul Rabinow (1982, pp. 102-103) chart Foucault's transition from prioritizing theory over practice in his earlier works, in which "the practices and the practitioners' theories of the human sciences were

subordinated to a theoretical structure which governed them" and "on the side of Foucault's methodology we find a similar favouring of theory over practice," to "Foucault's later works [in which] practice, on all levels, is considered more fundamental than theory."

125. Foucault (1980, p. 126).
126. See Foucault (1976/1978, p. 43) for the then radical view that homosexuality was a relatively modern socially constructed category.
127. On his activism, James Miller (1993/2000, p. 258) quotes Jean Le Bitoux, whom Foucault helped in setting up the gay magazine *Gai pied*, as asserting that Foucault fought "for gay rights." See too, the *Stanford Encyclopedia of Philosophy* entry on Michel Foucault: "He … often protested on behalf of homosexuals and other marginalized groups"; retrieved from http://plato.stanford.edu/entries/foucault/.
128. Retrieved from http://struggle.ws/mexico/ezln/1999/marcos_pride_june.html.
129. See, especially, Vanden Berghe (2007, pp. 398-401 & 406).
130. Retrieved from http://enlacezapatista.ezln.org.mx/sdsl-en/ and http://www.edinchiapas.org.uk/book/export/html/28.
131. Swier (2006) further notes that:
   In the invitation to take part in the Zapatistas' new Other Campaign, in the plenary meetings this past Fall 2005, and subsequently as the campaign has gotten underway, the visibility and participation of gays, lesbians and "other loves" has been noticeable. This has been significant not only because the historic sectors of revolutionary movements in Mexico (workers, students and campesinos) have excluded or ignored queer liberation politics, but also because beyond lip service, there hasn't been an opportunity previously to build connection and dialogue in such a way…
132. This quotation, and the one which follows, are to be found in Swiers (2006) who quotes from and translates a brief section of Tlahui's and Marcos' speeches.
133. In Yvon Le Bot (1997a, pp. 145-146).
134. Quoted and translated in John Holloway and Eloína Peláez (1998, p. 15).
135. In Marcos' Third Letter to Luis Villoro, retrieved from http://www.elkilombo.org/third-letter-to-don-luis-villoro-in-the-interchange-on-ethics-and-politics/.

5

Dogs Not Barking: Gramsci (and Others)[1]

There remains a final observation worthy of note regarding specifically Marcos' Marxist formation, and this concerns "dogs not barking" (as Arthur Conan Doyle put it); or, in other words, the absence of Marxist authors whom one might reasonably have expected to find in Rafael Guillén's thesis and Subcomandante Marcos' discourse. Concerning Guillén's thesis, Félix Hoyo (1995, p. 33) makes the following pertinent observation:

> A first inspection of the text's bibliography yields surprising results. We do not encounter the most lucid, sharp and penetrating Marxist authors … Antonio Gramsci, Herbert Marcuse, Ernst Bloch, Jean Paul Sartre and George Lukács are some of the great ignored.

Perhaps these results appear less surprising when one considers that all of the above belong to the tradition of Marxist Humanism, and when one knows that conversely, Althusser and Foucault, upon whose works Guillén's thesis was so heavily dependent, can reasonably be categorized as anti-Humanists.

Turning to the Subcommander's discourse, once again Gramsci and other Marxist luminaries are conspicuous by their absence. Indeed, Marcos' communiqués are notably free from references to such Marxist (or neo-Marxist) thinkers as Adorno, Badiou, Balibar, Fanon, Gramsci, Horkheimer, Mao, Marcuse, Negri, and Trotsky. (To provide some context, however, it should be pointed out that references to a great many eminent twentieth-century philosophers and political theorists are also not to be found in the pages of Marcos' missives, including: Baudrillard, Bourdieu, Chomsky (by some indices the most cited person alive[2]), Deleuze, Derrida, Guattari, Habermas, Hardt, Heidegger, Lacan, Laclau, Lévi-Strauss, Mouffe, and Pêcheux. Even the name of Foucault, one of the twentieth century's leading intellectual luminaries, only appears twice in all of Marcos' several hundred communiqués, and one of these is in a citation of Umberto Eco's novel *Foucault's Pendulum*, and so has nothing to do with the French philosopher.) Moreover, leaving aside his communiqués and instead focusing on statements made by Marcos in interviews, references to Marx, to subsequent Marxist philosophers such as Althusser, Gramsci or Poulantzas—or, in fact, any figures pertaining to the so-called "New Left"—or to more recent left-wing political philosophers such as Ernesto Laclau, Antonio Negri, or Michael Hardt, prove especially conspicuous by their absence. Finally in this context, I would re-emphasize the strikingly few Marxist texts, especially relative to the abundance of works of a literary nature, that were unearthed in the Subcommander's personal library when his camp was discovered during the Mexican military's February 1995 offensive.

In the pages that follow I will focus on the specific case of the curious incidence of Gramsci's absence in both Guillén's thesis and the Subcommander's discourse: I do so since the Italian Marxist's influence on the Latin American left was far-reaching and profound during the period that saw Rafael write his thesis and graduate from being a student to becoming a guerrilla, and also because several commentators have urged that the Zapatista movement in general, and even Marcos in particular, has been influenced by the Sardinian. Given this then, such an absence merits an attempt at explanation.

The Zapatista movement as a whole has on occasion come to be viewed through a Gramscian lens.[3] Furthermore, several scholars have proposed that the movement drew inspiration from, or was at least influenced by, Antonio Gramsci.[4] A handful of scholars have even seen in the Zapatistas' military leader and spokesperson, Subcomandante Marcos, an "organic intellectual" in the Gramscian mold.[5] Two scholars, however, stand out for their explicit assertions concerning Marcos' alleged exposure to the Italian Marxist. First, Kathleen Bruhn (1999, pp. 43–44) states that "Marcos sounds quite Gramscian…," adding "While Marcos has never declared himself a Gramscian, it is impossible to believe he has had no exposure to Gramsci …. An urban leftist intellectual educated during precisely these years, as a man of Marcos' age must have been, could hardly have failed to absorb this legacy." Second, and going one step further, José Rabasa (1997, p. 424) tentatively proposes that Marcos was not only acquainted with Gramsci's works but also, in fact, reacted against certain elements he found in them, stating: "In the case of Marcos ... there is a likelihood that he has read Gramsci and, perhaps, elaborated a critique of Gramsci's blindness toward the folkloric." Bruhn's and Rabasa's claims are interesting ones that merit testing against the available evidence.

Certainly the notion that Marcos encountered, and was influenced by, Gramsci is, *prima facie,* credible since one cannot ignore the existence of numerous works that detail the extent of Gramsci's diffusion in Latin America (more about this later). Caution must be exercised, however, when confronted with plausible, but technically circumstantial, evidence that appears to confirm a commonsense supposition. One must take the time to sift for compelling proof: It will not suffice simply to state, as Bruhn does, that "it is impossible to believe he has had no exposure to Gramsci ... Marcos ... could hardly have failed to absorb this legacy." Thus, closer inspection of the Subcommander's discourse throughout his life to date is perhaps the surest way to determine if Marcos has been in any way influenced by Gramsci.

A) Student Writings

Let us begin chronologically by looking at Marcos' writings before he became Subcommander and, in particular, at his award-winning graduation thesis submitted to the UNAM's *Facultad de Filosofía y Letras* in October 1980. The thesis does not contain a single reference to Gramsci or his writings throughout, nor is Gramsci listed in the bibliography. In fact, the sole sign that Rafael Guillén may have encountered Gramsci's thought is a bibliographic entry listing Angelo Broccoli's *Antonio Gramsci y la educación como hegemonía,* and notably this work is neither cited, nor quoted from, in the thesis' main text. (This is perplexing since Broccoli's book contains sections and chapters which discuss themes that appear to be directly relevant to Guillén's thesis which, entitled *Filosofía y educación: prácticas discursivas y prácticas ideológicas,* was concerned with education and ideology.) Significantly, however, another of Broccoli's works, *Ideología y educación,* which is also listed in Guillén's bibliography, is twice quoted in the thesis (pp. 26 and 90), with both quotations deriving from the book's first chapter, headed "Ideología y educación en el pensamiento moderno," which contains a very brief discussion of Gramsci (at pp. 35 and 46). In addition, *Ideología y ed-*

ucación's fourth chapter (pp. 139–193), bearing the heading "Filosofía de la praxis y educación" and, therefore, of obvious relevance to Guillén's thesis, has a lengthy section (pp. 159–193) devoted entirely to Gramsci.

Hence, although Guillén undoubtedly encountered the Italian Marxist, and was exposed to some of his ideas in and through Broccoli's books, he nonetheless failed to make any reference to Gramsci in his thesis and, indeed, the latter work bears not the slightest trace of any Gramscian influence.[6] (For example, absent are any of Gramsci's key concepts, such as "civil society," "historic bloc," "war of position," "war of maneuver," and "the modern prince.") True, Guillén's thesis twice (in 121 pages) employs the word *hegemony*, which is typically associated with Gramsci; however, his use of this term need not be attributed to Gramscian derivation. For one thing, Raúl Burgos notes how "The non-Gramscian use of the concept, viewing 'hegemony' simply as 'domination,' was common in the 1970s" (2002, p. 27).[7] For another, two authors to whom Guillén's thesis was heavily indebted, Louis Althusser and Nicos Poulantzas, employed the word *hegemony* in works that Guillén either quoted from or at least cited: hence, derivation in this case may be more convincingly attributed to Althusser and/or Poulantzas rather than to Gramsci. In fact, in this instance, I believe we can pinpoint the derivation to Poulantzas given that both sentences in which "hegemony" occurs in Guillén's thesis exhibit a Poulantzian "feel," containing reference to one of the Greco-French Marxist's core concepts, "class fractions."[8] Moreover, Poulantzas' 1977 *Poder político y clase sociales en el estado capitalista*, which is listed in the thesis' bibliography and to which Guillén directs his reader on page 36, note 1, has a subsection (iii) headed "Sobre el concepto de hegemonía" (pp. 169–175) in which Gramsci's use of the term is discussed.

Guillén's silence on Gramsci is, in fact, quite deafening when one considers that the central theme of his thesis, education, was an issue to which the Sardinian Marxist devoted considerable attention.[9] Of even greater relevance is a statement that appears much later on in Gramsci's (1971, p. 258) *Prison Notebooks* and that seems to have provided Althusser with inspiration concerning his theory of Ideological and Repressive State Apparatuses, on which Guillén's thesis heavily depended:

> The school as a positive educative function, and the courts as a repressive and negative educative function, are the most important State activities in this sense: but, in reality, a multitude of other so-called private initiatives

and activities ... form the apparatus of the political and cultural hegemony of the ruling classes.

How then can we explain this dog not barking? Certainly it was not a case of Gramsci passing Guillén by. On the contrary, as noted, Guillén listed in his bibliography two works by Broccoli that treated Gramsci and quoted from one of them twice in the main text of his thesis. Furthermore, Guillén would have encountered Gramsci in Poulantzas' two works (1977 and 1979), which he lists in his bibliography. Most significantly, however, we can conclude categorically that Guillén would have come into contact with Gramsci through his reading of Althusser. Of all the thinkers whose works influenced Guillén's thesis, Althusser undoubtedly had the most profound impact. As proof of this, if we examine the thesis' bibliography, ranking all the scholars appearing in it according to the number of their works that Guillén lists, Althusser is at the top with seven single-authored works plus two co-authored ones. Indeed, such was Guillén's indebtedness to Althusser that Professor Alberto Híjar, who presided over the judging panel of Guillén's thesis, dubbed Guillén "the Althusserian Rafael Guillén."[10]

Given the influence of Althusser's works on Guillén, it may be worth examining what the then university student and future guerrilla Subcommander would have encountered in the French philosopher's writings concerning Gramsci. In *For Marx*, Althusser (1965/1969, p. 114) asks and then answers: "Who has *really* attempted to follow up the explorations of Marx and Engels? I can only think of Gramsci," continuing in the accompanying footnote:

> *Gramsci* is of another stature .... There are ... some completely original and in some cases genial insights into the problem, basic today, of the superstructures. Also ... there are *new concepts*, for example, *hegemony*: a remarkable example of a theoretical solution in outline to the problems of the interpenetration of the economic and the political.

In his *Ideology and Ideological State Apparatuses,* an essay on which Guillén drew heavily for his thesis, Althusser (1971/2001c, p. 95) makes it clear that he had been influenced by Gramsci, writing admiringly of his Sardinian predecessor and acknowledging his debt to him:

> To my knowledge, Gramsci is the only one who went any distance in the road I am taking. He had the "remarkable" idea that the State could not be

reduced to the (Repressive) State Apparatuses, but included, as he put it, a certain number of institutions from "civil society": the Church, the Schools, the trade unions, etc.

Indeed, Michael Payne (1997, p. 38), commenting on the French philosopher's ISAs essay, goes so far as to write: "it is as though Althusser here is reading Marx through a lens provided by Gramsci's *Prison Notebooks*".[11]

Not all of Althusser's utterances on Gramsci were so complimentary, however. In *Reading Capital*, Althusser (1970/1997, pp. 134 and 126, respectively), while describing the Sardinian as possessing "enormous historical and political genius" and his *Prison Notebooks* as an "enormously delicate and subtle work of genius," and while cautioning his reader not to throw the baby out with the bathwater with regard to Gramsci's other theories, nonetheless levels a series of fundamental and damning criticisms at Gramsci. In addition to labeling some of Gramsci's pronouncements "disconcerting" and "disturbing" (pp. 129–130), Althusser produces a devastating critique of "Gramsci's historicism"; his "neglect[ing] to retain what distinguishes Marxist theory from every previous organic ideology: its character as *scientific* knowledge"; "his attribut[ing] to the concept 'superstructure' a breadth Marx never allowed"; and his "empiricis[m]" (pp. 131–134).

Thus, one must conclude that Guillén would have encountered Gramsci during his extensive reading of Althusser, but that he elected studiously to avoid him. We can only speculate as to the motives behind Guillén's rejection of Gramsci, but he may have chosen to shun him on account of having inherited a prejudice against Gramsci from Althusser: More specifically, to Guillén, arriving at Gramsci via Althusser, and thus viewing him through an Althusserian lens, the Sardinian would have appeared irredeemably tainted with historicist tendencies. It may also be worth noting here that Guillén would have found Althusser's accusations of historicism against Gramsci repeated in the works of the French philosopher's disciple, Poulantzas (1968/1977, pp. 35, 170, 173, 226, 247, 253, 255–256), who added to these another flaw, the Sardinian's "frequent conceptual confusion in his analyses" in connection with hegemony (pp. 260–262, 291), thus amplifying, or at least reinforcing, the negative image of Gramsci that Guillén may have formed from his study of *Reading Capital*.[12] (Note also that Guillén's anti-historicism appears to have persisted into later life. Hermann Herlinghaus

(2005, p. 60) claims that "the Subcomandante appears as one of the most consistent critics of historicism.")

In addition to being compelling per se, this hypothesis fits extremely well with the description of Gramsci's reception in Mexico afforded by Arnaldo Córdova, who notes that because "Gramsci's works were still not available in Spanish," and because Althusser was so popular, most of the Mexican left's contact with Gramsci occurred through the filter of Althusser.[13] Córdova (1987/1991, pp. 162–163) posits:

> Althusser made Gramsci fashionable in Mexico .... What is regrettable about that event is that ... [t]he French philosopher did not believe Gramsci could be considered a "true" Marxist. He was a "crociano," and Croce's teachings had led him to a neo-Hegelian historicism which was in resolute conflict with "true" Marxism .... As one can imagine, when Gramsci finally fell into the hands of the militants of the left, the reputation that preceded him was terrible, not just of his being a "crociano" and an "historicist," but even a "reformist"...

Ultimately, however, Córdova informs us, Gramsci's influence prevailed in Mexico:

> In spite of that, Gramsci finally imposed his presence in Mexico .... His works began being published in great abundance, especially in Mexico .... In just a few years there was hardly a Marxist who did not take pride in having one or two of Gramsci's books in his library ... Curiously, Gramsci began gaining authority as everyone was forgetting about Althusser. That was already evident by the mid-1970s.

Thus, provided we exercise a degree of flexibility concerning the date of Gramsci's eclipse of Althusser, and view it less as an event and more of a process (one which may have taken several years),[14] it appears that Guillén completed his thesis on the cusp of the waning of Althusser's and the waxing of Gramsci's influence. Perhaps, as with his contemporary compatriots, he had been infected by an inherited (from Althusser) prejudicial aversion to Gramsci. In this way, Guillén was very much a product of his time and his thesis provides a vivid snapshot of the intellectual predilections prevalent in Mexico in 1980.[155]

B)   *Guerrilla Writings*

Given that Gramsci appears to have exerted no influence on Rafael Guillén up to the point when he submitted his graduation thesis (October 1980), the question that next arises is whether there exists any evidence of his influence thereafter. Unfortunately, we hit a problem here. We know very little about what Guillén read or the intellectual currents he was exposed to both in the run-up to his embarking on the life of a rural guerrilla (August 1984) and for the decade he subsequently spent immersed in the mountains, jungles, and canyons of Chiapas. The only writings by the Subcommander that we possess from this period are a poem entitled "Problemas" (1987), his essay "Chiapas: el Sureste en dos vientos, una tormenta y una profecía" (1992), and the text of a speech he gave to a Tampico business association (1992).[16] Of these, the first two bear not a single reference to aid us in determining the political or philosophical influences at work on Marcos during that time, and the latter merely contains two quotations from José Martí. In addition to these writings, we know from an interview that Marcos (1995b, p. 72) gave which books he took with him to Chiapas. None of these, however, were works of a political-philosophical nature.

Again, as with his graduation thesis, the apparent total absence of Gramsci from Subcommander Marcos' reading and writings during the period from 1980 to 1994 is striking, especially if we consider the ascendancy of Gramsci's thought within Mexican left-wing circles during that period. After all, during the years immediately following Guillén's graduation, Mexico experienced a considerable sea change in the political-philosophical currents circulating throughout the country. In 1980, Althusser was institutionalized for strangling his wife following a mental breakdown, and with that came the end of what Michael Gane (1983, pp. 435–436) calls "the ISAs Decade" (1969–1979). Thus, as Gregory Elliott (1994, p. 178) has observed, "Althusser's effacement from the scene occurred no less rapidly than his rise to prominence within it." The void left by the waning of Althusser and later the death of Foucault (June 1984)—two philosophical giants who had dominated the 1960s and 1970s between them—would soon be filled by Gramsci, who had steadily been gaining ascendance in Latin America from the mid-to-late 1970s onward. Indeed, we can trace the Sardinian's trajectory in Mexico by observing the following: the publication of the proceedings of a colloquium on Gramsci edited by Carlos Sirvent, entitled *Gramsci y la política* (México: UNAM, 1980); the holding of a Gramsci-inspired symposium entitled "Hegemonía y alternativas políticas en América Latina" in Morelia (1980), the papers of which were published in 1985;[17] and the publication of Juan Carlos Portantiero's *Los usos de Gramsci* (México: Folios Ediciones, 1981), which brought together writings on Gramsci that had been composed during the years 1975 to 1981.

It comes as a surprise then to learn that during his short teaching career at the Universidad Autónoma Metropolitana (UAM) from January 1979 to February 1984, Guillén remained staunchly Althusserian. Indeed, a teaching colleague from that time observes that Guillén, and a small clique of fellow teachers in the Department of Theory and Analysis, "were big on Althusser ... on his theories of ideology and communication..."[18] Moreover, not only did Guillén continue to espouse Althusserian philosophy, but he also seems to have continued to hold himself aloof from Gramsci. A journalist who interviewed several of Guillén's students from his time at the UAM reports that Guillén prescribed them the works of Michel Foucault, Karl Marx, Louis Althusser, Mao Tse-Tung, and Armand Mattelart as reading material.[19] Again, the absence of Gramsci from the reading list is notable, the more so since Ilan Stavans (2002, p. 394), a student at the UAM while Guillén, only five years his senior, was teaching there, tells us that for those of his milieu "Our idols were Che Guevara, Felix Guattari, Antonio Gramsci, and Herbert Marcuse."

The mid-1980s saw a continuation and intensification of this trend: indeed, during this period Laclau and Mouffe, both early proponents of Gramsci's theories,[20] were writing their *Hegemony and Socialist Strategy*, which, its authors claimed, was "rooted ... in the Gramscian matrix and in the centrality of the category of hegemony,"[21] and which Richard J. F. Day (2005, pp. 70–71) has described as a "highly influential reworking of Gramsci's concept of hegemony ... which pushed Gramsci's theory to its limits." By 1984, Sheldon B. Liss (1984, p. 28) would claim "The thought of ... Antonio Gramsci (1891–1937) has of late surpassed that of Mao Zedong in terms of its popularity among Latin America's Marxists." The following year, 1985, saw the publication both of Laclau and Mouffe's aforementioned book and of the papers that had been delivered at the 1980 Morelia symposium, as well as the holding of the "International Seminar on Gramsci and Latin

America" organized by the Gramsci Institute in Ferrera, Italy, on September 11 to 13. The fiftieth anniversary of the Sardinian's death came in 1987 and, as such, was accompanied by international events and publications revisiting Gramsci, assessing his impact and gauging the applicability of his theories and frameworks to contemporary political situations throughout the world.[22] In that year, as Evelina Dagnino (1998, p. 38) observes:

> Interesting evidence of Gramsci's forceful diffusion [in Latin America] is found in an intelligence report presented to the Seventeenth Conference of American Armed Forces … in Mar del Plata in 1987, which conferred on him the status of "ideologue of the new strategy of the International Communist Movement."

Turning specifically to Mexico, the same year saw Córdova (1987/1991, p. 161) claim:

> It is certain that today in Mexico there are very few who speak about politics without mentioning Gramsci, and almost no intellectuals of the left who have not read or, at least, glanced at the works of Gramsci or some of the anthologies of his writings that have been published in the Spanish language.

Finally, also writing in 1987, Elliott (1987/2006, p. xvii) noted that "Althusserianism has found itself relegated politically, often in favor of a particular appropriation of the Gramscian legacy." By 1992, this process had gone so far that Robert Resch (1992, p. 385, n. 1) could claim: "The names of Gramsci and Foucault have become traces of the erasure of Althusser's impact on social theory."

Given the preceding, one might have expected to detect some traces of Gramsci's influence in the Subcommander's few writings from 1984 to 1994. Instead, we find none. Significantly, journalists who reported on the Mexican Federal Army's seizure of the Subcommander's camp during a February 1995 offensive, and who wrote about the discovery of a considerable stash—more than seventy—of Marcos' books on a variety of subjects, including political philosophy, make no mention of Gramsci's writings among the works found.[23] (Admittedly, none of the journalists provides a comprehensive list of the books found, and so the cache may have contained Gramsci's work but perhaps no reporter mentioned the fact.) Instead, we find Fernanda Navarro's interview with Louis Althusser, published as *Filosofía y Marxismo: Entrevista a Louis Althusser* (México: Siglo XXI editores: 1988). Of course, this tome may not have been acquired by Marcos himself but rather been brought to the Subcommander's camp by any one of a number of activists, journalists, intellectuals, and students who trekked into the jungle to meet Marcos during 1994. If, however, this was not the means of acquisition, but rather the Subcommander himself actively sought out a copy of *Filosofía y marxismo*, we may perhaps conclude that Marcos retained at least an academic interest in Althusserian philosophy until 1988 and possibly even thereafter.

It thus appears that the Gramsci boom that was enjoying such currency among the Mexican left simply passed by the Subcommander. Such a scenario, I urge, is far from unlikely given that Marcos, by dint of dwelling among the indigenous peasantry, immersed in the remote and isolated Chiapan hinterland, lived a cocooned existence, remaining impervious to prevailing intellectual currents, including the Gramsci boom, which were circulating among mainstream Mexican intellectuals. As Kara Zugman Dellacioppa (2009, p. 46) writes: "The ten years that the Zapatistas had been hidden in the jungles of Chiapas had isolated them from the political panorama in the rest of the country."[24] In support of this statement, Zugman quotes Frente Zapatista de Liberación Nacional (FZLN) founding member Sergio Rodríguez, whom she interviewed in 2000, as saying "There had been many political changes in Mexico since the early 1980s that the Zapatistas were not aware of."

This cultural and intellectual isolation meant that, unlike in the case of El Salvador's Ejército Revolucionario del Pueblo (ERP) guerrilla, Mexico's Ejército Zapatista de Liberación Nacional (EZLN) appears not to have been influenced by Gramsci. True, Marcos revealed to Yvon Le Bot (1997a, p. 197):

> [T]hat the Zapatista Army of National Liberation was adapting at the time it came out .... There were compañeros who were for orthodox Marxism, others who were for a Marxism which was closer to Trotskyism, others who were for a Marxism closer to Gramsci, for Euro-communism, others who were not Marxists but rather Social Democrats.

Of the numerous anecdotes related by Subcomandante Marcos concerning the EZLN's days as a rural guerrilla, however, none resemble the following by Comandante Jonás of the ERP:

> In May or June of 1992, by the San Salvador volcano, we had a meeting of cadres in which one of the things we discussed was precisely Gramsci. Many

of the compañeros said, "Yes, that's the direction we should take." ... From that point on, if not 100 percent, a good percentage of the ERP cadres would read works by Gramsci.[25]

Hence, even if some cadres belonging to the EZLN's mother-organization, the Fuerzas de Liberación Nacional (FLN), headquartered in Mexico City, "were for a Marxism closer to Gramsci," they appear to have exercised little influence over the geographically distant and culturally isolated EZLN. Indeed, one must seriously question the extent of any Gramscian influence even on the FLN, given that both its statutes, drawn up in 1980 and subscribed to by all cadres as late as January 1993, and its *Reglamento insurgente* ("Insurgent Rules"), drafted in 1985, bear not the slightest trace of any Gramscian influence.

C) *Rebel Writings*

If, as appears to have been the case, Marcos remained untouched by Gramsci's thinking throughout his university and guerrilla years, did he perhaps at least arrive late at the Sardinian's thought after January 1, 1994, when the Zapatistas were suddenly exposed to currents circulating in Mexican society at large, and the Subcommander began corresponding and interacting with journalists, intellectuals, and activists? To answer this question, examining the Subcommander's discourse in the form of communiqués and interviews is necessary, the more so since on initial inspection these appear to evince Gramscianesque traces.

Perhaps the first thing to note is how few references to Gramsci appear in Marcos' discourse. Indeed, in five volumes of communiqués (totaling over 1900 pages), and hundreds more of speeches and interviews, the sole reference to Gramsci I have been able to unearth is the one cited previously from the Subcommander's interview with Le Bot. Such scant reference is perhaps not so surprising, however, given that Marcos is remarkably reticent when it comes to mentioning influential political philosophers, especially when compared to his readiness to make reference to literary figures.[26] Indeed, even when, in a more candid than usual interview with journalist Laura Castellanos (2008, p. 96), Marcos was asked "Throughout these 14 years what other literary and philosophical sources have nourished you?" the Subcommander provided no examples of works pertaining to the canon of western political philosophy.

D) Perceived Affinities between Marcos and Gramsci

Given the near total absence of references to Gramsci, what, one must ask, have certain commentators seen in Marcos' discourse that has led them to perceive a Gramscian influence? Five aspects related to the Subcommander have encouraged commentators to propose an affinity with Gramsci, one of which concerns terminology and four of which relate to politico-philosophical concepts. Specifically, they are 1) Marcos' employment of terminology deployed extensively by Gramsci; 2) his decision to wage what some have described as a "war of position"; 3) his appreciation of the political importance of culture; 4) his role within the Zapatista movement, seen by some as being akin to that of an organic intellectual; and 5) his promotion of *mandar obedeciendo* as a key concept (and practice) of Zapatismo. Let us examine these in order.

The first aspect of Marcos' writings and utterances that has been perceived to exhibit a Gramscian affinity concerns the terminology that the Subcommander employs. Chief among these are his oft-repeated references and appeals to civil society. (This strongly contrasts with his thesis, which nowhere employs the phrase "civil society," perhaps an unsurprising omission given Althusser's (1970/1997, p. 162, n. 37) admonition that "The concept of 'civil society' ... constantly repeated by Gramsci ... is ambiguous and should be struck from Marxist theoretical vocabulary," and that, as Nicola Miller (1999, p. 16) notes, "...many on the Left remained suspicious of the idea of civil society into the 1980s."[27]) Indeed, María Elena Martínez-Torres (2001, p. 349) notes that "The Zapatistas ... have more of a Gramscian style than earlier revolutionaries, focusing more on strengthening civil society than on force of arms...," and calls attention to the movement's "Gramscian appeals to civil society" (p. 350).

There is ample reason, however, to question the assumption that consistent appeals to civil society betray any direct Gramscian influence. Ellen Meiksins Wood (1995, p. 242), for example, notes how "The concept of 'civil society' is being mobilized to serve so many varied purposes that it is impossible to isolate a single school of thought associated with it." Furthermore, Gustavo Esteva (1999, p. 158), although noting that "References to 'civil society' are a constant in the discourse of the Zapatistas," continues, "They find wide echo, but also are a source of confusion, given the long and convoluted conceptual and practical history of the expression…" Finally, Atilio Boron (2001, pp. 93–94), after observing that the term civil society is one that has been "utilized profusely in Latin American political discourse from the nineties," notes nonetheless that "it would be no exaggeration to affirm that, in its present meaning, it is one of the most confused and muddled in the social sciences" as well as one of "increasing conceptual vacuity." Boron continues, "from the particular situation of the countries of Eastern European and the Soviet Union, 'civil society' happened to be conceived, in Manichean form, as everything which was not the state and that, supposedly, was antithetical and opposite to it." Subsequently, with the fall of the socialist regimes, civil society became associated with freedom, whereas the state was deemed coercive. It is, Boron (2001, p. 94) argues, probably in this sense that Zapatismo began to use the expression, as he puts it, "to denote the deep organic crisis separating Mexican society from its system of hegemonized political representation by that 'perfect dictatorship,' in the words of Mario Vargas Llosa, which had converted into the PRI state." In short then, as several scholars have attested,[28] the term civil society enjoyed immense currency among the Latin American left throughout the 1980s and 1990s, evolving to take on a life of its own in the region,[29] and so the employment of this phrase cannot be taken to equate to an indebtedness to Gramsci on the part of those utilizing it.

Significantly, many of Gramsci's key phrases entered the Latin American left's parlance. Indeed, as Nicola Miller (1999, p. 14) observes: "During the 1970s and 1980s, Gramscian terms such as 'hegemony,' 'civil society,' 'political society' and 'national-popular' came to dominate the discourse of the Spanish-American Left, extending beyond intellectual circles (and even, at least in Mexico, becoming fashionable in government ranks)."[30] Given this, it is not unexpected to encounter such phrases in the Subcommander's discourse; one might even expect Marcos, at times, to sound quite Gramscian. With the exception of the phrase "civil society," however, which could be said to have become part of a generic Latin American left-wing lexicon that displays Gramscian trappings but does not necessarily entail derivation from or adherence to the Sardinian's key philosophical concepts, the Subcommander's discourse contains remarkably little in the way of Gramscian vocabulary. Indeed, a survey of five volumes of EZLN communiqués covering the seven years and three months from January 1, 1994, to April 4, 2001, reveals not a single reference to the key Gramscian concepts of "war of position," "war of manoeuvre," "modern prince," "hegemonic bloc," or "historic bloc." Regarding other key Gramscian phrases, Marcos does make mention of "common sense," writing, "What is the frame of reference of 'common sense'? Is it not that of the dominant ideology?," which Bruhn (1999, p. 43) interprets as "Marcos refer[ring] to the notion of common sense in Gramscian terms (without citing Gramsci)." One might expect, however, to encounter more than just a single use of this phrase in a corpus that spans more than 7 years and over 1900 pages. Similarly, the phrase "organic intellectual" appears three times and "political society" five times, again, perhaps indicating that Marcos had encountered Gramsci, but not that he was heavily indebted to him theoretically. Even "hegemony" and "hegemonic," although they appear in this corpus—perhaps introduced through the intermediary of Poulantzas—are hardly rife, occurring four times and once, respectively. True, in an interview with Gabriel García Márquez and Roberto Pombo (2001, pp. 70–71), Marcos, while discussing the role of the politico-military organizations of the 1960s and 1970s, talks about "a dispute between two hegemonies" involving "an oppressor power which decides on behalf of society from above, and a group of visionaries which decides to lead the country on the correct path and ousts the other group from power, seizes power and then also decides on behalf of society." He adds, "For us that is a struggle between hegemonies.... You cannot reconstruct the world or society, nor rebuild national states now in ruins, on the basis of a quarrel over who will impose their hegemony on society."

It should be noted, however, that hegemony, as it is employed by the Subcommander, is not the rather technical and specific "hegemony" of Gramscian theory, but the generic "hegemony" that has entered popular parlance among the Mexican left. As Adam David Morton (2011, p. 9) cautions:

> Any sojourn through the literature on Mexican studies thus reveals a repeated conflation of hegemony and authoritarianism, the use of hegemony as a synonym for dominance, or conceptually vague references to "contending hegemonic forces" and descriptions of the PRI losing its monopoly on power but still holding to some form of imprecise hegemony.... Across

the board, then, there seems something valid in the claim that there is indeterminacy in the way hegemony is understood, which reduces the term to a conceptual catchall and prevents clear theoretical and practical understanding...

Thus, a survey of the terminology employed throughout the EZLN's communiqués over an extended period reveals very little in the way of any Gramscian influence. On the contrary, rather than bearing the stamp of Gramsci, according to Carlos Monsiváis, who surveys "Marcos' thinking, distributed over hundreds of pages," the Subcommander's "discourse was initially very oversimplified, with too many paeans to the unreadable translations of Althusser and Poulantzas..."[31]

Let us now turn to discussing the first of the four politico-philosophical concepts that, on cursory inspection at least, exhibit an affinity between the thinking of Gramsci and that of Marcos. The first of these is the fact that the Zapatistas' strategy, as devised by Marcos (their chief military strategist) following the military reverses they suffered at the hands of the Federal Army during the first week of their uprising, mirrors closely what Gramsci termed the waging of a "war of position." Indeed, Josée Johnston (2000, p. 468) writes that "the Zapatistas' armed struggle was fought on the level of a Gramscian war of position," while Morton (2002, p. 41) states "the EZLN challenged the PRI by articulating a struggle based on a variety of strategies linked to the 'frontal attack' of a 'war of manoeuvre' as well as the prolonged tactics of a 'war of position'." Morton (pp. 42–43) elaborates: "the initial military assault in January 1994 was the transitory phase of a war of manoeuvre .... Since this phase ... it is possible to highlight the strategy of a shifting war of position conducted by the EZLN." Most recently, Daniela Di Piramo (2010, p. 107) writes:

> The other source of intellectual inspiration, possibly more directly related to what the Zapatistas are attempting to achieve, can be found in Gramsci's work. Its emphasis on the importance of ideas and of a "war of position" as a means to the contestation of hegemonic structures by civil society is particularly relevant to this movement.

In short, a host of scholars have viewed the Zapatistas' strategy as that of waging a Gramscian war of position,[32] and certainly it is hard to dispute the notion, shared by so many, that the Zapatistas' strategy can be analyzed utilizing a Gramscian framework and its attendant terminology. It is important to note, however, that just because a movement readily lends itself to Gramscian analysis, does not necessarily mean it derived any "intellectual inspiration" from the Sardinian Marxist.

The second concept that seems to connect Marcos with Gramsci is related to the first and involves the Subcommander's appreciation of the political importance of culture. In contrast to previous Latin American left-wing guerrillas, who adhered to what Nestor García Canclini (1988, p. 495) describes as "a revolutionary epic that repudiates culture," Marcos acknowledged, as did Gramsci, the political importance of culture and specifically its revolutionary potential. Hence, Kristine Vanden Berghe and Bart Maddens (2004, p. 137) note that "The fact that he [Marcos] reverts to works of fiction is indicative of a strong belief in the power of art and culture as a means to bring about political change," and Enrique Krauze (2011, pp. 440 and 441) writes of "the Gramscian creativity of Marcos' cultural revolution," adding, "Given the degree to which the Mexican left (even up to the present day) has been more cultural than social and more social than political, the discourse and symbols of Marcos had a truly revolutionary impact." Finally, Christopher Domínguez Michael (1999) writes that "The novelty of the political literature of Marcos would be that ... it is a cultural politics," and Ignacio Corona and Beth E. Jörgensen (2002, p. 244) state that "Marcos's communiqués and stories written from Chiapas certainly offer an opportunity to analyse ... the complex intermingling of aesthetic and political agency in cultural production."

Undeniably then, Marcos possessed a keen appreciation of the political importance of culture, and yet there is no reason to suppose that he inherited this from any direct exposure to Gramsci's works. Rather, could it not be that Marcos derived this trait from the way he arrived at politics, namely, as he himself tells us, after having received significant exposure to literature since his youth? In an interview with Gabriel García Márquez and Roberto Pombo (2001, p. 78) in which the Subcommander reflects on his childhood, when asked specifically "Didn't you read any political theory?" Marcos replied, "Not to begin with. We went straight from the alphabet to literature, and from there to theoretical and political texts..." Marcos also tells us (p. 78):

We didn't look out at the world through a news-wire but through a novel, an essay or a poem. That made us very different. That was the prism through which my parents wanted me to view the world...

Strictly speaking, we were already, as the orthodox would say, very corrupted by the time we got to ... revolutionary literature. So that when we got into Marx and Engels we were thoroughly spoilt by literature; its irony and its humour.

Furthermore, rather than attributing Marcos' appreciation of the political potential of culture to Gramsci, we should look to the tradition of Latin American intellectuals for whom culture, and especially literature, were inextricably intertwined. Indeed, Kristine Vanden Berghe (2006/1, p. 148) asserts:

Marcos is inspired by several convictions that usually are associated typically with Latin American intellectuals of the past. Like them, he thinks that the written word constitutes an effective weapon in social and political struggles ... that discourse constitutes a privileged place from where the marginalized can reply to those who dominate them.

If we were to look for a single figure who may have influenced the Subcommander in regard to his realization of the political significance of culture, we should look to fellow Mexican and, in the words of Enrique Krauze (2011, p. 439), Marcos' "literary mentor," Carlos Monsiváis.[33] Indeed, Christopher Domínguez Michael (1999) states that "Monsiváis endowed him [Marcos] with an effective notion of politics as a culmination of popular culture," whereas Julio Moguel (1998, pp. 31–32): claims

Marcos ... did not come to the world of war through the influence of Leninists or Maoists ... but rather through that generation of thinkers who, in Mexico, have Monsiváis as one of their most recognized representatives. They live and think of politics as culture...

The third concept related to Marcos that appears, on cursory inspection at least, to invite analogy with Gramsci concerns the Subcommander's role as an organic intellectual formulating an alternative "common sense" so as to produce a counterhegemonic discourse with which to challenge the dominant paradigm. Thus Vanden Berghe (2009, p. 57) writes:

Given that they believed they could put an end to the dominant hegemony by transforming the common way of thinking which sustained this hegemony, the Zapatistas can consider themselves true disciples of Gramsci. But Gramsci also pointed out that this subversive activity would only be successful if the intellectuals managed to elaborate new ideas which might reconcile the government with the civil society and impose an alternative common sense. In the ranks of the EZLN this role was occupied by … Subcomandante Insurgente Marcos.

Similarly, Stephon Boatwright (n.d., 27 and 29, respectively) writes:

> [Behind] the mask exists an organic intellectual with a mindset that seeks to create alternative definitions to the ones assigned by Power … Marcos identifies common sense in Gramscian terms, and speaks of the need to undermine its grip on civil society. By recognizing common sense as the ideological defence of the current order, a mandate is created in EZLN doctrine to debase Power's version of reality. This is the essence of many of Marcos' communiqués and poems; attempting to demystify the version of "truth" that Power promotes…
>
> Marcos has acted as the primary messenger of new ideas and conceptions, but what is particularly important here is the effort made to keep the intellectuals … close to civil society, a Gramscian requirement for organic intellectuals.

Again, as in the case of commentators describing the Zapatistas' strategy of waging a war of position, these passages appear plausible, even compelling, and I, too, have argued that Subcommander Marcos should be viewed as fulfilling the role of a Gramscian organic intellectual.[34] However, although I concur with Boatwright that "Subcomandante Insurgente Marcos embodies the 'organic intellectual' like no other" (p. 26), I believe that he goes beyond the evidence when he asserts that Marcos "may very well be [the] genesis of the Gramscian current in the Zapatistas movement," and that "the EZLN is following Gramscian thought quite closely" (pp. 26 and 29, respectively). Put simply, just because a phenomenon or person lends itself or his/herself readily to description in Gramscian terms this does not prove derivation from Gramsci.

The fourth and final politico-philosophical concept that may have the appearance of representing a point of convergence between the Sardinian's and the Subcommander's thinking is Marcos' emphasis on *mandar obedeciendo* (embodying autonomy and Councils of Good Government) as the Zapatistas' principle strategy of political organization.[35] This, when observed cursorily, may appear to bear a resemblance to Gramsci's promotion of *au-*

togestión and *consejismo*. Despite the appearance of similarity, however, the Zapatistas have asserted on several occasions that this primary tenet of Zapatismo, in fact, derived not from any proponent of western political philosophy but from Chiapas' indigenous communities.[366] Moreover, a number of prominent scholars have supported such a conclusion. For example, Walter D. Mignolo writes (2002, p. 256):

> [T]there is a principle from Amerindian wisdom among the Zapatistas that is both engrained in the intersubjective structure of their language and in their corresponding conception of social relations. In Spanish this principle reads: "Mandar obedeciendo" (in English: "To rule and obey at the same time"). This political principal is also engrained in the intersubjective logic of the Tojolabal language.[377]

So, too, Enrique Dussel (2003b, p. 173), when discussing what he dubs "Mayan Democracy," including the concept of command-obeying, quotes from several Zapatista documents and asserts that

> The[se] texts ... are not inspired on [*sic*] the political, "democracy" writings of Aristotle, Rousseau, or Bobbio. These texts are Maya, the creation of a millennial cultural experience as fundamental to world history as the Egyptian, Mesopotamian, Indian, Chinese, Inca, and Nahua ones.

Moreover, after quoting extensively from the first Zapatista communiqué to mention, and explain the meaning behind, the phrase *mandar obedeciendo*, Dussel (p. 174) concludes that this "text teaches what the Maya political system is and was, even from before the Conquest," adding "This system owes nothing to contemporary political science…" Hence Marcos' insistence that

> the real creators of zapatismo were the translators, the theoreticians of zapatismo, people like Major Mario, Major Moisés, Major Ana María, all of those people who had to translate in dialects. Tacho, David, Zevedeo, are really the theoreticians of zapatismo…[388]

E) Divergences between Marcos and Gramsci

Offsetting these five apparent Gramscian aspects of the Subcommander is the fact that certain facets of Marcos' thinking are at significant odds with the Sardinian's thought. For one thing, Gramsci's dismissive attitude toward the folkloric would certainly appear to conflict with Marcos' views; the Subcommander no doubt perceives Gramsci's rejection of the folkloric as a Eurocentric and exclusionary judgment on indigenous thought.[39] So, too, Gramsci's rather positive perception of political parties forming the "modern prince," is not one that the Subcommander shares, as Daniela Di Piramo (2010, p. 107) observes: "although the EZLN has followed Gramsci's innovative idea of the revolutionary potential of civil society, it does not insist on the importance of the revolutionary party as part of the transformative political process." Bruhn (1999, p. 49) goes even further, arguing that Marcos not only does not insist on the importance of the revolutionary party, but also, in fact, rejects it:

> An even more fundamental difference between Gramsci and Marcos concerns the role of the revolutionary party.... The EZLN ... denies that any existing party adequately represents the progressive forces and rejects the construction of a party of its own.... This exaltation of civil society functions well in the Mexican context, where cynicism about parties is widespread.

This rejection ought not surprise us. As Gideon Baker (2002, p. 61) notes, such a lack of faith in political parties was common among the Latin American left and was rooted in the continent's lived experience of left party politics:

> Finally, while Gramsci called for a "latter day Prince" (namely, some form of vanguard party) in order to coordinate the anti-hegemonical struggle in civil society, the Latin American left became generally suspicious of the party form itself for reasons of their wider critique of the state power sought by political parties as well as the vanguardism deployed in the process. (Not to mention that, in Latin American history, political parties had always co-opted and/or demobilized the very associational life that now seemed so important.)

In the case of Mexico in particular, Marcos' refusal to follow Gramsci in his assertion that the leading role in society-transforming politics should be played by a revolutionary party was no doubt fostered by the Subcommander having witnessed the Institutional Revolutionary Party (PRI) govern in the name of the Revolution for seventy-one years, during which time it became authoritarian and either coopted or murdered those organizing in opposition to it. Indeed, Marcos, in a March 1996 interview with Jorge Ramos (2006, pp. 78–80), explicitly denied the revolutionary potential of all of Mexico's political parties:

> J.R.: Is the PRD an alternative for you? If you were to vote, would you vote for the PRD?
>
> S.M.: Not for the PRD, not for the PRI, not for the PAN, nor for the Labor Party, insofar as their political relationships, at the electoral level, are not fair.
>
> J.R.: Do you not believe in anyone within the political system?
>
> S.M.: We do not believe in the Mexican political system, and that is what we are fighting against . ... The problem is not ... a problem vis-à-vis one individual but vis-à-vis a political system.

Marcos' rejection of Mexico's political parties became even more vehement following the legislative betrayal of 2001, when the legislature watered down, to the point of rendering it a travesty, the Indigenous Rights Bill that the Zapatistas had negotiated with the government.[40]

Significantly, however, although Marcos eschews the notion of a political party fulfilling the role of the "modern prince," he does not reject the need for such a role; rather, he merely disagrees on what entity will fulfill it. Indeed, the EZLN's attempts to establish the FZLN should perhaps be seen as an attempt to forge a "modern prince," although not from a "party" but from a newly constituted "force."[41]

There are other significant divergences between the Subcommander's thought and that of Gramsci. For example, Stephon Boatwright (n.d., pp. 27 and 30), after twice asserting that the Zapatistas employ Gramsci's tactics but not goals, continues:

> While Gramsci was attempting to create a more effective Leninism, those who most often appropriate his theory employ an anti-vanguardist, even anti-revolutionary discourse. A radical-democratic discourse has supplanted the "revolutionary party," the counter-hegemonic project no longer seeks to establish working-class supremacy, but to establish space for democratic and plural institutions and processes. These are departures Gramsci would quite certainly not welcome if he were walking among us today but maintained his early 20th century mindset. (p. 30)

By way of concluding this chapter, although certain commentators, having noted what they perceive to be the Subcommander's explicitly Gramscian vocabulary, his waging of what appears to be a war of position, his appreciation of the political importance of culture, his role akin to that of an organic intellectual articulating an alternative "common sense" to form a counterhegemonic discourse with which to combat the dominant hegemony, and his promotion of *mandar obedeciendo* as a key concept (and practice) of the Zapatismo, have drawn the inference that Marcos has been influenced by Antonio Gramsci, the above examination, although admittedly based predominantly on *argumenta ex silentio*, points to the tentative conclusion that although a Gramscian lens or framework may be a useful one through which to observe the Zapatista movement, there is no concrete evidence whatsoever—and the circumstantial evidence has been shown to be weak—to support the thesis, proposed by some, that the Subcommander was ever influenced by the Sardinian. (Conversely, as we have witnessed in the preceding chapters, plenty of hard evidence points to Marcos having been influenced, at least during his university years, by other European political philosophers, conspicuously Louis Althusser, but also others, such as Michel Foucault and Nicos Poulantzas.) Such a conclusion has significant implications.

The first, and widest of these, relates to the extent of the diffusion of Gramscian thought throughout Mexican academia. For how are we to explain the complete absence of the Sardinian Marxist, his thoughts and works, from an award-winning thesis presented in October 1980, at Mexico's top university, in a philosophy faculty, and on a subject which Gramsci's works were of not inconsiderable relevance? If Gramsci's penetration was so pervasive why, one must ask, did Guillén's thesis examiners not deem this absence of any reference to Gramsci a theoretical weakness? Furthermore, it is surely safe to assume that Guillén, although exceptional in his talents and achievements, must have been fairly typical of his peers in terms of the intellectual currents to which he was exposed. His shunning of Gramsci perhaps provides an insight into the political-philosophical influences that exerted themselves on a generation of university-educated, middle-class, left-wing Mexicans. Thus, when Eric Hobsbawm (2011, p. 334) writes "in the 1960s the vogue for Althusser in Latin America largely blocked the way for Gramsci…," in Mexico this phenomenon appeared to extend until at least 1980. As is clearly evidenced from the reading texts that Rafael Guillén set his UAM students to study, and possibly also from the Subcommander's possession of an edition of interviews Fernanda Navarro conducted with Althusser that was published in 1988, the French philosopher's thought continued to exert not inconsiderable influence over some on the Mexican left well after Gramsci had reached his ascendency. Consequently, we need to exercise caution when discussing the diffusion of Gramscian, and the eclipsing of Althusserian, thought in Mexico, for these processes appear to have been more uneven than have typically been described.

Second, in not having been influenced by Gramsci, Marcos resembles less his fellow contemporary Central American guerrilla counterparts, and especially the comandantes of El Salvador's ERP, and more his role model, Che Guevara, who appears to have remained largely ignorant of Gramsci throughout his life.[42] Such an observation carries with it wider implications, for it implies that Mexico's most renowned and successful guerrilla movement appears to have evolved in isolation, cocooned from the Gramscian currents that influenced other contemporary Latin American guerrillas. Instead, it was indigenous thought and practice more than recent trends in European political-philosophy that constituted the Zapatistas', and their Subcommander's, point of reference and source of inspiration during their years in the jungle. Thus, after examining the Rafael Guillén's thesis and claiming to have found traces of the influence of Gramsci, Foucault, and Poulantzas, Félix Hoyo (1995, p. 35) asks "if Guillén converted into Marcos, what was it that transformed him?," only to answer: "Apparently, it was fundamentally the strength of Mayan culture, present and active in indigenous groups of the region." In short, it appears that while European political philosophy played a large part in shaping Rafael Guillén, it was indigenous thought that played a large part in transforming him into Marcos.

In the last instance, it is surely ironical that the Subcommander, who so aptly fits the description of a Gramscian organic intellectual, appears to have escaped Gramsci's influence. Nonetheless, Gramsci may have impacted Marcos indirectly, in the form of the Sardinian's legacy to which the Subcommander was, in part, heir. Evelina Dagnino (1998, p. 38) quotes a leading Latin American proponent of Gramsci, José Aricó, as saying "For us, Gramsci represented that solid backing from which we could enter into a multiplicity of theoretical directions without having to abdicate our socialist ideas or the critical capacity of Marxism." Perhaps then, in this way at least, Gramsci can be said to have had an influence on Marcos—not directly, but by contributing to a prevailing atmosphere of what Dagnino calls "antiauthoritarian eclecticism" among those on the Latin American left (p. 40). It was just such an atmosphere that spawned both Guillén's thesis, which cites the works of, and quotes, many philosophers—Badiou, Balibar, Chomsky, Descartes, Engels, Foucault, Hegel, Kant, Lakoff, Lecourt, Lenin, Macherey, Marx, Pêcheux, Poulantzas, Weber, and so on—and the even less doctrinaire, more eclectic, and irreverent communiqués of Subcommander Marcos.

Notes

1. The following chapter, excepting the initial two paragraphs, previously appeared as a journal article: Henck, Nick. (2013, Summer). The Subcommander and the Sardinian: Marcos and Gramsci. *Estudios Mexicanos/Mexican Studies* 29(2), 428-458.
2. See (1992, April 15). Chomsky Is Citation Champ. MIT News. Retrieved from http://web.mit.edu/newsoffice/1992/citation-0415.html:
   [H]is [Chomsky's] 3,874 citations in the Arts and Humanities Citation Index between 1980 and 1992 make him the most cited living person in that period and the eighth most cited source overall—just behind famed psychiatrist Sigmund Freud and just ahead of philosopher Georg Hegel .... But that isn't all. From 1972 to 1992, Professor Chomsky was cited 7,449 times in the Social Science Citation Index—likely the greatest number of times for a living person there as well...
3. For a brief survey of Gramscian interpretations of the Zapatista movement, see Mihalis Mentinis (2006, pp. 32–36). Such interpretations include the following: a collected volume edited by Dora Kanoussi (1998); Kathleen Bruhn (1999); Adam David Morton (2000; 2002; 2007, pp. 171–200; 2011, pp. 199–235); and Nicolina Montesano Montessori (2009, pp. 87–89, 136, 274, 287). See also John Ross (1995, p. 292); René Báez (1996, p. 68); Peter Rosset, in George A. Collier and Elizabeth L. Quaratiello (1994/1999, p. viii); Josée Johnston (2000, pp. 467–468); Chris Gilbreth and Gerardo Otero (2001, p. 19); María Elena Martínez-Torres (2001, p. 349); Richard Gilman-Opalsky (2008, p. 254); and Stephon Boatwright (n.d., 20–30); who describe the Zapatista movement employing Gramscian terms. Note, however, the cautionary words of Steven P. Kanavel (2007, p. 55).
4. For example, Daniela Di Piramo (2010, p. 107) and Jen Couch (2001, p. 247).
5. For example, most notably Kristine Vanden Berghe (2009, p. 57) and Stephon Boatwright (n.d., 26), but also Ben V. Olguín (2002, pp. 172–173) and Claire Brewster (2005, p. 155).

6. Cf Félix Hoyo (1995, pp. 34–35) who writes:
   > Certain of Guillén's philosophical formulations we find are very close to the thesis of Gramsci, with whom he appears a little familiar … certain theories are close to Gramsci's conception …. The dialectic relation between philosophy and politics thus remains framed in Gramscian terms.

   In addition to finding these assertions far from conclusive, however, I would point out that Hoyo (p. 35) himself notes: "It appears that some of these Gramscian concepts came to Guillén via his reading of Poulantzas."
7. Burgos (2002, p. 27) notes that over time "however, the concept of hegemony adjusted to the Gramscian tradition."
8. See Guillén (1980, pp. 35 & 37, respectively). On Poulantzas' favorable reception in Latin America, and the wide and frequent employment of his concept of "class fractions" there, see Richard L. Harris (1979, pp. 66-70).
9. Gramsci (1971, pp. 26-43).
10. Quoted in Salvador Corro (1995, pp. 23 & 26).
11. Similarly, see Michael Gane (1983, p. 436): "It is not Marx or Lenin who are the direct influences on the formulations of the ISAs paper but Spinoza and Gramsci." On Gramsci's influence on Althusser, see Christine Buci-Glucksmann (1980, pp. 14–16, 59–60, 64–68, 340–343) and Margaret Majumdar (1995, pp. 109,152, & 165).
12. Note, however, Poulantzas (1979, p. 194).
13. Similarly, see Nicola Miller (1999, pp. 13–14 & 20).
14. I would propose a dating of "the mid-to-late 1970s" as most apt. Indeed, Córdova (1987/1991, p. 162) writes "Althusser, que todavia durante buena parte de los 70 siguio difundiendose extraordinariamente en los ambientes academicos y de la izquierda militante." See too, Francis Mulhern (1994, p. 167): "Throughout the 1970s, Althusser remained an inspirational influence."
15. Yvon Le Bot (1997a, p. 16) notes that Guillén's thesis was "tinged with a fairly stereotypical structuralist Marxism," and that in it the influence of Althusser could be detected "just like in thousands of theses at the end of the epoch in Latin American universities."
16. For the first two, see EZLN (1994, pp. 198-200 & 49-66, respectively); for the latter, see Rafael Sebastián Guillén Vicente (1992).
17. Raúl Burgos (2002, p. 12). José Aricó (1988, p. 31) tells us that a symposium dedicated to Gramsci had been held at the UNAM in September 1978.
18. Quoted in Alma Guillermoprieto (2002, p. 211).
19. Álvaro Delgado (1995, pp. 13 & 17).
20. Ernest Laclau's largely Gramscian *Politics and Ideology* and Chantal Mouffe's *Gramsci and Marxist Theory* had both been published in 1979.
21. See the "Preface to Second Edition"; the quotation cited appears on vii (see, too, ix). On the dating of the writing of the book, see vii and xiv.
22. In 1987, Laclau and Mouffe's aforementioned book was also translated into

Spanish.
23. See Juan Manuel Alvarado (1995, p. 10A), José Luis Ruiz (1995, p. 12), and Bertrand De la Grange (1995).
24. NB Marcos told Yvon Le Bot (1997a, pp. 139-141): "It was a solitary period because we weren't told anything, in terms of the world and national reality. As a guerrilla group we were very isolated, as much on the national terrain as on the local..." (The translation here is that of Christopher Gunderson (2013, pp. 462-3).) Cf, however, Alma Guillermoprieto (2002, p. 209), who tells us that when she interviewed Marcos in April 1994 she found him to be "uncannily well informed about the intellectual and media world beyond Chiapas."
25. Quoted in Raúl Burgos (2002, p. 25). Burgos (2002, p. 28) also quotes from a 1993 interview with Juan Ramón Medrano of the ERP in which the latter claimed to "have borrowed [central concepts] from Gramsci."
26. See the Subcommander's interviews with Gabriel García Márquez and Roberto Pombo (2001 pp. 77–79) and Laura Castellanos (2008, p. 96ff), in which he (respectively) recalls the literary authors he was exposed to during his childhood and lists those he continues to admire.
27. Norbert Lechner (1985, pp. 64–65) dates, by implication, the favorable reassessment of "civil society" that took place in Latin America to around 1980 and especially from 1982, that is, after Guillén had submitted his thesis.
28. For example, Nicola Miller (1999, p. 18) and Atilio Boron (2001, p. 93).
29. The same is true of other Gramscian terms. Nicola Miller (1999, p. 21) claims that "organic intellectuals" similarly took on a meaning among some Latin American intellectuals that "was not at all what Gramsci had meant."
30. See, too, Sebastiao Tigüera Sobrinho (1995, p. 44, fn. 49):
> It is common in Latin America to hear well known conservatives and even reactionaries use categories such as "hegemony," "civil society," etc. without any rigor as regards his [Gramsci's] work. What is regrettable, however, is observing that often intellectuals who claim to be of the left are also participating in the confusion.
31. In EZLN (2003, p. 22).
32. Similarly, Chris Gilbreth and Gerardo Otero (2001, p. 19), Richard Gilman-Opalsky (2008, p. 254), and Nicolina Montesano Montessori (2009, p. 274).
33. Carlos Fuentes (1994/1997, p. 93) convincingly claimed "that Subcommander Marcos ... has read more Carlos Monsiváis than Carlos Marx."
34. Nick Henck (2012).
35. For a book-length treatment of the political-philosophical concept of mandar obedeciendo, see Carlos Antonio Aguirre Rojas (2008).
36. See the Zapatistas' communiqué dated February 26, 1994 (Autonomedia 1994, pp. 236–237); Marcos (1995a); and the 2005 Sixth Declaration of the Lacandon Jungle (http://enlacezapatista.ezln.org.mx/sdsl-en/).

37. See, too, Antonio Paoli (2003, p. 30), who describes mandar obedeciendo as a fundamental principle of Tzeltal social organization, and Carlos Lenkersdorf (2004, p. 22), who claims that among the Tojolobales there was a common saying that "anticipates" the phrase *mandar obedeciendo*. Neil Harvey (1998, pp. 208–209) writes that "the principle of mandar obedeciendo … the EZLN drew from earlier practices within indigenous communities."
38. Marcos in Le Bot (1997a, pp. 338–339); my translation.
39. José Rabasa (1997, p. 405) has observed that "For Gramsci, notions of popular culture and indigenous knowledge were incompatible with his understanding of a Culture that could be established as a counterhegemony," continuing (406), "The 'folkloristic' would reduce all forms of knowledge not bound by Western criteria of truth to superstition at worst and to 'common sense' at best."
40. Marcos expressed the Zapatistas' utter rejection of Mexico's political class in the *Sixth Declaration of the Lacandon Jungle*.
41. The EZLN's *Fourth Declaration of the Lacandon Jungle* elaborates on this "force."
42. See Aricó (1988, p. 37, n. 7): "el Che Guevara … que tenía una amplísima curiosidad intelectual, no pareció haber leído nunca a Gramsci."

Conclusion

In the preceding chapters we have pieced together a profile of Marcos' political-philosophical formation. In the process of doing so we have unearthed some interesting and perhaps unexpected findings: namely, that for a left-wing Latin American guerrilla icon the Subcommander was rather unorthodox in his Marxist formation. For one thing, his exposure to Marxism was preceded, and in turn shaped, by literature, so that when he encountered the tenets of Marx these were experienced, one could even say mediated, through the pre-existing prism provided by his literary formation. For another, in terms of the underground guerrilla organization in whose ranks he was enrolled and by which he was to some extent formed, at least in terms of being inculcated with an Marxist-Leninist revolutionary ethos, the FLN appears to have been far less dogmatic and considerably more eclectic and heterogeneous in its ideology than other contemporary clandestine left-wing guerrilla groups such as the September 23rd Communist League. Furthermore, his graduation thesis, although Marxist, was extremely heavily indebted, not to the traditional Russian Marxism of Lenin or Trotsky or Stalin (or the Chinese Marxism of Mao either for that matter), but to the contemporary French structural Marxism of Althusser and Poulantzas, and post-Marxism of Foucault. (Interestingly, even in his Althusserianism he was atypical, since for him the philosophy of the French structural Marxist was not something to be mastered as some kind of intellectual exercise undertaken in the pursuit of attaining academic credentials; rather, it was, as Althusser himself put it, "class struggle at the level of theory," a means of experiencing directly "the reality of theoretical practice (science, philosophy) in its concrete life" as a precursor to embarking on "the reality of the *practice of revolutionary class struggle* in its concrete life, in close contact with the masses.") Finally, his reading of key anti-humanist, structuralist and post-structuralist works by Althusser (and his disciples) and Foucault caused him to shun Gramsci (and other influential humanist Marxists such as Lukács) and subsequently, in the relatively cocooned isolation of the Chiapan hinterland, the Subcommander would[1], unlike other Latin American guerrilla leaders of this era—one thinks, for example, of Comandante Jonás of the El Salvadoran Ejército Revolucionario del Pueblo (ERP)—remain insulated from the Gramsci boom that proved to exert such an influence on the continent's Left. In short, rather than adhering to a predictable pattern, Marcos' political-philosophical formation proves a somewhat curious affair.

It is my contention that this rather unorthodox, or at least unconventional, political-philosophical formation fostered in Marcos a flexibility of mind that aided him to no small degree in transforming himself when confronted in Chiapas with an indigenous reality that was so unexpected and so very alien. Had Marcos undergone a typical—by which I mean more dogmatic—formation, the EZLN *foco* would have remained a voice crying out in the Chiapan wilderness. Indeed, as the Subcommander himself succinctly puts it: "If we had been orthodox leftists, we would never have worked with Indigenous peoples … [since] not even in the Leninist conception of the weakest link was it thought that it might be the Indigenous people, right?"[2] In such a scenario, Marcos, for his part, would have continued to spout what he later describes as "the absurdities that we had been taught; of imperialism, social crisis, the correlation of forces and their coming together, things that nobody understands…",[3] while the indigenous chiapanecans, for their part, would have simply walked away, turning their backs on a movement whose "words were not understandable," being as they were "very tough."[4] Indeed, despite having experienced a less rigid or doctrinaire formation, the Subcommander relates how hard it was, nonetheless, to accept the need to modify his ideology, describing it as "a forced … learning process,"[5] and telling another interviewer:

> It's very difficult when you have a theoretical scheme that explains the whole of a society and then you arrive in that society and you realize that your scheme explains nothing. It's difficult to accept; to recognize that you have dedicated all of your life to a project, and that this project is fundamentally warped. It can't even explain the reality into which you are trying to integrate yourself. It was something truly serious.[6]

— Conclusion —

And yet, ultimately, despite the difficulty involved, and certainly without there being any sense that it was a foregone conclusion, Marcos effected a dramatic transformation. Thus, as Walter D. Mignolo (2002, p. 247) observes:

> Rafael Guillén became Subcomandante Marcos at the moment of his recognition that … his Marxist ideology needed to be infected by Amerindian cosmology, and that Amerindians had their own equivalent of what Marx meant to Rafael Guillén and the urban intellectuals who went to the Lacandon Forest in the 1980s with the hope of propagating revolution.

This phenomenon, one that is perhaps unique in the annals of the Latin American left, has been oft related but seldom (if ever) explained, with commentators instead tending to focus on the dazzling transformation itself, and what emerged from it, and neglecting what had preceded it and made it possible. The examination of Marcos' formation that has been undertaken in the previous chapters seeks to rectify this and to contribute significantly to our understanding of how this transformation was able to take place. In addition to this, and crucially, such an examination also permits us to identify the components in Marcos' formation and to ascertain the extent to which these influences persisted in the Subcommander's discourse.

More concretely, we have witnessed the persistence in the Subcommander of key aspects of his political-philosophical formation which he had engaged with and imbibed during his formative years as Rafael Guillén. First, and arguably most striking of all, is the way his exposure to literature impacted on how he subsequently approached and engaged with Marxism, and how it ultimately shaped the couching of his political-philosophical discourse—one of the most novel, inspirational and commented upon aspects of the Zapatismo. In terms of his Marxism and Leninism, in the case of the former, it is evident that Marcos continues to be Marxist at least in some sense: for example, he utilizes Marxist analysis as one of his tools with which to critique neoliberal capitalism and the current state of Chiapas, Mexico, and the world at large; while he also retains elements of a class-based focus in his discourse, although in his terminology he replaces the *la clase obrera* (the proletariat or working class) with *los de abajo* (those of below or the underdogs). In the case of the latter, although there is little (if anything) to suggest that his Leninism persisted—and much that points to his rejection of certain central tenets of it, i.e. the creating of a vanguard party, the seizing of power, and the establishment of a dictatorship of the proletariat—we can witness in the Subcommander's discourse a small handful of references to the Russian revolutionary, showing at the very least that he had clearly not forgotten all his Lenin. Moreover, whereas Marcos points out that Lenin's "weakest link" theory had failed to take into account indigenous peoples, he defends the Russian's *Materialism and Empirio-criticism*. We can also witness the emergence of varying degrees of conceptual continuity, or at least the persistence of political-philosophical preoccupations, between the writings of Rafael and the discourse of Marcos in relation to certain contemporary French philosophers of the structural Marxist and post-structuralist/post-Marxist school. Specifically, in the case of Althusser this is related to the philosopher's work emphasizing the nature and crucial import of ideology, and also his concern with the relationship between theory and praxis. When it comes to Foucault's legacy, the situation is less straightforward, for we can witness here both a degree of continuity between Rafael's writings and Marcos' discourse, most notably concerning the power of discourse and the discourse of power, but also a phenomenon which, we will see, is even more pronounced with regard to Poulantzas: namely, the emergence in the Subcommander's discourse of theories and preoccupations that he would have encountered when he read Foucault's works as the student Rafael Guillén, but which do not reveal themselves in the latter's thesis. These latent Foucauldian concepts which appear to emerge newly (i.e. without having been foreshadowed in Rafael's thesis) in the Subcommander's writings and utterances, chiefly involve the conducting of a genealogical approach, an attack on grand narratives, and the promotion of gay rights. Turning, finally, to Poulantzas, we can see from Rafael's writings that he took on certain of the Greco-French thinker's preoccupations; specifically, those related to economic, political, and ideological crises, and the crisis of the State; class factions and the power bloc; and bourgeois ideology's masking of its inherently class exploitative nature in its discourse. However, crucially we cannot perceive the continuation of these specific influences in the discourse of Marcos. (We can, however, detect a Poulantzian stylistic and terminological continuity between the writings of Rafael Guillén and the discourse of Subcommander Marcos.) Instead, examination of the latter reveals other crucial Poulantzian concerns, ones not readily apparent in Rafael's thesis and other writings, but which he would have encountered in his reading and which lay dormant within him. Such "latent legacies" (as I would call them) include a keen appreciation of the importance of a) the role of social movements in bringing about radical social transformation, and b) the need for the left to be democratic, i.e. to take the lead in promoting democratic practices and to privilege democracy above all else (including revolution). (Needless to say, the above is testament to the continued influence, if not enduring legacy, of Althusser's, Foucault's, and Poulantzas' thought upon contemporary political thinking, discourse, and practice.)

The persistence or retention of these elements, I would urge, ought not to surprise us, for it is surely counterintuitive to suppose that the Subcommander's confrontation with indigenous reality should have completely obliterated all aspects of his previous political-philosophical formation. As profound as the culture shock that he experienced undoubtedly was, and as radical as the transformation that it provoked may have been, Marcos did not emerge from it a *tabula rasa*. Indeed, there can be, I believe, no such thing as a complete rupture when it comes to one's intellectual formation, residual traces will persist, and there is always a degree of continuity. It is for this reason that I chose to preface this book with the following quotation from Juan Villoro's *From Carthage to Chiapas: An Untimely Chronicle*: "Intellectual integration in alien surroundings has elements of the shipwreck. Does acceptance mean casting aside everything that went before? Not necessarily."[7] Two sets of evidence, the one experiential the other empirical, sustain and indeed confirm me in this belief. The first is my own experience of living for the last decade-and-a-half in Japan, where certain cultural values and ways of thinking (and arriving at decisions) which I have encountered have proven very foreign to me at times. This has instilled in me the conviction that in order to effect a degree of "intellectual integration" when cast adrift "in alien surroundings," one tends to fall back on pre-shipwreck cultural and intellectual baggage which one salvages in an attempt to assimilate the new values one is suddenly confronted with. The second comes from observation of the natural world, since even in the case of the spectacular metamorphosis whereby larvae transform themselves into butterflies or moths, imaginal discs that are present, but often dormant, in the former survive the transformation process to persist in the latter. Not only that, but of particular pertinence here, one scientific study, while noting that those "[i]nsects that undergo complete metamorphosis experience enormous changes in both morphology and lifestyle," has found evidence to suggest that "larval experience can persist through pupation into adulthood," and even "that associative memory survives metamorphosis in Lepidoptera."[8] Returning to the Subcommander, in sum, just as Marcos' literary formation was not completely expunged by his steeping himself in Marxism, neither was his Marxism, in turn, totally erased in the confrontation with indigenous reality.

Crucially, given, as noted in the introduction, that Marcos' discourse is largely (though not completely) inseparable from the Zapatistas' discourse, the discovery of these political-philosophical continuities in the Subcommander's writings has important implications regarding Zapatismo: namely, it aids in the identification of certain influences that informed, and elements that contributed to (and thus helped constitute), the Zapatistas' political philosophy. Moreover, in doing so it enables us to re-evaluate the Subcommander's role in this process, for while Marcos may not be "the very core of Zapatismo, as Mao was for Maoism and Che for Guevarism,"[9] there has been a prevailing tendency, at least on the part of scholars,[10] to neglect the Subcommander's political-philosophical contribution to Zapatismo.[11] This tendency has a long pedigree, dating back to the first detailed and nuanced examination of the Zapatistas' ideological underpinnings produced by Michael Löwy (1998), who, in a concise and otherwise incisive piece on Zapatismo, identified five "threads"[12] that constitute the Zapatistas' political philosophy: (1) *Guevarism*, (2) *the legacy of Emiliano Zapata*, (3) *liberation theology*, (4) *the Mayan culture*, and (5) *the democratic demands made by Mexican civil society*.[13] Notably, Löwy's schema entirely ignored the person of Marcos, resulting in the neglect of two significant dimensions in the development of Zapatismo: the first being Marcos' role as the shuttle by which the majority of non-indigenous (i.e. the Guevaran, Mexican civil society, and possibly also the Zapatan—though not the liberation theology[14]) threads were woven into the existing fabric of indigenous thought to create what we today call Zapatismo[15]; and the second being the Subcommander's own political-philosophical formation which contributed yet another thread in the tapestry that is Zapatismo. Indeed, by charting these continuities we can see that the Subcommander's role with regard to Zapatismo far exceeds that which it has frequently been reduced to: that is, of mere *traductor* (translator)[16] between the rural indigenous communities of Chiapas and Mexico's urban mestizo society (and the wider world which lies beyond it). For while there is no doubt that Marcos, as he himself has acknowledged,[17] fulfills that function, a role

— CONCLUSION —

the enormous importance of which should not be underestimated,[18] the Subcommander is much more than this: he contributed significant political-philosophical threads to the Zapatismo tapestry—something that hitherto has been almost completely ignored.

Ultimately, it is hoped that a fundamentally more nuanced picture of the Subcommander and his role emerges from the pages of this book, one in which Marcos brought with him to Zapatismo an understanding of the current world, and a devastating critique of the state of it, that was influenced by his exposure to both literature and structural Marxist and post-structuralist post-Marxist political-philosophy during his formative years as Rafael Guillén. That Marcos, as were so many of the Left of his generation, was influenced by these schools of thought is perhaps neither surprising nor, certainly, does it make Zapatismo any less valid as a political philosophy: thinkers belonging to those political-philosophical schools have been rich in their thought and analysis, and although no single one of them may be considered to offer a definitive political philosophy that provides all the answers to all the questions, it cannot be said that they provide no answers whatsoever. Hence, instead of avoiding discussion of Marcos' indebtedness to structural Marxism and post-structural post-Marxism, I have maintained the position that it proves far more productive to try and ascertain the extent to which these influences persisted in the Subcommander and the degree to which he wove these into the tapestry that is Zapatismo. In sum, through my adopting an approach that utilizes elements drawn from literary theory and criticism, and political theory and practice—i.e. that examines Marcos' literary formation, traces the socio-political background of the FLN, conducts a close textual analysis of the graduation thesis of Rafael Guillén, and carries out a discourse analysis of the Subcommander's writings, speeches, and interviews—a multi-layered, richly textured portrait of the Subcommander has been composed, one which constitutes an intellectual biography (of sorts) of the Subcommander. In a sense then, it can be seen as complementing my previous biography of this iconic insurgent.

Notes

1. As Marcos told Yvon Le Bot (1997a, pp. 139-141):
    It was a solitary period because we weren't told anything, in terms of the

world and national reality .... As a guerrilla group we were very isolated, as much on the national terrain as on the local, because we had no contact with the indigenous communities ... we were the prime example of solitude, of isolation in every sense...

(The translation here is that of Christopher Gunderson (2013, pp. 462-3), with the final clause after the second ellipsis being that of my own.)

2. In Autonomedia (1994, p. 294).
3. In an interview with Adolfo Gilly (1995, p. 137); the English translation here is that of Nicholas P. Higgins (2004, p. 159).
4. Ibid.
5. In Autonomedia (1994, p. 294).
6. Le Bot (1997a, pp. 149-150); the English translation here is that of Nicholas P. Higgins (2004, p. 162).
7. This translation is that of The Creative Crossroads of the Americas.org, and is retrieved from http://creativecrossroadsofamericas.org/from-carthage-to-chiapas-an-untimely-chronicle-part-2-by-juan-villoro/.
8. Blackiston, Douglas J., Casey, Elena Silva, and Weiss, Martha R. (2008). Retention of Memory through Metamorphosis: Can a Moth Remember What It Learned As a Caterpillar? *PLoS ONE 3*(3). Retrieved from http://www.plosone.org/article/fetchArticle.action?articleURI=info:doi/10.1371/journal.pone.0001736.
9. The quotation is from Gustavo Esteva (2004, p. 20) who poses the question: "is he [i.e. Marcos] the very core of Zapatismo, as Mao was for Maoism and Che for Guevarism?"
10. Media commentators, conversely, have predominantly (though not exclusively) tended to focus on the figure of Marcos, often in a sensationalist manner.
11. There have been several works on Zapatismo; for example, in Spanish: Dora Kanoussi (1998), Guillermo Michel (2001a) and (2003), Iván Molina (2000), Hernán Ouviña (2007), Guiomar Rovira (2009), and Eugene Gogol (2014); in English: Thomas Olesen (2005), and Alex Khasnabish (2008) and (2010); and in French, Jérôme Baschet (2002). None of these however focus on the Subcommander's contribution to Zapatismo's political-philosophical formulation.
12. Löwy (1998, p. 2): "What is Zapatism composed of? It is a subtle mixture, an alchemistic fusion, an explosive cocktail made up of several ingredients, several traditions, each of them indispensable, each of them present in the final product. Or rather, it is a carpet made of threads of different colors, old and new, interwoven in a wonderful design whose secret is known only to the Mayan Indians."
13. Italics in the original.
14. See Legorreta Díaz (1998, p. 225) and Nick Henck (2007, pp. 21 & 118-120), for Marcos' at best lukewarm, and according to others even hostile, attitude towards Christianity.

15. Isolated geographically, culturally, linguistically and philosophically from Mexican mainstream society, Chiapas' indigenous peasants were likely introduced to Che Guevara, the Cuban and Nicaraguan revolutionary experiences, Mexican civil society, and possibly also Zapata, predominantly by the Subcommander. NB however, that while the rank and file indigenous EZLN recruits would have been introduced to these external icons by the three regional Subcommanders (i.e. Marcos, Daniel, and Pedro), indigenous cadres who belonged to the upper echelons of the movement received more in-depth instruction through FLN schools for cadres in Mexico City.
16. For commentators' references to Marcos as an "interpreter," "translator," or "bridge," see: Gunther Dietz (1995, p. 35), Enrique Dussel (1995b, pp. 87, 96-97), René Báez (1996, p. 68), Manuel Castells (1997/2004, p. 83), Tanius Karam (2000), Ezequiel Maldonado (2001, p. 144), Cynthia Steele (2002, p. 248), Walter D. Mignolo (2002, p. 247), Jorge Lora Cam (2003, p. 258), Valeria Wagner and Alejandro Moreira (2003, p. 196), Gustavo Esteva (2004, p. 22), Clifford Bob (2005, p. 162), Kevin McDonald (2006, p. 126), Analisa Taylor (2009, p. 1), and Jeff Conant (2010, p. 187). Similarly, Régis Debray (1996/2002, p. 342) dubs Marcos an "interface," Ann Carrigan (2001, p. 418) states "Marcos has built bridges between 'two Mexicos'," and, most recently, Alex Khasnabish (2010, p. 115) has termed Marcos "a conduit." Walter D. Mignolo (2002, p. 247) and Mignolo and Schiwy (2003, pp. 13-14) perhaps go furthest in elaborating on Marcos as a *traductor*, providing an insightful and nuanced, though brief, account of his role.
17. In a communiqué dated May 5, 1995, and published in *La Jornada* (May 11, 1995), the Subcommander wrote that "The need for a translator (*traductor*) between the indigenous Zapatista culture and the national and international culture caused the obvious nose [i.e. Marcos], in addition to sneezing, to talk and to write;" retrieved from http://palabra.ezln.org.mx/comunicados/1995/1995_05_05_b.htm (Spanish) and http://flag.blackened.net/revolt/mexico/ezln/marcos_absence_exp_may95.html (English).
18. See Jorge Lora Cam (2003, p. 258), who, while noting how the Subcommander "gradually transformed himself from a translator into a mirror," writes that "This does not mean that Marcos has become an accessory for the indigenous world."

Appendix I: The Althusserian Preamble to Rafael Guillén's Thesis

As Marx did *not* say in the Communist Party Manifesto:

> "A spectre is haunting the history of philosophy: the spectre of non-existent 'Althusserianism.' All the Powers of old and new philosophy have entered into a holy alliance to exorcise this spectre: neo-positivists and metaphysics, Marxist-logicians and existentialists, Latin American ones and neo-philosophers.

Two things result from this fact:

1. Non-existent 'Althusserianism' is already acknowledged by all the powers of philosophy.

2. It is high time that non-existent 'Althusserians' (with the exception of Althusser himself) should openly, in the face of the whole world, publish their views, their aims, their aspirations, and meet this nursery tale of the spectre of non-existent 'Althusserianism' with a manifesto of their own philosophical work: a new practice of philosophy: PHILOSOPHY AS A REVOLUTIONARY WEAPON."

Appendix II: The Preface to Rafael Guillén's Thesis

PREFACE

The Theoretical Horizon of Discourse Analysis

    Regarding the analysis of the various discourses constructed around the specific Objects of Discourse according to the regulations and specifications of the different Discursive Formations, the archaeology of this discursive operation (rules of formation, organization, preventive incursion of discourses, etc.) inside the School Ideological System in Mexico has yet to be carried out and could give some general signs concerning the problems it would confront.

    What this is about here is establishing the broad terms which allow the analysis of how the various Discursive Formations inside the Mexican School System are organized among themselves and how they produce their effects-practices according to the specific situations of the process of reproduction-transformation of the relations of production. The specifically discursive has not been confronted in this research, we have preferred to focus on the DISCOURSE-IDEOLOGY relationship in so far as it is related to Ideological Discursive-Practices.

    It has to do with detecting the mechanisms of power which allow the philosophical, administrative, pedagogical, legal-political, etc. discourses inside the space-time situations in the Mexican ideological (educational) system. In sum, if what discursive practices are about is forming the practices of subjection, how is this carried out in the educational system? From what place is the discourse "said?" How are the questions carried out? What about the contradictions which arise in the educational system? How is it formed in partnership with the family ideological system? What is at stake in the organization established by the Discourse of Power?

The archaeology of the discursive practices should "track" the appearance of the various most important Discursive Objects, of the modification and/or continuance of its relationship of Domination/subordination, of the modifications in the organization of the discourses and of the various Discursive Formations.

But not only that. It is also necessary to analyze the mechanisms of power which are put into play in the discursive-practice non-discursive practice relationship. The present research project tries to be in keeping with this perspective. Nothing has been exhausted, there is nothing definitive in this discourse *which recalls discourse, the permanent crisis of theory is assumed as such and is expected to continue producing effects in specific analyses carried out, or, like this one, outlined.*[1]

What's at stake is not simply an academic requirement; rather what's at stake is the possibility of a new site for the functioning of philosophy, of theory, of politics…

Notes

1. The original text reads: "que vuelve sobre el discurso, la permanente crisis de la teoría es asumida como tal y se espera que siga produciendo efectos en los análisis concretos realizados o, como éste, esbozados."

Appendix III: Subcommander Marcos' *Letter to Adolfo Gilly*[1]

To: Güilly [sic][2]

From: Sup Marcos

October 22, 1994

    I received the photocopies of the article by Carlo Ginzburg, "Clues. Roots of an Evidential Paradigm" (look: undated, although one can guess that it is around 1978), with a dedication from you, illegible, about something having to do with Old Antonio's thoughts (and Heriberto's), also undated. Excuse my repeated demand for dates (and even for hours, if possible). It so happens that, upon leaving the mountains, I met with several surprises: one of them was finding out that "theoreticians," revolutionaries for ten years, are now sad apologists for neoliberalism. So, after my scolding (don't laugh, I know quite well that my fame for being rude and grumpy is spreading like wildfire), I'll go on to what occurred to me while reading the aforementioned Ginsburg.

    I remember having read the book by T. S. Kuhn about the structure of scientific revolutions, I think it was in an edition of the Economic Culture Fund (breviaries?). At that time there was a discussion about whether there were differences or similarities between the natural and the social sciences, the epistemological "slant," the "paradigms" and their "rupture" and the etceteras which, as always, have nothing to do with reality. Now I read that this Carlo Ginzburg person trawls for signs in psychoanalysis, detective literature and the aesthetics of the late 19th century, the coincidences of a new paradigm: the evidential. All that makes me sleepy. What would happen, for example, if the ears, the fingers or the fingernails (which so terrified the aesthetics theoreticians of the late 19th century, Morelli dixit), don't belong to anyone, that is, they could be anybody's?

I mean that this analysis or "search" ("tracking the animal," Old Antonio said) needs a frame of reference. Something with which to compare or contrast the gathered signs. And if there isn't anything in that frame of reference against which to contrast the sign? I mean, Old Antonio could know the time and the route of the paca, of the "white-tailed" deer, even of the mountain lion, but there was a referent for paca, for deer, for lion. And if not? What would Old Antonio have deduced if he had found the tracks of one of those automobiles that archbishops and drug traffickers use?

In sum, said paradigm is a tautology. Its assumption is taken as truth (the frame of reference with which the "signs" are contrasted), and, ergo, the conclusion is true (the "collection of signs" method).

The author tries to get out "of the predicament of the contraposition of rationalism and irrationalism." But where does that get anyone? I mean, the supposed fight between "rationalism" and "irrationalism" is just a variant of an idealist position: the subject, the individual, as the basis of knowledge. This dispute is just for resolving whether the subject is rational or irrational about knowledge. In reality, the problem in the sciences takes place in the struggle between materialism and idealism. (Ah, the now vituperated Lenin! Ah, the forgotten *Materialism and Empirio-criticism*! Ah, Mach and Avenarius resuscitated! Ah, the fool, Vladimir Ilych!).

Just look at how the historic referent of this scientific "paradigm" is consigned to the last part of the text in order to "complete" the analysis of the discovery of fingerprints and their use in police control. If I remember correctly, at the end of the 19th century the dominant social sciences were quite disconcerted by that new theory which was demanding its scientific place: the Science of History. It had developed over a critique of idealism (and a political practice) and of the system of domination which sustained and provided "foundation" for the bourgeois sciences. A counteroffensive was necessary. Stripping the social classes of the leading role which that irreverent theory, by that equally irreverent German Jew, gave them and returning it to the guarantor of the system: the individual and the idea which moved him (rationally or irrationally). Isn't this Morelli's objective in seeking a method in order to be able to award a work of art to the individual creator? The purpose

— APPENDICES —

of the search for details is to reconstitute the individual who created them. Pure science, no?

The similarities with criminal methods (we look for the criminal, we individualize him, we take him out of the social context which makes him possible, but, above all, we hide, within the shiny crime, the "other" crime: that of exploitation) lead to the same results: the search for, and the discovery of, the "special" individual, the one who creates a work of art or commits a criminal act. (By the way, why don't you apply this method for discovering the "special" individual who produced that criminal "work of art" that was the electoral process of August 21st?)

Fine, Ginzburg is difficult to follow. I imagine that now the intellectual fashion is this everythingology, mixing all kinds of social "sciences" in order to make reality explicable in an incomplete theoretical framework which, in order to be complete, resorts to other theoretical frameworks, even contradictory ones. That constant leap of knowledge from "common sense" to scientific knowledge to aesthetic products is a way in which the dominant ideology dominates in the sciences. Given that "common sense" jumps to scientific knowledge, it's worth asking oneself: what is the frame of reference for "common sense?" Isn't it the dominant ideology? The author manages to be sublime: the law and medicine are referred to as two "sciences." With such forceful arguments he "forgets" the central problem: how are the indicators "read?" From what class position? If you make the leap from hunters' anecdotes to the science of history, what are the "historical readings" of the collected signs? Don't you have to question the method of collecting the signs? Isn't there a class position in choosing some signs and not others? Isn't there a relationship with a political position on "reading" those signs? Isn't, ultimately, that criteria for selecting the signs, and for reading them, a criterion of class?

For example, the author says that "relationships between the doctor and the patient ... have not changed much since the times of Hippocrates." Relationships between doctor and patient? No! It's something more complicated: the institutional medical-body relationships and all those "scientific" concepts such as "normalcy." Examples? AIDS, wasn't it a curiosity while it was limited to affecting homosexuals? Didn't the "real" concern about AIDS start when it began affecting heterosexuals? Didn't interest increase when it began "striking" distinguished persons?

But you cannot sit down and argue with this Ginzburg, he keeps jumping from science to aesthetics, to history, to medicine, to literature, to psychoanalysis. It's fun—just kidding. During the first years of the guerrilla, we had three laws of the dialectic: the first is "everything has to do with everything else." The second is "a thing is a thing, and another thing is don't screw with me." The third is "there's no problem so big you can't go around it." And the fourth (yes, I know I said there were three, but, since they are dialectics, you don't have to ask them for a lot of formality) is "screw your mother, the world and the material." (You don't know how amused I am at how "conflicted" you'll be in deciding whether to publish this part of the letter). So, this Ginzburg is perfectly singular for his obscurantism.

Since we are talking about "scientific" paradigms, look at the current one. In what paradigm does the theory fall that supports and justifies (for some time now, the role of the dominant social theories has been to "justify" [that is, "make just"] the dominant system) the brutal process of appropriation of wealth, conscience and history that was begun again with the end of the century? Because that is neoliberalism, the "highly original" theory of the new dividing up of the world … and of its corners. You don't have to go to Italy and the neo-ascension of the right. Just look here. Take the completely tax-free pearls that Salinas, Aspe or Serra Puche give us. Here the paradigm is that, if reality does not correspond to what the theory says and orders, then a new "reality" must be invented, the reality of the media. For example, that myth of the country's "industrialization" with NAFTA and the real growth of micro-industry, the real correspondence with the international division of labor: countries which produce raw materials (and with cheap labor) and industrialized countries. The 19th century? No way, just before the 21st! There are at least two Mexicos (I say there are four, but neither you nor I are going to fight over two more or less, there could be three): one is that of the presidential reports, the official speeches, the big news programs, the commercials and the tourism promotions. The other is the one that really takes place, the one that allows for the regrettable "confusion" of vehicles in the Jalisco May, the Chiapas January, the March of Colosio, the September of Ruiz Massieu, the October of … who's next? The one of the 4%, of the 50-26-16 percent. You already knew that? Yes? Fine, but why is it that the more festive the official discourse, the more violent the reality? No, I'm not going to answer.

That is the work of the theoreticians, not of the guerreros. Missing the third Mexico? Fine, it is the one which fights … I believe.

Another thing. Here is a serious problem for Morelli-Doyle-Ginzburg-Guilly: let's try to apply the "evidentiary" paradigm to "neozapatismo." According to said "science," we should look for the individual "author" of plans, direction, conception, etceteration. Let us imagine the big-nosed ski-mask ("and quite a wanker," the guys say) who calls himself "Marcos." Let's take note of his signs: the obvious nose, the dubious eye color, crow's feet, the clumsy way of walking and writing (believe me, it's the same), the lies or truths they say about his past and—of course!—his fingernails (it is more difficult to make conclusions about his ears).

P.S. out of place and doesn't go here, but which is relevant, given the fingernails and etcetera:

Instructions For Going Forward

In front of any mirror, realize that one is not the best of oneself. But something can always be saved: a fingernail, for example…

Let us imagine that a more or less complete image may be composed of the man who is behind the large-nosed ("and a wanker," the guys repeat) ski-mask. The moment arrives to compare him with a frame of reference. Let me imagine, for signs, what happens in each case: in the Department of Government, they are reviewing the files of Liberation Theology sympathizers, yearbooks from the Ibero-Itam-Unam, and, of course, the reserves of the "Monterrey" football team. In the PRI they are reviewing the agendas of resentful, irrelevant or resurrected members of the PRI, in the CIA-FBI, the lists of Cubans-Nicaraguans-Libyans-Fedayeen-ETA-etceteras. In the left they are reviewing their memories, in intellectual circles their grudges. In Mexican homes, they are reviewing the mirror. The result? "Marcos" could be anyone or no one, he could be all or none, he doesn't exist, he's an unfinished invention, a model to be assembled according to anyone's liking. A faceless man is not necessarily a man with a covered face. He is, above all, a man with any face, who says nothing, who doesn't lead us to anything. A useless face, a mere skeleton for giving form to the large-nosed ("and a wanker," the guys confirm) ski-mask.

About the ski-mask. The same. I don't know how many different and contradictory arguments I've made over the use of the ski-masks. Now I remember: the cold, security, anti-caudillismo (paradoxically), homage to Old Antonio's black god, aesthetic difference, embarrassing ugliness. Probably none of those arguments would be true. The fact is that now the ski-mask is a symbol of rebellion. Just yesterday it was a symbol of criminality or terrorism. Why? Certainly not because we would have proposed it.

(It's 14:00 [according to your watch], they just let me know about a new incursion by a patrol of federal police, next to the Toniná ruins, in Ocosingo now. We won't make the denuncia now. We're tired now, and, besides, we're going to end up like the shepherd crying "wolf!," "wolf!" and they'll stop believing us…)

Now let's go to a paradigm in disuse. It will be necessary to go to the wastebasket, smooth out that crumpled old piece of paper which is called "The Science of History," historical materialism. Why did they throw it out? Because of the moral hangover after the collapse of the socialist camp? A tactical "retreat" in the face of the overwhelming force of the "marine boys" and neoliberalism? The "end of history?" Did it go out of fashion along with the desire to fight? Why, today, is a revolution quickly consigned to the place of utopias? What happened to them, Güilly? Did they get tired? Did they get bored? Did they sell out? Did they surrender? Wasn't it worth it? Isn't it worth it? Or did that theory take them down the blind alley (for the theoreticians) of having to be consistent in practice? What happened to them, Güilly? I see that now cynicism is the flag of the left. "Realism," a columnist will correct me, "realpolitik," another will add. Perhaps the most elaborate theories didn't end up being a search through the old manuals. At the end of the day, why am I telling you all this? I was just going to write you the aforementioned article which I promised you on an off-day for the irregular *Vientos del Sur*, and then you come across with this article by this Ginzburg (whose last name carries its own punishment). Perhaps you didn't send it, and it was another "Güilly" [sic] who did. The fact is the aforementioned letter is going to take a while, so you should wait for it sitting down. In exchange, and, in the meantime, I'm sending you this delightful letter which you can use as filler in the missing section, "The Readers Belch," regrettably absent from the irreverent *Vientos del Sur*.

— Appendices —

Vale, Güilly. Salud and look for a name that's easier to write, because I've heard six different versions of this name in our patrols.

From the mountains of the Mexican Southeast.

Subcomandante Insurgente Marcos.

P.S. always yes. Fine, I'll start explaining. We didn't propose it. In reality, the only thing we have proposed is changing the world, the rest we've been improvising as we go along. Our rigid conception of the world and of revolution was left rather dented in the confrontation with the indigenous Chiapas reality. Something new (which doesn't mean "good") came out of the blows, what is now known as "neozapatismo."

P.S. always no. Better that you wait for a while again. Here comes the airplane again. Smile. It's 20:46, "southeastern time," as Tacho says.

Notes

1. The following translation is the work of the late Irlandesa, from whom I personally commissioned the piece. There remains, to the best of my knowledge, no other complete translation of this important epistle. For an interesting discussion of this letter and Gilly's response to it, see Stephanie Jed (2001, p. 377ff).
2. For some (inexplicable) reason Marcos misspells Gilly's name throughout.

Works Cited

Aguirre Rojas, Carlos Antonio. 2008. *Mandar obedeciendo: Lecciones políticas del neozapatismo mexicano.* Bogotá, D.C., Colombia: Ediciones desde abajo.

Aguirre Rojas, Carlos Antonio. 2011. "La guerra, la política y la ética: Reflexiones sobre una Carta," *Rebeldia* 77 (mayo 6): 43-50; retrieved from http://revistarebeldia.org/revistas/numero77/08aguirre.pdf.

Althusser, Louis. [1965] 1969. *For Marx*, translated by Ben Brewster. London: Penguin. Retrieved from http://www.marx2mao.com/Other/FM65NB.html.

Althusser, Louis. [1965] 1990. "Theory, Theoretical Practice and Theoretical Formation: Ideology and Ideological Struggle," pp. 1-42 in his *Philosophy and the Spontaneous Philosophy of Scientists and Other Essays*. London: Verso. Retrieved from http://www.marx2mao.com/Other/PSPS90i.html.

Althusser, Louis. [1967] 1990. "Philosophy and the Spontaneous Philosophy of Scientists," pp. 69-165 in his *Philosophy and the Spontaneous Philosophy of Scientists and Other Essays*. London: Verso. Retrieved from http://www.marx2mao.com/Other/PSPS90.html.

Althusser, Louis. [1968a] 2001. "Philosophy as a Revolutionary Weapon," pp. 11-22 in *Lenin and Philosophy and Other Essays*, translated by Ben Brewster. New York: Monthly Review Press.

Althusser, Louis. [1968b] 2001. "Lenin and Philosophy," pp. 23-70 in *Lenin and Philosophy and other essays*, translated by Ben Brewster. New York: Monthly Review Press.

ALTHUSSER, LOUIS. [1970] 1997. *Reading Capital*, translated by Ben Brewster. London: Verso. Retrieved from http://www.marxists.org/reference/archive/althusser/1968/reading-capital/index.htm.

ALTHUSSER, LOUIS. [1971] 2001. "Ideology and Ideological State Apparatuses," pp. 85–126 in *Lenin and Philosophy and other essays*, translated by Ben Brewster. New York: Monthly Review Press. Retrieved from http://www.marx2mao.com/Other/LPOE70ii.html.

ALTHUSSER, LOUIS. [1974] 1990. *Philosophy and the Spontaneous Philosophy of Scientists and Other Essays*. London: Verso. Retrieved from http://www.marx2mao.com/Other/PSPS90.html.

ALTHUSSER, LOUIS. 1976. *Essays in Self-Criticism*. London: New Left Books.

ALTHUSSER, LOUIS. [1976] 1990. "The Transformation of Philosophy," pp. 241-265 in his *Philosophy and the Spontaneous Philosophy of Scientists and Other Essays*. London: Verso. Retrieved from http://www.marx2mao.com/Other/PSPS90iii.html.

ALTHUSSER, LOUIS. 2006. *Philosophy of the Encounter: Later Writings, 1978-87*. London: Verso.

ALVARADO, JUAN MANUEL. 1995. "En un 'Lugar de la Selva'." *Reforma* (February 17): 10A.

ALVAREZ, SONIA E., DAGNINO, EVELINA, AND ESCOBAR, ARTURO (eds.). 1998a. *Cultures of Politics: Politics of Cultures*. Boulder, Colorado: Westview Press.

ALVAREZ, SONIA E., DAGNINO, EVELINA, AND ESCOBAR, ARTURO. 1998b. "Introduction: The Cultural and the Political in Latin American Social Movements," pp. 1-29 in Alvarez, Dagnino and Escobar (1998a).

ANDERSON, JON LEE. 1997. *Che Guevara: A Revolutionary Life*. London: Bantam.

ANDERSON, PERRY. 1983. *In the Tracks of Historical Materialism*. London: Verso.

ANDERSON, PERRY. 1992. *A Zone of Engagement*. London: Verso.

ARICÓ, JOSÉ. 1988. *La cola del Diablo: Itinerario de Gramsci en América Latina*. Caracas: Editorial Nueva Sociedad.

Aubry, Andrés. 2005. *Chiapas a contrapelo: Una agenda de trabajo para su historia en perspectiva sistémica*. México: Contrahistorias.

Autonomedia. 1994. *¡Zapatistas! Documents of the New Mexican Revolution*. New York: Autonomedia.

Autonomedia. 2005. *Conversations with Durito: Stories of the Zapatistas and Neoliberalism*. New York: Autonomedia.

Badiou, Alain. 2013. "The Althusserian Definition of Theory." Lecture given at Princeton University on December 6; an audio recording is available on the Internet at: http://progressivegeographies.com/2013/12/10/alain-badiou-the-althusserian-definition-of-theory-audio-recording/.

Báez, René. 1996. *Conversaciones con Marcos*. Quito: Eskeletra.

Bahn, Josh. 2009. "Marxism in a snail shell: Making history in Chiapas," *Rethinking History*, Vol. 13, No. 4 (December): 541–560.

Baker, Gideon. 2002. *Civil Society and Democratic Theory: Alternative Voices*. London and New York: Routledge.

Baker, Gideon. 2003. "'Civil society that so perturbs': *Zapatismo* and the Democracy of Civil Society." *Space and Polity*, Vol. 7, No. 3 (December): 293–312.

Barajas, Rafael. "'El Fisgón.' El 68 marcó la ruptura de la opinión pública con los medios," pp. 121-132 in Eduardo Cruz Vázquez (ed.), *1968–2008. Los silencios de la democracia*. México: Planeta.

Bardach, Ann Louise. 1994. "Mexico's Poet Rebel," *Vanity Fair* 57 (July): 68-74 & 130-135.

Barnes, Barry. [1985] 2000. "Thomas Kuhn," in Quentin Skinner ([1985] 2000b:83-100).

Barret, Patrick Chávez, Daniel and Rodríguez-Garavito, César. 2008. *The New Latin American Left: Utopia Unborn*. London: Pluto Books.

Barros, Robert. 1986. "The Left and Democracy: Recent debates in Latin America," *Telos* 68: 49-70.

Bartra, Roger. 2002. *Blood, Ink, and Culture* (trans. Mark Alan Healey). Durham, North Carolina: Duke University Press.

Baschet, Jérôme. 2000. "(Re) discutir sobre la historia," in *Chiapas* 10: 7-40.

Baschet, Jérôme. 2002. *L'Étincelle Zapatiste*. Paris: Éditions Denoël.

Baschet, Jérôme. 2005. "Los Zapatistas: ¿'Ventriloquia india' o interacciones creativas?," *istor*, Año VI, Número 22 (otoño): 110-128.

Benjamin, Medea. 1995. "Interview: Subcomandante Marcos," pp. 57-70 in Elaine Katzenberger, *First World, ha ha ha!*. San Francisco: City Lights Books.

Benton, Ted. 1984. *The Rise and Fall of Structural Marxism*. London: Macmillan.

Besancenot, Olivier and Löwy, Michael. 2009. *Che Guevara: His Revolutionary Legacy*. New York: Monthly Review Press.

Blackledge, Paul, and Kirkpatrick, Graeme (eds.). 2002. *Historical Materialism and Social Evolution*. Houndmills: Palgrave Macmillan.

Boatwright, Stephon. n.d. "Common Sense." Retrieved from http://www.oswego.edu/Documents/wac/Deans'%20Awards,%202012/politics1.pdf.

Bob, Clifford. 2005. *The Marketing of Rebellion*. Cambridge: Cambridge University Press.

Boron, Atilio A. 2001. *"La selva y la polis*. Interrogantes en torno a la teoría política del zapatismo." *Chiapas* 12: 89–114.

Brand, Ulrich and Hirsch, Joachim. 2004. "In Search of Emancipatory Politics: The Resonances of Zapatism in Western Europe," *Antipode*, Vol. 36, Issue 3 (June): 371-382.

Brewster, Claire. 2005. *Responding to Crisis in Contemporary Mexico: The Political Writings of Paz, Fuentes, Monsiváis, and Poniatowska*. Tucson: The University of Arizona Press.

Broccoli, Angelo. 1977. *Antonio Gramsci y la educación como hegemonía*. México: Ed. Nueva Imagen.

Broccoli, Angelo. 1978. *Ideología y educación*. México: Ed. Nueva Imagen.

BRUHN, KATHLEEN. 1999. "Antonio Gramsci and the Palabra Verdadera: The Political Discourse of Mexico's Guerrilla Forces," *Journal of Interamerican Studies and World Affairs*, Vol. 41, No. 2 (Summer): 29-55.

BUCI-GLUCKSMANN, CHRISTINE. 1980. *Gramsci and the State*. London: Lawrence and Wishart, Ltd.

BURBACH, ROGER AND NÚÑEZ, ORLANDO. 1986. *Democracia y revolución en las Américas: agenda para un debate*. Managua: Editorial Vanguardia; updated and translated into English as *Fire in the Americas* (London: Verso, 1987).

BURGOS, RAÚL. 2002. "The Gramscian Intervention in the Theoretical and Political Production of the Latin American Left," *Latin American Perspectives*, 29, 1 (January): 9–37.

CALLAHAN, MANUEL. 2004. "Zapatismo beyond Chiapas," in David Solnit (ed.) (2004:217-228).

CALLINICOS, ALEX. [1987] 2004. *Making History: Agency, Structure, and Change in Social Theory*. Leiden: Brill.

CARLSEN, LAURA. 2007. "Introduction: An Uprising Against the Inevitable," pp. 13-31 in Subcommander Marcos (2007d).

CARR, BARRY. 1985. "Mexican Communism 1968-1981: Eurocommunism in the Americas?," *Journal of Latin American Studies*, Vol. 17, No. 1 (May): 201-228.

CARRIGAN, ANA. 1998. "Why is the Zapatista Movement so Attractive to Mexican civil society?," *Civreports*, Vol. 2, No. 2 (March-April): 1-22.

CARRIGAN, ANA. 2001. "*Afterword:* Chiapas, the First Postmodern Revolution," pp. 417-443 in Juliana Ponce de León, *Our Word is Our Weapon*. New York: Seven Stories Press.

CASTAÑEDA, JORGE. 1997. *Campañero: The Life and Death of Che Guevara*. New York: Alfred A. Knopf.

CASTAÑEDA, JORGE. [2011] 2012. *Mañana Forever?: Mexico and the Mexicans*. New York: Vintage Books.

CASTELLANOS, LAURA. 2008. *Corte de Caja. Entrevista al Subcomandante Marcos*. México: Grupo Editorial Endira México.

CASTELLS, MANUEL. [1997] 2004. *The Power of Identity* Vol. II. Second edition. Oxford: Blackwell Publishing.

CAVALLARI, HÉCTOR MARIO. 1994. "*Savoir* and *Pouvoir*: Michel Foucault's Theory of Discursive Practice," pp. 209-223 in Barry Smart (ed.), *Foucault (2) Critical Assessments*. London: Routledge.

CECEÑA, ANA ESTHER. 2001. "Civil Society and the EZLN," pp. 23-43 in Midnight Notes Collective (eds.), *Auroras of the Zapatistas*. Second edition. New York: Autonomedia.

CECEÑA, ANA ESTHER. 2004. "The Subversion of Historical Knowledge of the Struggle: *Zapatistas* in the 21st Century," *Antipode*, Volume 36, Issue 3, (June): 361–370.

CEDILLO, ADELA. 2008. "El fuego y el silencio: Historia de las fuerzas de liberación nacional mexicanas (1969-1974)." Tesis para obtener el título de Licenciado en Historia por la Facultad de Filosofía y Letras-UNAM.

CEDILLO, ADELA. 2010. "El fuego y el silencio. Historia de las FLN (1979-1974), El suspiro del silencio. De la Reconstrucción de las Fuerzas de Liberación Nacional a la fundación del Ejército Zapatista de Liberación Nacional (1974-1983)." UNAM MA thesis (November).

CEDILLO, ADELA. 2012. "Armed Struggle Without Revolution: The Organizing Process of the National Liberation Forces (FLN) and the Genesis of Neo-Zapatism (1969-1983)," pp. 148-166 in Fernando Herrera Calderón and Adela Cedillo (eds.), *Challenging Authoritarianism in Mexico: Revolutionary Struggle and the Dirty War, 1964-1982*. New York: Routledge.

CHOAT, SIMON. [2010] 2012. *Marx Through Post-Structuralism: Lyotard, Derrida, Foucault, Deleuze*. London and New York: Continuum.

CHOMSKY, NOAM AND MICHEL FOUCAULT. [1971] 2006. "Human Nature: Justice vs. Power (1971) A Debate Between Noam Chomsky and Michel Foucault," in Noam Chomsky and Michel Foucault (2006:1-67).

CHOMSKY, NOAM AND MICHEL FOUCAULT. 2006. *The Chomsky-Foucault Debate on Human Nature*. New York and London: The New Press.

— Works Cited —

Cohen, G. A. 1978. *Karl Marx's Theory of History: A Defense*. Oxford: Clarendon Press.

Collier, George A. 2000. "Zapatismo resurgent: Land and Autonomy in Chiapas," *NACLA Report on the Americas*, Vol. 33, Issue 5 (March): 20-22.

Collier, George A., and Collier, Jane F. 2005. "The Zapatista rebellion in the context of globalization," *Journal of Peasant Studies*, Special Issue: Rural Chiapas Ten Years After The Zapatista Uprising, Volume 32, Issue 3-4: 450-460.

Collier, George A., and Quaratiello, Elizabeth L. [1994] 1999. *Basta!: Land and rebellion in Chiapas*. Revised edition. Oakland, CA: Food First Books, Institute for Food and Development Policy.

Conant, Jeff. 2010. *A Poetics of Resistance: The Revolutionary Public Relations of the Zapatista Insurgency*. California: AK Press.

Córdova, Arnaldo. [1987] 1991. "Gramsci y la izquierda mexicana," *Nueva Sociedad* No. 115 (September-October): 160-163; retrieved from http://www.nuso.org/upload/articulos/2043_1.pdf. Originally published under the same title in *La Ciudad Futura* No. 6, Suplemento/4 (1987): 14-15.

Corona, Ignacio and Jörgensen, Beth E. (eds.). 2002. *The Contemporary Mexican Chronicle*. New York: New York State University.

Correa-Díaz, Luis. 2000. "América como Dulcinea: Cervantes, el *Che* y el Subcomandante Marcos," *Taller de Letras* No. 28: 23-40.

Correa-Díaz, Luis. 2001. "Cervantes in America: Between New World Chronicle and Chivalric Romance," pp. 210-224 in Santiago Juan-Navarro and Theodore Robert Young's *A Twice-Told Tale: Reinventing the Encounter in Iberian/Iberian American Literature and Film*. Newark: University of Delaware Press.

Corro, Salvador. 1995. "Cesáreo Morales y Alberto Híjar evocan los años setenta, cuando se gustaba la insurrección," *Proceso* No. 979 (August 7): 22-27.

Couch, Jen. 2001. "Imagining Zapatismo: the Anti-globalisation Movement and the Zapatistas." *Communal/Plural* 9, 2: 243–260.

CRESPO, LUIS AND RAMONEDA, JOSEP. 1974. *Sobre la filosofía y su no-lugar en el marxismo*. Barcelona: Laia.

DAGNINO, EVELINA. 1998. "Culture, Citizenship, and Democracy: Changing Discourses and Practices of the Latin American Left," in Alvarez, Dagnino and Escobar (1998a:33-63).

DAVID, MIRIAM E. 1980. *The State, the Family and Education*. London: Routledge.

DAY, RICHARD J. F. 2005. *Gramsci is Dead*. London: Pluto Press.

DE HUERTA, MARTA DURAN AND HIGGINS, NICHOLAS. 1999. "An interview with Subcomandante Insurgente Marcos, spokesperson and military commander of the Zapatista National Liberation Army (EZLN)," *International Affairs*, Vol. 75, Issue 2 (April): 269-279.

DE LA COLINA, JOSÉ. 2002. "As Time Goes By: 'Marcos,' or The Mask is the Message," in Tom Hayden (ed.) (2002:363-367).

DE LA GRANGE, BERTRAND. 1995. "L'armée mexicaine a repris sans combat le contrôle du territoire zapatiste," *Le Monde* (février 22).

DE LA GRANGE, BERTRAND. 1999. "El otro subcomandante: Entrevista con Salvador Morales Garibay," *Letras Libres* No. 2 (February): 76-83.

DE LA GRANGE, BERTRAND AND RICO, MAITE. 1998. *Subcomandante Marcos: la genial impostura*. México: Aguilar.

DE LA PEÑA MARTÍNEZ, LUIS. 2004. "¿Qué hay de peligroso en el hecho de que las gentes hablen?: Foucault, el zapatismo y la crítica de la modernidad," *EspacioLatino*; Retrieved from http://letras-uruguay.espaciolatino.com/aaa/de_la_pena/foucault.htm.

DEBRAY, RÉGIS. 1995. "*A demain, Zapata!*," *Le Monde* (March 17, 1995).

DEBRAY, RÉGIS. [1996] 2002. "A Guerrilla with a difference," in Tom Hayden (ed.) (2002:340-52); first published as "Le guerilla autrement," in *Le Monde* (May 14, 1996); translated into English and reprinted in *New Left Review* 218 (July/August), pp. 128-137, as "Talking to the Zapatistas: A guerrilla with a difference."

DELGADO, ALVARO. 1995. "Rafael Guillén, en la UAM-Xochimilco de los años 80: 'inteligencia filosa y certera,' 'humor privilegiado,' 'desmadroso y chacotero.'" *Proceso* No. 981 (agosto 21): 12-13 & 17-20.

DERRIDA, JACQUES. 1993. "Politics and Friendship: An Interview with Jacques Derrida," pp. 183-231 in E. Ann Kaplan and Michael Sprinkler, *The Althusserian Legacy*. London and New York: Verso.

DEWS, PETER. 1994. "Structuralism and the French Epistemological Tradition," in Elliott (1994:104-141).

DI PIRAMO, DANIELA. 2010. *Political Leadership in Zapatista Mexico: Marcos, Celebrity, and Charismatic Authority*. Boulder, Colorado: FirstForumPress.

DI PIRAMO, DANIELA. 2011. "Beyond Modernity: Irony, Fantasy, and the Challenge to Grand Narratives in Subcomandante Marcos's Tales," in *Mexican Studies/Estudios Mexicanos*, Vol. 27, Issue 1 (Winter): 177-205.

DÍAZ, CARLOS TELLO. [1995] 2001. *La rebelión de las Cañadas*. México: Cal y Arena.

DIETZ, GUNTHER. 1995. "Zapatismo y movimientos: étnico-regionales en México," *Nueva Sociedad* No. 140 (Noviembre-Diciembre): 33-50.

DOMÍNGUEZ MICHAEL, CHRISTOPHER. 1999. "El prosista armado," *Letras Libres* (January); retrieved from http://letraslibres.com/revista/libros/el-prosista-armado.

DREYFUS, HUBERT L., AND RABINOW, PAUL. 1982. *Michel Foucault: Beyond Structuralism and Hermeneutics*. Chicago: University of Chicago Press.

DURÁN, MARTA (compiladora). 1994. *Yo, Marcos*. México: Milenio.

DUSSEL, ENRIQUE. 1995a. "Ethical Sense of the 1994 Maya Rebellion in Chiapas," *Journal of Hispanic/Latino Theology*, Vol. 2, No. 3: 41-56.

DUSSEL, ENRIQUE. 1995b. "Marcos, ein Übersetzer zwischen Maya und Moderne. Ein Gespräch," pp. 87-101 in Anne Huffschmid, *Subcomandante Marcos: Ein maskierter Mythos*. Berlin: Elefanten Press.

DUSSEL, ENRIQUE. 2003a. "Philosophy in Latin America in the Twentieth Century: Problems and Currents," pp. 11-53 in Eduardo Mendieta (ed.), *Latin American Philosophy: Currents, Issues, Debates*. Indiana: Indiana University Press.

DUSSEL, ENRIQUE. 2003b. "Ethical Sense of the 1994 Maya Rebellion in Chiapas," pp. 167–183 in Enrique Dussel (ed.), *Beyond Philosophy: Ethics, History, Marxism, and Liberation Theology*. Maryland: Rowman & Littlefield Publishers.

EL KILOMBO. 2007. *Beyond Resistance: Everything: An Interview with Subcomandante Insurgente Marcos*. Durham, N.C.: PaperBoat Press.

ELLIOTT, GREGORY. [1987] 2006. Second edition. *Althusser: The Detour of Theory*. Historical Materialism Book Series, No. 13. Leiden: Brill.

ELLIOTT, GREGORY. 1990. "Introduction," pp. viii-xx in Louis Althusser, *Philosophy and the Spontaneous Philosophy of Scientists and Other Essays*. London: Verso.

ELLIOTT, GREGORY. 1993. "The Lonely Hour of the Last Instance: Louis Pierre Althusser, 1918-1990," in E. Ann Kaplan and Michael Sprinkler (1993:33-239).

ELLIOTT, GREGORY (ed.). 1994. *Althusser: A Critical Reader*. Oxford: Blackwell.

ERIBON, DIDIER. [1989] 1991. *Michel Foucault*. Betsy Wing (translator). Cambridge, MA: Harvard University Press.

Esteva, Gustavo. 1999. "The Zapatistas and People's Power," *Capital & Class* 68 (Summer): 153-182.

ESTEVA, GUSTAVO. 2004. *Celebration of Zapatismo*. Dissenting Knowledges Pamphlet Series (no. 1). Penang, Malaysia: Multiversity & Citizens International.

ESTEVA, GUSTAVO AND PRAKASH, MADHU SURI. 1998. *Grassroots Post-Modernism*. London and New York: Zed Books Ltd.

EZLN. 1994. *Documentos y comunicados*. Vol. 1. México: Ediciones Era.

EZLN. 1995. *Documentos y comunicados*. Vol. 2. México: Ediciones Era.

EZLN. 1997. *Documentos y comunicados*. Vol. 3. México: Ediciones Era.

EZLN. 2003. *Documentos y comunicados*. Vol. 4. México: Ediciones Era.

FLN. [1980] 2003. *Estatutos de las Fuerzas de Liberación Nacional*. Aug. 6, 1980 (México); translated into English as *Statutes of the Forces of National Liberation*. Montreal: Abraham Guillen Press & Arm The Spirit.

FLYNN, THOMAS. 2003. "Foucault's Mapping of History," in Gary Gutting (ed.), *The Cambridge Companion to Foucault*. 2nd edition. Cambridge: Cambridge University Press.

FORAN, JOHN. 1997. "Discourses and Social Forces: The role of cultural studies in understanding revolution," pp. 203-226 in his (ed.), *Theorizing Revolutions*. London and New York: Routledge.

FORAN, JOHN. (ed.). 2003. *The Future of Revolutions: Rethinking Radical Change in the Age of Globalization*. London and New York: Zed Books.

FOUCAULT, MICHEL. [1966] 2002. *The Order of Things*. Oxford: Routledge.

FOUCAULT, MICHEL. [1969] 1972. *The Archaeology of Knowledge and the Discourse on Language*. Trans. A. M. Sheridan Smith. New York: Pantheon Books.

FOUCAULT, MICHEL. [1969] 1996. "Foucault Responds to Sartre," pp. 51-56 in Sylvère Lotringer (ed.), *Foucault Live: Collected Interviews, 1961-1984*. New York: Semiotext(e).

FOUCAULT, MICHEL. [1970] 1972. "The Discourse on Language," in Michel Foucault ([1969] 1972:215-237).

FOUCAULT, MICHEL. [1976] 1978. *The History of Sexuality. Volume 1: An Introduction*. New York: Random Vintage.

FOUCAULT, MICHEL. 1977. *Language, Counter-Memory, Practice*. Ithaca, New York: Cornell University Press.

FOUCAULT, MICHEL. [1978] 2006. "'*Omnes et Singulatim*:' Toward a Critique of Political Reason," in Noam Chomsky and Michel Foucault (2006:172-210).

FOUCAULT, MICHEL. 1979. *Microfísica del poder* (Genealogía del Poder No.1). Madrid: Ediciones de la Piqueta.

Foucault, Michel. 1980. *Power/Knowledge: Selected Interviews and Other Writings 1972-1977*. New York: Pantheon Books.

Foucault, Michel. 1982. "Afterword: The Subject and Power," in Hubert L. Dreyfus and Paul Rabinow (1983:208-226).

Foucault, Michel. 1984. "Politics and Ethics: An Interview," pp. 373-380 in Paul Rabinow (ed.), *The Foucault Reader*. New York: Pantheon.

Foucault, Michel. [1984] 1997. "The Ethics of the Concern for the Self as a Practice of Freedom," pp. 281-301 in Paul Rabinow (ed.), *The Essential Works of Michel Foucault. Volume I: Ethics: Subjectivity and Truth*. New York: New Press.

Fuentes, Carlos. 1994. "Chiapas: Latin America's First Post-Communist Rebellion," *New Perspectives Quarterly*, Vol. 11, no. 2, (Spring): 54-58.

Fuentes, Carlos. [1994] 1997. *A New Time for Mexico*. Berkeley: University of California.

Galván, Valentín. 2010. *De vagos y maleantes: Michel Foucault en España*. Barcelona: Virus editorial.

Gane, Michael. 1983. "The ISAs Episode." *Economy and Society* 12, 4: 431–467.

García Agustín, Oscar. 2009. "Ni centro ni periferia: La construcción del Tercer Espacio en los textos del Subcomandante Marcos," *Discurso & Sociedad*, Vol. 3, No. 2: 280-315.

García Canclini, Néstor. 1988. "Culture and Power: the state of research," *Media, Culture and Society*, Vol. 10, No. 4: 467-497.

García de León, Antonio. 2005. "From Revolution to Transition: the Chiapas Rebellion and the Path to Democracy in Mexico," *Journal of Peasant Studies*, Vol. 32, Nos 3 & 4 (July-October): 508-527.

García Márquez, Gabriel, and Roberto Pombo. 2001. "The Punch Card and the Hour Glass: interview with Subcomandante Marcos," *New Left Review* 9 (May/June): 69-79.

Garfield, Eugene. 1987. "A Different Sort of Great Books List: The 50 Twentieth-Century Works Most Cited in the *Arts & Humanities*

Citation Index, 1976-1983," *Current Contents*, No. 16 (April 20): 101-105.

GELMAN, JUAN. 1996. "'Nada que ver con las armas.' Entrevista exclusiva con el Subcomandante Marcos;" retrieved from http://www.elortiba.org/gelman1.html#EL ENTREVISTADOR.

GIDDENS, ANTHONY. [1983] 1995. *A Contemporary Critique of Historical Materialism, Vol. 1 Power, Property and the State*. Second edition. London: The Macmillan Press Ltd.

GIDDENS, ANTHONY. [1985] 2000. "Jürgen Habermas," in Quentin Skinner ([1985] 2000b:121-139).

GILBRETH, CHRIS AND OTERO, GERARDO. 2001. "Democratization in Mexico: The Zapatista Uprising and Civil Society," *Latin American Perspectives*, Vol. 28, No. 4, Mexico in the 1990s: Economic Crisis, Social Polarization, and Class Struggle, Part 2. (July): 7-29.

GILLY, ADOLFO. 1995. *Discusión sobre la historia*. México: Taurus.

GILLY, ADOLFO. 1998. "Chiapas and the Rebellion of the Enchanted World," pp. 261-333 in Daniel Nugent (ed.), *Rural Revolt in Mexico*. Durham, North Carolina: Duke University Press.

GILMAN-OPALSKY, RICHARD. 2008. *Unbounded Politics: Transgressive Public Spheres, Zapatismo, and Political Theory*. Plymouth: Lexington Books.

GINZBURG, CARLO. [1979] 1989. "Clues: Roots of an Evidential Paradigm," pp. 96-125 in *Clues, Myths, and the Historical Method*. Transl. John and Anne C. Tedeschi. Baltimore: Johns Hopkins University Press.

GOGOL, EUGENE. 2014. *Ensayos sobre Zapatismo*. México: Juan Pablos Editor.

GOLDEN, TIM. 1994. "The Voice of the Rebels Has Mexicans in His Spell," *New York Times* (February 8).

GOLDSTEIN, PHILIP. 2005. *Post-Marxist Theory: An Introduction*. New York: State University of New York Press.

GOLLNICK, BRIAN. 2008. *Reinventing the Lacandón: Subaltern Representations in the Rain Forest of Chiapas*. Tucson: University of Arizona Press.

González Casanova, Pablo. 1980. "The Crisis of the State and the Struggle for Democracy in Latin America," *Contemporary Marxism*, Vol. 1 (Spring): 64-69.

González Casanova, Pablo. [1994] 1996. "Causas de la rebelión en Chiapas," *Política y sociedad*, No. 17, Madrid. (Ejemplar dedicado a: Gobernabilidad y Democracia en América Latina): 83-96; translated into English and published as "Causes of the Rebellion in Chiapas," in *Identities: Global Studies in Culture and Power*, Vol. 3, No. 1-2 (October, 1996): 269-290.

González Casanova, Pablo. [2003] 2005. "The Zapatista 'Caracoles': Networks of Resistance and Autonomy," *Socialism and Democracy*, Vol. 19, No. 3: 79-92. (First published in Spanish in, *La Jornada*. Perfil. septiembre 26, 2003; retrieved from http://www.jornada.unam.mx/2003/09/26/per-texto.html.

González Oropeza, Manuel. 1996. "The Administration of Justice and the Rule of Law in Mexico," pp. 59-78 in Mónica Serrano and Victor Bulmer-Thomas (eds.), *Rebuilding the State: Mexico After Salinas*. London: The Institute of Latin American Studies, University of London.

González Ortega, Nelson. 2006. "La recuperación de la palabra indígena testimonial: el *Popol Vuh* en los comunicados insurgentes de Marcos," pp. 223-240 in his *Relatos mágicos en cuestión*. Madrid / Frankfurt am Main: Iberoamericana / Vervuert.

Gordon, Colin. 1980. "Afterword," in Foucault (1980:229-259).

Graeber, David. 2007. *Possibilities: Essays on Hierarchy, Rebellion, and Desire*. Oakland, CA: A.K. Press.

Graebner, Cornelia. 2011. "Subcomandante Insurgente Marcos," *The Literary Encyclopedia* (online); portal located on the Internet at: http://www.litencyc.com/.

Gramsci, Antonio. 1971. *Selections from the Prison Notebooks,* edited and translated by Quintin Hoare and Geoffrey Nowell Smith. New York: International Publishers.

Guevara, Ernesto "Che". [1965] 2009. *Socialism and Man in Cuba.* Third edition. Atlanta, GA: Pathfinder Press.

Guillén Vicente, Rafael Sebastián. 1980 (October). *Filosofía y educación: prácticas discursivas y practícas ideológicas. Tesis de licenciatura.* Facultad de Filosofía y Letras. México: UNAM. A copy of Guillén's thesis can be found posted on the Internet at: http://132.248.9.195/ptd2014/anteriores/0011253/0011253.pdf.

Guillén Vicente, Rafael Sebastián. 1992. "El empresario del siglo XX y los retos de su circunstancia." Aparecido en *el Boletín Ventas y Mercadotecnia.* Organo informativo de EVMAC Tampico. Republished in *Revista Impacto.* 19 de marzo de 1995. pp. 56-57; and posted on the Internet at: http://www.lahaine.org/index.php?p=22817.

Guillermoprieto, Alma. 1995. "The Shadow War," *New York Review of Books,* Vol. 42, No. 4 (March 2): 34-43.

Guillermoprieto, Alma. 2002. "The Unmasking," pp. 207-223 in her *Looking for History: Dispatches from Latin America.* New York: Vintage Books.

Gunderson, Christopher. 2013. "The Provocative Cocktail: Intellectual Origins of the Zapatista Uprising, 1960-1994." Doctoral Thesis. The City University of New York.

Gutiérrez Carlin, Ivonne. 1996. *Pólvora En La Boca, Chiapas, Que hay detrás de las mascaras?* México: Editorial Diana.

Gutting, Gary. 2005. *Foucault: A Very Short Introduction.* Oxford: Oxford University Press.

Gutting, Gary. 2011. *Thinking the Impossible: French Philosophy Since 1960.* Oxford: Oxford University Press.

Halliday, Fred. 2003. "Afterword: Utopian Realism: The Challenge for 'Revolution' in Our Times," in John Foran (ed.) (2003:300-309).

Hardt, Michael. 2000. "The Withering of Civil Society," pp. 158-178 in Mike Hill and Warren Montag (eds.), *Masses, Classes, and the Public Sphere.* London & New York: Verso.

Harnecker, Marta. 2007. *Rebuilding the Left.* London: Zed Books.

HARRIS, RICHARD L. 1979. "The Influence of Marxist Structuralism on the Intellectual Left in Latin America," *Insurgent Sociologist*, Vol. 9, No. 1: 62-73.

HARVEY, NEIL. 1994. "Rebellion in Chiapas: Rural Reforms, Campesino Radicalism, and the limits to Salinismo," pp. 1-49 in *Transformation of Rural Mexico*, no. 5. Ejido Reform Research Project, Center for U.S.-Mexican Studies. San Diego: University of California.

HARVEY, NEIL. 1998. *The Chiapas Rebellion: The Struggle for Land and Democracy*. Durham, North Carolina: Duke University Press.

HAYDEN, TOM (ed.). 2002. *The Zapatista Reader*. New York: Thunder's Mouth Press.

HEARSE, PHIL. 2007. "Change the world without taking power?," pp. 23-37 in his (ed.), *Take the Power to Change the World: Globalisation and the Debate on Power*. London: Socialist Resistance.

HENCK, NICK. 2007. *Subcommander Marcos: the Man and the Mask*. Durham, North Carolina: Duke University Press.

HENCK, NICK. 2009. "Laying a ghost to rest: Subcommander Marcos' playing of the indigenous card," *Estudios Mexicanos/Mexican Studies*, Vol. 25, No. 1 (Winter 2009): 155-170.

HENCK, NICK. 2011. "Subcommander Marcos and Mexico's Public Intellectuals: Octavio Rodríguez Araujo, Carlos Monsiváis, Elena Poniatowska and Pablo González Casanova," *A Contracorriente*, Vol. 9, No. 1 (Fall): 287-335.

HENCK, NICK. 2012. "Subcommander Marcos' Discourse on Mexico's Intellectual Class," *Asian Journal of Latin American Studies*, Vol. 25, No. 1: 35-73.

HENCK, NICK. 2013. "The Subcommander and the Sardinian: Marcos and Gramsci," *Estudios Mexicanos/Mexican Studies*, Vol. 29, No. 2 (Summer): 428-458.

HENCK, NICK. 2014. "Subcomandante Marcos: The Latest Reader," *The Latin Americanist*, Vol. 58, Issue 2 (June): 49-73.

Henck, Nick. 2015. "Subcomandante Marcos," pp. 556-562 in Eric Zolov (ed.), *Iconic Mexico: An Encyclopedia from Acapulco to Zócalo*. California: ABC-CLIO, LLC.

Herlinghaus, Hermann. 2005. "Subcomandante Marcos: Narrative Policy and Epistemological Project," *Journal of Latin American Cultural Studies*, Vol. 14, No. 1 (March): 53-74.

Hernández, Gabriela. 1999. "Una historia de familia." *Proceso edición especial* (January 1): 62-63.

Hernández Martínez, Laura. 2002. "Detrás de nosotros estamos ustedes: la ironía en el discurso del subcomandante Marcos." *Signos Literarios y Lingüísticos* iv.2 (julio-diciembre): 101-115; retrieved from http://148.206.53.230/revistasuam/signosliterariosylinguisticos/include/getdoc.php?id=130&article=130&mode=pdf.

Hernández Millán, Abelardo. 2007. *EZLN: Revolución para la Revolución (1994-2005)*. Madrid: Editorial Popular.

Hernández Navarro, Luis. 1997. *Chiapas: La nueva lucha india*. Madrid: Talasa Ediciones.

Hernández Navarro, Luis. 2007. *Sentido contrario*. México: La Jornada Ediciones.

Higgins, Nicholas P. 2004. *Understanding the Chiapas Rebellion: Modernist Visions and the Invisible Indian*. Austin: University of Texas Press.

Hiller, Patrick T. 2009. "Contesting Zapata: Differing Meanings of the Mexican National Idea," *Journal of Alternative Perspectives in the Social Sciences*, Vol. 1, No. 2: 258-280.

Hirsh, Arthur. 1982. *The French Left*. Montréal, Québec: Black Rose Books Ltd.

Hobsbawm, Eric. 2011. *How to Change the World: Tales of Marx and Marxism*. London: Little, Brown Book Group.

Holden, Adam and Elden, Stuart. 2005. "'It cannot be a Real Person, a Concrete Individual:' Althusser and Foucault on Machiavelli's Political Technique," *borderlands ejournal* vol. 4, no. 2.

HOLLOWAY, JOHN. 1998. "Dignity's Revolt," pp. 159-198 in John Holloway and Eloína Peláez (eds.), *Zapatista! Reinventing Revolution in Mexico*. London: Pluto Press.

HOLLOWAY, JOHN. 2005. "Zapatismo Urbano," pp. 168-178 in Manuel Callahan (ed.), "Zapatismo as Political and Cultural Practice," *Humboldt Journal of Social Relations Special Issue* 29.1. California: Humbolt.

HOLLOWAY, JOHN AND ELOÍNA PELÁEZ. 1998. "Introduction: Reinventing Revolution," pp. 1-18 in their (eds.), *Zapatista! Reinventing Revolution in Mexico*. London: Pluto Press.

HONNETH, AXEL. 1994. "History and Interaction: On the Structuralist Interpretation of Historical Materialism," in Elliott (1994): 73-103.

HOYO, FELIX. 1995. "De Filósofo a Subcomandante," *La Guillotina*, Vol. 31 (Aug-Sept): 33-35.

HUFFSCHMID, ANNE. 1995. *Subcomandante Marcos: Ein maskierter Mythos*. Berlin: Elefanten Press.

HUGHES, JONATHAN. 2000. *Ecology and Historical Materialism*. Cambridge: Cambridge University Press.

IGNACIO TAIBO II, PACO. 1997. *Guevara Also Known as Che*. Translated by Martin Michael Roberts. New York: St. Martin's Press.

JAMES, SUSAN. [1985] 2000. "Louis Althusser," in Quentin Skinner ([1985] 2000b:141-157).

JAMESON, FREDERIC. 1981. *The Political Unconscious: Narrative as a Socially Symbolic Act*. London: Methuen.

JED, STEPHANIE. 2001. "Proof and Transnational Rhetorics: Opening up the Conversation," *History and Theory*, Vol. 40, No. 3 (October): 372-384.

JEFFRIES, FIONA. 2001. "Zapatismo and the Intergalactic Age," pp. 129-144 in Roger Burbach (ed.), *Globalization and Postmodern Politics: From Zapatistas to High-Tech Robber Barons*. London: Pluto Press.

JESSOP, BOB. 1985. *Nicos Poulantzas: Marxist Theory and Political Strategy*. London: Macmillan.

JESSOP, BOB. 1991. "The Originality, Legacy, and Actuality of Nicos Poulantzas," *Studies in Political Economy* 34 (Spring): 75-107.

JESSOP, BOB. [2007] 2014. "Political Economy, Political Ecology, and Democratic Socialism," First Annual Nicos Poulantzas Memorial Lecture. Delivered at Panteios University of Economics and Political Sciences (December 7, 2007); posted on the Internet (February 26, 2014) at: http://bobjessop.org/2014/02/26/political-economy-political-ecology-and-democratic-socialism/.

JESSOP, BOB. 2007. *State Power*. Cambridge: Polity.

JESSOP, BOB. 2014. "Althusser, Poulantzas, Buci-Glucksmann: Elaborations of Gramsci's Concept of the integral State;" retrieved from http://bobjessop.org/2014/02/01/althusser-poulantzas-buci-glucksmann-elaborations-of-gramscis-concept-of-the-integral-state/.

JOHNSTON, JOSÉE. 2000. "Pedagogical Guerrillas, Armed Democrats, and Revolutionary Counterpublics: Examining Paradox in the Zapatista Uprising in Chiapas Mexico," *Theory and Society*, Vol. 29, No. 4 (August): 463-505.

JOHNSTON, JOSÉE. 2003. "'We Are All Marcos'? *Zapatismo*, Solidarity and the politics of Scale," pp. 85-104 in Gordon Laxer and Sandra Halperin (eds.), *Global Civil Society and Its Limits*. Houndmills, Basingstoke: Palgrave Macmillan.

JUNG, HWA YOL. 1987. "The Question of the Moral Subject in Foucault's Analytics of Power," *Canadian Journal of Political and Social Theory*, Vol. XI. No. 3: 28-45.

KANAVEL, STEVEN P. 2007. "The Rhetorical Weapons of the Zapatistas," *The Chico Historian* 17: 55–64.

KANOUSSI, DORA. 1998. *El Zapatismo y La Política*. México: Plaza y Valdés.

KARAM, TANIUS. 2000. "El Subcomandante Marcos y el horizonte de la traducción intercultural," *Razón y Palabra* No. 18 (mayo-julio); retrieved from http://www.razonypalabra.org.mx/anteriores/n18/18tkaram4.html.

KAPLAN, E. ANN AND SPRINKLER, MICHAEL. 1993. *The Althusserian Legacy*. London and New York: Verso.

Khasnabish, Alex. 2008. *Zapatismo Beyond Borders*. Toronto: University of Toronto Press.

Khasnabish, Alex. 2010. *Zapatistas: Rebellion from the Grassroots to the Global*. London: Zed Books.

King, Patricia and Villanueva, Francisco, Javier. 1998. "Breaking the Blockade: The Move from Jungle to City," pp. 104-125 in John Holloway and Eloína Peláez (eds.), *Zapatista! Reinventing Revolution in Mexico*. London: Pluto Press.

Klein, Hilary. 2015. "The Zapatista Movement: Blending Indigenous Traditions with Revolutionary Praxis," pp. 22-43 in Barry Maxwell and Raymond Craib (eds.), *No Gods, No Masters, No Peripheries: Global Anarchisms*. Oakland, CA: PM Press.

Krauze, Enrique. 2001. "The view from La Realidad," *The New Republic* (August 13): 27-33.

Krauze, Enrique. 2011. *Redeemers: Ideas and Power in Latin America*. New York: HarperCollins.

Kuhn, Thomas S. [1962] 1996. *The Structure of Scientific Revolutions*. Chicago: University of Chicago Press.

La Botz, Dan. 2007. "Review: On Marcos, Man and Mask," *Against The Current* No. 130 (Sept./Oct.); retrieved from http://www.solidarity-us.org/node/734.

Laclau, Ernesto. [1977] 1979. *Politics and Ideology in Marxist Theory*. London: Verso.

Laclau, Ernesto, and Mouffe, Chantal. [1985] 2001. *Hegemony and Socialist Strategy: Towards a Radical Democratic Politics*, 2nd Ed. London and New York: Verso.

Le Bot, Yvon. 1997a. *El sueño zapatista*. Barcelona: Plaza & Janés Editores.

Le Bot, Yvon. 1997b. "Los zapatistas lograron conquistar su propio espacio de libertad: Ivon Le Bot," *Proceso* 1069 (April 27): 28-30.

Lechner, Norbert. 1985. "De la Revolución a la Democracia. El debate intelectual en America del sur," *Opciones* 6 (May-August): 57-72.

LEGORRETA DÍAZ, MARÍA DEL CARMEN. 1998. *Religión, política y guerrilla en Las Cañadas de las Selva Lacandona*. México: Cal y Arena.

LENKERSDORF, CARLOS. 2004. *Conceptos tojolabales de filosofía y del alter mundo*. México: Plaza y Valdés.

LEWIS, WILLIAM S. 2005. *Louis Althusser and the Traditions of French Marxism*. Oxford: Lexington Books.

LINSTROTH, J. P. 2005. "An Introductory Essay: Are We in 'The Age of Resistance' in a Post-9/11 World?," *Peace and Conflict Studies* 12 (2): 1-54.

LISS, SHELDON B. 1984. *Marxist Thought in Latin America*. Berkeley: University of California Press.

LORA CAM, JORGE. 2003. *Radicalismo de izquierda y confrontación político-militar en América Latina*. Segunda edición. Lima: Juan Gutemburg Editores-Impresores.

LORENZANO, LUIS. 1998. "Zapatismo: Recomposition of Labour, Radical Democracy and Revolutionary Project," pp. 126-58 in John Holloway and Eloína Peláez (eds.), *Zapatista! Reinventing Revolution in Mexico*. London: Pluto Press.

LÖWY, MICHAEL. [1973] 2007. *The Marxism of Che Guevara: Philosophy, Economics, Revolutionary Warfare*. Second edition. Lanham, Maryland: Rowman & Littlefield Publishers, Inc.

LÖWY, MICHAEL. 1998. "Sources and Resources of Zapatism," in *Monthly Review*, Vol. 49, No. 10 (March): 1-4.

MACEY, DAVID. 1993. *The Lives of Michel Foucault*. London: Hutchinson.

MÁIZ, RAMÓN. 2010. "The Indian Heart of the Nation: The Evolution of the Political Discourse of the EZLN in Mexico (1993–2009)," *Latin American and Caribbean Ethnic Studies*, Vol. 5, No. 3 (November): 245–272.

MAJUMDAR, MARGARET A. 1995. *Althusser and the End of Leninism*. London: Pluto Press.

MALDONADO, EZEQUIEL. 2001. "Los Relatos Zapatistas y su Vínculo con la Oralidad Tradicional," *Convergencia*, año 8, número 24 (enero-abril): 141-153.

Mann, Michael. 1986. *The Sources of Social Power.* Cambridge: Cambridge University Press.

Marcos, Subcommander. 1994. "Interview with Marcos before the Dialogue," pp. 196-210 in Autonomedia (1994).

Marcos, Subcommander. 1995a. "Interview with Marcos about neoliberalism, the national State and democracy;" retrieved from http://flag.blackened.net/revolt/mexico/ezln/inter_marcos_aut95.html.

Marcos, Subcommander. 1995b. "Por Radio UNAM. 18 de marzo," pp. 72-139 in *Chiapas: la palabra de los armados de verdad y fuego,* Volume II. Barcelona: Ediciones de Serbal.

Marcos, Subcommander. 1996. "Intervención de Marcos en la Mesa 1 del Encuentro Intercontinental," (June 30); retrieved from http://palabra.ezln.org.mx/comunicados/1996/1996_07_30.htm.

Marcos, Subcommander. 1998. *Cuentos para una soledad desvelada.* México: Ediciones del Frente Zapatista de Liberación Nacional.

Marcos, Subcommander. 1999. *Relatos de El Viejo Antonio.* México: Centro de Información y Análisis de Chiapas.

Marcos, Subcommander. 2003. "The World: Seven Thoughts in May of 2003," *Rebeldía* Magazine, Issue #7; Retrieved from (in Spanish) http://palabra.ezln.org.mx/comunicados/2003/2003_05_b.htm; and (in English) at: http://www.cuestiones.ws/revista/n15/ago03-mex-eng-marcos.htm.

Marcos, Subcommander. 2004. "Reading a Video (Part II): Two Flaws," (August); retrieved from http://alainet.org/active/6725&lang=es.

Marcos, Subcommander. 2007a. "Part I. Arriba, pensar el blanco. La geografía y el calendario de la teoría," the first of Subcomandante Marcos' seven presentations under the general title of "Neither Center Nor Periphery," given at the Andres Aubry Colloquium, CIDECI, San Cristobal de las Casas, Chiapas, Mexico, December 17, 2007. Marcos' presentation can be heard, and a typescript of it read, on the internet at: http://enlacezapatista.ezln.org.mx/2007/12/13/conferencia-del-dia-13-de-diciembre-a-las-900-am/.

— Works Cited —

Marcos, Subcommander. 2007b. "Parte V. Oler el Negro. El Calendario y la geografía de la guerra," the fifth of Subcomandante Marcos' seven presentations under the general title of "Neither Center Nor Periphery," given at the Andres Aubry Colloquium, CIDECI, San Cristobal de las Casas, Chiapas, Mexico, December 17, 2007; retrieved from (in Spanish) http://enlacezapatista.ezln.org.mx/2007/12/16/parte-v-oler-el-negro-el-calendario-y-la-geografia-del-miedo/.

Marcos, Subcommander. 2007c. "Part VII. Sentir el rojo. El Calendario y la geografía de la guerra," the final of Subcomandante Marcos' seven presentations under the general title of "Neither Center Nor Periphery," given at the Andres Aubry Colloquium, CIDECI, San Cristobal de las Casas, Chiapas, Mexico, December 17, 2007; retrieved from (in Spanish) http://enlacezapatista.ezln.org.mx/2007/12/17/parte-vii-y-ultima-sentir-el-rojo-el-calendario-y-la-geografia-de-la-guerra/; and (in English) http://www.naomiklein.org/shock-doctrine/communique-english.

Marcos, Subcommander. 2007d. *The Speed of Dreams*. San Francisco: City Lights Books.

Marcos, Subcommander. 2011. "Third Letter to Don Luis Villoro in the Interchange on Ethics and Politics," (July-August); retrieved from http://www.elkilombo.org/third-letter-to-don-luis-villoro-in-the-interchange-on-ethics-and-politics/.

Marcos, Subcommander. 2012. "We Don't Know You Yet?" (December 29); retrieved from http://enlacezapatista.ezln.org.mx/2013/01/07/we-don't-know-you-yet/.

Marcos, Subcommander. 2013. "EZLN: Rewind 1, When the Dead Silently Speak Out," (December 31); retrieved from http://www.elkilombo.org/ezln-rewind-1-when-the-dead-silently-speak-out/.

Marcos, Subcommander. 2015. "The Method, the Bibliography, and a Drone Deep in the Mountains of the Mexican Southeast," (May 4); retrieved from http://enlacezapatista.ezln.org.mx/2015/06/19/the-method-the-bibliography-and-a-drone-deep-in-the-mountains-of-the-mexican-southeast/.

Martin, James. 2008a. "Introduction," in James Martin (2008b:1-24).

Martin, James. 2008b. *The Poulantzas Reader: Marxism, Law and the State*. London and New York: Verso.

Martínez, Elizabeth (Betita) and García, Arnoldo. 2004. "What is Zapatismo? A Brief Definition for Activists," in David Solnit (ed.) (2004:213-216).

Martinez-Torres, Maria Elena. 2001. "Civil Society, the Internet, and the Zapatistas," *Peace Review*, Vol. 13 Issue 3: 347-355.

Matamoros Ponce, Fernando. 1996. "Marcos, l'homme masqué de la forêt. L'éthique de l'information," pp. 233-242 in Luis E. Gomez (ed.), *Mexique de Chiapas á la crise financière*. Paris: Editions L'Harmattan.

Matamoros Ponce, Fernando. 2009. *Memoria y utopía en México: imaginarios en la génesis del neozapatismo*. Buenos Aires: Ediciones Herramienta.

Mauriac, Claude. 1976. *Le temps immobile 3: Et comme l'esperance est violente*. Paris: Bernard Grasset.

McCaughan, Michael. 2002. "King of the Jungle," in Tom Hayden (ed.) (2002:72-75).

McDonald, Kevin. 2006. *Global Movements: Action and Culture*. Oxford: Blackwell.

Meiksins Wood, Ellen. 1995. *Democracy Against Capitalism: Renewing Historical Materialism*. Cambridge: Cambridge University Press.

Mentinis, Mihalis. 2006. *Zapatistas: The Chiapas Revolt and what it means for Radical Politics*. London: Pluto.

Meyer, Jean. 2002. "Once Again, The Noble Savage," in Tom Hayden (ed.) (2002:367-373).

Meyer, Lorenzo. 1994. "Turbio lenguaje del poder," *Excélsior* (March 17): 1, 10 & 36; retrieved from http://www.lorenzomeyer.com.mx/documentos/pdf/17marzo1994.pdf.

Michel, Guillermo. 2001a. *Votán Zapata*. México: Rizoma.

MICHEL, GUILLERMO. 2001b. "No morirá la flor de la palabra. La Utopía zapatista: Teoría y Praxis," pp. 7-24 in Michel Guillermo and Fabiola Escárzaga (eds.), *Sobre La Marcha*. México: UAM-Xochimilco.

MICHEL, GUILLERMO. 2003. *Ética política Zapatista*. México: UAM.

MIGNOLO, WALTER D. 2002. "The Zapatistas' Theoretical Revolution: Its Historical, Ethical, and Political Consequences," *Review (Fernand Braudel Center)*, Vol. 25, No. 3: 245-275.

MIGNOLO, WALTER D. 2005. *The Idea of Latin America*. Oxford: Blackwell.

MIGNOLO, WALTER D. 2015. "Foreword," pp. viii-xlii in Hamid Dabashi, *Can Non-Europeans Think?* London: Zed Books.

MIGNOLO, WALTER D. AND FREYA SCHIWY. 2003. "Double Translation: Transculturation and the Colonial Difference," pp. 3-29 in Tullio Maranhão and Bernhard Streck (eds.), *Translation and Ethnography: The Anthropological Challenge of Intercultural Understanding*. Tucson: University of Arizona Press.

MILLER, JAMES. [1993] 2000. *The Passion of Michel Foucault*. Harvard: Harvard University Press.

MILLER, NICOLA. 1999. *In the Shadow of the State: Intellectuals and the Quest for National Identity in Twentieth-Century Spanish America*. London: Verso.

MOGUEL, JULIO. 1998. *Chiapas: la guerra de los signos*. México: Juan Pablos Editor/La Jornada Ediciones.

MOLINA, IVÁN. 2000. *El Pensamiento del EZLN*. México: Plaza y Valdés.

MONSIVÁIS, CARLOS. [2009] 2011. *Apocalipstick*. México, D.F.: Debols!llo.

MONTAG, WARREN. 1995. "'The Soul is the Prison of the Body': Althusser and Foucault, 1970-1975," *Yale French Studies*, No. 88, entitled *Depositions: Althusser, Balibar, Machery, and the Labor of Reading*: 53-77.

MONTAG, WARREN. 2003. *Louis Althusser*. Houndmills: Palgrave Macmillan.

MONTALBÁN, MANUEL VÁZQUEZ. 2000. *Marcos: El señor de los espejos*. Madrid: Aguilar.

Montalbán, Manuel Vázquez. 2002. "Marcos: Mestizo Culture on the Move," in Tom Hayden (ed.) (472-483).

Montaner, Carlos Alberto. 2001. "Marcos, la máscara y los idiotas sin frontera," *Firmas Press* (March 18), at http://www.firmaspress.com/115.htm.

Montesano Montessori, Nicolina. 2009. *A discursive analysis of a struggle for hegemony in Mexico: The Zapatista movement versus President Salinas de Gortari*. VDM Verlag Dr. Müller: Saarbrücken.

Mora, Mariana. 2003. "The Imagination to Listen: Reflections on a Decade of Zapatista Struggle," *Social Justice*, Vol. 30, No. 3: 17-31.

Morales, Cesáreo. 1975. "Poder del discurso o discurso del poder," *Historia y Sociedad* (segunda época) no. 8: 38-48.

Morton, Adam David. 2000. "Mexico, Neoliberal Restructuring and the EZLN: A Neo-Gramscian Analysis," pp. 255-279 in Barry K. Gills (ed.), *Globalization and the Politics of Resistance*. New York: St. Martin's.

Morton, Adam David. 2002. "'La Resurrección del Maíz': Globalisation, Resistance and the Zapatistas." *Millennium: Journal of International Studies* 31, 1: 27–54.

Morton, Adam David. 2007. *Unravelling Gramsci: Hegemony and Passive Revolution in the Global Political Economy*. London and Ann Arbor: Pluto Press.

Morton, Adam David. 2011. *Revolution and State in Modern Mexico*. Lanham: Rowman and Littlefield Publishers, Inc.

Morúa, Jorge Fuentes. 1999. "Raíces del pensamiento zapatista o la crítica al Neoliberalismo," *Revista Nueva Antropología*, Vol. XVII, No. 56 (noviembre): 109-125.

Muir, Edward. 1991. "*Clues, Myths, and the Historical Method.* By Carlo Ginzburg: a Review," *Journal of Social History* 25:1 (Fall): 123-125.

Mulhern, Francis. 1994. "Althusser in Literary Studies," in Gregory Elliott (ed.) (1994:159–176).

NAIL, THOMAS. 2012. *Returning to Revolution: Deleuze, Guattari and Zapatismo*. Edinburgh: Edinburgh University Press.

NAVARRO, FERNANDA. 1988. *Filosofía y marxismo: Entrevista a Louis Althusser*. México: Siglo XXI editores.

NAVARRO, FERNANDA. 1998. "A New Way of Thinking in Action: The Zapatistas in Mexico – A Postmodern Guerrilla Movement?," *Rethinking Marxism* 10 (4): 155-165.

NEWMEYER, FREDERICK J. 1994a. "The Chomskyan Revolution," pp. 422-442 in Carlos P. Otero (ed.), *Noam Chomsky: Critical Assessments Volume III: Anthropology: Tome* II. London: Routledge.

NEWMEYER, FREDERICK J. 1994b. "Are Marx and Chomsky Compatible?," pp. 443-451 in Carlos P. Otero (ed.), *Noam Chomsky: Critical Assessments Volume III: Anthropology: Tome II*. London: Routledge.

NOLA, ROBERT. 2003. *Rescuing Reason: A Critique of Anti-Rationalist Views of Science and Knowledge*. Dordrecht, The Netherlands: Kluwer Academic Publishers.

O' FARRELL, CLARE. 2005. *Michel Foucault*. London: Sage Publications Ltd.

OLESEN, THOMAS. 2005. *International Zapatismo*. London: Zed Books.

OLESEN, THOMAS. 2007. "The Funny Side of Globalization: Humour and Humanity in *Zapatista* Framing," *International Review of Social History*, Vol. 52, Suppl. S15: 21-34.

OLGUÍN, BEN. V. 2002. "Of Truth, Secrets, and Ski Masks Counterrevolutionary Appropriations and Zapatista Revisions of *Testimonio*." *Nepantla: Views from South* 3, 1: 145–178.

OPPENHEIMER, ANDRÉS. [1996] 1998. *Bordering on Chaos*. Boston: Little, Brown and Company.

ORTEGA REYNA, JAIME. 2015. "'El cerebro de la pasión': Althusser en tres revistas mexicanas," *Revista Izquierdas* N° 25 (Octubre): 143-164.

OUVIÑA, HERNÁN. 2007. *Zapatismo para Principiantes*. Buenos Aires: Era Naciente SRL.

OUWENEEL, ARIJ. 2002. *The Psychology of the Faceless Warriors: Easten Chiapas, Early 1994*. Cuadernos del Cedla Series, Vol. 10. Amsterdam: Centre for Latin American Research and Documentation.

PAOLI, ANTONIO. 2003. *Educación, Autonomía y lekil kuxlejal: Aproximaciones sociolingüísticas a la sabiduría de los tseltales*. México: UAM-X, CSH.

PAYNE, MICHAEL. 1997. *Reading Knowledge*. Oxford: Blackwell.

PELLICER, JUAN. 1996. "La gravedad y la gracia: el discurso del Subcomandante Marcos," *Revista Iberoamericana* Vol. 62, No. 174 (January-March): 199-208.

PELLICER, JUAN. 2001. "El subcomandante Marcos: posdata de las armas y las letras," *Universitas Humanistica* 51/XXIX (January-June): 115-125.

PELLICER, JUAN. 2006. "De la Mancha a la Lacandona. Provocación y generación de interminable lecturas," *Revista Iberoamericana* Núm. 215-216, vol. LXXII. (abril-septiembre): 689-696.

PELLICER, JUAN. 2011. "Zapatismo y neozapatismo. Entre la modernidad y la literature," pp. 161-187 in Kristine Vanden Berghe, Anne Huffschmid and Robin Lefere (eds.), *El EZLN y sus intérpretes: Resonancias del zapatismo en la academia y en la literatura*. México: Universidad Autónoma de la Ciudad de México.

PETRAS, JAMES. 1999. *The Left Strikes Back. Latin American Perspectives Series, number 19*. Boulder, Colorado: Westview Press.

PHILP, MARK. 1985. "Michel Foucault," in Quentin Skinner ([1985] 2000b:65-81).

PITARCH, PEDRO. 2004. "The Zapatistas and the art of ventriloquism," *Journal of Human Rights*, Vol. 3, No. 3 (September): 291-312.

PITARCH, PEDRO. 2005. "*Ventriloquia confusa*," *istor*, Año VI, Número 22 (otoño): 129-144.

PIZARRO, FERNANDO ORTEGA. 1995a. "Sea o no su hijo, el subcomandante Marcos ha revitalizado a Alfonso Guillén," *Proceso* No. 959. (marzo 20): 22-23.

Pizarro, Fernando Ortega. 1995b. "'La Raíz Oculta,' la revista que Rafael Sebastian Guillén dirigió en Tampico al final de la prepa," *Proceso* No. 979 (agosto 7): 20.

Ponce de León, Juliana. 2001. *Our Word is Our Weapon*. New York: Seven Stories Press.

Poulantzas, Nicos. [1968] 1973. *Political Power and Social Classes*. Trans. Timothy O'Hagan. London: New Left Books.

Poulantzas, Nicos. [1968] 1977. *Poder político y clase sociales en el estado capitalista*. México: Siglo XXI editores.

Poulantzas, Nicos. [1976] 1977. "Las transformaciones actuales del Estado, la crisis política del Estado," pp. 33-76 in his (ed.), *La crisis del Estado*. Barcelona: Editorial Fontanella.

Poulantzas, Nicos. [1976] 2008. "The Political Crisis and the Crisis of the State," in James Martin (ed.) (2008b:294-322).

Poulantzas, Nicos. [1978] 1979. *Estado, Poder, Socialismo*. México: Ed. Siglo XXI editores.

Poulantzas, Nicos. [1978] 2014. *State, Power, Socialism*. London: New Left Books.

Poulantzas, Nicos. 1979. "Interview with Nicos Poulantzas," *Marxism Today* (July): 194-201.

Prakash, Madhu Suri and Esteva, Gustavo. 2008. *Escaping Education: Living as Learning within Grassroots Cultures*. Counterpoints: Studies in the Postmodern Theory of Education, Vol. 36. New York: Peter Lang Publishing.

Quintero, Jesús. 2007. *Entrevista*. Madrid: Aguilar.

Rabasa, José. 1997. "Of Zapatismo: Reflections on the Folkloric and the Impossible in a Subaltern Insurrection," pp. 399-431 in Lisa Lowe and David Lloyd (eds.), *The Politics of Culture in the Shadow of Capital*. Durham, North Carolina: Duke University Press.

Radio El Espectador de Uruguay. 2001. "Entrevista con el subcomandante Marcos, del EZLN," (March 15); retrieved from http://riie.com.mx/?a=23100.

RAMONET, IGNACIO. 2001. "Marcos marche sur Mexico," *Monde Diplomatique* (March): 1, 16-17.

RAMOS, JORGE. 2006. *Detrás la máscara*. México: Random House Mondadori.

RESCH, ROBERT PAUL. 1989. "Modernism, Postmodernism, and Social Theory: A Comparison of Althusser and Foucault," *Poetics Today*, Vol. 10, No. 3 (Fall): 511-549.

RESCH, ROBERT PAUL. 1992. *Althusser and the Renewal of Marxist Social Theory*. Berkeley: University of California Press.

REYNOSO, RAYMUNDO. 2007. "Entrevista con el Subcomandante Marcos," (jan. 9); retrieved from http://cedoz.org/site/content.php?doc=518&cat=16.

RIDING, ALAN. 1994. "The World: Letter From Mexico; How Peasants Lit the Fires Of Democracy," (Feb. 27) *The New York Times*; retrieved from http://www.nytimes.com/1994/02/27/weekinreview/the-world-letter-from-mexico-how-peasants-lit-the-fires-of-democracy.html.

ROBINET, ROMAIN. 2012. "A Revolutionary Group Fighting Against a Revolutionary State: The September 23rd Communist League Against the PRI-State (1973-1975)," pp. 129-147 in Fernando Herrera Calderón and Adela Cedillo (eds.), *Challenging Authoritarianism in Mexico: Revolutionary Struggle and the Dirty War, 1964-1982*. New York: Routledge.

RODRIGUEZ, RENÉ. 1996. "Portrait de Rafael Guillén, *alias* le sous-commandant Marcos," *Esprit*, no. 222 (juin): 129-146.

RODRÍQUEZ LASCANO, SERGIO. 2002. "Zapatismo: A Bridge to Hope," *Rebeldía* 1 (November); retrieved from http://web.tiscali.it/coll_tiromancino/ezln/rebeldia/001/art03_en.html.

RODRÍGUEZ LASCANO, SERGIO. 2006. "A Message for the Intellectuals and their 'Magnificent Alibi to Avoid Struggle and Confrontation': An Exclusive Interview with Zapatista Subcomandante Marcos: Part II," *Rebeldía* Magazine (May 31, 2006); retrieved from http://www.narconews.com/Issue41/article1857.html.

ROMERO, CÉSAR JACOBO. 1994. *Marcos: ¿un profesional de la esperanza?* México: Planeta.

ROMERO, RAÚL. 2014. "A brief history of the Zapatista Army of National Liberation," *Roar Magazine* (January 1); retrieved from https://roarmag.org/essays/brief-history-ezln-uprising/.

ROSS, JOHN. 1995. *Rebellion from the Roots: Indian Uprising in Chiapas.* New York: Common Courage Press.

ROSS, JOHN. 2000. *The War Against Oblivion: the Zapatista Chronicles 1994-2000.* Monroe: Common Courage Press.

ROSS, JOHN AND BARDACKE, FRANK. 1995. *Shadows of a Tender Fury: The Communiqués of Subcomandante Marcos and the EZLN.* New York: Monthly Review Press.

ROSSET, PETER. [1994] 1999. "Foreword," in Collier and Quaratiello ([1994] 1999: vii–viii).

ROVIRA, GUIOMAR. 1994. *¡Zapata Vive! La rebelión indígena de Chiapas contada por sus protagonistas.* Barcelona: Virus Editorial.

ROVIRA, GUIOMAR. 2009. *Zapatistas sin fronteras.* México: Ediciones Era.

RUBIN, JEFFREY W. 2002. "From Che to Marcos," *Dissent* (Summer): 39-47.

RUIZ, JOSE LUIS. 1995. "Sin dejar rastros, abandonando casi todo, Marcos desapareció," *El Universal* (February 17): 1 and 12.

RUPERT, MARK. (ed.). 2002. *Historical Materialism and Globalisation: Essays on Continuity and Change.* London: Routledge.

RYDER, ANDREW. 2013. "Foucault and Althusser: Epistemological Differences with Political Effects," *Foucault Studies*, No. 16 (September): 134-153.

SÁEZ ARRECEYGOR, HUGO ENRIQUE. 2012. "La tesis de filosofía del sub Marcos: una lectura de Althusser", *Pacarina del Sur* [En línea], año 3, núm. 12 (julio-septiembre); retrieved from http://www.pacarinadelsur.com/home/alma-matinal/472-la-tesis-de-filosofia-del-sub-marcos-una-lectura-de-althusser.

SALDAÑA-PORTILLO, MARÍA JOSEFINA. 2001. "Who's the Indian in Aztlán? Re-Writing Mestizaje, Indianism, and Chicanismo from the Lacandón," pp. 402-423 in Ileana Rodríguez (ed.), *The Latin American Subaltern Studies Reader*. Durham, North Carolina: Duke University Press.

SAMPERIO, GUILLERMO. 2011. *Marcos, el enmascarado de estambre*. México: Lectorum.

SAWICKI, JANA. 1991. *Disciplining Foucault*. Routledge: London.

SCHAFFER, SCOTT. 2004. *Resisting Ethics*. New York: Palgrave Macmillan.

SCHERER GARCÍA, JULIO. 2001. "La entrevista insólita," *Proceso* No. 1271 (March 11): 10-16.

SERNA, JUSTO AND PONS, ANACLET. 2000. *Cómo se escribe la microhistoria: Ensayo sobre Carlo Ginzburg*. Madrid: Ediciones Cátedra.

SHERIDAN, ALAN. 1980. *Michel Foucault: The Will to Truth*. London and New York: Routledge.

SKINNER, QUENTIN. [1985] 2000a. "Introduction," in Quentin Skinner ([1985] 2000b:1-20).

SKINNER, QUENTIN. [1985] 2000b. *The Return of Grand Theory in the Human Sciences*. Cambridge: Cambridge University Press, Canto edition.

SOLNIT, DAVID (ed.). 2004. *Globalize Liberation: How to uproot the system and build a better world*. San Francisco: City Lights Books.

SOLNIT, REBECCA. [2004] 2006. *Hope in the Dark: Untold Histories, Wild Possibilities*. New York: Nation Books.

SPEED, SHANNON AND REYES, ALVARO. 2008. "'Asumiendo Nuestra Propia Defensa': Resistance and the Red de Defensores Comunitarios," pp. 279-304 in Pedro Pitarch, Shannon Speed, and Xochitl Leyva Solano (eds.), *Human Rights in the Maya Region*. Durham and London: Duke University Press.

STAHLER-SHOLK, RICHARD. 2001. "Globalization and Social Movement Resistance: The Zapatista Rebellion in Chiapas, Mexico," *New Political Science*, Vol. 23, No. 4: 493-516.

STAHLER-SHOLK, RICHARD. 2007. "A World in Which Many Rebellions Fit." Book review: Thomas Olesen, *International Zapatismo: The Construction of Solidarity in the Age of Globalization* (London & New York:

Zed Books, 2005), in *A Contracorriente*, online journal of Latin American studies, North Carolina State University, Vol. 4, No. 2, Winter 2007: 187-198; retrieved from http://www.ncsu.edu/project/acontracorriente/winter_07/Stahler-Sholk.pdf.

STAVANS, ILAN. 2002. "Unmasking Marcos," in Tom Hayden (ed.) (2002:386-395).

STEELE, CYNTHIA. 2002. "The Rainforest Chronicle of Subcomandante Marcos," pp. 245-255 in Ignacio Corona and Beth E. Jörgensen (eds.), *The Contemporary Mexican Chronicle*. New York: New York State University.

STEPHEN, LYNN. 1997. "Pro-Zapatista and pro-PRI: Resolving the contradictions of Zapatismo in rural Oaxaca," *Latin American Research Review*, Vol. 32, Issue 2: 41-70.

STEPHEN, LYNN. 2002. *Zapata Lives!* California: University of California Press.

STURROCK, JOHN (ed.). 1979. *Stucturalism and Since: From Lévi-Strauss to Derrida*. Oxford: Oxford University Press.

SWIER, MARK. 2006. "'Other Loves' in the 'Other Campaign': Oaxaca's Queer Community Looks for Common Ground with the Latest Phase of Zapatista Struggle," *The Narco News Bulletin* (March 24); retrieved from http://narconews.com/Issue40/article1691.html.

TANGEMAN, MIKE. 1995. *Mexico at the Crossroads*. New York: Orbis Books.

TAUSSIG, MICHAEL. 1999. *Defacement*. California: Stanford University Press.

TAYLOR, ANALISA. 2009. *Indigeneity in the Mexican Cultural Imagination*. Arizona: University of Arizona Press.

THELEN, DAVID. 1999. "Mexico's Cultural Landscapes: A Conversation with Carlos Monsiváis," *The Journal of American History*, Vol. 86, No. 2 (Sept.): 613-622.

TIGÜERA SOBRINHO, SEBASTIAO. 1995. "El zapatismo y la democracia popular en Nuestra América," pp. 19–80 in Noam Chomsky, Sebastião Tigüera Sobrinho and Héctor Díaz Polanco, *Chiapas Insurgente: 5 Ensayos sobre la realidad Mexicana*. Navarra: Txalaparta.

TORMEY, SIMON. 2006. "'Not in my Name:' Deleuze, Zapatismo and the Critique of Representation," *Parliamentary Affairs*, Vol. 59, No. 1: 138–154.

VANDEN BERGHE, KRISTINE. 2005. *Narrativa de la rebelión zapatista. Los relatos del Subcomandante Marcos*. (Colección Nexos y Diferencias No. 13) Iberoamericana / Vervuert: Madrid / Frankfurt am Main.

VANDEN BERGHE, KRISTINE. 2006/1. "Los 'sin voz' y los intelectuales en México. Reflexiones sobre algunos ensayos de Mariano Azuela, Octavio Paz y el EZLN," *Latinoamérica* 42: 131-152.

VANDEN BERGHE, KRISTINE. 2007. "Cambios y constantes en la narrativa del Subcomandante Marcos: De los relatos a la novela *Muertos incómodos (falta lo que falta)*," *Mexican Studies/Estudios Mexicanos*, Vol. 23, Issue 2 (Summer): 387-408.

VANDEN BERGHE, KRISTINE. 2009. "The Quixote in the Stories of Subcomandante Marcos," pp. 53-69 in Theo D'haen and Reindert Dhondt, *The International Don Quixote*. Amsterdam: Rodopi.

VANDEN BERGHE, KRISTINE. 2012. *Las novelas de la rebelión zapatista*. Bern: Peter Lang.

VANDEN BERGHE, KRISTINE, AND BART MADDENS. 2004. "Ethnocentrism, Nationalism and Post-nationalism in the Tales of Subcomandante Marcos," *Mexican Studies/Estudios Mexicanos*, Vol. 20 (1): 123-144.

VASCONI, TOMÁS A. 1990. "Democracy and Socialism in South America," *Latin American Perspectives*, Issue 65, Vol. 17, No. 2 (Spring): 25-38.

VILLORO, JUAN. 2011. *De Cartago a Chiapas: crónica intempestiva*. Barcelona: Centre de Cultura Contemporánea de Barcelona.

VODOVNIK, ŽIGA. 2004. *Ya Basta! Ten Years of the Zapatista Uprising*. Oakland, CA: A.K. Press.

VOLPI, JORGE. 2003. "La novela del alzamiento Zapatista," *El País*, Opinión (December 28); retrieved from http://www.elpais.com/articulo/opinion/novela/alzamiento/zapatista/elpepiopi/20031228elpepiopi_7/Tes.

VOLPI, JORGE. 2004. *La guerra y las palabras*. Barcelona: Editorial Seix Barral.

— Works Cited —

WAGNER, VALERIA, AND MOREIRA, ALEJANDRO. 2003. "Toward a Quixotic Pragmatism: The Case of the Zapatista Insurgence," *boundary 2*, Vol. 30, No. 3 (Fall): 185-212.

WATSON, IAIN. 2002. "Rethinking Resistance: Contesting Neoliberal Globalisation and the Zapatistas as a Critical Social Movement," pp. 108-138 in Jason P. Abbott and Owen Worth (eds.), *Critical Perspectives on International Political Economy*. Houndmills, Basingstoke: Palgrave, Macmillan.

WILLIAMS, RAYMOND. 1994. *"Selections* from Marxism and Literature," pp. 585-608 in Nicholas B. Dirks, Geoff Eley, Sherry B. Ortner (eds.), *Culture/Power/History: A Reader in Contemporary Social Theory*. Princeton, N.J.: Princeton University Press.

WOLFSON, TODD. 2014. *Digital Rebellion: The Birth of the Cyber Left*. Urbana, Chicago: Univ. of Illinois Press.

WOMACK JR., JOHN. 1999. *Rebellion in Chiapas: An Historical Reader*. New York: The New Press.

YOUNG, ROBERT. 1981. *Untying the Text: A Post-Structuralist Reader*. Boston, London and Henley: Routledge & Kegan Paul.

ZUGMAN, KARA. 2008. "The 'Other Campaign:' The EZLN and New Forms of Politics in Mexico and the United States," *New Political Science*, Vol. 30, No. 3 (September): 347-367.

ZUGMAN DELLACIOPPA, KARA. 2009. *This Bridge Called Zapatismo: Building Alternative Political Cultures in Mexico City, Los Angeles, and Beyond*. Lanham, Maryland: Lexington Books.

ZUGMAN DELLACIOPPA, KARA. 2012. "Local Communities and Global Resistance: Social Change and Autonomy Struggles in the Americas," pp. 1-20 in Kara Zugman Dellacioppa and Clare Weber (eds.), *Cultural Politics and Resistance in the 21st Century*. New York: Palgrave Macmillan.

Index

(*The index below is a somewhat skeletal one, being intended to be used as a quick reference to enable the user to locate rapidly key themes, concepts, organizations, and works, as well as individuals who influenced Marcos significantly: it is not intended as a comprehensive general index.*)

A

Althusser, Louis 16, 19-21, 34, 36-37, 51, 56, 64, 66-67, 71, 75-82, 84-89, 91-99, 104-105, 109, 112-115, 118, 120-127, 131, 135, 140-148, 153, 155-156, 158, 161-162, 164, 177, 193, 197-198, 201, 217-218, 220-226, 229, 232, 239-240, 242, 245, 248-249, 255

Anti-capitalism 11, 58-61, 193, 200

Anti-globalization 11, 58, 60, 183, 193, 198, (see also Neoliberal)

Anti-humanism 81, 86, 96, 142 nn. 18 & 19, 217, 245

Archaeology 79, 161-162, 164-167, 202, 257-258

Autonomy 24, 235

B

Benedetti, Mario 29, 34, 43

Bourgeoisie, the 56, 61, 90, 129-131, 135, 139

C

Capital 56-57, 62, 123, 129, 134, 145, 198, 202, 222

Carta a Adolfo Gilly (see *Letter to Gilly*)

Chomsky, Noam 34, 43, 56, 72, 140, 162, 202, 205, 217, 241

Civil society 32, 71, 73, 103, 127, 136, 193, 203, 212, 220, 229-230, 237, 243, 250, 253

Class consciousness 37, 68 n. 7, 91, 148 n. 72

Class factions 131, 248

Class struggle 55-56, 61, 86-87, 92, 96, 105, 146, 203, 245

Command obeying (see Mandar obedeciendo)

Common sense 155, 231, 234, 239, 244, 261

Communist Manifesto, The 85, 255

Correlation of forces 41, 246

Cortázar, Julio 29, 31, 34-35, 37

Councils of good government (see Juntas de Buen Gobierno)

Crisis of the State 129-130, 248

D

Declaration of the Lacandón Jungle: First, ; Second, ; Fourth, ; Fifth, ; Sixth, 17, 23 n. 18, 126, 131-140, 174, 193, 236, 248-249

Democracy (see also Maya democracy) 17, 23 n. 18, 126, 131-140, 174, 193, 236, 248-249

Dialectical materialism 65-66

Dictatorship of the proletariat 22, 45, 48, 51-52, 55, 61, 132, 177, 247

Dignity 17, 23, 102, 176-177, 207

Discipline and Punish 81-82, 153, 182, 202, 214

Discursive formations and/or practices and/or relations 56, 77-79, 164, 166-167, 209 n. 8, 257-258

Don Quixote 33-35

E

Eclecticism 49, 56, 75, 241

Education system, the 56, 81, 89-90, 115, 124, 161-162, 164

Engels, Friedrich 19-20, 28, 41, 47, 55-56, 62-63, 69, 73, 75, 221, 241

ERP, the (Salvadoran) 227, 240, 243, 246

Ethics 54-55, 109, 111, 200-201, 216

EZLN (Ejército Zapatista de Liberación Nacional) 11-15, 17, 18, 31, 39, 44 n. 28, 48, 51-53, 58, 62, 101, 103, 107, 112, 134, 137, 140, 170, 173, 176, 181, 183-185, 207 n. 60, 227-228, 231-232, 235, 237-238, 246, 253-254 n. 15

F

FLN (Fuerzas de Liberación Nacional) 14, 18-19, 29, 47-55, 66-67, 96, 105, 114-115, 132-133, 184, 228, 245, 251, 253-254 n. 15

Foco (including *foquismo*) 14, 50, 52, 54, 246

For Marx 92, 142, 153, 221

Foucault, Michel 20-21, 34-35, 56, 64, 67, 71, 75-82, 84-85, 98, 118, 127, 130-131, 140-144, 152-153, 155-156, 161-168, 170-175, 177-179, 181-185, 188-194, 196-209, 211-215, 217-218, 224-226, 239-241, 245-246, 248-249

G

Galeano, Eduardo 32-33

Gay activism/rights 198-200, 215 nn. 127 & 131, 248

German Ideology, The 56, 113

Gramsci, Antonio 15, 21, 34, 36, 76, 91, 104, 140-141, 148, 155, 201, 217-244, 246

Guevara, Ernesto "Che" (including Guevarism) 11, 37, 42, 50, 52-53, 152, 225, 240, 244, 253

H

Hegemony 104, 115, 141, 208, 220, 222, 225, 230-231, 239, 242

Historical materialism 66, 115-117, 124, 153-154, 264

History, made by the masses 86-87, 96, 210 n. 87

History of Sexuality, The 171, 174, 182, 202, 208

Humanism (see also, anti-humanism) 76, 81, 86-87, 96, 104, 142 nn. 18 & 19, 202 n. 6, 217, 245

I

Idealism vs materialism 65-66, 114-115, 153 n. 126, 154 n. 134, 260

Ideological State Apparatuses (ISAs) 56, 78, 81, 84, 87-90, 99, 124, 146 nn. 46 & 49, 148 n. 72, 161, 221

Ideology 14-15, 22-23, 39-40, 45, 49, 56-57, 64, 69, 78-79, 81, 85, 87-88, 90, 93-94, 96, 99-101, 104, 113, 121, 128-131, 145-146, 148, 155-157, 194, 219, 221-222, 225, 231, 242, 245-246, 248, 257, 261

Inconvenient Dead, The (see *Muertos incómodos*)

Indigenous, peoples, reality, thought and/or practices, (see also, Maya) 11-18, 23-24, 28, 31-32, 35-36, 39-40, 44-45, 48, 50-51, 65, 70, 74, 100-102, 107, 112, 134, 138, 149-150, 177, 183-186, 188, 190, 192, 198, 204, 208-212, 227, 236-238, 240, 244, 246, 248-250, 252-253, 265

Intercontinental Encuentro for Humanity and Aagainst Neoliberalism 71, 127, 136, 171, 180-181, 204 n. 37, 209 n. 76

Interpellation 56, 79, 80, 81, 87-88, 99, 143, 165

Inverted Periscope (or Memory, A Buried Key), An 179, 187

Irony, Marcos' use of 28, 40-41, 44, 100, 195, 204

J

Juntas de Buen Gobierno 25 n. 24, 126, 176, 235

K

Kuhn, Thomas S. 117-120, 122, 154-155, 259

L

Lenin, V.I. 15-16, 19-20, 28, 35, 40, 47, 50-52, 55-56, 63-66, 68-69, 75, 91-92, 114, 141, 146, 153, 241-242, 245, 248, 260

Letter to Gilly 12, 21, 40-41, 64-65, 113-124, 196, 259-265

Liberation theology 71, 250, 263

M

Macherey, Pierre 84-85, 127, 145, 241

Mandar obedeciendo (see Command obeying) 17, 134, 176, 229, 235-236, 239, 243 nn. 35 & 37

Mao (including Maoism) 12, 13, 15, 17, 23 n. 18, 34, 43 n. 21, 49, 52, 62, 217, 225, 234, 245, 250, 252 n. 9

Martí, José 50, 70, 224

Marx, Karl 15-16, 19-20, 28, 35-36, 40-41, 47, 50-52, 55-58, 61-64, 66, 68-69, 72-73, 75, 82, 91-92, 96-97, 115, 125, 142, 145-146, 153-154, 156, 198, 201-202, 218, 221-222, 225, 241-243, 245, 255

Masses, the 37, 86, 96, 135, 148, 173, 198, 245

Materialism and Empirio-criticism 65-66, 114, 260

Maya culture and political system (including Maya democracy) 23 nn. 18 & 19, 24 nn. 21 & 23, 25 n. 26, 71 n. 26, 236, 240, 250, 252 n. 12

Memory (including historical memory and memory vs. oblivion) 97, 149 n. 78, 179, 182-190

Mestizaje 99-102, 104, 149, 193

Mexican Revolution, The 99, 101, 104, 193, 196, 210

Militancy 197, 214

MLN (Movimiento de Liberación Nacional) 49

"Modern prince" 220, 231, 237-238

Modernity 99, 101-102, 104, 150, 193-195, 213

Monsiváis, Carlos 27, 32, 35, 40, 43, 64, 97, 101, 131, 147, 160, 207, 232, 234, 243

Muertos incómodos 193, 199, 212 n. 104

N

Neoliberalism (including anti-neoliberalism) 11, 35-36, 58, 60, 99-100, 102, 104, 115, 124, 127, 171, 180-181, 187, 193, 198-199, 247, 262, 264

Networks of power and/or resistance 174, 177, 179-181

O

Organic intellectual(s) 243

P

Paradigm(s) 122, 155, 259, 262

Pêcheux, Michel 34, 84-85, 118, 144, 217, 241

Philosophy as class struggle 87, 92-93, 104-105, 146 n. 50, 245

Philosophy as a Revolutionary Weapon 92-93, 96, 104, 114, 146, 255

Poetry 19, 27-28, 30-32, 36-38, 41

Political economy 57, 61, 63, 72

Poulantzas, Nicos 16, 20, 34, 36, 51, 56, 75-80, 82, 84, 97, 104, 127-135, 137-141, 143-144, 157-158, 160, 177, 204, 207, 218, 220-222, 231-232, 239-242, 245, 248-249

Power bloc 128-131

Praxis, theory and 68 n. 7, 91-97, 99, 105-113, 123, 198, 248

Proletariat, the 22, 45, 48, 51-52, 55-56, 61, 70, 90, 92, 132, 177, 247

R

Reading Capital 123, 145, 222

Revolution 23, 38-39, 51-52, 64, 68, 70, 85, 99, 101, 104, 111-112, 123, 132-134, 140, 175, 178, 181, 193, 196, 205, 209-210, 213, 233, 237, 249, 264-265

Rule of Law 99, 103-104, 150-151, 193

S

Sandinistas 52, 132, 134

September 23 Communist League

Social movements 132, 138-140, 248

Social relations 90, 174-177

Socialism 51, 61, 68, 70, 77, 129-130, 132-135, 139, 143, 157-158, 160, 204

Stalin, and Stalinism 12, 15, 115, 144 n. 26, 158, n. 175, 245

State, the (including statism and state theory) 78, 82-83, 89-91, 99-104, 119, 129-130, 138, 163, 166, 173-174, 176-177, 190-191, 230, 237, 248

State power, the taking of 12, 15, 53, 107, 171-177, 231

Stories and storytelling 39, 101, 183-184, 191-195, 199, 233

Subjugated knowledge(s) 182-183, 190

T

The World: Seven Thoughts of May 2003 105, 108, 188

Theory and praxis 68 n. 7, 91-97, 99, 105-113, 123, 198, 248

Thesis on Feuerbach 91, 96, 153 n. 126

U

Uncomfortable Dead, The (see *Muertos incómodos*)

V

Vanguardism 12, 22 n. 6, 52, 73 n. 39, 95, 107, 136, 158 n. 175, 194, 237-238, 247

W

War of position 149 n. 74, 220, 229, 231-232, 235, 239

"Weakest link," theory of 45 n. 32, 66, 107, 153 n. 125, 246, 248

Z

Zapata, Emiliano 71 n. 26, 101, 185-188, 250
Zapatistas and the Other: The Pedestrians of History, The 58

www.ingramcontent.com/pod-product-compliance
Ingram Content Group UK Ltd.
Pitfield, Milton Keynes, MK11 3LW, UK
UKHW041432180426
11947UKWH00007B/394

9 781945 234033